THEORIES OF THE PROPOSITION

*Ancient and medieval conceptions
of the bearers of truth and falsity*

NORTH-HOLLAND
LINGUISTIC SERIES   8
Edited by S. C. DIK *and* J. G. KOOIJ

THEORIES OF
THE PROPOSITION

Ancient and medieval conceptions of the bearers of truth and falsity

GABRIEL NUCHELMANS

University of Leiden

1973

NORTH-HOLLAND PUBLISHING COMPANY
AMSTERDAM · LONDON

259461

Library of Congress Catalog Card Number: 72-93495

ISBN of this series: 0 7204 6180 4
ISBN of this volume: 0 7204 6188 X

Publisher:
NORTH-HOLLAND PUBLISHING COMPANY – AMSTERDAM

PRINTED IN THE NETHERLANDS

PREFACE

This book is intended as the first part of a history of those problems and theories in the domain of philosophical semantics which nowadays are commonly referred to as problems and theories about the nature and the status of propositions. Although the conceptual apparatus and the terminology by means of which questions concerning propositions were asked and answered have considerably varied from period to period, the main types of disputes and solutions have remained remarkably constant. One of the aims of this study is precisely to trace the vicissitudes of the vocabulary in which this refractory topic was treated in the remote past. As is evident from the Bibliography, many parts of the field have been explored by predecessors. Guided by their results, I have tried to fill in more details and to design a provisional map of the area as a whole.

It gives me great pleasure to acknowledge my indebtedness to Professor Norman Kretzmann of Cornell University, who has been kind enough to undertake the tedious task of improving the English of an earlier version. I am no less grateful to him for many valuable substantive comments and criticisms. He is not, of course, in any way responsible for my views or for any shortcomings which remain for others to discover.

I should also like to thank my colleague Professor L.M. De Rijk, who let me profit from his vast knowledge of medieval logic whenever I felt the need of consulting him.

University of Leiden, July 1972

CONTENTS

1. INTRODUCTION

1.1. A preliminary map of the field in which philosophical reflection on the bearers of truth and falsity originates

By way of introduction to the actual subject of this monograph and confining myself to what seems useful for that purpose I shall first give a very rough description, as uncontroversial as possible, of the areas in which problems concerning the bearers of truth and falsity can be expected to arise, and of the factors that are likely to play some role in attempts to solve these problems. There seem to be at least three aspects which have to be taken into account in drawing such a sketch: the acts or attitudes of holding something true and their objects; the language in which some of these acts or attitudes and their objects find expression; and the elements of reality outside thought and language that are of decisive importance in the process of verifying or falsifying beliefs and assertions.

1.1.1. There is a kind of human acts and attitudes that may be called holding something true (in the sense of the German term *für wahr halten* as it is found, for instance, in Kant and Bolzano). When we characterize someone as judging, thinking, or believing that something is the case, we ascribe to him an act or attitude which may but need not be expressed in some kind of language. When, on the other hand, we describe a person as asserting, stating, or declaring that something is the case, we also attribute to him an act or attitude of holding something true, but now it is implied that his judgment, thought, or belief is made known by means of language. Accordingly, we may say that one species of acts or attitudes of holding something true belongs to the mental sphere; and that another species of such acts or attitudes belongs to the verbal sphere, in so far as they are expressed in spoken or written words.

1

There are also modes of holding something true. Both in the mental and in the verbal sphere acts and attitudes of holding something true may be qualified in one way or another. People are described not only as judging, thinking, believing, asserting, stating, or declaring that something is the case, but also as, for instance, knowing, surmising, concluding, admitting that something is the case. Languages have a more or less extensive and refined stock of verbs by means of which the user is enabled to characterize, in different respects, acts or attitudes of holding something true, either in a predominantly descriptive manner ('He admits that ---', 'I have admitted that ---') or by way of indicating explicitly the precise nature of his own acts or attitudes ('I admit that ---').

Such verbs have as their natural complement a 'that'-clause expressive of the object of the act or attitude of holding something true. The same type of act or attitude, for instance believing, may have different objects. And different acts or attitudes may have the same object; I can first suspect that something is the case and then come to believe it. It is, therefore, quite natural to make a distinction between, on the one hand, acts or attitudes of holding something true and, on the other, the objects of such acts or attitudes, the alleged states of affairs.

Now what is held true need not, of course, be true. It can always be subjected to some kind of critical scrutiny. At least one of the uses of the expression '--- is true (false)' is to state the outcome of such a critical examination. The open place in this sentence-frame may be filled by such phrases as 'What he asserted', 'That Zeno is the father of dialectic'. What these phrases stand for we may call the bearers of truth or falsity, the possessors of truth-values.

From this central case, in which the object of an act or attitude of holding something true is seen as the bearer of truth or falsity, we can go on to other cases that seem to be more or less closely connected with the central case. We could, for example, find reason to suppose that the subject which, as the bearer of one of the truth-values, is designated by a phrase that can fill the open place in the sentence-frame '--- is true (false)' is identical with the subject that is designated by that phrase in the open space of the sentence-frame '--- is necessary (possible, contingent)', as that of which one of the so-called modalities is predicated.

Further, we can ask ourselves whether that which, as the object of an act or attitude of holding something true, is a bearer of truth or falsity can also be the object of other acts or attitudes which have to do with truth-values in a more indirect way. As an extreme case we might take the situation in which one merely entertains a proposition, putting before one's mind the thought that something is the case without either accepting or rejecting that thought. The state of affairs conceived in such a neutral attitude might be regarded as the potential object of acts or attitudes of a more committing kind. And among these latter could also be reckoned acts or attitudes of wishing, regretting, and even commanding, where the connection with truth-values still is a rather remote one.

As intermediate cases between the acts or attitudes which we have just mentioned and the full-blown acts or attitudes of holding something true we have such acts or attitudes as asking, doubting, supposing, assuming. The objects of the acts or attitudes of supposing and assuming are particularly important in so far as they can be considered as the terms of logical relations, such as the relation of entailment between premisses and conclusion, the relation of implication between antecedent and consequent, or the relations of contradiction and contrariety.

So there seems to be a continuous transition from the extreme case of merely entertaining a proposition to acts or attitudes of actually holding something true. In the open places of sentence-frames like 'He believes (asserts) ---', '--- is true (false)', '--- is necessary (possible, contingent)', 'He supposes ---', '--- implies . . .', phrases can be filled in that designate something which, on the one hand, takes on, as it were, the colour of its environment, but which, on the other hand, may be thought to maintain its identity through the differences of its surroundings.

This question of identity and difference and of the criteria by which they are determined becomes even more important in the light of the fact that it is very natural to say that several persons believe or assert the same thing; or that the same person, at different times, believes or asserts the same thing; or that the same person has, at different times, different attitudes (of doubting, believing, knowing) towards the same object; or that different persons display, for instance in a debate, different attitudes towards the same issue. As this kind of identity seems to be preserved in spite of various differences in the linguistic expression given to acts or attitudes of holding something true and their objects, it is advisable to turn now to the linguistic side of the matter.

1.1.2. As a rule the linguistic signs by means of which acts or attitudes of holding something true and their objects are expressed will be more or less independent utterances. If we take the word 'utterance' in the sense of a product of an act of uttering, we can still distinguish at least three nuances in this sense. The concrete product of a particular act of uttering the words 'The king is dead' is usually called an utterance-token. Utterance-tokens of the same linguistic form are then said to be instances of one utterance-type, for example 'The king is dead' as a sentence of the English language which, in different circumstances, is used for a variety of purposes. As an intermediate case between utterance-types in general and utterance-tokens we may consider the sentence 'The king is dead' in so far as it is used, possibly by different persons at different times and places, for the special purpose of making one definite statement, for instance that Charles I of England is dead.

Parallel to these distinctions on the side of the linguistic signs which are used to express acts or attitudes of holding something true and their objects there are different levels on which the meaning of such signs can be discussed. First of all, there is a general meaning of the utterance-type. This general meaning is a function of the general meanings of the parts out of which the utterance-type as a whole is compounded. Compared to the composite whole these parts are necessarily characterized by varying degrees of imperfection or incompleteness. Further, in the case of an utterance-type which is used, possibly by different persons at different times and places, for the special purpose of asserting the same determinate content the general meaning of the utterance-type may be narrowed to a particular thing meant. This particular meaning is a resultant of the general meaning of the utterance-type and the special determinants that are found in the context and the situation in which the utterance-token is used. As the thing meant is assumed to be the same, there is no need to make a distinction between the particular meaning of an utterance-type used for a definite purpose and the meaning of one of the utterance-tokens of that specific utterance-type. Perhaps the person who produces an utterance-token which contains the same particular information as utterance-tokens produced by other persons has certain intentions of his own in uttering it, but in general there will be no need to take these subjective intentions into account when only questions of linguistic meaning are considered.

With the aid of these and other distinctions it is possible to get a clearer insight into the way in which the objects of verbal acts of holding something true are connected with the linguistic means of expressing them and, in particular, into the extent to which the identity of such objects is influenced by differences in the form or meaning of the expressions in which acts of asserting are performed. At one end of the scale of possible answers we may put the view that it is the utterance-token which determines the sameness and difference of things asserted; in the sense that difference of utterance-token necessarily implies difference of what is asserted. At the other extreme it may be maintained that the thing asserted is the same as long as the factors which determine its truth or falsehood remain the same. In that conception differences of linguistic form, either in the same language or in different languages, are taken to be irrelevant in so far as they do not bring about a change of meaning. And differences of meaning are taken to be irrelevant in so far as they are not accompanied by changes in the factors which determine the truth or falsehood of what is said. The linguistic meanings of the utterances 'He will be hungry when he arrives', 'I am hungry', and 'You were hungry yesterday afternoon' are no doubt different; but as long as the persons who use them do so in order to refer to the same situation there are, according to this view, no corresponding differences in what is asserted. Between these two extremes there are several other possibilities, according to the extent to which variations in form or meaning are taken into consideration.

One consequence of the close relations between acts or attitudes of holding something true and their expression in language is worth mentioning. We have adduced such phrases as 'What he asserted', 'That Zeno is the father of dialectic' as suitable fillers of the open place in the sentence-frame '--- is true (false)'. These phrases stand for objects of acts or attitudes of holding something true, which objects are taken to be the bearers of truth or falsity. In so far as acts or attitudes of holding something true are expressed in language, however, it is not unnatural to say that the utterance which is used for that purpose, for instance 'Zeno is the father of dialectic', is true or false. It is easy to understand how this comes about: the predicates 'true' and 'false' (and similar expressions) are transferred from the content of the act of asserting to the linguistic expression by means of which the speech act is accomplished.

1.1.3.   I shall be very brief about the third of the aspects mentioned in the beginning, namely the elements of reality outside thought and language that determine the truth or falsehood of beliefs and assertions. What precisely these elements are, what it is in the world that renders thoughts or statements about the world true or false, has proved to be a very difficult question. Do these elements of reality possess the character of things, in some sense of that rather vague word, or of states and events as they occur at certain times and places, or are they perhaps timeless facts? The issue is complicated by the circumstance that in some languages it is very hard to make a clear distinction between the content of an act or attitude of holding something true and, on the other hand, the feature of reality that renders this content true or false. In Greek and Latin the question 'What does he believe (assert)?' and the question 'What makes his belief (assertion) true?' tend to be answered in exactly the same way, for example by the equivalent of 'That Hannibal defeated the Romans at Cannae'.

1.2.   Impasses of the first attempts at theoretical reflection

1.2.1. In many fields of human activity a distinction can be drawn between
a stage or level of mere practice and a stage or level of theoretical reflection
on that practice. Applied to acts or attitudes of holding something true this
would mean that people believe or assert that certain things are the case
before they start to reflect on what they do and try to make explicit what is
involved in their doings; or, if there is no chronological succession, that it is at
least possible to discern some borderline between just believing or asserting
that something is the case and reflecting upon these activities. There is little
doubt that also in the case of acts or attitudes of holding something true
some such distinction between practice and reflection is indeed applicable.
But, as so often, it turns out to be difficult to decide where exactly the line
should be drawn. We have seen that even the most unreflective language-user
has at his disposal a rather refined vocabulary by means of which he can
discriminate between various kinds of acts or attitudes of holding something
true. To be able to employ this vocabulary in a correct way he must have an
implicit notion of the necessary and sufficient conditions to which the proper
application of the words is subject. Further, it is obvious that even on the
level of the common affairs of practical life matters of truth and falsehood
are so important that rudimentary discussions about these concepts and what
they imply are well-nigh inevitable. And the same applies to the form and
meaning of the linguistic expressions that play a part in acts or attitudes of
holding something true. Long before the beginning of professional grammatical and semantical studies there were more than enough occasions on which
some point of linguistic usage could, for one reason or another, become the
subject of conversation and thereby expose the need of an adequate terminology for the most essential aspects of the problem.

   Although the transition from practice to critical reflection is therefore a
very gradual one, it is nevertheless possible, I think, to indicate a point at
which such occasional and imperfect comments have gained the character of a
regular philosophical discussion, carried on with the aid of a conceptual apparatus and a vocabulary which are steadily growing in adequacy and systematic
coherence. The period during which this development took place is the fourth
century B.C. It can hardly be a coincidence that this is also the time at which
Greek philosophy came of age; on the contrary, it would be more accurate to
say that increased preoccupation with problems concerning acts and attitudes
of holding something true and their objects was an essential part of that
coming of age.

   Normally the reaching of maturity is preceded by a stage of trial and error, of feeling one's way in unfamiliar surroundings. In the case of our topic this has led to certain impasses which are caused by a kind of clash between the results of reckless theorizing and the implicit knowledge that one has of the object of theoretical reflection, the acts and attitudes of holding something true. The evidence of apparently valid abstract arguments is seen to be incompatible with the equally evident awareness of what one is actually practising all the time. Of such blind alleys there are in fact some remarkable examples in the history of Greek philosophy. They are symptoms of a crisis which no doubt was not exclusively brought about by abortive attempts to make sense of acts and attitudes of holding something true, but which nonetheless testifies to a growing interest in those questions and, at the same time, to the inability to give satisfactory answers to them.

1.2.2. Aristotle (*Metaphysics* 1010 a 10) tells us that Cratylus, a younger contemporary of Socrates, criticized the Heraclitean doctrine that one cannot step twice into the same river, because one cannot do so even once. From the observation that everything is constantly changing and moving he apparently drew the conclusion that identification, either individual or qualitative, is impossible and that therefore the use of language, which in its referring and predicating functions presupposes the possibility of identification, is vain. Accordingly, he finally decided that he ought to say nothing at all and only moved his finger. Theoretical reflection convinced Cratylus that what he did in practice could not be done, and consequently he gave up the practice.

1.2.3. A little earlier the sophist Gorgias had defended some theses that are hardly less radical. According to Sextus Empiricus (*Adversus mathematicos* VII, 65–87) and the pseudo-Aristotelian treatise *De Melisso, Xenophane, Gorgia* (979 a 10 – 980 b 21) he set out to prove that nothing exists; that even if anything exists, it cannot be comprehended; and that even if it can be comprehended, it cannot be communicated to others. It is clear that the second and third theses deny the possibility of acts or attitudes of holding something true, both in the mental and in the verbal sphere.

Gorgias tries to establish the second proposition in the following way. If the things thought are not existent, the existent is not thought; the things thought are not existent; therefore, the existent is not thought. The second premiss is supported by three arguments. The first two are counterexamples against the Parmenidean thesis that the things thought are existent. If someone thinks of a man flying or of a chariot running over the sea, it does not follow that the things thought are existent. And if the things thought are existent, then the non-existent things will not be thought; but Scylla and

Chimaera and many other non-existent things are thought. The third argument points out the absurdity of a line of thinking according to which each object ought to be judged by its own special sense and not by others, and that therefore the things thought will exist even if they should not be viewed by the sight nor heard by the hearing, because they are apprehended by their own proper criterion. It is obvious that these arguments do not establish the truth of the second premiss of the main reasoning. What Gorgias needs is the proposition that no things thought are existent. What he proves is that it is not the case that all things thought are existent or, in other words, that some things thought are not existent.

In defence of his third thesis — that even if anything can be comprehended, it cannot be communicated to other persons — Gorgias adduces arguments of two different kinds. In the first place, he holds that there can be no semantical relation between speech and things in the world, on the following grounds. If it is true that each externally existing sensible thing is apprehensible only by its own special sense, visible things by sight and audible things by hearing, then we cannot 'speak' these things to another person; the only object of speaking is speech and speech is different from the external things. And even if we reckon speech among the externally existing things, it differs so much from the rest that it cannot serve to indicate them to another person, just as they themselves do not make plain one another's nature. Moreover, it is not speech that reveals the externally existing things, but since speech itself is caused by the impressions of external things, it is the external object that proves to be explanatory of speech. In the second place, Gorgias denies the possibility of another necessary condition of successful communication, namely that the speaker and hearer come to share the same thought. The same thing cannot be in two persons at the same time, for then it would be two things. And even if the same thing could be in two persons at the same time, the fact that these persons are different would cause some difference in the way the thing appears to each of them. Moreover, even in the case of one person there is no sense in speaking of his having the same thing before his mind, either at the same time or at different times; what he sees by his sight will be different from what he hears by his hearing, and at different times he will have different impressions.

Notwithstanding the intentional or unintentional flaws that can be discovered in these reasonings it is undeniable that the problems which Gorgias propounds in such a striking manner are of the utmost importance: how are the linguistic expressions which we use in speaking about the world related to the intended objects, and how does a speaker succeed in informing the hearer of the same thing as he himself believes to be true?

1.2.4. Next, we shall consider three more specific theses from antiquity, which are alike in that they appear to be conclusions of cogent arguments but are nevertheless inconsistent with the evidence of an indisputable practice. The three theses are: (1) that it is impossible to believe or assert something negative; (2) that it is impossible to believe or assert something false; (3) that it is impossible to contradict.

Thesis (1) has its origin in Parmenides's poem on the way of truth and the way of seeming. There it is repeatedly urged that it is not to be said or thought that 'it is not', for it is the same thing that can be thought and can be, and what can be spoken and thought of must be[1]. Parmenides may have arrived at his view by taking the verbs for thinking (*noein, gignōskein*) and saying (*phrazein, legein, phasthai, phatizein*) as success-verbs, like seeing or pointing at something, and by concentrating upon only one sense of the verb for being (*einai*). In any case, it took a long time before Parmenides's dogma was refuted; it was Plato who, in *Sophist* 251–259, showed a way out of the impasse by suggesting an interpretation of negative statements which at least saves them as meaningful utterances.

According to Plato (*Cratylus* 429 d) proposition (2) was an old and much-discussed thesis. In particular it is attributed to Protagoras[2] and to Antisthenes[3]. Plato examines the thesis more than once: *Euthydemus* 283 e – 287 c; *Cratylus* 429 b – 430 a; *Republic* 478 b – c; *Theaetetus* 187 d – e, 188 d – 189 c; *Sophist* 236 e – 239 c, 240 d – 241 b, 259 e. It is perhaps worth mentioning that there were also defenders of the opposite thesis, that it is impossible to believe or assert something true. Sextus Empiricus (*Adversus mathematicos* VII, 53) mentions Xeniades of Corinth as one of them[4].

Thesis (3), that it is impossible to contradict, is ascribed to Antisthenes[5], but also to Protagoras[6] and, in a papyrus from the fourth century A.D., even to Prodicus[7]. It is obvious that thesis (3) follows logically from thesis (1) and also from thesis (2); if I cannot say '*x* is not *A*', I cannot contradict '*x* is *A*',

---

[1] Diels-Kranz, *Die Fragmente der Vorsokratiker* I, 28, B 2, 7–8; B 3; B 6, 1; B 8, 7–9, 34–36.

[2] Plato, *Euthydemus* 286 c; Diogenes Laertius, *Vitae philosophorum* IX, 51. Cf. also Plato, *Theaetetus* 167 a, 170 c; Aristotle, *Metaphysics* 1009 a 6; Sextus Empiricus, *Adversus mathematicos* VII, 60, 64, 388.

[3] Aristotle, *Metaphysics* 1024 b 34; and perhaps Isocrates, *Helena* X, 1.

[4] Cf. also VII, 388, 399, VIII, 5; and *Pyrrhōneioi hypotypōseis* II, 18, 76.

[5] Aristotle, *Topics* 104 b 21; *Metaphysics* 1024 b 34; Diogenes Laertius, *Vitae philosophorum* IX, 53.

[6] Diogenes Laertius, *Ibidem*; Plato, *Euthydemus* 286 c.

[7] Cf. G. Binder & L. Liesenborghs, 'Eine Zuweisung der Sentenz *ouk estin antilegein* an Prodikos von Keos', *Museum Helveticum* 23 (1966), 37–43.

and if there are no false statements, both *p* and not-*p* will be true and so there will be no contradiction between the two.

1.2.5.   Instead of analyzing in detail all the arguments that were supposed to lead to such paradoxical results I shall confine myself to calling attention to some distinctions which are of vital importance in these matters but are nonetheless apt to be neglected. Let us take as our example the thesis that to think what is not the case (*doxazein to mē on*) or to say what is not the case (*legein to mē on*) is impossible. I shall first make a few remarks about the verbs *doxazein* and *legein* and then about the expression *to mē on*.

The verbs *doxazein* and *legein* (and verbs with similar meanings) can have objects of several different kinds.

A. I.   If they are taken to designate cases in which one intends to think of something or to refer to something by means of a linguistic expression, there is always at least an internal object: the thought one thinks and the referring expression one uses.

A. II.   If they are taken to designate cases in which one succeeds in thinking of something or in referring to something by means of a linguistic expression, there will also be an external object, the thing thought of or referred to. In these cases *doxazein* and *legein* are used as success-verbs, comparable to verbs for seeing, hearing, or touching (Cf. Plato, *Theaetetus* 188 e).

B. I.   If they are taken to designate cases in which one thinks or says that something is the case, there is always at least an internal object: the thought that something is the case (*doxa*) or the assertion that something is the case (*logos*).

B. II.   While there are, of course, circumstances in which what is held true or claimed to be the case proves to be the case in the objective world of facts, this success has not been built into the meaning of the verbs *doxazein* and *legein*. There are, however, verbs of knowing, whose meaning does entail that what is held true is indeed true. Such verbs are, in this respect, comparable to verbs of seeing, hearing, or touching.

Accordingly, at least three fundamental distinctions should be kept in mind. (a) The distinction between A and B: cases in which the acts of *doxazein* and *legein* are directed to things which may be components of states of affairs but are not themselves complete states of affairs, and cases in which it is thought or said that something is the case. (b) The distinction between, on the one hand, intending to think of something or to refer to something and holding something true and, on the other hand, succeeding in these endeavours and being right about the alleged state of affairs. (c) The distinction between internal objects and external objects.

As for the expression *to mē on,* it is worth noting that it is highly ambiguous. It may designate that which does not exist, in some sense of that word, or it may be used for that which is not the case, either in the sense of a false *doxa* or *logos* or in the sense of that which does not actually occur as a state of affairs in reality.

1.2.6.   As I remarked before, it is not unlikely that Parmenides took the verbs he uses for thinking and saying as success-verbs. But it can now be seen that at the same time he must have overlooked the distinction (a) and the ambiguity of the expression *to mē on.* Awareness of the logical impossibility of thinking of something which does not exist or referring to something which is not there (in the success-sense of 'thinking of' and 'referring to') thus led him to the mistaken idea that it is also impossible to think or say that something is not the case.

The key-word of Gorgias's second thesis is the verb *phronein.* In his counterexamples against the Parmenidean proposition that the things thought are existent he takes it for granted that existent things are things that exist in the objective world outside thought; he then shows that it is not the case that all things thought are existent in that sense, and that things which do not exist in that sense are as a matter of fact thought. He concentrates upon the external objects, if any, of *phronein* and does not regard the internal objects, the produced thoughts, as existent things; otherwise he would not have concluded that the existent things are not thought. So far so good. But in his arguments for the third thesis he admits only internal objects: what one says is a saying and what one thinks is a thought, just as what one sees is a sight and what one hears is a sound. It then becomes analytically true that one cannot think a sound or tell what one sees. It is hard to believe that such a move would have been possible if there had been a clear awareness of distinction (c).

If we study the passages in which Plato discusses the thesis that it is impossible to believe or assert something false, we can discern at least three ways in which neglect of essential distinctions makes arguments for this thesis look plausible. First, one can assimilate *doxazein* and *legein* to success-verbs of knowing that something is the case by pointing out the analogies with success-verbs of seeing, hearing, or touching in cases where *doxazein* and *legein* are used in connection with thing-like objects. By disregard of distinction (a) one is led to the conclusion that if it is impossible successfully to refer to something which is not there, then it is also impossible to say something which is not the case. Second, one may set out from the truism that every act of thinking or saying has an internal object. If there is no internal object, there is no act of thinking or saying either. So *doxazein* or *legein to mē on,* understood as thinking a non-existent thought or asserting a non-existent assertion, is readily seen to be impossible. And then the similarity of outward form easily deceives one into believing that it is also impossible in the sense of thinking or saying something which is not the case. Third, there is a more positive line of thinking which starts from the impeccable expressions *doxazein ti* and *legein ti* in which *ti* stands for some kind of object, and then proceeds somewhat as follows: if what one thinks or says is something, then it is one thing (*hen ti*); and if it is one thing, then it is an existing thing (*on ti*); and if it is an existing thing, then it is that which is (*to on*) or that which is the case.

It is highly improbable that many people were convinced by this kind of reasoning to such a degree that they actually became doubtful of the possibility of what they all did in practice − using negative statements, believing or saying things which proved to be false, and contradicting each other − and even more unlikely that they went as far as Cratylus did and gave up what they had been practising. But remaining unconvinced by an argument is not the same as being able to refute it. And the fact that the paradoxical propositions which we have mentioned remained the subject of heated debates for so long and in so many circles is sufficient proof that the participants did not yet possess the proper tools to handle such issues. On the other hand, the strangeness and incredibility of the propounded theses must have been a strong stimulus to search for the exact points where the reasoning had gone wrong and, more positively, to develop a conceptual apparatus and a terminology in which it would be possible to discuss these matters in a more satisfactory way. As far as we know, it was Plato who took the first steps in the right direction.

2. PLATO

2.1. Introductory remarks

2.1.1. It has usually been thought that in certain passages of Plato's *Cratylus* (notably 425 a) the word *logos* already has more or less the same meaning as is elucidated in the famous passage *Sophist* 261–264: the meaning namely of a statement or statement-making utterance which is constructed out of a noun and a verb and is either true or false in a straightforward sense. Those who hold this interpretation are confronted with the difficulty that Plato concludes from the fact that such a *logos* is true or false that its parts too are true or false, a conclusion that seems hard to justify. In view of this difficulty Prauss (1966 : especially 43–60) has argued for a quite different rendering of *logos*, namely as an aggregate consisting of single words (*onomata*) as smallest parts and of *rhēmata* as combinations of *onomata*, by which aggregate something is characterized in the way of a complex name and not in the way of a statement. As I find Prauss's arguments convincing, I shall disregard the *logos*-passages in the *Cratylus* as not concerned with bearers of truth and falsity in our sense, and confine myself to *Sophist* 261–264.

2.1.2. In attempting to give a definition of the sophist, which is at least one of the aims of the dialogue of that name, Plato comes across the following obstacle. If the sophist is said to create a false belief in his own wisdom by false statements, he will object that it is impossible to think or state something which is not the case. Consequently, it becomes necessary to meet this objection with a satisfactory account of falsity in thought and speech. This account itself, however, has to be given in speech and therefore Plato wants to make sure that discourse in general is possible. In 251–259 he has considered three hypotheses: that no form combines with any other; that every

13

form combines with every other; that some forms combine with one another and others do not. The second possibility can be eliminated at once; it is absurd. But fortunately the first possibility too is found to be without any plausibility. If everything were isolated from everything, all discourse would be impossible. That we can have discourse is due to the fact that it is not the case that everything is isolated from everything but that the forms can be combined with one another, although, of course, not in complete promiscuity (This, I think, is the correct interpretation of the much-discussed phrase *dia tēn allēlōn tōn eidōn symplokēn* in 259 e 5—6). After this reassuring conclusion that the possibility of discourse in general is not in danger, Plato turns to the problem of explaining the existence of a special kind of discourse, false statements.

2.2.   *Sophist* 261 c 6 — 262 e 2

2.2.1.   As a first part of his account of the possibility of falsity in speech Plato puts forward two fundamental theses: that there is an essential difference between two levels of speech activity, the *onomazein*-level and the *legein*-level; and that certain units of the *onomazein*-level must be combined in a definite way in order to get a unit of the *legein*-level, a *logos*. The two units which Plato introduces on the *onomazein*-level are *onomata* (in the narrow sense of nouns) and *rhēmata*. Both are means of naming or designating something: *rhēmata* of indicating actions or states (*praxeis*) and *onomata* of specifying the subjects of those actions and states.

   Now there is a criterion by which all possible combinations of *onomata* and *rhēmata* can be divided into two groups. Some of them yield a *logos* and some of them, such as 'Walks runs sleeps' or 'Lion stag horse', do not. That some of the combinations yield a *logos* means that they essentially occur in a speech act of *legein*, of saying that something is the case. This speech act of *legein* and the *logos* which goes with it are of a character fundamentally different from the activity of *onomazein* by means of *onomata* and *rhēmata*. When someone says 'A man understands', he gives information about a certain state of affairs and asserts something.

2.2.2.   The key-words in this passage are of a rather unspecialized nature. *Onoma* is used in the sense of a name for an agent; but also in the broader sense of a word. The verb *onomazein* is construed with an internal object, *onomata*, or with an external object, the thing indicated by means of an *onoma* or *rhema*; the subject may be a person or a word. The verbs *dēloun* and *sēmainein* take as their subjects persons or linguistic expressions and the things signified are either actions and agents or states of affairs. *Legein* is used in the sense of uttering *onomata* and *rhēmata* or a *logos*, with a person as subject; or in the sense of saying that something is the case, with a person or a *logos* (263 b 4) as subject. Correspondingly, a *logos* may be an utterance, as the words spoken, or a statement, either in the sense of an act of asserting that something is the case or in the sense of that which is asserted.

This lack of differentiation in the vocabulary tends to obscure the distinctions between internal object and external object, between things and actions and states and, on the other hand, states of affairs, between act and content, and between what is properly done by persons and what is properly done by linguistic expressions.

2.2.3. A phrase which needs some special comment is *ti perainei* in 262 d 4. Cornford (1935: 305) regards *perainein ti* as the opposite of *ouden perainein,* 'to get nowhere', and translates: 'it (*sc.* a *logos*) --- gets you somewhere'. Prauss (1966: 186) renders it by 'fügt etwas zur Ganzheit', taking *logos* as subject and referring to *Theaetetus* 207 b 4–5 and c 3–4 (where persons are the subject of *perainein*). I think that Prauss's rendering is correct except for the minor point that to me it seems more natural to take the *tis* of 262 c 9 as the subject of the verbs in 262 d 2–4 and as the referent of *auton* in 262 d 5. But perhaps some more light can be shed on the manner in which Plato intends the phrase to be understood.

Plato apparently wants to say that someone who asserts that something is the case, on the *legein*-level, brings about something that is a complete and independent whole, in contrast with somebody who only calls attention to something by means of an *onoma* or *rhēma*, on the *onomazein*-level. The completeness and independence of a saying is, no doubt, always relative to a great variety of factors; but an utterance which is used for making a statement is at any rate complete and independent to the extent that no room is left for the questions of whom or of what something is said and what is said of something. It is one of these questions which typically remains open in the case of an isolated *onoma* or an isolated *rhēma.* While Plato probably regarded the completeness of a *logos* in the first place as the relative independence of the thought conveyed in making the statement, the fact that he lays great stress on the necessity of a specific combination of a *rhēma* with an *onoma* seems to show that he was not altogether unaware of the formal aspects of such a completeness.

Now it is noteworthy that Aristotle (*Rhetoric* 1408 b 26 and 1409 a 29) repeatedly uses the word *perainein* in connection with the thesis that the form of prose composition should be neither metrical nor destitute of rhythm, and with the difference, in prose, between a free-running style and the compact style in periods. In the first passage it is said that unrhythmical language is too unlimited (*aperanton*); and what has no clear limits (*apeiron*) is unpleasant and unintelligible. Therefore, prose should have limitations (*dei peperanthai*), though not those of metre. And everything is limited (*peperainetai*) by number. In the second passage Aristotle contrasts the free-running style, which has no end in itself (*telos kath'hautēn*) and is unsatisfying because it goes on indefinitely (*dia to apeiron*), with the compact style in periods. A period is a portion of speech that has in itself a beginning and an end and is easily taken in at a glance. It is satisfying because it is the reverse of indefinite (*aperanton*) and the hearer feels that he is grasping something and is confronted with a well-rounded whole (*peperanthai ti hautōi*). Finally, Aristotle adds that the period must also be complete as regards the sense or thought (*dianoia*), using the verb *teleioun* instead of *perainein*.

That Plato was not entirely unfamiliar with rhetorical studies of this kind is made plausible by passages like *Phaedrus* 267 c–d, where he parodies Thrasymachus of Chalcedon, who introduced the rhythmical period into Greek prose literature (Cf. Norden 1915: 41–43). We may, therefore, hazard the hypothesis that the phrase *ti perainei* in *Sophist* 262 d 4 has been borrowed from the terminology of rhetoric and that Plato used this expression because he was struck by a close resemblance between the essential characteristics of a *logos* in his sense and those of a period in rhetoric. This hypothesis is corroborated by the fact that the verbs *perainein* and *teleioun* are prominent members of a semantic field whose elements keep recurring, as we shall see later (Cf. 6.2), in connection with the theme of the *perfectio sensus,* a theme which has to do with the completeness of a thought not only in so far as it determines a certain unit of speech but also as a decisive factor in questions of prose-rhythm and interpunction. This theme of the *perfectio sensus,* with the corresponding vocabulary, has its natural complement in the theme of what may be called the *imperfectio sensus* and the words that express the idea of defectiveness and incompleteness, or of the 'not yet'. And it is precisely this last expression that we find in *Sophist* 262 c 1, where it is said that mere strings of *onomata* or *rhēmata* do not yet make up a *logos* (*oudeis pō synestē logos*). In comparison with the relative completeness and independence of the units that belong to the *legein*-level the units of the *onomazein*-level are seen to be defective; with respect to the *legein*-level they stand in need of some kind of completion. From there it is only one step to the realization that *onomata* and *rhēmata* are accompanied by an open place. The schemata 'A man ---' and '--- understands' become a complete *logos* only when the open places are filled by an appropriate verb or noun. Then the mind is put at rest having full information about what is done and who or what does it. The 'not yet'-phrase is a sign of some dim awareness that *onomata* and *rhēmata* are functional units destined to be used in a wider frame in which they contribute as organic parts to the constitution of a unit of an altogether different nature.

If this is right, the phrases *oudeis pō* and *ti perainei* are the starting-points of the twin themes of the imperfection and perfection of sense whose growth and maturation we shall have occasion to watch in the following chapters.

2.3.   *Sophist* **262 e 3 – 263 d 5**

2.3.1.   Every *logos* that something is the case, Plato goes on to say, must be of something or about something; for example, both the *logos* 'Theaetetus sits' and the *logos* 'Theaetetus flies' are of or about Theaetetus. Probably by noticing that we often say quite different things of the same subject and also say the same thing of different subjects Plato has gained a clear insight into the compound and articulate character of a statement. A statement is not something monolithic which admits of only one question: does the thing meant exist or does it not exist? It has parts; and one of these parts is here identified as the referring part, by means of which the speaker indicates what it is about which he is going to say something. That this referring part is an essential component of a *logos* is explicitly stated twice: it is impossible that there should be a *logos* unless it is a *logos* of something (262 e 6, 263 c 10).

At the same time, Plato assigns a certain character to the *logos*: it is the bearer of truth and falsehood. As the word *logos*, however, is highly ambiguous, there is from the beginning a certain obscurity in the notion of the bearer of truth and falsehood. On the one hand, *logos* can be taken as that which is stated, just as *doxa* can be understood in the sense of that which is believed. There is, for instance, a passage in the *Philebus* (39 b 9 – c 5) where *doxai* and *logoi* are clearly identical with *ta doxazomena* or *doxasthenta* and *ta legomena* or *lechthenta,* the things which are believed and asserted. On the other hand, *logos* can also stand for the utterance which is used in making the statement. At the end of 1.1.2 we noted that the predicates 'true' and 'false' tend to be transferred from the content of an act of asserting to the linguistic expression by means of which the act of asserting is accomplished. It is obvious that this tendency is considerably strengthened when one and the same word is used both for the asserted content and for the linguistic expression.

2.3.2.   Plato is now sufficiently equipped to deal with the paradoxical thesis that it is impossible to assert something which is false. By distinguishing the *onomazein*-level from the *legein*-level he is able to separate the question whether the objects of *onomazein* are existing things from the quite different question whether that which is indicated by the *rhēma* is something which is the case about that which is referred to by means of the *onoma*. One of the fatal ambiguities in the phrase *legein to (mē) on* was, as we saw in 1.2.5, the use of *legein* both in the sense of *onomazein* and in the sense of saying what is (not) the case. The easy transition from one sense to the other is now obstructed by Plato's constant use of *onomazein* for designating things and actions or states and his reserving the verb *legein* as much as possible for the sense of saying that something is the case. This enables him to grant that in making a statement we always indicate things that exist in some way, by means of the *onoma* and the *rhēma* on the *onomazein*-level, and to maintain at the same time that it is nonetheless possible that we assert something which is not the case, namely by ascribing an existing property to an existing subject which does not possess that property. By regarding the *logos* as an articulate whole, constructed out of parts, Plato can distinguish between two senses of the word *einai* and the word *on* and consequently between two fundamentally different questions: whether the objects designated by the parts exist or do not exist and, on the other hand, whether that which is said in the predicate belongs to the subject or does not belong to it. In the first instance the *logos* is true because it says something which is the case, in the second it is false because it says something which is not the case.

2.4.   *Sophist* 263 d 6 – 264 b 8

2.4.1.   After refuting the thesis of the impossibility of falsehood with re-spect to verbal acts of holding something true Plato naturally wants to extend the result of his investigation to mental acts or attitudes of holding something true. As cases in point he mentions *dianoia, doxa,* and *phantasia.* As *phantasia* is a species of *doxa,* namely a belief that is caused by some present percep-tion, I shall ignore it and concentrate on *dianoia* and *doxa.*

According to *Theaetetus* 189 e 4 and *Sophist* 263 e 3 *dianoia* is a *logos*, in the wide sense of discourse, and *dianoeisthai*, the process of thinking, is a dialogue (*dialegesthai*) of the mind with itself, without spoken words. The mind is, as it were, talking to itself, asking questions and answering them, saying yes or no, until finally it reaches a decision and judges that something is the case. The whole process of thinking and forming a judgment is de-scribed in terms which are borrowed from the field of spoken language, and represented as mental speech. That the association between thinking and speaking has always been a close one is proved by such facts as that the word *phanai*, as used by Homer, has the sense of thinking as well as of saying. But, as far as we know, Plato was the first writer who indulged in this 'lingualization' of mental phenomena in connection with the problems concerning acts and attitudes of holding something true. Thereby he introduced another theme which was predestined for a great future, the theme of what may be called *oratio mentalis*.

2.4.2. A *doxa* is the result of a process of thinking. This result is reached when the inner dialogue issues in a clear yes or no, in a definite assent or dissent. For this act of judging that something is the case or is not the case in *Theaetetus* 170 d 4 the verb *krinein* is used, which precisely means separating one thing from others, preferring one thing to another, coming to a decision in favour of something. In *Theaetetus* 190 a 2, on the other hand, Plato employs the verb *horizein* for this inward saying yes or no to one of several possibilities: in forming a judgment one marks out, by drawing boundaries around it, as it were, that one of the considered states of affairs which, after due deliberation, seems to have the best credentials. Here we encounter again the idea of setting limits to something. But, more importantly, it is noteworthy that Plato uses exactly that word from which in later times the name for the indicative mood will be derived. Dionysius Thrax (*Ars grammatica* 13, ed. Uhlig p. 47) calls the indicative mood *horistikē enklisis*; and Apollonius Dyscolus (*De syntaxi*, ed. Uhlig p. 346) explains this name by pointing out that in using this mood we make known an opinion and assert something definite (*apophainomenoi horizometha*). Some more light is shed on this meaning of *horizein* by two remarkable passages in Sextus Empiricus (*Pyrrhōneioi hypotypōseis* I, 197) and Diogenes Laertius (*Vitae philosophorum* IX, 74) on the skeptics' use of the phrase *ouden horizō*. Sextus informs us that *horizein* is not simply to put something into words (*legein ti*), but to put forward something combined with assent (*meta synkatatheseōs*), in a declaration which is accompanied by confident belief (*meta pepoithēseōs apophainomenos*). It is just this element of assent or belief, the assertive force, which is supposed to be absent when the skeptic pronounces the words *ouden horizō*; all he does is give expression to a certain state of mind, without affirming or denying anything. In all these contexts, we may safely conclude, *horizein* has the sense of forming or pronouncing a definite judgment, of reaching a point at which one's assent or dissent is firmly fixed on one alternative.

2.4.3. *Doxazein*, then, is a kind of *legein*, and *doxa* is a *logos* pronounced not aloud to someone else but silently to oneself (*Theaetetus* 190 a 4–6). But often one will want to communicate one's belief to others, by means of genuine language. This process of giving verbal expression to what one holds true in one's mind is described by Plato in various ways. He uses the verbs *apophainesthai, emphanē poiein, endeixasthai* (*Theaetetus* 170 d 4, 206 d 1–2, 8), in the sense of making known (manifest, plain) what one thinks. As a fable is put into verse or a poem is set to music, so what one has first said to oneself is put into words spoken aloud (*Philebus* 38 e 1–2). The expression of thought in speech is also likened to casting an image of one's *doxa* on the stream that flows through the mouth, like a reflection in a mirror or in water (*Theaetetus* 206 d 3–4). The *logos* is, as it were, the image (*eidōlon*) of thought in spoken sound (*Theaetetus* 208 c 5), the stream which flows from the mind through the mouth with sound (*Sophist* 263 e 7–8).

So, on the one hand, it is the thought or belief which precedes overt speech and gives meaning and content to its sounds. In this sense thought is prior, both in time and importance, to speech. On the other hand, it is the familiar and public process of overt discourse that serves to throw light upon the mysterious phenomena of private thought and judgment, by supplying the vocabulary in which those are characterized.

2.5. Summary

In spite of understandable shortcomings in Plato's treatment of problems concerning acts and attitudes of holding something true and their objects it is undeniable that he has succeeded in making some distinctions and initiating some themes that are of the utmost importance for the further history of these problems. We may sum up the results of his reflections in the following points.

He has called attention to a fundamental difference between two levels of speech activity: the level on which a speaker designates something by means of a noun or a verb and the level on which a speaker asserts that something is the case. The units of the second level, the *logoi*, have a certain completeness and independence which is not found in the units of the first level, the *onomata* and *rhēmata*.

Onomata and *rhēmata* are parts of speech which, in a particular combination, make up a *logos*. Plato's recognition of the importance – and the difference – of the roles that these two kinds of words play in statements is the beginning of the traditional view that nouns and verbs have a privileged status in comparison with the other parts of speech (to which Plato does not yet pay any attention).

Plato tries to make the process of thinking and in particular the mental acts and attitudes of holding something true more intelligible by applying to them the terminology of spoken language and treating them as mental speech.

The dualistic conception of thought and speech was considerably strengthened by Plato's way of representing the relation between judging and believing and their expression in words. Verbal communication to others is manifestly regarded by him as secondary to what occurs in the privacy of the mental sphere.

As the bearers of truth and falsity Plato has now come to consider the *doxa* and the *logos,* the judgment or belief and the utterance that, in making a statement, is used to give expression to such a judgment or belief. He did not yet make these terms as clear and precise as would have been desirable. In particular, he has not found occasion to say anything about the identity conditions of a *logos.* We may, however, conjecture that for him a *logos* was primarily of a concrete and individual character, a token rather than a type, if this modern distinction is applicable at all.

3. ARISTOTLE

In the first chapter of his *De interpretatione* (16 a 3) Aristotle indicates the
three principal dimensions in which acts and attitudes of holding something
true should be studied: the affections of the soul or the mental sphere, the
sounds and marks of spoken and written language, and the world of things of
which the affections of the soul are likenesses. I shall begin with the mental
sphere. About this rather little is said in those treatises of Aristotle's that
were most influential during the period with which we are concerned, the
Categories and the *De interpretatione*. To get more detailed information we
have to consult other works, in particular the *De anima,* to which Aristotle
himself refers us.

3.1.   Thought, judgment, and belief

3.1.1.   The soul of human beings is characterized by the powers of local
motion and of discerning (*to kritikon*). To the latter belong the capacities of
perceiving (*aisthēsis*) and imaging (*phantasia*), and, more importantly for our
purposes, the faculties of immediate apprehension and of discursive thinking,
of judging by means of combining and separating concepts. Although the
names for these faculties vary, it is clear that Aristotle attaches great importance to the distinction between them (*De an.*   408 b 24, 413 b 24, 415 a 8,
430 b 27). We are chiefly interested in the faculty of discursive thinking, of
that kind of thinking which is susceptible of being called true or false (*De an.*
427 b 8). In the exercise of this faculty three stages can be distinguished: a
preparatory phase, in which one attempts to arrive at a definite judgment; the
act of judging that something is or is not the case; and the dispositional state,
such as believing or being of the opinion that something is or is not the case,
which results from making up one's mind about a certain issue.

23

3.1.2. The preparatory phase is touched upon in a passage of the *Nicomachean Ethics* (1142 a 31) in which Aristotle investigates the nature of deliberation and of the quality which enables a man to deliberate well. Excellence in deliberation is neither knowledge nor opinion. It is, rather, a correctness in thinking (*dianoia*). Thinking is not yet a definite assent or dissent (*phasis*), while *doxa*, on the contrary, has got beyond the stage of investigation and is already a form of assent or dissent (*phasis*). There is no doubt, in my opinion, that Aristotle alludes here to the two passages in Plato's *Theaetetus* (189 e 4) and *Sophist* (263 e 3) which were discussed in 2.4.1. He employs exactly the same criterion to separate the stage of *dianoia* from the actual arrival at a *doxa*; the word *phasis* comprehends both *kataphasis,* affirmation, and *apophasis,* denial (Plato's *phasis* and *apophasis* in *Sophist* 263 e 12). It is by an inward saying yes or no that the soul or the activity of thinking concludes the preparatory phase of deliberation and reaches a definite judgment and opinion which are either true or false (*Nic. Eth.* 1139 b 15; *Met.* 1012 a 2).

3.1.3. In the verbal sphere of speech activity Plato had drawn a fundamental distinction between the *onomazein*-level and the *legein*-level. Analogously, Aristotle distinguishes between thoughts in the soul that are without combination and separation and are, therefore, neither true nor false and, on the other hand, thoughts that are susceptible of truth and falsity (*De int.* 16 a 9). Elsewhere (*Met.* 1051 b 17; *De an.* 430 a 26) Aristotle speaks about incomposites which are simply apprehended by the mind in a kind of intuitive grasping comparable, in certain respects, to the perception of sensible objects; this apprehension of incomposites is contrasted with a level of thought on which the incomposites are combined in such a way that the compound becomes capable of being called true or false. Just as there are acts of *onomazein* by means of *onomata* and *rhēmata* standing for things and actions or states, there are acts of thinking directed towards incomposite objects; and just as there are acts of *legein* in which *onomata* and *rhēmata* are put together in such a manner that a true or false *logos* is brought about, there are acts of thinking in which incomposite thoughts are made parts of a whole that is true or false.

For Plato the decisive factor in the genesis of a *logos* was a specific kind of combination of a *rhēma* with an *onoma*, a *symplokē*. Aristotle uses the same word for the essential factor in the formation of a composite thought which is true or false: it is a *symplokē noēmatōn* (*De an.* 432 a 11). This *symplokē* is an act of thinking incomposites together or apart in such a way that they form a unity (*Met.* 1027 b 25; *De an.* 430 a 28, 430 b 5). Instead of the mental saying yes or no, the *phasis* which is reminiscent of Plato, Aristotle introduces the terms *synthesis* and *dihairesis* for the composition and division typical of the kind of thought that is true or false.

In *De an.* 430 a 28 Aristotle aptly refers the reader to Empedocles who said: 'On the earth many heads sprang up without necks, arms wandered bare, bereft of shoulders, and eyes strayed alone in need of foreheads'. This state of things, in which the single-limbed members wandered about longing to combine with each other, was remedied by the activity of *Philia*: 'as the elements mingled, a myriad kinds of mortal creatures were brought forth, endowed with all sorts of shapes, a wonder to behold'[1].

The synthesizing act of assenting or dissenting occurs in the mind; falsity and truth are not in things but in thought (*Met.* 1027 b 25, 30, 1065 a 21). On the other hand, truth and falsehood depend, on the side of the objects, on their being combined or separated, so that he who thinks the separate to be separated and the combined to be combined has the truth, while he whose thought is in a state contrary to that of the objects is in error (*Met.* 1051 b 2, 1027 b 20). It is the state of things in the world that determines the truth or falsity of the judgment; but the judgment itself, as the actual bearer of truth and falsehood, is in the mind.

3.1.4. For the dispositional states of holding something true which are the results of acts of judging Aristotle usually employs the verbs *doxazein* and *hypolambanein* (also *dianoeisthai, oiesthai, nomizein, gnōmēn echein* etc.). I have found no indications that he ever uses them for the preparatory phase. In the aorist, with an inchoative aspect, they may have the sense of arriving at an opinion or coming to hold an opinion; a sense that is also sometimes expressed by the phrase *lambanein (labein) hypolēpsin* or *doxan* (*Posterior Analytics* 79 b 27; *Met.* 983 b 22, 25; *Physics* 191 a 35; *Rhetoric* 1417 b 10). But apart from these specially marked cases those verbs indicate a more or less permanent state of mind which is originated by an act of judging. Once this act has been accomplished, one has the belief or holds the opinion that something is or is not the case.

3.1.5. Finally, we may ask ourselves what kind of expressions Aristotle uses for that which is thought or believed. Sometimes we find *doxazomenon, doxaston, hypolambanomenon, hypolēpton,* passive participles of the verbs *doxazein* and *hypolambanein.* The nouns *doxa* and *hypolēpsis* (which does

---

[1] Diels-Kranz, *Die Fragmente der Vorsokratiker* I, 31, B 57, 58; B 35, 16−17.

not occur in Plato's works) are occasionally employed in a verbal sense, with the object in the genitive case: the belief of the contrary (*De int.* 23 a 33), the judging of an immediate proposition (*Posterior Analytics* 88 b 37, 89 a 3). But they can also stand for that which is held to be the case: that the sum of the angles of a triangle is equal to two right angles (*Nic. Eth.* 1140 b 13), or that contradiction is impossible (*Topics* 104 b 19). In that sense *doxa* and *hypolēpsis* (and also *dianoia*) are practically synonyms and are rather neutral, generic terms for that which is believed; axioms, for instance, are universal *doxai* (*Met.* 996 b 28, 997 a 21).

Often it is far from easy to decide whether *doxa* and *hypolēpsis* are to be taken in the verbal sense of *doxazein* and *hypolambanein* or in the sense of the objects of those verbs. It is, however, not implausible to assume that if they are qualified by the attributes 'true' or 'false', it is normally the content of *doxazein* and *hypolambanein* that is regarded as the bearer of truth or falsity. It is that which is believed to be the case which is true or false in the primary sense; only in a secondary sense can the act or state of judging or believing be called true or false. This also applies to a case like *De an.* 432 a 11, where it is said that the true or false is a *symplokē* of thoughts. It is not so much the act of combining, by composition or division, that is true or false, but rather the object of the assent or dissent. This seems to be confirmed by the fact that elsewhere (*De int.* 16 a 13; *De an.* 430 a 26) Aristotle expresses himself in a more careful way: truth and falsity have to do with a combination or separation of thoughts; they presuppose a certain kind of *synthesis*.

Although *doxa* and *hypolēpsis* are sometimes of a generic nature, they can also acquire a more special character, by being contrasted with such states as scientific knowledge (*epistēmē*) and intuitive reason (*nous*), in which we always grasp the truth. Compared with these superior cases of knowledge *doxa* and *hypolēpsis*, which admit of falsity, are only opinion, only something which is held to be true but may prove to be false (*Posterior Analytics* 100 b 5; *Nic. Eth.* 1139 b 16). Similarly, Plato uses *doxa* in a generic sense in *Theaetetus* 190 a 3 and *Sophist* 264 a 2, and elsewhere, in a more special sense, for a mere opinion.

3.2.   The expression of thought in speech

3.2.1.   As we saw in 2.4.3, one of the words that Plato uses for giving verbal expression to what one holds true in one's mind is the verb *apophainesthai*. This verb, with *gnōmēn* or *doxan* as the expressed or unexpressed object, was familiar to every Greek and had the quite ordinary meaning of making known one's opinion. It is this word that plays a central role in Aristotle's treatment of the expression of thought in speech, at least in *De interpretatione*. Together with the noun *apophansis,* it becomes a more or less technical term for the speech act of making known to others what one holds true in one's mind, of asserting that something is the case. This speech act is either an affirmation or a denial: a *kataphasis* is an *apophansis* in which it is asserted that one thing belongs to another, an *apophasis* is an *apophansis* in which one thing is separated from another (*De int.* 17 a 25). Both *kataphasis* and *apophasis* are species of the genus *phasis*: they are forms of saying (*phanai*) that something is or is not the case.

All these nouns suffer from a process-product ambiguity. Sometimes they indicate the activity of making known one's opinion by means of affirming or denying that something is the case. But they may also designate the utterance which is produced in the course of that activity. So an *apophansis* is defined as a significant spoken sound about whether something does or does not hold (*De int.* 17 a 23). The two species of the genus *phasis, kataphasis* and *apophasis,* are defined as *logos kataphatikos* and *logos apophatikos,* as an affirmative or negative utterance (*Cat.* 12 b 8). Each is a *logos apophantikos,* an utterance used in the activity of revealing one's thought (*De int.* 17 a 8).

It is this utterance, as used for a special purpose, that is the typical unit of the *legein*-level, the Platonic *logos*. In contrast with other sorts of expressions which do not yet admit of truth or falsity, a *kataphasis* or *apophasis* and a *logos apophantikos* are the kind of units that are rightly called true or false (*Cat.* 2 a 7; *De int.* 17 a 3, 20 a 35).

3.2.2.   The other sorts of expressions, which do not yet admit of truth or falsity and are for that reason incomplete and defective, are the units of Plato's *onomazein*-level, the *onomata* and *rhēmata*. By uttering an *onoma* or a *rhēma* one cannot reveal anything by one's utterance in such a way as to be making a statement (*De int.* 17 a 17). This 'not yet'-character of *onomata* and *rhēmata* is a point to which Aristotle remarkably often returns.

In *Cat.* 1 a 16 he distinguishes between expressions whose utterance involves a combination (*symplokē*) and expressions that are uttered without combination. As examples are given: 'Man runs', 'Man wins'; 'Man', 'Ox', 'Runs', 'Wins'. The expressions formed without any combination designate something belonging to one of the categories, and none of them is either true or false (*Cat.* 2 a 8, 13 b 10).

In *De int.* 16 a 9 a parallel is drawn between the mental sphere and the verbal sphere. In the mental sphere two kinds of thoughts are found, those unaccompanied by truth or by falsity and those that necessarily have one or the other. In the verbal sphere *onomata* and *rhēmata* which are pronounced without any addition – for instance, 'Man', 'White' – are like thoughts that are formed without any combination; they are not yet true or false. Even a word such as 'Goat-stag' does not yet signify anything true or false. It does so only when 'is' or 'is not' is added.

That the *symplokē* must be of a special kind is shown by *De int.* 16 b 1. When 'is' or 'is not' is added to a genitive or dative case ('Philo's' or 'to-Philo'), the combination does not yet yield a truth or falsehood. The oblique cases cannot play the role of naming the subject in a statement-making utterance.

Further examples of the 'not yet'-terminology are *De int.* 16 b 19 and 17 a 9. Verbs uttered by themselves signify something but they do not yet signify whether something is the case or not (Compare *De int.* 16 b 28: a word like 'Man' signifies something but not that something is the case or is not the case). The definition (*logos*) of man, without 'is' or 'was' or 'will be' or something of that kind, is not yet a statement-making utterance.

These passages are sufficient proof that Aristotle, probably inspired by Plato, is fully aware of the incomplete and defective character of *onomata* and *rhēmata*. Measured against the relative independence of utterances by means of which expression is given to a belief that something is the case, and which therefore admit of truth or falsity, the meaning of *onomata* and *rhēmata* is imperfect. A composite unit of the *legein*-level, which has the complete sense of a true or a false thought, is formed only when the open place accompanying each separate *onoma* or *rhēma* is occupied by a proper complement.

Aristotle defines *onomata* and *rhēmata* as spoken sounds significant by convention none of whose parts is significant in separation (*De int.* 16 a 20, 16 b 6; *Poetics* 1457 a 10, 14). The difference between the two is that an *onoma* signifies without any reference to time, whereas a *rhēma* additionally signifies time. Moreover, the *rhēma* is a sign of something said of something else, the subject. The verb *legein* which Aristotle uses in this connection indicates both the predicative and the assertive function of the *rhēma*; if someone says 'Callias runs', the component 'runs' is a sign that the speaker connects the activity of running with Callias, but also that he holds that this predicate actually belongs to Callias, at the time indicated. As for cases like 'Callias is running' or 'Man is just', where the word 'is' occurs as a third element, there the verb 'is' by itself is nothing, but it additionally signifies some combination (*synthesis*) which cannot be thought without the components (*De int.* 16 b 25). This *synthesis*, of which the spoken sounds 'is' or 'is not' are the appropriate sign, is the mental activity of bringing together or separating two concepts which, at the same time, is an act of assenting to the combination, or of dissenting from it. Aristotle does not seem to distinguish between merely conceiving of a certain combination, in a neutral state of mind, and actually accepting or rejecting it; for him a *synthesis* is always a mental assertion. That the copula 'is' has this assertive force is confirmed by *Met.* 1017 a 31; although Aristotle speaks there of an emphatic use of 'is' and 'is not', in the sense of 'Socrates *is* educated, he really is so', there is reason to believe that this emphatic use is only a strengthening of what is normally present in all cases. For in *De int.* 21 b 31 it is said that in utterances of the form 'Man is white', 'Man is not white' the parts 'is' and 'is not' determine the true; this presumably means that they lend assertive force to these utterances (The passage is, however, far from clear).

De int. 16 b 20 is also interesting because it is in these lines that we find the first trace of a distinction that later came to be known as the distinction between categorematic and syncategorematic words. Although verbs by themselves do not yet signify whether something is the case or not and therefore do not possess the degree of completeness and independence which is characteristic of the units of the *legein*-level, it is still true that most of them have a meaning of their own in the sense that both the speaker and the hearer, in pronouncing or hearing the word, will have a definite thought in their minds, a thought that has some kind of self-sufficiency. The copula 'is', on the contrary, is not accompanied by any such distinct and relatively self-sufficient thought; it only adds a certain nuance to the meaning of the words to which it is joined. For this additional way of signifying Aristotle uses the word *prossēmainein.* This verb also occurs in *De int.* 20 a 13, in connection with 'every' and 'no'; these words additionally signify nothing other than that the affirmation or negation is about the name taken universally. Thus we have here the beginning of a trichotomy: expressions signifying that something is the case; verbs and nouns, which do not yet signify that something is the case but have some meaning of their own; and words like 'is', 'every', 'no', which do not signify (*sēmainein*) in either of those ways but only contribute to the meaning of other words.

3.2.3. While *onomata* and *rhēmata* are significant sounds none of whose parts is significant in separation, a *logos,* according to *De int.* 16 b 26 and *Poetics* 1457 a 23, is a significant spoken sound some part of which is significant in separation. As that part can be any expression from a noun or a verb upwards, a *logos* is a meaningful group of words extending from phrases like 'two-footed land animal' to complete utterances of various length and complexity; even the *Iliad* is a *logos* (*Poetics* 1457 a 29). Among the complete *logoi* some are utterances which are used for the purpose of making known an opinion and are therefore true or false; others — for instance, prayers — are not used for this particular purpose and cannot be characterized as true or false. Consideration of the latter group belongs to the study of rhetoric or poetry.

About this subject of the kinds of speech we find some more detailed information in *Poetics* 1456 a 33. Aristotle has already discussed plot and character and now comes to diction (*lexis*) and thought (*dianoia*). Thought belongs more properly to the province of rhetoric; the thought of the characters in a play is shown in everything to be effected by their language, in every effort to prove or disprove, to arouse emotion (pity, fear, anger, and the like), or to maximize or minimize things. Next, he mentions, only to dismiss them as irrelevant, the *schēmata tēs lexeōs*. This expression does not designate the figures of speech here, but Aristotle indicates by it certain ways in which the meaning of a phrase may be determined by the speaker's intonation. The theory of these manners of speaking belongs to the art of delivery or elocution (*hypokritikē*), in which questions are raised concerning the difference between, for instance, command and prayer, simple statement and threat, question and answer. In *Poetics* 1457 a 21 some examples are given. The verbal form *ebadisen* may be used as a statement or as a question, according to the tone in which it is uttered: '(He) walked' or '(He) walked?'. And the imperative *badize* may be used for commands of different degrees of urgency, according to the mode of utterance.

In this connection Aristotle informs us that Protagoras had criticized the first verse of Homer's *Iliad* ('Sing, Goddess, of the wrath') as being a command instead of a prayer. Apparently Protagoras had noticed that the imperative mood is usually associated with the tone of command and this led him to object that a commanding tone of voice in a prayer is improper. That he took a lively interest in this sort of problem is confirmed by Diogenes Laertius (*Vitae philosophorum* IX, 53; cf. Quintilian, *Institutio oratoria* III, 4, 10), who says that Protagoras was the first to divide speech into four fundamental kinds: prayer, question, answer, and command. According to Diogenes others distinguished seven kinds: statement, question, answer, command, report, prayer, calling; but Alcidamas, a rhetorician from the first half of the fourth century B.C., adhered to a division into four kinds: affirmation, denial, question, address.

The fact that Aristotle relates Protagoras's criticism to his own remarks about the manners of speaking which are treated by the professors of elocution makes it plausible that the above-mentioned divisions had at least something to do with the art of delivery. On the other hand, it would be unwise to exclude the possibility of influences from other quarters; from dialectic, for instance, where the difference between question and answer is conspicuous, or from rhetoric (Aristotle pays special attention to question and answer in *Rhetoric* 1418 b 40). That interest in classifying uses of language was aroused by very different considerations we know, moreover, from other sources. In Plato's *Phaedrus* (271 c 10) it is urged that the true orator must understand how each type of discourse (*logōn eidē*) affects different types of temperament. According to *Sophist* 222 c 9 the art of persuasion can be exercised in forensic pleading, in speeches in public assemblies, and in ordinary conversation. The first two are also mentioned in the first chapter of the so-called *Rhetorica ad Alexandrum*, as the two genera (*genē*) of political speeches, to which seven kinds (*eidē*) are added: hortatory, dissuasive, panegyrical, censorious, accusatory, apologetic, investigatory. Quintilian (*Institutio oratoria* III, 4, 9) ascribes the same division to Anaximenes of Lampsacus, a contemporary of Aristotle and probably the author of the *Rhetorica ad Alexandrum*.

Aristotle's remark about the difference between the utterance which is used for making a statement and a prayer has to be seen against the background of these passages, which show that the classification of uses of language was a much-discussed theme in several branches of investigation. Aristotle has related it to the question of the bearers of truth and falsity and in this connection we shall meet it time and again.

3.2.4.   It is worthwhile to look again at some of the words of Aristotle's vocabulary for dealing with the expression of thought in speech and, in particular, to ask ourselves what kind of subject and object the verbs *sēmainein, dēloun, apophainesthai, kataphanai,* and *apophanai* may take.

In contexts pertinent to our topic the verb *sēmainein* always has a linguistic expression for its subject. From the cases in which it is said that an expression signifies something but not yet that something is the case or is not the case, we may conclude that it would also be correct to say that an expression signifies that something is the case or is not the case, perhaps as an abbreviated way of saying that some person indicates, by means of that expression, that something is the case. The verb *dēloun* is synonymous with *sēmainein*, as is easily shown by juxtaposing *De int.* 17 a 16 and *Poetics* 1457 a 28, 30. In *De int.* 17 a 18 it is used in the sense of revealing, by spoken sounds, that something is the case, with a person as subject.

In contrast with *sēmainein* and *dēloun*, whose more general meaning makes them applicable to a rather wide range of cases, *apophainesthai* and its species *kataphanai* and *apophanai* stand for definite speech acts, performed by persons and directed to states of affairs. Compared to Plato's term *legein* with its great variety of meanings, *apophainesthai* has the advantage of being much more precise and specific. It is also a gain in precision and clarity that Aristotle determines the Protean word *logos* by means of adjectives which are derived from the verbs for the speech acts in which the *logos* is used: he nearly always speaks of a *logos apophantikos,* a *logos kataphatikos,* or a *logos apophatikos.* These additions make it probable that in such phrases the word *logos* has for Aristotle the sense of an utterance; and the suffix *-tikos* in the adjectives indicates that the utterance is fit to be used or is properly used in a speech act of making known an opinion or of affirming or denying that something is the case.

3.2.5. Finally, a few remarks should be made about the very important term *protasis.* This word, which does not occur before Aristotle, originally belongs, together with *problēma,* to the context of dialectical disputations. The nouns are derived from the verbs *proteinein* and *proballein,* with the sense of putting forward or propounding something for acceptance or rejection. While a *problēma* is stated in the form 'Is *A B*, or not?', a *protasis* has the form 'Is *A B*?' (*Topics* 101 b 28). The partner in the debate has to make his choice between a positive and a negative answer; and the chosen answer serves as the starting-point of the argument.

Now the word *protasis* designates not only the activity of propounding such a question or the propounded question itself, but also the thesis to which the answerer commits himself, either assuming it for the sake of argument or taking it as a true premiss for a demonstration. In the latter cases a *protasis* is a *logos* in which something is affirmed or denied of a subject, in other words, a *logos apophantikos* or *apophansis* (*De int.* 20 b 22; *Prior Analytics* 24 a 16; *Posterior Analytics* 72 a 8). It is obvious that a *protasis* can be a bearer of truth or falsity only in its role as a *logos apophantikos.*

Since a *protasis* in the sense of a *logos apophantikos* will usually be an element of an argument, in particular one of the statements from which another is inferred, the word *protasis* also becomes the technical term for a premiss. Sometimes Aristotle distinguishes the minor premiss from the major premiss by calling it the other or the last *protasis* (*Nic. Eth.* 1143 b 3, 1147 b 9). This association with a certain place in the structure of an argument, as well as the association with the questioner in a debate, will long remain typical of the term *protasis* and of its Latin equivalent *propositio.*

3.3.   States of affairs, alleged and real

3.3.1.   In 3.1.5 we saw that the content of a belief can be designated by a 'that'-clause: that the sum of the angles of a triangle is equal to two right angles, or that contradiction is impossible. In these two cases in Greek the conjunction *hoti* is used, followed by a verb in the indicative mood. Another construction which is very common in Greek is an accusative and infinitive phrase, both with verbs of believing and asserting and with expressions of the type 'is true (false, necessary, possible)'. Now it is worth noticing that such accusative and infinitive phrases do not only stand for that which is believed or asserted to be the case but can also be used to designate that which actually is the case in the world. A clear instance of the latter use is found in *Met.* 1051 b 6: it is not because we think truly that you are white, that you are white, but because of the fact that you are white (*dia to se einai leukon*) we who say this have the truth. This double use of the accusative and infinitive phrase, combined with the obscurity of the word *pragma* which Aristotle sometimes employs in this connection, is the source of some difficulties which for a long time have beset the discussion of problems concerning the bearers of truth and falsity. The nature of these difficulties may be illustrated by the following examples.

3.3.2.   In *Cat.* 14 b 14 Aristotle points out that there is a mutual implication between the fact that there is a man and the truth of the *logos* about it: if there is a man, the *logos* whereby we say that there is a man is true, and if the *logos* whereby we say that there is a man is true, there is a man. This does not mean, however, that the true *logos* is the cause of the circumstance that the *pragma* is (*tou einai to pragma*). On the other hand, the *pragma* does seem in some way the cause of the truth of the *logos*; for it is because the *pragma* is or is not that the *logos* is called true or false (Cf. also *Cat.* 4 b 8). Now it looks as if this can be interpreted in two ways. One may take *pragma* as referring to a thing or an object, in this case to the man in question. This interpretation might seem to be supported by *De int.* 21 b 28, where 'white' and 'man' are called the underlying things (*ta hypokeimena pragmata*) of utterances such as 'Man is white' and 'Man is not white'. The meaning of the passage then becomes: the true *logos* is not the cause of that man's existence, but that man (or, rather, that man's existence) is the cause of the truth of the *logos*. For it is because the man (or, in general, the thing referred to) exists or does not exist that the *logos* is called true or false. We shall see later that in some medieval texts Aristotle's words were indeed read in this manner.

It is, however, more likely that the word *pragma* here has the same sense as in *De int.* 16 b 23, namely that of a state of affairs. In support of this interpretation at least two other passages from Aristotle's works may be cited. First of all, *Met.* 1051 b 6, where it is stated that because of the fact that you are white we who say this have the truth. This might also be expressed by saying that the *logos* is true because the *pragma* that you are white is in fact part of the world. Next, we may adduce *Cat.* 14 a 13: if it is the case that Socrates is well (*ontos tou Sōkratēn hygiainein*), it would not be the case that Socrates is sick (*ouk an eiē to nosein Sōkratēn*). In other words, if the *pragma* that Socrates is well is in fact part of the world, then the *pragma* that Socrates is sick would not belong to the world of facts. If we assume, in the light of these passages, that a *pragma* is that which is designated by an accusative and infinitive phrase, then *Cat.* 14 b 19 has to be read as follows: the true *logos* is not the cause of the circumstance that it is the case that there is a man, but that (it is the case that) there is a man is the cause of the truth of the *logos*. For it is because it is the case or is not the case that there is a man that the logos is called true or false. If this reading is correct, it is obvious that *pragma* can also refer to a state of affairs which is held to be part of reality but is nevertheless not the case. Even if in the cases in which the *logos* is true one goes so far as to identify the *pragma* (considered as the content of the *logos*) with the factual state of affairs as it is found in the world, this identification is impossible when the *logos* is false, since in that case the *pragma* is not part of the world. It is hard to tell whether Aristotle identified the *pragma* of a true *logos* with the actual fact or considered it as a conceived state of affairs which happens to be the case in reality. But in the case of a false *logos* he has no choice; there is nothing in the world with which the *pragma* can be identified, and he must therefore take it in those cases at least as the state of affairs which is believed or asserted.

There is still another relevant passage in which the word *pragma* occurs, namely *Cat.* 4 a 35. There it is said that the *logos* and the *doxa* that somebody is seated remain absolutely the same; we call them now true and now false because of a change in the *pragma* (*tou pragmatos kinoumenou* or *kinēthentos*). It is perhaps just possible to take *pragma* as referring to the person who first sits and then gets up. But it is hard to see how this interpretation can be harmonized with the formula which follows a bit further on in the text: it is because the *pragma* is or is not that the *logos* is said to be true or false. For here it is not the existence of the person in question which renders the *logos* true or false but his sitting or not sitting. On the other hand, it is also difficult to tell what exactly changes if the *pragma* is not the person. Surely not the conceived state of affairs or the actual fact. The best translation would perhaps be: because the situation changes. But then again it seems difficult to fit this meaning of the word *pragma* into the above-mentioned formula. The truth of the matter appears to be that Aristotle uses a very vague word rather loosely. In particular, he might have differentiated more clearly between a thing or object which exists or does not exist and a state of affairs which is the case or is not the case, and between a merely believed state of affairs and a state of affairs which actually is part of the world.

3.3.3. In the tenth chapter of the *Categories* Aristotle points out that there is a difference between privation and possession on the one hand and being deprived and possessing on the other. Nevertheless, being deprived and possessing seem to be mutually opposed in the same way as privation and possession are. Similarly, he continues in 12 b 6, what underlies a negation or affirmation (*to hypo tēn apophasin kai kataphasin*) is not itself a negation or affirmation; for that which underlies an affirmation or negation is not a *logos*. But in these cases too the manner of opposition is the same: as the affirmation 'He is sitting' is opposed to the negation 'He is not sitting', so the *pragma* underlying the one is opposed to the *pragma* underlying the other, his sitting to his not sitting.

What does Aristotle mean by the phrase *to hypo tēn apophasin kai kataphasin* and by the phrase *to hyph' hekateron pragma* used in 12 b 15? Let us look at two other passages where more or less similar expressions occur. In *Met.* 1067 b 18 (Cf. *Physics* 225 a 6) he calls the positive termini presupposed by change *hypokeimenon* and explains that by *hypokeimenon* he means that which is indicated by a *kataphasis* (*to kataphasei dēloumenon*). In *De int.* 19 b 7 he says that what is in a *kataphasis* (*to en tēi kataphasei*) must be one and about one thing. In both cases he seems to mean by *kataphasis* a term which is or may be used as the predicate-term in an affirmative *logos*. But as Aristotle does not always clearly distinguish between affirming that something is the case and affirming something of a subject, and as in *Cat.* 12 b 15 he mentions only the predicates (*to kathēsthai tōi mē kathēsthai*), we may ignore this difference. But even so, we are still faced with the question whether he intends his expressions to be understood in an intensional or in an extensional way. Does he mean the thought-content associated with the words or the actual things and states of affairs in the world outside thought and language? *Met.* 1067 b 18 might incline us to opt for the latter alternative; apart from the context we could also take into account the fact that *hypokeimenon* is often used of a thing which exists in external reality, in contradistinction to the word that refers to it. On the other side, in *Cat.*

12 b 6 Aristotle speaks of an opposition between the affirmation 'He is sit-ting' and the negation 'He is not sitting'. If we take him to mean that these two utterances cannot be true at the same time, it follows that the underlying states of affairs cannot both be part of the world of facts at the same time. Only the content of the true utterance could be identified with an actual state of affairs in the world; the content of the false utterance must be a state of affairs that is merely believed to be the case but does not belong to reality. We have to conclude again, I think, that Aristotle expresses himself in such a way that no definite answers to our questions can be given. Concentrating on some aspects one can read him in one way, concentrating on other aspects one can read him in another way.

Finally, it may be noted that still another sense of the expression *ta hypokeimena* (*pragmata*) is found in *De int.* 21 b 26. There Aristotle uses it for the concepts or terms 'white' and 'man' as the matter to which 'is' or 'is not' must be added in order to get the affirmation 'A man is white' or the negation 'A man is not white'. This passage is the source of the doctrine that the concepts signified by the subject-term and the predicate-term are the matter of the judgment and that the mental composition or division signified by an affirmative or negative copula is the form. Now just as 'white' and 'man' are the underlying matter of 'A man is white' or 'A man is not white', so '(that) a man is white' is the matter of such expressions as 'It is possible that a man is white' or 'It is not possible that a man is white', where 'It is possible' and 'It is not possible' are the additions that transform this matter into a new affirmation or negation. It is clear that this kind of underlying *pragma* has nothing to do with the underlying *pragma* of *Cat.* 12 b 15. In the latter passage Aristotle obviously means by it the state of affairs associated with utterances such as 'Socrates is sitting' and 'Socrates is not sitting': Socrates's sitting and Socrates's not sitting. According to *De int.* 21 b 26, however, the underlying *pragmata* of 'Socrates is sitting' would be the notions of Socrates and of being seated; and '(that) Socrates is sitting' itself would be the underlying *pragma* of 'It is (not) possible that Socrates is sitting'.

3.4.   The relation between thought and language

As Aristotle himself does not pay much attention to written language and the way in which it is a symbol of spoken language, I shall leave written language aside and confine myself to the connection between thought and spoken language.

3.4.1. First of all, it should be remarked that Aristotle apparently feels less inclined to 'lingualize' thought than Plato does. We have seen that once or twice he uses words that mean saying yes or no for the act of judging that something is the case (*Nic. Eth.* 1142 b 13; *Met.* 1012 a 2, 4; perhaps also *Nic. Eth.* 1139 b 15). There is also one passage, *Posterior Analytics* 76 b 24, where he contrasts overt speech (*ton exō logon*) with discourse in the soul (*ton esō logon* or *ton en tēi psychēi logon*), in connection with axioms which are necessarily thought to be true, although they may be denied in words. But on the whole he prefers a terminology without metaphors from the field of spoken language, the terminology of the *symplokē noēmatōn*. The most general term of this special vocabulary is *ta en tēi psychēi pathēmata*, 'the affections of the soul'. This rather vague phrase may be supposed to comprehend acts of conceiving incomposites, with their contents, the *noēmata*, acts of *synthesis*, of thinking these *noēmata* together or apart, in a composition or division, and the attitudes of believing or thinking that something is the case which result from these acts of judging, together with their content, that which is believed or thought to be the case.

The affections of the soul are, according to *De int.* 16 a 8, the likenesses (*homoiōmata*) of the *pragmata* in the external world. Even if we restrict these affections of the soul to the incomposite *noēmata*, it is hard to tell what Aristotle means by the word 'likenesses'. One may be inclined to think of sense-impressions and mental images, but this interpretation seems to be excluded by what Aristotle himself says in *De an.* 432 a 10: both combined and uncombined *noēmata* differ from *phantasmata*. However this may be, the units of the *doxazein*-level, with which we are primarily concerned, the beliefs as combinations of *noēmata,* contain an element, the *synthesis,* which cannot be thought of without the components (*De int.* 16 b 25). So there must at least be a difference between the way in which the separate *noēmata* are related to the things in the world and the way in which the units that are built by means of a *synthesis* are related to the world. As these units are characterized by the fact that they are susceptible of truth or falsity, it is most natural to assume that their relations to the world are determined by the general conditions of truth and falsity which Aristotle elsewhere states, for instance *Met.* 1051 b 2 and 1027 b 20.

Next, we have to consider what is comprehended by the equally vague phrase *ta en tēi phōnēi*, 'the sounds of spoken language', and the way in which the elements of this field are related to the sphere of thought and to the world. The spoken sounds that Aristotle has in mind are the *onomata* and *rhēmata*, the copula 'is' or 'is not', and the *logoi* that one forms by combining these elements in an appropriate manner. Those different units of spoken language are signs or symbols (*sēmeia, symbola*) of units of thought: *onomata* and *rhēmata* signify incomposite *noēmata,* the copula signifies the mental *synthesis,* either a composition or a division, and the complex *logos* indicates a thought or belief that something is the case, true or false. From the point of view of the linguistic expressions it may be said that they signify (*sēmainein, dēloun*) thoughts of different kinds. From the point of view of the users of the language we may say that the speaker reveals, by means of the linguistic expressions, what he is thinking of. For this activity of revealing one's thoughts the same verbs *sēmainein* and *dēloun* can be used, but Aristotle also employs the verb *apophainesthai* which is, however, restricted to cases in which the speaker makes known a complete thought or a belief that something is the case. It is this act of *apophainesthai* which gives to spoken words the special character of an affirmative or negative utterance used for the purpose of making known one's belief; and the utterance can be used for this purpose because the spoken sounds are conventional signs of mental phenomena.

As Aristotle says in *De int.* 23 a 32, the spoken sounds follow things in the mind; they are in the first place (*prōtōs; De int.* 16 a 7) signs of the affections of the soul. It is only in an indirect way, *via* the thoughts which they express, that they can be said to signify things or states of affairs in the outside world. Asserting that something is the case is making known to others a belief that one has previously formed in one's own mind. The utterance used in the act of asserting has a definite meaning in so far as it is the verbal expression of a prior belief; whether it reveals something about the actual world or not depends entirely upon the way in which the expressed belief is related to the world.

3.4.2.   There are two questions with which every student of the relation between thought and language will be confronted sooner or later. Can the same thought be expressed by means of different wordings or, to put it in another way, are certain variations in the verbal expressions irrelevant to the identity of the expressed thought? And, conversely, can the same verbal utterance be used to express quite different thoughts?

There are some indications that Aristotle was faintly aware of the possibility of asking the first question on the abstract level of explicit reflection. In *De int.* 20 a 39 he says that the utterance 'Every not-man is not-just' signifies the same (*tauton sēmainei*) as the utterance 'No not-man is just'. In the following sentence he uses the same expression, *tauton sēmainei,* for utterances in which the *onomata* and *rhēmata* are transposed, for instance 'White is a man' and 'A man is white'. In *De int.* 21 b 9, *Prior Analytics* 51 b 13, and

Met. 1017 a 27 we find the phrase *ouden diapherei,* indicating that there is no difference between such utterances as 'A man walks' and 'A man is walking'. In the light of Aristotle's general conception of the relation between thought and language we have to conclude, I think, that by the same thing which is signified by the various utterances he means the thought that remains one and the same through the different ways of expressing it in words. However slight the evidence is, it proves that there was at least a beginning of theoretical reflection on the fact that some variations on the verbal side do not alter the identity of the thought that is expressed.

As to the second question, there are no signs that Aristotle made any explicit distinction between, for example, utterances such as 'The sum of the interior angles of a triangle is equal to two right angles' and utterances such as 'I am hungry', between *logoi* that practically always stand for the same thought and *logoi* that express different thoughts according to the circumstances of their utterance. The fact that he ascribes truth and falsehood to utterances as well as to beliefs suggests that in general he regarded the relation between the two as a one-one correspondence and did not pay attention to cases in which one *logos* can be used to express many different thoughts.

Both questions have to do with the sameness of thoughts and utterances and it seems therefore desirable to add some remarks about this important notion.

3.5. Conditions of sameness and difference

3.5.1. In the *Dissoi logoi,* an anonymous treatise on twofold arguments dating from about 400 B.C., the fourth chapter deals with the question whether a false *logos* and a true *logos* are different *logoi* or the same *logos*[2]. The author first presents some arguments for the latter view. A false *logos* and a true *logos* are the same *logos* because they are both uttered by means of the same words and, secondly, because whenever a *logos* is uttered, if things have happened as stated in the *logos*, the *logos* is true, but if things have not happened in that way, the same *logos* is false. A *logos*, for instance, which accuses a person of temple-robbery is true if such a deed actually took place, but false if it did not. The same applies to the *logos* which is uttered by the defendants. And the law-courts judge the same *logos* both true and false. Or suppose that we are all sitting in a row and that each of us says 'I am an

---

[2] Diels-Kranz, *Die Fragmente der Vorsokratiker* II, 90, 4.

initiate'; we all utter the same words, but I am the only person saying something true, because I alone actually am one. From these examples it is clear that the same *logos* is false when it is uttered in relation to the false, and true when it is uttered in relation to the true. The author concludes this line of argument with a simile: the *logos* is the same just as a man is the same person when he is a child and a young man and an adult and an old man.

What the author intends to say is, I think, that utterance-types containing indexical words, such as 'He committed temple-robbery', or 'I did not (commit temple-robbery)', or 'I am an initiate', are called true and false not because the utterances themselves somehow take on a different character as they are pronounced at different times or by different persons at the same time, but only because of the external circumstance that they happen to be used to assert different things which are true or false according to what is found to be the case in the outside world. It is, admittedly, strange to call an utterance-type true or false; it is likely that the author was led to do so by the ambiguity of the word *logos*. But once this way of speaking has been adopted, it is not unnatural to hold that one and the same utterance-type may be both true and false: true when it is used to assert something true and false when it is used to assert something false.

It is, however, also possible to argue that a false *logos* and a true *logos* are different *logoi*; that there is not only a difference in the things that are asserted (*to pragma*) but also in the words (*tōnyma*). In the first place, one may ask those who say that the same *logos* is both false and true whether their own *logos* is true or false. If they answer that it is false, then they concede that a true *logos* and a false *logos* are two different *logoi*. If they answer that it is true, then it follows that it is also false; its truth has the absurd consequence that if a man has said certain things which are true, then these same things are also false, and that if we know that some man can be relied upon to speak the truth, we also know that this same man says things which are false. At this point the author (who is in favour of the first thesis) inserts an objection: those who defend the thesis that the same *logos* is true and false are led by the consideration that the *logos* is true if that which is asserted has really happened (*genomenō men tō pragmatos*), and false if it has not happened (In other words, they do not mean that the same *logos* in so far as it is used to make one definite statement can be both true and false at the same time; they are speaking about a *logos* used to make many different statements). There is, therefore, no difference on the verbal side (*tōnyma*), but only on the side of the things that are asserted (*to pragma*). But if that is so, the opponents can ask again what the judges in the law-courts are judging, because they are not present at the actual events (*tois pragmasin*) which determine the truth and falsehood of what is said. Moreover, the defenders of the first thesis themselves agree that a *logos* in which the false is mingled is false and that a *logos* in which the true is mingled is true; and that, surely, constitutes a total difference.

If this paraphrase is faithful to the author's intentions, we can easily see that the opponents' main argument does not really come to grips with the first thesis. The party contending that there is no difference on the *onoma*-side, but that the difference between a true and a false *logos* is wholly restricted to the *pragma*-side (the things asserted which are found to be true or false) takes *logos* in the sense of an utterance-type such as 'I am an initiate' which is used to make many different statements. The party which maintains that there is a difference on the *onoma*-side as well tries to bring off a *reductio ad absurdum* by taking *logos* in a different sense, namely either in the sense of an utterance-token or in the sense of an utterance-type in so far as it is used by different persons at the same time to make one and the same statement; both these kinds of utterance, of course, can never be true and false at the same time. The primitive and very misleading dichotomy *onoma/ pragma,* name and thing named, leaves no room for the distinctions that must be made to reduce the issue to its right proportions.

3.5.2. At two places Aristotle touches upon similar problems of sameness and difference. In *Met.* 1051 b 13 he says that regarding contingent facts the same *doxa* and the same *logos* come to be false and true, and it is possible for them to be at one time true and at another false. Regarding things that cannot be otherwise, however, it does not happen that something is now true and now false, but the same things are always true or always false. In *Cat.* 4 a 22 he discusses a possible counterexample against the thesis that only a substance is able to receive contraries while it remains numerically one and the same. Someone might object that one and the same *doxa* and *logos* can be true and false; the *doxa* or *logos* that somebody is seated, for instance, may be true at a certain moment, but the same *doxa* or *logos* will be false after that person has got up. Aristotle points out that even if one were to grant this, there is still a difference in the way contraries are received. A substance that receives contraries undergoes change. A *logos* and a *doxa*, on the other hand, themselves remain completely unchanged in every respect; it is because of a change in the *pragma* that they come to be true at one time and false at another. Actually, it is misleading to say that a *doxa* and a *logos* receive contraries; it is not because anything happens in the *doxa* or *logos* or because they themselves receive anything that they are called true and false, but they are qualified in these different ways because of what has happened to something else.

First, it is worthy of note that in both passages the *doxa* and the *logos* are taken to be of the same number, as it were; it is not the relation between one *doxa* and different *logoi* or the relation between one *logos* and different *doxai* that is at issue, but there seems to be a one-one correspondence between the two. Next, we may ask the question what exactly is meant by the phrases 'the same *doxa*' and 'the same *logos*'. Let us take 'Callias is in Athens' as an example of what Aristotle must have had in mind in *Met.* 1051 b 13. If this is to be a *doxa*, it must be definite to the extent that the person who believes it must be thinking of a certain individual as being in a certain town; what is left unspecified is the period during which that individual is in the town. This semi-definite *doxa* may be expressed, at different times and by different speakers, by means of the utterance-type 'Callias is in Athens'. As long as Callias happens to be in Athens the semi-definite *doxa* and the utterance-type used to express this *doxa* will be true; as soon as Callias leaves the town, the *doxa,* precisely because it remains the same, and the utterance-type that gives expression to that same *doxa* become false. That the *logos* in question must be an utterance-type as far as it is used to give expression to a semi-definite *doxa* is confirmed by the consideration that it can hardly be an utterance-token or an utterance-type in general. The *logos* as utterance-token seems to be too momentary and fugitive to admit of changing truth-values; once it has been uttered it can no longer be recaptured (*Cat.* 5 a 34; cf. 4 b 33). And if we take *logos* in the sense of an utterance-type that can be used to express many different *doxai* (for example, about different individuals all bearing the name 'Callias'), the parallelism between the *logos* and the *doxa* is lost; it is difficult to see how there could be one and the same *doxa*-type in the sense in which there is one and the same utterance-type that can be used to make different statements. I conclude, therefore, that in the first passage by 'the same *doxa*' Aristotle means a semi-definite belief and by 'the same *logos*' an utterance-type that is used to express such a belief.

Next, we have to look again at *Cat.* 4 a 22. As for *doxa,* I think that here too it must be the belief that a certain individual is seated, without any specification of time. As long as the individual thought of is as a matter of fact seated the belief is true; from the moment that individual has risen the same belief is false. If this is correct, it is most plausible to interpret *logos* in the same way as we did above: it is the utterance-type in so far as it is used to express this semi-definite *doxa,* and neither an utterance-token nor an utterance-type in general. From this interpretation it follows that we must suppose that somebody first utters the words 'He is seated', as a token of an utterance-type used to express a semi-definite belief, at a moment when the person referred to is seated; and that he utters another token of that same utterance-type at a later moment when the person concerned is no longer seated.

It is interesting to compare the passage in the *Categories* with the first thesis of the chapter on truth and falsehood in the *Dissoi logoi*. In a way Aristotle and the anonymous author of the *Dissoi logoi* make use of the same kind of argument. The circumstance that a *logos* is true or false is wholly external to the *logos* itself; the truth or falsehood is determined by features of the outside world which make that which is asserted by means of the *logos* now true and now false, but these differences in the actual world do not affect the identity of the *logos* as the expression used either to make completely different statements or to make one not fully specified statement at different times. The formula that is characteristic of the first thesis of the *Dissoi logoi* and which, in my interpretation, is repeated no less than four times, has in one of its versions a striking resemblance to Aristotle's formula in *Cat.* 4 b 8 (and 14 b 21): the *logos* is true when the *pragma* has happened (is the case) and false when the *pragma* has not happened (is not the case). Besides these similarities there is, however, also a difference. The author of the *Dissoi logoi* apparently concentrates upon examples which are utterance-types that can be used to make many different statements, while Aristotle, no doubt because he wants to include *doxa* as well, confines himself to an utterance-type that is used to express one semi-definite belief.

Although I have argued that in *Met.* 1051 b 13 and in *Cat.* 4 a 22 the word *logos* stands for an utterance-type that is used to express one *doxa*, it should not be forgotten that there are also passages in Aristotle's works where there can be no doubt that this word designates an utterance-token. Two passages that were very influential in later periods are those I have already mentioned: *Cat.* 4 b 33 and 5 a 34. There we learn that the *logos* in the sense of spoken sounds is a discrete quantity that can be measured by long and short syllables. None of its parts endures, and once the sounds have been uttered they can no longer be recaptured. If we take into account that in *De int.* 16 b 26 the *logos* is explicitly defined as a spoken sound (*phōnē*), it becomes highly probable that as a rule it is the utterance-token that is foremost in Aristotle's mind when he speaks of expressions used to make statements.

3.6.   Summary

This chapter clearly shows that the treatment of problems concerning acts and attitudes of holding something true and their objects with which Plato had made a modest but hopeful beginning in *Sophist* 261-264 was considerably extended and refined by Aristotle's efforts. By way of conclusion I shall give a synopsis of what we have found out about his conception of the bearers of truth and falsity.

In the first place that is true or false which is thought or believed to be the case. This bearer of truth or falsity may be designated by such expressions as *doxa, hypolēpsis, doxazomenon (doxaston), hypolambanomenon (hypolēpton)*, or by a *hoti*-clause or an accusative and infinitive phrase. In so far as a thought or belief is expressed in words it is perhaps also referred to as the *pragma* that underlies an affirmation or negation; but Aristotle does not seem to make a clear terminological distinction between the thing believed or asserted and that which is actually the case in reality.

Although it is not denied that *logos* sometimes stands for that which is asserted, in the contexts that are most relevant to our subject the word usually has the sense of utterance. Utterances that are used to make statements are the second category of bearers of truth and falsity, designated by such expressions as *logos apophantikos, logos kataphatikos, logos apophatikos, apophansis, kataphasis, apophasis,* and *protasis.* It is probable that Aristotle in speaking of utterances commonly has in mind what would nowadays be called utterance-tokens. There are, however, some passages in which the bearer of truth or falsity must be taken to be an utterance-type of a certain kind. [3]

As some of the terms for that which is thought or believed and for the utterances used to express it are also employed for the acts or attitudes of judging and believing and for the acts of uttering words with a special intention, the qualifications 'true' and 'false' can easily come to be applied to those acts and attitudes as well. Such cases are, however, exceptional and at any rate derivative.

---

[3] For the problem of the so-called future contingencies see Dorothea Frede, *Aristoteles und die 'Seeschlacht'. Das Problem der Contingentia Futura in* De interpretatione 9, Göttingen, 1970.

4. THE STOIC *LEKTON*

The Stoic conception of the bearers of truth and falsity centres around the notion of *axiōma*. As an *axiōma* is a species of the genus *lekton,* I shall first discuss the nature of the *lekton.* It will be maintained that the word *lekton* must have had several shades of meaning, although the deplorable state of our sources[1] makes it impossible to reach a high degree of certainty about the exact borderlines between these different nuances and their ascription to definite authors or periods.

4.1. The *lekton* as what is said or predicated of something

4.1.1. According to *SVF* I, 89, Zeno of Citium, the founder of the Stoic school, made a distinction between a cause, which is a body or *sōma,* and that of which it is the cause, which is called *symbebēkos,* consequence, or *katēgorēma,* predicate. Stobaeus, who gives this information, cites as examples of causes or bodies practical wisdom (*phronēsis*), the principle of life (*psychē*), and self-control (*sōphrosynē*); and as examples of what is caused by these bodies being wise (*phronein*), living (*zēn*), and being temperate (*sōphronein*). For the Stoics a body or *sōma* is everything that acts or undergoes action (*SVF* II, 336, 340). What is done or undergone by such agents or patients, the action or passion, is a *katēgorēma,* which in contrast with the somatic agents

---

[1] I shall refer to Diogenes Laertius, *Vitae philosophorum,* by means of the letters DL; to Sextus Empiricus, *Pyrrhōneioi hypotypōseis,* by SE, *PH*; to Sextus Empiricus, *Adversus mathematicos,* by SE, *AM*; and to fragments in Ioannes ab Arnim, *Stoicorum veterum fragmenta,* by *SVF,* followed by volume and number of fragment (and page for the fragments in III, pp. 209–269).

45

or patients is characterized as asomatic (*asōmaton*). Sextus (*AM* IX, 211) gives the following examples. The lancet and the flesh are bodies; the lancet is the cause of an asomatic *katēgorēma*, namely being cut, with respect to the flesh. Fire and wood are bodies; the fire is the cause of an asomatic *katēgorēma*, namely being burnt, with respect to the wood. Further examples can be found in *SVF* II, 349, where it is also added that the flesh is the cause of the cutting with respect to the lancet.

The verbal character of that which is caused was stressed by the Stoics against those who maintained that it could be indicated by nominal expressions (SE, *PH* III, 14). If the sun or the sun's heat makes the wax melt, we have to say that the sun is the cause, not of the melting of the wax (*tēs chyseōs*), but of the wax being melted, of a *katēgorēma* which is indicated by an infinitive (*tou cheisthai*). Clement of Alexandria (*SVF* III, 8, p. 263) even makes an explicit distinction, in a somewhat similar context, between 'is cut' (*temnetai*), which is the actual *katēgorēma*, and the infinitive 'to be cut', which is the name (*ptōsis*; cf. 4.6) of the *katēgorēma*.

There are some very instructive passages in which a distinction is mentioned between good things (*ta agatha*) and the consequences or effects of good things (*ta ōphelēmata*). The good things are such virtues as practical wisdom and self-control, which are bodies, and the consequences or effects of good things are asomatic *katēgorēmata* such as being wise and being temperate. Now our inclinations and appetitions have as their objects these *katēgorēmata*. What we want is to have the good things, wisdom or self-control; and having wisdom or self-control, being wise or temperate, are *katēgorēmata* (*phronein, sōphronein*)[2]. But we do not want to have the *katēgorēmata*, namely having wisdom or self-control, for these *katēgorēmata* are only asomatic and not the good things themselves, which are *sōmata*. This distinction is also expressed by saying that the good things are *haireta*, whereas the effects of the good things are *hairetea*. This must mean that the good things are what we want to have, and that the asomatic *katēgorēmata* are what we want, namely to have the good things (*SVF* III, 89, 90, 91; cf. 16, 171, 494, 501, 503, 587).

It is no wonder that many thinkers found it difficult to understand this subtle doctrine. In *Epistula* 117 Seneca struggles with a question that has been put to him by Lucilius, namely whether it is true, as the Stoics maintain, that wisdom (*sapientia*) is a good but that being wise (*sapere*) is not a good.

---

[2] Cf. Cicero, *Tusculanae disputationes* IV, 21: — *ut libido sit earum rerum, quae dicuntur de quodam aut quibusdam, quae* katēgorēmata *dialectici appellant, ut habere divitias, capere honores* —.

Although Seneca does not agree with the doctrine, he tries to elucidate it by explaining that wisdom is a good in so far as it is a body (*corpus*) and has certain effects; being wise, on the other hand, is not a good, since it is that which is caused and therefore not a body (*incorporale*), but only the consequence (*accidens*) of the working of a body.

4.1.2. We are told by Clement of Alexandria (*SVF* I, 488 = III, 8, p.263) that Cleanthes and Archedemus of Tarsus called the *katēgorēmata* by the name of *lekta*. As Cleanthes wrote a book on predicates with the title *Peri katēgorēmatōn* (DL VII, 175), it seems most likely that he used both terms but was the first to employ *lekton* as a synonym of *katēgorēma*. However this may be, his choice was a natural one. A *katēgorēma* is defined (DL VII, 64) as that which is said of something (*to kata tinos agoreuomenon*). We know that Aristotle (*De int.* 16 b 6) considered a *rhēma* as the sign of the things which are said of something else (*tōn kath' heterou legomenōn*; cf. 3.2.2) and that in his works the phrase *legein ti kata tinos* occurs frequently. It was, therefore, not far-fetched to introduce the term *lekton*, 'that which has been said or predicated (of something)', as an equivalent of *katēgorēma*. The word *lekton* is not used by Aristotle and it is possible that Cleanthes, being aware of the radical difference between the Aristotelian and Stoic theories of predication, came to feel the need of replacing the term *katēgorēma*, which does occur in Aristotle's works, by another word. If this speculation is right, his proposal was only a partial success; *lekton* was accepted as a synonym of *katēgorēma* but certainly did not put it out of use.

4.1.3. In DL VII, 64, a *katēgorēma* is also defined as a *pragma* which occurs in a construction about one or more subjects (*syntakton peri tinos ē tinōn*). To answer the question what the word *pragma* means in this context we have to note, I think, the way in which it is frequently used by grammarians. Dionysius Thrax (*Ars grammatica* 13, ed. Uhlig p. 46) offers a definition of the verb (*rhēma*) which includes the claim that it is a word which sets before the mind an action or a passion (*energeian ē pathos*). A variant of the definition has it that the verb is a word that indicates a *katēgorēma*. In the *Scholia* on Dionysius Thrax (ed. Hilgard p. 215, 28) it is pointed out that it is typical of a verb to indicate a *pragma*; and these *pragmata* are accomplished by persons in so far as they act or undergo actions (*ē hōs energountōn ē hōs paschontōn*). Further, the infinitive is commonly called the name of the *pragma* (*Scholia* on Dionysius Thrax, ed. Hilgard p. 245, 13, p. 399, 34, p. 558, 22; Apollonius Dyscolus, *De adverbiis*, ed. Schneider p. 129, 16, p. 131, 24). Optative forms such as *graphoimi* and *philologoimi* signify an attitude of wishing or praying with respect to the action (*pragma*) of writing or studying (Apollonius Dyscolus, *De syntaxi*, ed. Uhlig p. 351, 9). In contrast with the expression *age* ('Come on'), which only signifies a command, an imperative such as *grapson* ('Write') also contains, besides the included command, information about the *pragma*, the action which is the object of the commanding attitude (*Ibidem* p. 353, 3). If somebody asks 'Which man has won?', he is ignorant about the man, but he has comprehended the *pragma*, namely the having won (*Ibidem* p. 108, 11)[3].

Latin grammarians translated *pragma*, in the sense of an action or passion, by *res*. Charisius (*Ars grammatica*, ed. Barwick, p. 209) defines the verb as a part of speech that signifies the application of a *res* (*administrationem rei significans*). Priscian uses *res* three times in a passage about impersonal verbs where his source, Apollonius Dyscolus (*De syntaxi*, ed. Uhlig p. 431, 2, 11), has *pragma* (*Institutiones grammaticae*, ed. Hertz II, p. 231, 19, p. 232, 1, 3). *Ibidem* p. 235, 16, he explains that the indicative mood has acquired that name because it usually signifies *essentiam ipsius rei*, that the action or passion of the verb is true of the subject[4]. The indicative may be accompanied by adverbs or conjunctions which help to signify the *substantiam vel essentiam rei* (p. 236, 4). The same phrase occurs I, p. 422, 1, where it is added that in the case of other moods the speaker does not signify *substantiam actus vel passionis* but only various states of mind concerning an action or passion which lacks the character of being true of a subject (*de re carente substantia*). Finally, Priscian renders what Apollonius says about optative forms by stating that optative forms of verbs indicate both the *res* and the attitude of wishing (*cum re et votum*), while the adverb *utinam* only signifies the attitude of wishing (II, p. 239, 13).

The phrase *substantia* or *essentia rei* has to be interpreted, I think, in the light of such passages as *SVF* I, 89, and *SVF* II, 509. In the first passage, which we already discussed at the beginning of 4.1.1, Zeno says that it is impossible that the cause is present without that of which it is the cause

---

[3] Cf. also *Scholia* on Dionysius Thrax, ed. Hilgard, p. 72, 25, p. 515, 12; Apollonius Dyscolus, *De syntaxi*, ed. Uhlig p. 43, 6, p. 44, 11, p. 45, 15, p. 323, 6, p. 325, 1, p. 346, 4, p. 349, 3, p. 352, 7, p. 375, 1, 10, p. 403, 7, p. 431, 2, 11, p. 456, 4, p. 467, 10; *De pronomine*, ed. Schneider p. 23, 20, p. 68, 2, p. 108, 27, 29, p. 109, 1, p. 114, 27; Choeroboscus, ed. Hilgard p. 6, 20, 22, p. 7, 12, 17, p. 8, 5, 10; Sophronius, ed. Hilgard p. 410, 15.

[4] Cf. Macrobius, *Excerpta Parisina, Grammatici Latini*, ed. Keil V, p. 611, 1: *indicativus habet absolutam de re quae agitur pronuntiationem*; *Excerpta Bobiensia, Ibidem* p. 636, 5: *indicativus --- habet absolutissimam ac perfectam de re quae agitur pronuntiationem*.

belonging to it and being true of it (*hyparchein*). And in the second passage we read that only those *katēgorēmata* which are actual consequences (*symbebēkota*) are said to belong to something: for instance, walking belongs to me and is true of me (*hyparchein*) when I walk, but when I am lying down or sitting, it does not belong to me and is not true of me. It must be this kind of *hyparxis tou pragmatos,* the circumstance that the action or passion which is signified by the verb is true of something or belongs to something, that is translated by *substantia* or *essentia rei.* This use of *hyparchein* reminds one of the many places in Aristotle where the predicate is said to belong to the subject (*De int.* 16 b 9, 17 a 24; *Prior Analytics* 24 a 19, and *passim*). The Stoics seem to have taken over the word *hyparchein* but, as we shall see in a moment, they used it in the context of a totally different theory of predication.

At this point one may also remember the formula that Aristotle puts forward in *Cat.* 4 b 8 and 14 b 21: it is because the *pragma* is or is not that the *logos* is called true or false. Is it not possible that Aristotle too employs the word *pragma* in the sense of an action or passion which is true of something or is not true of something? It is probable that for a Greek the word *pragma* had a strong association with the verb *prattein,* in one or another of its meanings; it would, therefore, be rash to assume that this aspect of the meaning of the word *pragma* is altogether irrelevant to Aristotle's use of it in the contexts which we have discussed. On the other hand, I cannot discover any indication that Aristotle had in mind anything as precise and clear as what we have found in the above-mentioned texts. It is practically certain, in my opinion, that his use of the term *pragma* has to be understood in the light of the opposition between *onoma* and *pragma* or, in general, between language and the things of which linguistic expressions are the signs, either the things designated by nouns and verbs or the states of affairs designated by combinations of nouns and verbs. It should be noted, however, that in later treatises on logic the phrase *hyparxis tou pragmatos* (*tōn pragmatōn*) came to be used for that which is expressed by categorical statements in contradistinction to hypothetical (conditional or disjunctive) statements (Cf. Galen, *Institutio logica* III, 1; John Philoponus, *In Analytica priora,* ed. Wallies p. 244, 22). This usage seems to be connected with the Aristotelian formula and probably became dominant in the Peripatetic tradition.

4.1.4.   So far I have defended the hypothesis that *lekton* can have the same meaning as *katēgorēma.* Both words indicate that which is said or predicated of something; and that which is said of something is a *pragma,* an asomatic action or passion which is held to be true of some agent or patient, of a body or *sōma* by which the *pragma* is caused. In order to appreciate the very peculiar character of the Stoic theory of predication one has to take into account the difficulties which had been raised in connection with conceptions of predication in which the copula is predominant.

Plato (*Sophist* 251 b) mentions a theory according to which it is impossible that many things are one or one thing many. Only identical predication is possible; we can call a man a man, or a good a good, but we cannot say that a man is good. It has often been thought that Plato is here hinting at a doctrine which Aristotle (*Metaphysics* 1024 b 32) ascribes to Antisthenes: that a thing can only be spoken of by its proper *logos*, one expression for one thing. But as a *logos* is a many-worded formula, rather than a single name, it is doubtful if the identification of the theory mentioned by Plato with the thesis ascribed to Antisthenes is right.

According to Aristotle (*Physics* 185 b 25) some philosophers were disturbed by the thought that the same thing would simultaneously be one and many. In order to avoid making the one many by adding the verb *esti* ('is') the sophist Lycophron decided to use only predications in which *esti* was omitted (a correct construction in Greek). Others altered the form of the expression in such a way that the verb *esti* disappeared, saying 'The man has-been-whitened' (*leleukōtai*) instead of 'The man is white' and 'The man walks' instead of 'The man is walking'.

In his commentary on Aristotle's *Physics* (I–IV, ed. Diels p. 120, 12) Simplicius informs us that the philosophers of the Megarian school assumed as an obvious premiss that things having a different *logos* are different, and that different things are divided from each other. From this premiss, they thought, it could be proved that everyone is divided from himself: for instance, that Socrates is divided from himself, because the *logos* of 'educated Socrates' is different from the *logos* of 'white Socrates'. In other words, we cannot attribute different things to one and the same subject (Cf. Aristotle, *Sophistici elenchi* 166 b 28). A similar view is ascribed by Plutarch (*Adversus Colotem* 1119 d) to Stilpo of Megara, who said that one should not predicate of any subject things which are different from it (*heteron heterou mē katēgoreisthai*). It is wrong to say that a man is good, since either being a man and being good are identical and then we cannot predicate good of other things; or they are different and then we have no right to say that the one is the other. We can say only that a man is a man, that a good is a good, and so on.

The Eretrians seem to have been of the same opinion. Simplicius, in his commentary on Aristotle's *Physics* (I–IV, ed. Diels p. 91, 28), tells us that they were so afraid of difficulties that they did not allow any real predication at all; only statements of the form 'The man is a man', 'The white is white' were regarded as safe. This is confirmed by DL II, 134, where we read that Menedemus of Eretria tried to prove that being of use (*ōphelein*) is not good, by pointing out that the subject and the predicate are two different things.

These examples may suffice to show that many philosophers regarded predication by means of the verb 'is' with strong suspicion, mainly because they considered 'is' as a sign of identity. The Stoics seem to have sought a way out of these difficulties by proposing a theory of predication in which the verb 'is' does not play any part. While Aristotle tends to assimilate utterances such as 'A man walks' to utterances of the type 'A man is just', by interpreting them as 'A man is walking' etc., the Stoics nearly always confine their attention to cases in which the subject is combined with another verb than 'is'. For them the verb signifies an action or passion, a *pragma*, which is said to hold of an agent or patient, a body or *sōma* which is the cause of the *pragma*.

It is not unlikely that in developing this view they were at least partly inspired by what Plato says in *Sophist* 262. There he defines a *rhēma* as an expression which is applied to *praxeis*, actions or states, and an *onoma* as the spoken sign applied to what performs those actions or is in those states. In 262 e 12 he uses *praxis* for the action or state which is predicated of the subject, whereas for the subject he uses the word *pragma*, in the sense of the thing which acts in a certain way or is in a certain state. But that *pragma* could also be a synonym of *praxis* is shown by Plutarch (*Platonicae quaestiones* 1009 b) who, commenting upon *Sophist* 262, draws a clear parallel between the Platonic and Stoic ways of representing predication. For the actions or passions that are signified by *rhēmata* Plutarch uses both *praxeis/pathē* and *pragmata/pathē*. Further, he points out (1010 a) that there is a difference between, on the one hand, such expressions as *typtei* ('beats'), *typtetai* ('is beaten'), *Sōkratēs, Pythagoras*, and, on the other hand, such expressions as *gar* ('for') and *peri* ('about') occurring in isolation. Expressions of the first kind make us think of something, but expressions of the second sort are not accompanied by any thought of either a *pragma* or a *sōma*. From this it may be concluded that in the utterances *Sōkratēs typtei* or *Sōkratēs typtetai* the *onoma* stands for the *sōma* and the *rhēma* for the *pragma*. Plutarch interprets Plato by means of Stoic terminology. This may be taken as evidence of his tendency to fuse different doctrines; but at the same time it shows that there must have been a certain resemblance.

The strongest proof that the term *lekton* was used to designate that which is said or predicated of something, as a synonym of *katēgorēma* and in the typical frame of the Stoic theory of predication, is the fact that it is so often qualified by the attribute *asōmaton*. In many contexts one can make sense of this characterization only by taking *lekton* as standing for the action or passion, the *pragma* which is signified by the verb, in contrast with the *sōmata* which perform or undergo the action. It is therefore time to try to throw more light upon the ontological and psychological aspects of that which the Stoics called *asōmaton*.

4.1.5. As for the ontological aspects, I shall confine myself to a rough outline; for details and controversial points I refer to Bréhier (1962), Gold-schmidt (1969), Hadot (1968 and 1969), and Rist (1969). At the top of the Stoics' ontological hierarchy we find the *ti*. These somethings are divided into the *on* and the *mē on,* the sphere of the existent and the sphere of the non-existent. To the *on* belong the *sōmata,* the things that can perform or undergo actions. In terms of the Stoic categories a *sōma* is composed of *hylē,* matter, and *poiotēs,* determining quality. To the *mē on* belong the void, place, time, and the *lekta.* These four *asōmata* do not have an independent existence of their own; they are only thought and said. A *lekton,* as we have seen, belongs to a *sōma* (*hyparchein*) when the *sōma* actually performs or undergoes the action concerned, but in itself it does not have the same kind of existence as a *sōma* has. What is predicated of a *sōma* is an event that occurs at the periphery of the domain in which bodies act and are acted upon; the actuality of the event entirely derives from the body by which it is caused. In terms of the Stoic categories the *lekton* has to be associated with the *pōs echon,* the ways of behaving of a body, and the *pros ti pōs echon,* its ways of behaving in relation to something else.

4.1.6. Turning now to the psychological side of the asomatic *lekton,* I first call attention to a passage (DL VII, 51) in which two divisions of presenta-tions (*phantasiai*) are mentioned. One is into those of living beings possessed of reason and speech (*logikai*) and those of living beings that are deprived of these faculties (*alogoi*). The presentations of the first group are also called *noēseis,* in a broad sense of that word (Cf. *SVF* II, 89). The second division divides presentations into those of sense-perception (*aisthētikai*) and those of thought in the narrower sense (*dia tēs dianoias*). To the latter group belong the presentations of *asōmata* and of the other things that are apprehended only by means of the *logos.* Parallel to this second division into presentations of sense-perception and presentations of thought we often find a distinction between *periptōsis* and *metabasis*: between direct acquaintance by means of the senses (for instance, with something white or black, sweet or bitter) and the formation of ideas, which consists in a kind of transition from sense-perception to something else. The *metabasis* is characteristic of man (SE, *AM*

VIII, 276, 288; Epictetus, *Dissertationes* I, 6, 10). This creative power of the human mind amounts, however, to no more than the faculty of compounding, transposing, augmenting, or diminishing the materials afforded us by the senses; it is impossible to find in thought anything which one does not possess as known by experience (SE, *AM* VIII, 58, 60). Sextus gives the following examples of *metabasis* (*AM* I, 25, III, 40, VIII, 59, IX, 393, XI, 250). Because of a likeness of Socrates, which has been seen, we conceive of Socrates, who has not been seen. Starting from the common man we move on to a conception of a giant. By decreasing the size of the common man we grasp a conception of a pygmy. By way of composition we derive from man and horse the conception of a thing we have never perceived, a centaur. DL VII, 52–53, gives a more extensive list of possibilities. The queer thing is that he contrasts *periptōsis* not with *metabasis* generally, but with such species of *metabasis* (in Sextus's sense) as resemblance, analogy, transposition, composition, and opposition. *Metabasis* occurs as one of the species: some ideas are formed by transition, for instance *lekta* and place, both *asōmata*. This may be just a mistake; or the word *metabasis* may have been used by some in a generic sense and by others in a more special sense, without much further difference of meaning.

Now the *lekton* was defined as that which exists *kata logikēn phantasian*, by way of a presentation which is typical of a living being possessed of reason and speech (DL VII, 63; SE, *AM* VIII, 70). Sextus adds that a *logikē phantasia* is a presentation in which it is possible to set the thing presented before the mind by means of speech (*logos*). This can be connected with what DL, VII, 49, says: first comes the presentation and then follows thought (*dianoia*), which is capable of expressing things in speech (*eklalētikē*) and expresses that which it undergoes by the influence of the presentation, by means of an utterance. From elsewhere (*SVF* II, 236) we know that the Stoics called the *noēmata* by the name of *ekphorika*, things capable of being expressed in words.

The view that the thinking faculty is capable of forming, on the basis of the materials offered by sense-perception, new presentations which are arrived at by a process of *metabasis* and exist only in so far as they are thought and expressed in words, was illustrated by means of the following simile (SE, *AM* VIII, 409). A trainer or drill-sergeant who is teaching a boy rhythm and how to make certain motions sometimes takes hold of the boy's hands and at other times stands at a distance and offers himself as a model for the boy's imitations, by making certain rhythmical motions. In the same way some of the objects presented produce the impression in the soul as it were by touching and contact with it (such as white and black and *sōmata* generally), whereas others are not of this nature, since in their case the principal part of the soul has presentations which are not caused by them but are formed on the occasion of their occurrence (*tou hēgemonikou ep'autois phantasioumenou kai ouch hyp'autōn*), as is the case with asomatic *lekta*. Sextus cites this simile in connection with the question of how presentations of asomatic *lekta* are possible. Since an *asōmaton* neither effects nor suffers anything, it cannot produce presentations in the soul. The Stoics apparently solved this problem by pointing out that just as the boy makes both movements which are caused by the trainer and spontaneous movements, so the soul has both presentations that are caused by *sōmata* and spontaneous presentations – for instance, of *lekta*. The *lekta* do not cause their presentations, but those presentations are produced by the soul itself, although this spontaneous production is limited to certain operations on the impressions of sense-perception.

That *lekta* are merely thought and that nothing directly corresponds to them in the world of existing *sōmata* is confirmed by *SVF* II, 521. The Stoics considered time and *asōmata* generally as existing only in thought, without the reality of bodies which consists in causal activity. It looks as if this were contradicted by a passage in Plutarch (*De communibus notitiis contra Stoicos* 1084 c), where such activities as walking and dancing (*ton peripaton, tēn orchēsin*) are counted among the *sōmata*. This can be connected with what Seneca (*Epistula* 113, 23; *SVF* II, 836) tells us about a controversy between Cleanthes and Chrysippus concerning the nature of walking (*ambulatio*). Cleanthes contended that it is *pneuma* which has been sent down from the principal part of the soul into the feet; Chrysippus maintained that it is the principal part of the soul itself (a *sōma*). To solve the apparent contradiction we probably have to distinguish between the *sōma* as far as it is in a certain state or is disposed in a certain way (*pōs echon*) and that state itself, considered on its own. If the action or passion is regarded as realized in a *sōma*, it is, as it were, an aspect of that *sōma*. This point of view was strongly emphasized by Chrysippus, here and elsewhere. But if the action or passion is contrasted with the *sōma*, as that which is caused or undergone by it, it is seen to have a status of its own; from this point of view it is something asomatic and a mere product of thought.

4.1.7. It may be concluded, I think, that at least one of the ways in which the word *lekton* was used by Stoic philosophers was to designate that which is said or predicated of something. The *lekton* or *katēgorēma* is an asomatic *pragma*, an action or passion which is performed or undergone by a *sōma*. From an ontological point of view the *lekton-katēgorēma-pragma* is totally different from the *sōma*. *Sōmata* are the real things which are characterized by their capacity of acting and being acted upon. The actions or passions themselves are merely thought and expressed in words; they are presentations which are spontaneously formed by a transition from sense-experience and made known by spoken sounds, without having a direct counterpart in somatic reality. Given this ontological and psychological peculiarity of the *lekton*, it is not unlikely that almost from the beginning the word *lekton* could also be taken as referring to that which is only (thought and) said. If the *lekton* as such does not really exist and is nothing but a spontaneous product of thought, it is quite natural to see it not only as that which is said of a *sōma*, but also as that which is merely an expressed thought, only something said.

4.2. The *lekton* as what is said or expressed in an assertion

4.2.1. According to DL VII, 62, Chrysippus took dialectic to be concerned with things which signify (*sēmainonta*) and things which are signified (*sēmainomena*). This division of the subject-matter of logic seems to have become traditional. It is also mentioned by SE, *PH* II, 214. DL VII, 43, says that dialectic is divided into a part which deals with things signified and a part which deals with spoken sounds (*phōnē*). And Seneca (*Epistula* 89, 17) draws the same distinction between sounds (*verba*) and significations (*significationes*), between things which are said (*res quae dicuntur*) and the words by means of which they are said (*vocabula quibus dicuntur*).

DL VII, 63, is worthy of note for two reasons. In the first place, Diogenes now describes the part that deals with things signified as the part about the *pragmata* and the *sēmainomena*. The phrase 'the part about the *pragmata*' also occurs in the enumeration of books written by Chrysippus in DL VII, 190, apparently for that part of logic that deals with things signified. In the second place, Diogenes specifies the subjects which are treated in this part of logic as complete and defective *lekta*. To the complete *lekta* belong *axiōmata* and arguments (*syllogismoi*); the defective *lekta* comprise the *katēgorēmata* and their species. That the *lekta* were considered as things signified is confirmed by SE, *AM* VIII, 69, where we read that the Stoics assumed truth and falsehood to lie in the *sēmainomenon*, that is to say in the asomatic *lekton*. And by SE, *AM* VIII, 264, where it is stated that vocal sounds signify but that *lekta*, which include *axiōmata,* are signified (*sēmainetai*). This may be compared to DL VII, 57: the vocal sounds are uttered (*propherontai*), but what is said (*legetai*) are the *pragmata,* which then are *lekta.*

One thing seems to be certain: the word *lekton* could be used not only in the sense of that which is said or predicated of something but also in the sense of the thing said or meant, of that which is signified or expressed by vocal sounds. 'The thing said' could be taken as 'the thing predicated of something' or as 'the thing expressed by means of words'. A bridge between the two meanings is perhaps found in the nuance of meaning which was touched upon at the end of 4.1.7. As a predicate a *lekton* is merely an expressed thought, something which is only said. From there it is only one step to the interpretation of the *lekton* as the thought expressed or that which is signified by words, without any qualification. After all, predicates are among the things which are expressed by words.

4.2.2. Besides *katēgorēmata*, which are called defective *lekta*, we now find among the *lekta* also *axiōmata* and arguments, which are complexes of *axiōmata*. It is difficult to decide whether Chrysippus was the first writer who characterized *axiōmata* as *lekta*. From DL II, 112, we know that Clinomachus of Thurii, a pupil of Euclides of Megara, was the first to write books about *axiōmata* and *katēgorēmata* and kindred subjects. As there are no indications that Zeno or Cleanthes reckoned the *axiōmata* among the *lekta,* it is possible that the identification of *axiōmata* as *lekta* was inaugurated by Chrysippus. In any case as one of the pioneers of the logic of propositions Chrysippus must have been particularly interested in the nature and status of *axiōmata,* which are the elements of the reasoning studied in that logic.

Although the word *lekton* was used also in the sense of that which is expressed by vocal sounds, it can, I think, be argued that the first meaning we have discussed − the sense of that which is said or predicated of something − could easily be preserved when the word was applied to *axiōmata*. There are reasons to believe that the distinction between *katēgorēmata* and *axiōmata* was not a very sharp one. First, among the examples given by Clement of Alexandria of *katēgorēmata* in the sense of an action or a passion (*SVF* II, 349, 353, III, 8, p. 263) there are some which have the form of an *axioma*: the state of the spleen is not the cause of the fever, but of the circumstance that the fever arises; the cause is present at the process caused, for instance the shipbuilder and the architect are present when the ship and the house are built; the sculptor is the cause of the circumstance that the statue comes into being. It is true that in *SVF* III, 8, p. 263, a distinction is made between causes of *katēgorēmata* such as 'is cut' (*temnetai*) and of *axiōmata* such as 'A ship comes into being' (*naus ginetai*); but this proves only that *axiōmata* as well as *katēgorēmata* could be taken as the effects of causal influence exercised by bodies.

In the second place, Hadot (1969) has called attention to the fact that the term *hyparchein* is used not only of *katēgorēmata* which are true of something but also of *axiōmata*. According to SE, *AM* VIII, 10, and 85, an *axiōma* is true when it is the case (*hyparchei*) and false when it is not the case. In *AM* VIII, 100, Sextus says that the *axiōma* 'This (man) sits' is the case as something true (*alēthes hyparchein*) when the *katēgorēma* actually belongs to the object indicated. Another example is *AM* VIII, 277, where it is stated that in a proof the conjunction of the premisses wil be a sign of the fact that the conclusion is true (*tou hyparchein to symperasma*). One has only to remember Plato, *Sophist* 263 a, where the *logoi* 'Theaetetus sits' and 'Theaetetus flies' are said to be of and about Theaetetus, to realize how natural this shift of meaning in the verb *hyparchein* is. 'What is said' can be taken as designating a predicate which is said of a subject and is true or false of that subject. But it can also be taken as designating the whole statement, for instance 'Theaetetus sits'; in this case too we can say that the statement is made about Theaetetus and is thus true of him, although as a rule we omit the addition 'of him' and just declare that the statement is true, *sans phrase*. The fact that both *katēgorēmata* and *axiōmata* could be the subject of the verb *hyparchein*, together with the fact that both were regarded as actions or passions which are caused or undergone by bodies, is a strong indication that they had enough in common to call both of them *lekta* in the sense of an action or passion which is said of something.

4.2.3.   There is, however, also a difference between *katēgorēmata* and *axiōmata*; the former are incomplete and defective *lekta,* the latter are complete and self-sufficient *lekta*. It is important, I think, to note that only *katēgorēmata* are called defective *lekta*; there is not a single passage where, for instance, the subject is called a defective *lekton*. This means that in this context the *lekton* is not just any thing signified, but rather that which is said of something. This point is corroborated by the definitions which are given of a *katēgorēma*: it is that which is said of something, or a *pragma* which occurs in a construction about something (DL VII, 64). Further, it is highly probable that the incompleteness of a *katēgorēma* was primarily measured against the completeness of an *axiōma* rather than of any other independent utterance-content. In the third definition given by DL VII, 64, the *katēgorēma* is said to be a defective *lekton* which can be constructed with a nominative case in order to get an *axiōma* (*pros axiōmatos genesin*). A *katēgorēma* was seen as a kind of schema for *axiōmata*: by filling in the name-positions around the given predicate one forms a full-blown assertion.

The difference between *katēgorēmata* and *axiōmata* is sometimes expressed by the pair 'imperfect/perfect' (*ateles/teleion*; *SVF* II, 182), sometimes by 'defective/full' (*ellipes/plēres*; *SVF* II, 99) and also, in a passage with predominantly Aristotelian terminology, by 'needing some addition/self-sufficing' (*prosthēkēs tinos deomenon/autarkes*; *SVF* II, 184). The standard terminology, however, appears to have been 'defective/complete in itself' (*ellipes/autoteles*). DL VII, 63, explains that the defective *lekta* are those where the expression of thought remains uncompleted (*ta anapartiston echonta tēn ekphoran*[5]): if someone says only 'Writes', we ask him 'Who?'. The complete *lekta* are those where the expression of thought leaves nothing to be desired (*ta apērtismenēn echonta tēn ekphoran*), such as 'Socrates writes'. The verb *apartizein* which is used in this connection means: to make complete in such a way that there is neither too much nor too little. It is also applied to definitions (DL VII, 60; *SVF* II, 390, III, 24, p. 247) and to arguments (SE, *PH* II, 155, *AM* VIII, 446); if, for instance, only the premisses of an argument are given, there is not yet any proof, since no sensible man would maintain that such a combination is a *logos* or renders a complete thought (*dianoian holōs apartizein* or *dianoian sōzein*; SE, *PH* II, 176, *AM* VIII, 389). This shows that the criteria by means of which the completeness of *lekta* is tested are different in the case of *axiōmata* and in the case of arguments.

4.2.4.   According to DL VII, 64, and *SVF* II, 184, a *katēgorēma* was also called *symbama*. This term must have had the same meaning as the word *symbebēkos* which, as we saw in 4.1.1, was used by Zeno for that which is caused by a body. A *katēgorēma* or *symbama* is the action or passion which is indicated by an intransitive verb and said of something signified by a noun in the nominative case. We might say that in *Sōkratēs peripatei* ('Socrates walks') the verb indicates a (nominative) predicate. A *parasymbama* or *parakatēgorēma* is said of something signified by a noun in an oblique case: in *Sōkratei metamelei* ('It grieves Socrates') the verb indicates an (oblique case) predicate. Apart from these two kinds of predicates there are also cases in which the verb indicates something which is less than a predicate (*elatton ē katēgorēma*). The form *philei* ('likes'), for example, is not only accompanied by a name-position for a subject-term in the nominative case but also by a name-position for a grammatical object in an oblique case. In *Platōn philei Diōna* ('Plato likes Dion') the verb designates something less than a predicate; the action has to be supplemented by a patient before we obtain a full predicate which can be said of an agent. Similarly, there is an *elatton ē*

---

[5] The *Suda*, *s.v. katēgorēma*, has *dianoian* instead of *ekphoran* (*Suidae lexicon*, ed. A. Adler, Pars III, Leipzig, 1933, pp. 74–75).

parasymbama; in *Sōkratei Alkibiadou melei* ('In Socrates there is affection for Alcibiades') the verb indicates something that has to be supplemented by a patient before we obtain a full predicate which can be said of an agent signified by a noun in an oblique case. What is predicated of Plato is not that he likes, but that he likes Dion; and what is predicated of Socrates is not that he cares for, but that he cares for Alcibiades.

4.2.5. In the passages in which the *axiōma* is defined (DL VII, 65, 66; SE, *PH* II, 104, *AM* VIII, 12, 71, 73; *SVF* II, 192, 194, 196, 197) we find, in various combinations, four features that were regarded as distinctive of the definiendum. From a generic point of view the *axiōma* is a *pragma* or *lekton*. As such it differs from a *katēgorēma* by being complete and independent (*autoteles, hoson eph' heautōi*). It can be distinguished from other complete and independent contents of utterances in so far as it is associated with a speech act of asserting or making known one's opinion (*axioun, apophaines-thai*). And as a complete and independent *pragma* or *lekton* which is said of something in an act of asserting it is that which is true or false[6].

The most important division of *axiōmata* is that into those which are simple and those which are not simple. Simple *axiōmata* are those which are neither compounded of one *axiōma* twice repeated nor of different *axiōmata* by means of some one or more conjunctions (DL VII, 68; SE, *AM* VIII, 93). DL VII, 69, gives two divisions of simple *axiōmata*. First, some are negative (*apophatikon*), such as 'It is not the case that it is day' (*ouchi hēmera estin*); some are denials (*arnētikon*), consisting of a denying part and a *katēgorēma*, such as 'Nobody walks' (*oudeis peripatei*); others again are privative (*sterēti-kon*), consisting of a part expressing privation and a potential (*kata dynamin*) *axiōma*, such as 'Unkind he is' (*aphilanthrōpos estin houtos*), which is there-fore analyzed as 'Un (kind he is)'. The second division enumerates three kinds of affirmative *axiōmata*: (1) those which consist of a name in the nominative case and a *katēgorēma*, such as 'Dion walks'; (2) those which consist of a demonstrative pronoun in the nominative case and a *katēgorēma*, such as

---

[6] DL VII, 65, cites a line from the *Dialectical Definitions* of Chrysippus: *axiōma esti to apophanton ē kataphanton hoson eph' heautōi*, and adds that the *axiōma* has acquired its name from the fact that it is asserted or denied (*axiousthai ē atheteisthai*). There can hardly be any doubt that *ē kataphanton* and *ē atheteisthai* are interpolations. The examples which follow the definition are both affirmative ('It is day' and 'Dion walks'). And it is evident that the name *axiōma* has not been derived from *atheteisthai* but only from *axiousthai*. Somebody must have taken *apophanton* as a form of *apophanai* and then have felt the need of adding *ē kataphanton*; this idea of denial and affirmation made him also add *ē atheteisthai* to *axiousthai*.

'This (man) walks' (*houtos peripatei*); (3) those which consist of an indefinite part or indefinite parts and a *katēgorēma*, such as 'Someone walks' or 'He moves' (*ekeinos kineitai*), presumably when 'he' (*ekeinos*) is used in an indefinite way, as in 'If anyone walks, then he moves'. Diogenes calls these kinds *katēgorikon, katagoreutikon*, and *ahoriston*. SE, *AM* VIII, 96, uses names which suggest a certain order of importance: for group (2) 'definite' (*hōrismena*), for group (1) 'intermediate' (*mesa*), and for group (3) 'indefinite' (*ahorista*). According to Sextus group (2) contains *axiōmata* in which the *katēgorēma* is said of something which is present and can be pointed at; group (1) contains *axiōmata* in which the *katēgorēma* is said of something which is only named or described and may be absent; and group (3) contains *axiōmata* in which the *katēgorēma* is said of an individual which is left unspecified. An indefinite *axiōma* is true when the corresponding definite *axiōma* is found to be true.

Denials and the three kinds of affirmative *axiōmata* can be regarded as constructions built upon the basis of a *katēgorēma* which has been completed by filling in the open place for the subject-term. Negative and privative statements of the type 'It is not the case that (it is day)' and 'Un (kind he is)' are simple *axiōmata* which have been formed out of a potential *axiōma* by prefixing to it a negation or a privative particle. It is not clear how the Stoics analyzed such statements as 'It is day' and 'Kind he is'. Galen (*Institutio logica* II, 1) calls such statements as 'There is providence' and 'There is no centaur' statements about simple existence (*hyper haplēs hyparxeōs*) and also gives a list of statements having predicates from each of the ten Aristotelian categories, many of which contain the copula 'is', but he does not say anything which could help us to answer the question how the Stoics analyzed such statements. Further, it is remarkable that, while indefinite *axiōmata* and denials roughly correspond to what in syllogistic are called particular statements and universal negative statements, no mention is made of *axiōmata* of a universal affirmative character. There are indications that the Stoics interpreted universal affirmative statements of the type 'Every man is mortal' as conditionals with an indefinite subject: 'If something is a man, then it is mortal'. Such conditionals do not belong to the class of simple *axiōmata* (SE, *AM* XI, 8; for details see Hay 1969).

It is not necessary to discuss in detail the division of compound *axiōmata* given by DL VII, 71. I shall confine myself to three points. First, from DL VII, 68–69, it can be seen that the Stoics used the name *axiōma* for the antecedent and consequent of a conditional (*synēmmenon*) as well as for the whole conditional. This might mean that they did not make a very sharp distinction between the non-assertoric character of the antecedent and consequent and the assertoric character of the whole. This seems to be confirmed by Ammonius (*SVF* II, 237), when he says that the Stoics called the Aristotelian *protaseis* by the name of *axiōmata* and *lēmmata* because they are assumed or taken to be true, just like the *axiōmata* in geometry. But it is also possible that in the case of the antecedent and consequent they used the word *axiōma* in the sense of *axiōma kata dynamin* (DL VII, 70).

Second, in connection with the disjunctive *axiōmata* (*diezeugmena*) it is worthy of note that both Dionysius Thrax (*Ars grammatica* 20, ed. Uhlig p. 91, 1) and Apollonius Dyscolus (*De coniunctionibus*, ed. Schneider p. 216, 6) call the parts which are disjoined by such conjunctions as *ē* ('or') the *pragmata*. This usage may originate from Stoic texts in which a disjunction was defined by means of a disjunctive particle and *axiōmata*.

Third, among the compound *axiōmata* there is also mentioned a quasi-causal (*aitiōdes*) *axiōma*, with the example 'Because it is day, it is light'. Diogenes explains the name by saying that the first *axiōma* is, as it were, the cause of the second (VII, 72). In *SVF* II, 345, we find the remark that the Stoics considered only the *sōma* as a cause in the strict sense of the word, whereas according to them an *asōmaton* was called a cause by a misuse of language, being merely something which resembles a cause. Again it is evident that for the Stoics an *axiōma* was that which is caused and can, therefore, not itself be a cause in any strict sense.

4.2.6. Looking back at what we have found so far we may, I think, draw the conclusion that also in connection with *axiōmata* the words *lekton, pragma,* and *asōmaton* preserve to a certain extent the meanings that were discussed in 4.1. There are many indications that *axiōmata* were considered mainly from the point of view of the action or passion signified by the verb. This action or passion is the *pragma* which, as the asomatic thing caused, is said of the *sōma* which performs or undergoes that *pragma*. The asomatic *pragma* or *lekton* may be viewed in abstraction from the particular context in which it is or can be used; in that case it is seen to be defective. Besides such defective *pragmata* or *lekta*, the *katēgorēmata*, there are also *pragmata* or *lekta* which are complete and independent in the sense that they are the nucleus of a content which is the object of an act of asserting and is true or false. Being the principal part of the asserted content, the *pragma* or *lekton* easily lends its name to the whole of which it is the kernel.

On the other hand, it should not be overlooked that the passages in which the *axiōma* is discussed also show features which make it difficult to uphold this interpretation in all cases and in all respects. In the first place, *axiōmata* of the type 'It is day', 'He is kind', which contain forms of the verb 'to be', are not easily fitted into the model of an action or passion which is caused or undergone by a *sōma*. Further, once the whole *axiōma* had been characterized as an asomatic *pragma* or *lekton,* a characterization which presumably had its origin in the peculiar nature of that part which is the *katēgorēma,* there must have been a strong tendency to regard the other parts as sharing that character as well. Now it is obvious that the things which are added to a *katēgorēma* in order to get a complete *axiōma* of some kind by means of such linguistic expressions as proper names, common nouns, negations, privative particles, and conjunctions, can hardly be considered as asomatic *pragmata* or *lekta* in the sense of actions or passions which are said of a *sōma*. They can be accommodated as *lekta* only if the *lekton* is taken as that which is signified, as the *sēmainomenon* in general. And the words *pragma* and *asōmaton* will be applicable to them only in a meaning which is considerably different from the meaning we have highlighted so far. But before this point is elaborated I want to say a few words about those complete *lekta* which are not *axiōmata*.

4.3.   The *lekton* as what is said or expressed in other complete speech acts

4.3.1.   DL VII, 42, and 62, mentions a definition of dialectic according to which it is the science of the true and the false and of that which is neither. In 42 this definition is brought up in connection with another one, namely that dialectic is the science of arguing correctly by way of question and answer, in contrast with rhetoric which is the science of speaking well in a continuous exposition. We may therefore conclude that by that which is neither true nor false yes-or-no questions (*erōtēmata*) are meant, which in VII, 66, are defined as a complete *pragma* that demands an answer (*aitētikon apokriseōs*; cf. Aristotle, *De int.* 20 b 22) and is neither true nor false. Such yes-or-no questions, together with the answers, which are *axiōmata* and can be characterized as true or false, are the most salient part of a dialectical debate and form the main subject-matter of the science of dialectic. As we have seen in the case of the Aristotelian *protasis*, question and answer are so closely connected in the sphere of dialectical disputes that it is highly probable that the starting-point of the Stoic doctrine of complete *lekta* was the study of yes-or-no questions and the answers that are given to them. From a grammatical point of view too yes-or-no questions and assertions have much in common. The *pragma* is exactly the same and also everything that complements the *pragma*. The only difference is that in the one case the complex is used to express a question, which cannot be true or false, and that in the other case it is used to express a true or false assertion. As Apollonius Dyscolus (*De syntaxi,* ed. Uhlig p. 349, 1–10) shows, grammarians were fully aware of this close resemblance.

Once yes-or-no questions and assertions had become the object of a special branch of study, it was only natural to pay some attention to other complete *lekta* as well, if only to contrast them with the two privileged ones. In this connection the first candidate for consideration was perhaps the question which cannot be answered by 'yes' or 'no': a *pysma* such as 'Where does Dion live?'. At any rate, DL VII, 63, enumerates under the head of complete *lekta* exactly four kinds: *axiōmata*, arguments, yes-or-no questions, and *pysmata*.

4.3.2. Starting from the domain of dialectic and probably utilizing already existing divisions of kinds of speech the Stoics developed rather elaborate classifications of complete *lekta*. From the several passages in which such lists are given[7] we learn that apart from *axiōmata* and the two kinds of questions the following varieties of complete *lekta* were distinguished.

(a)   That which is more than an *axiōma* or is like an *axiōma*, for example: 'How beautiful the Parthenon (is)', 'How like to Priam's sons the cowherd (is)'. It differs from an *axiōma* in so far as it includes some emotional reaction, usually expressed by the particle *hōs* ('How'). It is also called *thaumastikon,* the *lekton* of admiration or astonishment; as such it may be contrasted with the *psektikon,* the *lekton* of censure.

(b)   Another sort of question, put to oneself in order to express doubt or despair (*epaporētikon*): 'Are sorrow and life something akin?'.

(c)   A command (*prostaktikon*), for instance: 'Come thou hither, O lady dear'.

(d)   An oath (*horkikon, omotikon, epōmotikon*), for instance: 'By this sceptre', 'Let earth be my witness in this'.

(e)   A prayer (*aratikon, euktikon*), for example: 'Zeus, my father, who rulest from Ida, majestic and mighty, victory grant unto Ajax and crown him with glory and honour'. Sometimes a distinction is drawn between prayer (*euktikon*) and deprecation or curse (*aratikon*); an instance of the latter is 'Even as this wine is spilt, so may their brains be spilt earthwards'.

(f)   An address or greeting (*prosagoreutikon*), for example: 'Most honoured son of Atreus, lord of the warriors, Agamemnon'.

(g)   A supposition or assumption (*hypothetikon*), for instance: 'Let it be supposed that the earth is the centre of the sphere of the sun'.

---

[7] DL VII, 66; SE, *AM* VIII, 71; Ammonius, *In De interpretatione,* ed. Busse p. 2, 10; Simplicius, *In Categorias,* ed. Kalbfleisch pp. 406–407; *In Hermogenis Peri staseōn,* ed. Rabe p. 186.

(h) An exhibition of a particular instance (*ekthetikon*): 'Let this be a straight line'. According to DL VII, 196, Chrysippus had written a treatise about *ektheseis.*

(i) An explanation or elucidation (*diasaphētikon*).

4.3.3. In Greek most of the names of these complete *lekta* are adjectives in the neuter gender. They may be used substantivally, but originally they determined *lekton* and *pragma,* as is shown by DL VII, 66, where *pragma* constantly occurs in the definitions, and by SE, *AM* VIII, 71, where only *lekton* is found. The definitions display a more or less fixed pattern: a *prostaktikon*, for instance, is a *pragma* or *lekton* which we say in giving a command (*ho legontes prostassomen*). There is a *pragma* which is said and there is a certain kind of speech act which determines the specific character of the *pragma* said. That the *pragma* or *lekton* was at least originally the asomatic action or passion signified by the verb is, in my opinion, shown by the following passages, two of which were already touched upon in 4.1.3. Apollonius Dyscolus (*De syntaxi,* ed. Uhlig p. 351, 9, and p. 353, 3) makes similar distinctions between the *pragma* of writing or studying and the attitude of wishing or praying (which is signified by the endings of the optative mood and certain particles), and between the *pragma* of writing and the commanding attitude (signified by the imperative mood). In these cases, which in spite of some differences are strongly reminiscent of the Stoic definitions, there cannot be the slightest doubt that *pragma* stands for the neutral action or passion of the verb, viewed in abstraction from the different speech acts in which it can play a role. In a third passage, Origen, *Selecta in Psalmos* 4:5 (ed. Migne 12, 1141 D), we read that the form *orgizesthe* signifies both *to prostaktikon katēgorēma* and *to horistikon* or *diabebaiōtikon katēgorēma*: it can be used to issue a command ('Be angry') and to make a statement ('You are angry'). What is common to both significations is the *katēgorēma,* the neutral action or passion of the verb, being angry[8]; what is different are the speech acts in which the *katēgorēma* is said. I think that the same kind of distinction is intended by Plutarch (*De Stoicorum repugnantiis* 1037 d; *SVF* II, 171), when he states that the Stoics hold that those who forbid something say one thing (*legein*), forbid another thing (*apagoreuein*), and command a third thing (*prostassein*). He who says 'You ought not to steal' (*mē klepsēis*) says just that (this, I take it, means that he expresses the thought of the action of refraining from stealing). But at the same time he performs a speech act

[8] And not the mood, as the Latin translation and *A Patristic Greek Lexicon* (ed. G.W.H. Lampe, Oxford, 1961) *s.v. katēgorēma,* have it.

which can be characterized either as a prohibition of stealing or as a command not to steal.

I submit, then, that in those cases in which the complete *lekton* contains a *pragma* in the sense of an action or passion which is said of something the definition was constructed out of this *pragma* or *lekton* as the generic element and a reference to a speech act as the specific difference. In general the principle of division was difference of speech activity. Formal differences, of mood for instance, play only a secondary role. An imperative, for example, can be used to express a command, an oath, a prayer, a supposition, or the exhibition of a particular instance.

It is not difficult, however, to find instances of complete *lekta* which do not contain a *pragma* in the sense of an action or passion that is said of something. The Greek versions of four of the examples that have been cited have no verb at all. Nevertheless they are called *pragmata* and *lekta*. Thus we have again reached a point where the facts force us to give up the interpretation of *lekton* and *pragma* (and *asōmaton*) on which we have concentrated so far. As regards *lekton*, we can fall back upon the meaning: that which is signified. All the examples can be said to be *lekta* in the sense of *sēmainomena*, thoughts expressed or things meant; for even those instances to which the characterization as asomatic *lekton* or *pragma* in the sense which has been brought into prominence up to now is readily applicable can of course also be regarded as *sēmainomena* in general. But then we are still confronted with the question of how to interpret the words *pragma* and *lekton* in the recalcitrant cases.

4.4.   The *lekton* as the thought expressed

4.4.1. Dionysius Thrax (*Ars grammatica* 12, ed. Uhlig p. 24, 3–6) defines the *onoma* as a part of speech that is capable of inflexion and signifies either a *sōma* (for instance *lithos*, 'stone') or a *pragma* (for instance *paideia*, 'education'). Some of the *onomata* are common nouns ('man', 'horse'), others are proper names ('Socrates'). In the *Scholia* on Dionysius Thrax (ed. Hilgard p. 360, 5, p. 524, 8, p. 572, 14) and by Choeroboscus (ed. Hilgard p. 105, 24) this distinction between *sōma* and *pragma* is explained in the following way. A *sōma* is something which is accessible to the senses; it is an *aisthēton* and can be seen, heard, or touched. A *pragma*, on the other hand, is a *noēton* and can only be thought. Apart from 'education' the nouns 'rhetoric', 'philosophy', 'god', 'reason', and 'grammar' are also cited as examples of *onomata* that signify *pragmata*. In Latin *sōma* is translated by *corpus, res corporalis*, or *corporale*; *pragma* by *res, res incorporalis,* or *incorporale*[9]. Common nouns signifying a *res* (*incorporalis*) are *pietas, iustitia, dignitas, disciplina, ars, virtus, sapientia, doctrina, facundia, eloquentia, dolor, prudentia, perfidia, clementia*; proper names signifying a *res* (*incorporalis*) are *Arithmetica, Arithmetica Nicomachi, Grammatica Aristarchi, Pudicitia.*

This technical use of the pair *sōma/pragma*, which seems to have been peculiar to the grammarians, was in all probability derived from Stoic sources. The semantical development of the terms *sōma* and *pragma* may perhaps be reconstructed as follows. In a first stage a *sōma* was contrasted with a *pragma* in the context of the distinction between agents or patients and the actions or passions which they cause or suffer. The *pragma* is then an action or passion signified by a verb and predicated of a *sōma*; as such it is something asomatic that is only thought. In a second stage the word *pragma* was gradually released from the association with cause and effect and came to designate anything that is only thought. At the same time the word *asōmaton*, which originally characterized the *pragma* as something that is not a cause but rather the thing caused, came to be used in the more general sense of incorporeal; a sense that it already had in certain passages of Plato's and Aristotle's works[10]. As an incorporeal thought in general, the *pragma* is also the *lekton* or *sēmainomenon*, that which is expressed by means of words. In a third stage, finally, the pair *sōma/pragma* was taken over for a special purpose by the grammarians: they used it to distinguish between two kinds of things signified by proper names and common nouns, namely things which are accessible to the senses and abstract things that are incorporeal and can be grasped only by thought. In certain respects this last conception is very different from what the old Stoics held: for them a combination such as *hē phronēsis phronei* (*SVF* III, 306) or *sapientia sapit* (Cf. Seneca, *Epistula* 117) is a typical example of the relation between a *sōma* (the virtue of practical wisdom) and a *pragma* (being wise). But what the old Stoics and the grammarians have in common is the use of the word *pragma* for something which is merely thought.

Let us now return to the problem with which we found ourselves con-

---

[9] Cf. Charisius, *Ars grammatica,* ed. Barwick pp. 193–194; Diomedes, *Ars grammatica,* ed. Keil p. 320, 10, p. 322, 10; Priscian, *Institutiones grammaticae,* ed. Hertz I, p. 56, 22, p. 57, 4, p. 59, 10; *Grammatici Latini,* ed. Keil I, p. 533, 6, IV, p. 119, 21, p. 373, 1, p. 429, 15, p. 489, 20, p. 490, 10, V, p. 34, 26, p. 137, 24, p. 338, 10, p. 549, 21, 30; Augustine, *De magistro* 8, 7 (*res visibiles/res intelligibiles*); Alcuin, *Grammatica,* ed. Migne 101, 859 B.

[10] *Sophist* 246 b, *Politicus* 286 a, *Phaedo* 85 e, *Philebus* 64 b; *Physics* 209 a 16, *De anima* 404 b 31.

fronted at the end of 4.2.6 and 4.3.3: how are we to interpret the words
pragma and *asōmaton* in cases in which there is no action or passion signified
by a verb and said of a *sōma*? The answer is, I believe, that in such cases
pragma has the sense that I have assigned to the second stage, namely of
something that is merely thought; and *asōmaton* has the sense of incorporeal,
of that which is not accessible to the senses. In so far as such an incorporeal
thought is put into words, it is a *lekton* or *sēmainomenon*, a thought expressed by means of speech. DL VII, 57, draws a distinction between *propherein* and *legein*; what we utter are the vocal sounds, but what we say or
express are the *pragmata*, the things thought, which then are *lekta*, thoughts
expressed. And SE, *AM* VIII, 80, gives the following Stoic definition of
legein; it is to utter sounds which signify the *pragma* which is thought (*tou
nooumenou pragmatos*). When DL VII, 67, says that an address such as 'Most
honoured son of Atreus, lord of the warriors, Agamemnon' is a *pragma* of
such a kind that if a person says it he will address somebody, this must
therefore mean that it is a thought which a person expresses in the speech act
of addressing somebody, or that it is that which a person means when he
addresses somebody in those words. All the examples of complete *lekta* can
be read in this way. A yes-or-no question, for instance, is a complete thought
(*pragma*), just like an *axiōma*, but it differs from an *axiōma* in being a
complete thought that is expressed in the speech act of demanding an answer.
Or a command is a thought (*pragma*) that we express in the speech act of
giving a command. But in those cases in which the complete *lekton* contains
an action or passion that is said of something, *pragma* could preserve the
additional nuance of an action or passion which is thought, a nuance that is
necessarily absent from the cases in which complete *lekta* without any element of action or passion are characterized as *pragmata*. There must have
been a gradual transition from 'an *action or passion* thought' to 'a thing
thought', with perhaps a revival of the ordinary sense of thing in such combinations as *to nooumenon pragma*: 'the *thing* thought'.

4.4.2. As I remarked in 4.2.6, once *katēgorēmata* and all sorts of complete
thoughts expressed had come to be characterized as asomatic *pragmata* and
lekta, there must have been a strong tendency to consider in the same way
those parts that have to be added in order to get a full *katēgorēma* or a
complete thought expressed. Given the fact that, for instance, the division of
axiōmata into definite, intermediate, and indefinite species turns entirely
upon the nature of the subject that is combined with the predicate, it must
have seemed natural to view the subject as an integral part of the *axiōma* and
therefore of the complete *pragma* or *lekton*, on the same footing as the
katēgorēma.

As a matter of fact, this conception is found in a famous passage of Sextus Empiricus (*AM* VIII, 11–13), where we read that the Stoics held that three things are linked together, the thing signified (*to sēmainomenon*), the thing signifying (*to sēmainon*), and the real object (*to tynchanon*)[11]. The thing signifying is the sound, for instance 'Dion'; the thing signified is the very thought (*auto to pragma*) which is expressed by the sound and which we apprehend as it arises in our mind, but of which the barbarians, although they hear the sound, are not aware; the real object is that which is given in the outside world, such as Dion himself. Of these, two are *sōmata,* the sound and the real object, and one, namely the thought that is signified (*to sēmainomenon pragma*), is *asōmaton* and a *lekton.* To *lekton* Sextus adds that it is that which is true or false. But then he seems to have realized that the thought expressed by the word 'Dion' is not a *lekton* that is true or false, and he corrects himself by saying that not every *lekton* is true or false, but that some are defective and some complete and that in the latter category only the *axiōmata* are true or false. In fact, his example is very badly chosen. He is speaking of a controversy about truth: some (the Stoics) place truth and falsehood in the thing signified, others in the sound, others in the motion of the intellect. What he should have offered as an illustration of the Stoic doctrine is of course an *axiōma.* The same confusion is found in VIII, 74–75. In general the fact that most authors in treating the Stoic *lekton* give pride of place to this passage has been an obstacle to getting a correct insight into the nature of the *lekton.* Nevertheless, it is evident that the terms *pragma, asōmaton,* and *lekton* were also applied to that which is signified by a proper name like 'Dion'. Elsewhere (*SVF* II, 164) the term *noēma* is used: if we want to express the thought of Socrates which we have in mind, we utter the name 'Socrates'. All four words occur in connection with a common noun in Clement of Alexandria (*Stromateis* VIII, 4, 13, 1). If we have to answer the question whether an embryo (*kyoumenon*) is a living being, we must make certain distinctions: the noun itself is not a living being but a sound and a *sōma* and an existent (*on*) and a something (*ti*); and that which is signified by the noun (*to sēmainomenon*) is not a living being either but an *asōmaton* and a *lekton* and a *pragma* and a *noēma.* There is another very interesting passage in Clement of Alexandria (*Stromateis* VII, 11, 61, 4). In connection with the

---

[11] Plutarch (*Adversus Colotem* 1119 f) contrasts the sounds and the real objects (*tynchanonta*) with the *lekta* as the intervening thoughts signified (*ta metaxy sēmainomena pragmata*). In a somewhat different sense the *lekton* is called intermediate by Ammonius (*SVF* II, 168), namely as the thought expressed which lies between the thought as such (*noēma*) and the real object (called *pragma* in the Aristotelian sense).

biblical story of Joseph and Potiphar's wife (*Genesis* 39, 7 ff.) Clement offers
a variation of the saying in I *Samuel* 16, 7, and *Jeremiah* 17, 10, in purely
Stoic terminology which is strongly reminiscent of SE, *AM* VIII, 11–13. We
only hear the sound (*phōnē*) and see the bodies (*sōmata*), but God examines
the *pragma* from which the speaking and seeing proceed (Cf. *Ibidem* 60, 4).

Let us try to connect this with some other data. *Logoi* of the sort 'Plato
likes Dion', 'A man sits' are defined (DL VII, 56) as significant sounds which
are sent forth from thought (*apo dianoias ekpempomenē*). The *dianoia* or the
principal part of the soul is the source of the *logos* (*SVF* II, 840, 894, 903,
III, 29, p. 215); there is a *logos* which resides in the mind (*endiathetos*)
besides the *logos* which is uttered (*prophorikos*; *SVF* II, 135). The *logos* and
its parts are *sōmata*. According to DL VII, 58, the verb or *rhēma* signifies a
katēgorēma; a proper name or *onoma* signifies an individual property (*idian
poiotēta*), and a common noun or *prosēgoria* signifies a common property
(*koinēn poiotēta*). The nature of the *katēgorēma* was discussed in 4.1.6: it is
something that is merely thought and to which nothing in the outside world
directly corresponds. Thus it is clear what kind of thought is associated with
the *rhēma*; it is the action or passion, the asomatic *pragma* which becomes a
lekton in so far as it is expressed by means of a *rhēma*. But the individual and
common properties that are signified by proper names and common nouns
are *sōmata* and we cannot, therefore, consider them as the thoughts or
noēmata which are expressed when someone utters a proper name or common noun. They are rather what the Stoics called the *tynchanonta,* the things
in the outside world which are denoted by the names. The thoughts which are
associated with proper names and common nouns have to be sought elsewhere.

As we saw in 4.1.6, DL VII, 51, gives as examples of presentations of
thought the *asōmata* and the other things that are apprehended only by
means of the *logos*. In all probability these presentations of thought are the
ideas which are formed by the transition (*metabasis*) from sense-perception to
something else. And one of the standard examples of such *noēta* or spontaneous products of thought is the mental image of Socrates which is formed
by somebody who sees a likeness of him. It must be such a mental image of
Socrates which we have in mind when we utter the proper name 'Socrates' in
order to refer to the person. As for the thought expressed by a common
noun, that can be identified, I believe, with the *ennoēma* which DL VII, 61,
defines as a presentation of thought (*phantasma dianoias*), giving as an example the situation in which we form a mental image (*anatypōma*) of a horse
even if it is not present (Cf. also *SVF* II, 83). Such *ennoēmata* are neither
sōmata nor *asōmata* in the technical meaning of these Stoic terms, and conse-

quently not even 'somethings'. They are neither 'somethings' nor of a certain nature, but only images of the mind which present themselves as if they were 'somethings' and of a certain nature (*SVF* II, 329, 278, I, 65).

When someone utters the *logos* 'Plato likes Dion' in order to make a statement, what he utters, the *logos* and its parts, two proper names and a verb, are vocal sounds and therefore *sōmata*. The *logos* has a meaning in so far as it gives expression to a thought. This thought is a complete *pragma,* an asomatic action said of *sōmata* which are specified in full. As thought expressed, it is a *lekton* or *sēmainomenon*; as thought expressed in a speech act of asserting, it is an *axiōma*. The complete thought can be analyzed into a *katēgorēma* and the thought of something of which the *katēgorēma* is said. The full *katēgorēma* is expressed by the words 'likes Dion'. What the verb 'likes' signifies is something less than a *katēgorēma*, an action or asomatic *pragma* which has to be supplemented by the thought of a body that is the object of the action. The full *katēgorēma* is not yet a complete thought; it has to be supplemented by the thought of another body which is the subject of the action. The whole utterance and the verb each signify only one thing: the complete thought and the action, to which nothing directly corresponds in the outside world. The proper names, on the other hand, signify both a thought (a mental image of the persons referred to) and some object in the outside world, namely the person himself. The same applies to common nouns; they express a vague and generalized mental image of the thing concerned and they denote the thing itself. If used in connection with a complete *logos* or a verb, the word *sēmainein* can have only one meaning: to express a thought. Since there is nothing in the somatic world that directly corresponds to an *axiōma* or *katēgorēma,* the *sēmainomenon* can only be the *lekton,* the thought expressed. If used in connection with a proper name or common noun, however, the verb *sēmainein* is ambiguous: it has either the sense of expressing a thought, of being the sign of some mental image, or the sense of denoting something in the outside world. Only in the first sense is the *sēmainomenon* a *lekton,* a thought expressed. Since for the Stoics the word *pragma* had the technical sense of something thought, in particular the action or passion thought, they could not use it in the way it was ordinarily used in Greek, for the thing denoted. That is why they introduced the term *tynchanon* (*SVF* II, 236). Such passages as *SVF* I, 65, and Clement of Alexandria, *Stromateis* VIII, 9, 26, 5, give the impression that they took this word in the sense of that which gets the name.

Apart from verbs and proper names or common nouns the utterances which express complete thoughts may also contain such expressions as 'nobody', 'that (man)', 'someone', 'he', 'not', 'un-', 'and', 'or', 'if'. Although these parts are of the utmost importance for the differentiation of the complete thoughts which they help to express, the Stoics do not seem to have developed a theory concerning the exact way in which they are involved in the process of expressing thoughts. All they say about the meaning of the conjunctions 'if' and 'or', for instance, is that they 'announce' (*epangellesthai*) that the second part logically follows from the first, or that one of the *axiōmata* is false (DL VII, 71–72; SE, *AM* VIII, 111).

4.5.   Summary of the hypothesis concerning the meaning of *lekton*

In the meanings of the words *pragma, asōmaton,* and *lekton* at least two nuances can be distinguished, which I propose to call A and B.

A. In the context of the Stoic theory of predication the meanings of the words *pragma, asōmaton, katēgorēma,* and *lekton* are determined by the opposition in which they stand to the term *sōma.* In contrast with the really existing agents or patients to which the Stoics apply their technical term *sōma,* the action or passion which is ascribed to those bodies as that which they cause or suffer, the *pragma,* is one of the things which are *asōmata,* not really existing agents or patients but only things thought. In so far as such an asomatic *pragma* is regarded as something said of a *sōma,* it is a *katēgorēma* or *lekton,* a predicate. The *lekton* as the thing said is then either the asomatic *pragma* only thought and said of a *sōma* or the asomatic *pragma* only thought and said by means of a linguistic expression.

B. In the context of the theory of signification the meanings of the words *pragma, asōmaton,* and *lekton* are determined by the opposition in which they stand to the term *sēmainon* and also, sometimes, to the term *tynchanon. Pragma* now comes to designate the thing thought in general; *asōmaton* is used to characterize the thing thought as incorporeal and immaterial; and *lekton* becomes a synonym of *sēmainomenon,* indicating the incorporeal thought expressed.

A and B are linked by the fact that an asomatic *pragma* and *lekton* in sense A are, apart from their essential association with causality, at any rate also an incorporeal thought and a thought expressed, and as such a species of the genus that is designated by *asōmaton, pragma,* and *lekton* in sense B.

Given the fragmentary character of our sources, it is impossible to trace the details of the semantical development of *lekton* by assigning A and B to definite authors or periods. All that can be gathered with some probability is that the peculiarly Stoic nature of *pragma, asōmaton,* and *lekton,* their typical association with the theory of predication in terms of cause and thing caused, gradually became less prominent by merging into a wider notion that was present from the beginning as a secondary aspect but finally became primary. This process would parallel the development of other parts of Stoic doctrine. As it is, I can say only that there are some passages which require an A-interpretation, that there are others of which I can make sense only under a B-interpretation, and that there is also a third kind, the *changeant* passages which lend themselves to both interpretations.

4.6.   Appendix

Finally, I would like to call attention to some problems concerning the distinction between things signifying and things signified. Although the Stoics had begun to develop an adequate terminology to designate each of those categories, there are indications that their efforts were not altogether successful.

The *katēgorēma* which is signified by a *rhēma* or finite verb is designated in the same way as the finite verb itself, namely by, for instance, *graphō* ('(I) write'), *graphei* ('(He) writes'): DL VII, 58, 63. This applies equally to the *logos* and the *axiōma* expressed by the *logos*: both are designated by, for instance, *hēmera estin* ('It is day'). We also find an accusative and infinitive phrase for the *axiōma* (SE, *PH* II, 97, *AM* VIII, 255; DL VII, 52) or an infinitive for the *katēgorēma* (*SVF* II, 349, III, 91). Clement of Alexandria (*SVF* III, 8, p. 263) says that the name (*ptōsis*) of such a *katēgorēma* as *temnetai* ('is cut') is the infinitive *to temnesthai* and that the name of such an *axiōma* as *naus ginetai* ('A ship comes into being') is the accusative and infinitive phrase *to naun ginesthai*. Both expressions, however, can also serve to designate the forms themselves, an infinitive or an accusative and infinitive phrase. In these circumstances it could easily happen that designations of forms were used for contents and designations of contents for forms. As a matter of fact, we learn from Porphyry (*SVF* II, 184) that the Stoics called the *katēgorēmata* or *symbamata* and their varieties, *rhēmata*. Apollonius Dyscolus (*De syntaxi*, ed. Uhlig p. 43, 14), on the other hand, informs us that the Stoics gave different names to the infinitive and to such finite verbs as *peripatei* or *graphei*: the infinitive they called *rhēma*, the finite verb *katēgorēma* or *symbama*.

Another source of uncertainty are the designations for those elements that have to be added to a *katēgorēma* in order to get an *axiōma*. The usual name for such an element seems to have been *ptōsis* ('case'). Plutarch (*Platonicae quaestiones* 1009 c) says that the Stoics called the parts of an *axiōma* by the

names of *ptōsis* and *katēgorēma*; but apparently he does not see much difference between the two parts of an *axiōma* and the *onoma* and *rhēma* of which
a *logos* and a *protasis* consist. At any rate, it is not at all clear how the word
ptōsis has to be interpreted in this connection. Does it stand for a thing
signifying or for a thing signified? On the one hand, there is good evidence for
the view that a *ptōsis* is a linguistic expression. In *SVF* I, 65, *ptōseis* are
contrasted with *ennoēmata* and identified with *prosēgoriai* or common nouns.
This identification with *prosēgoriai* is confirmed by *SVF* II, 278, and by the
following passages. Clement of Alexandria (*SVF* III, 8, p. 263) calls the infinitive the *ptōsis* of the *katēgorēma* 'is cut' and the accusative and infinitive
phrase the *ptōsis* of the *axiōma* 'A ship comes into being'. Galen (*SVF* II,
153) reports that the utterance *anthrōpos estin* ('Man exists') was held to be
ambiguous: it means either that the thing (*ousia*) exists or that the noun
(*ptōsis*) exists. And SE, *PH* II, 227, speaks of the noun (*prosēgoria*) 'man'
being introduced as an element in the construction of an *axiōma*. Furthermore, the Stoics justified their view that the nominative is a case just as well
as the oblique cases by pointing out that the nominative too has 'fallen' from
the thought in the mind. From this we may conclude that the nominative
cannot be identified with the thought but rather is the linguistic form that
gives expression to the thought (*SVF* II, 164).

On the other side, there are also indications that *ptōsis* was used for the
thought signified by a noun in a certain case. In the *Scholia* on Dionysius
Thrax (ed. Hilgard p. 230, 34) it is urged that the five cases be reckoned
among the *sēmainomena* and not among the sounds; otherwise a word like
Atreidēs ('son of Atreus'), whose genitive has no less than four variants,
would have more than five cases. Moreover, in DL VII, 190, 192, a treatise by
Chrysippus on the five cases is put into that department of logic that deals
with the *pragmata*, the thoughts. Finally, one might be tempted to adduce a
passage in Clement of Alexandria (*Stromateis* VIII, 9, 26, 1), where he cites
the sophism 'What you say goes through your mouth; you say house; therefore, (a) house goes through your mouth' (Cf. DL VII, 186) and refutes it by
pointing out that we do not say (*legomen*) the house, which is a *sōma*, but
that we say the *ptōsis* which the house gets (*hēs oikia tynchanei*); and the
ptōsis is generally regarded as *asōmatos*. Now it is of course true that the
ptōsis, if it is regarded as the thought that is signified by a noun, is *asōmatos*. But what may be seriously doubted is whether the solution which
Clement offers is at all plausible. Actually there is no need to appeal to the
thought signified by the noun 'house'; on the contrary, it is positively misleading. What goes through the mouth is not the thought which is expressed
by the noun, but the noun itself; and that is a *sōma*, namely battered air. That

the correct solution was considered to be on these lines is made probable by Augustine (*De quantitate animae* 32, ed. Migne 32, 1071), who seems to allude to the same sophism and only mentions a distinction between the sun itself and the noun 'sun', between the thing denoted and the sound.

It appears that, on the one hand, there was a tendency to interpret the word *ptōsis* as standing for the thought signified by a noun in a certain case and thus to bring it into line with the term *katēgorēma,* which in normal Stoic usage stood for something that is only thought. On the other hand, the association of the word *ptōsis* with the things signifying could also work in the opposite direction and favour the interpretation of *katēgorēma* in the sense of the finite verb which is combined with a noun in a certain case. Thus it became easy to identify the Stoic *ptōsis* and *katēgorēma* with the Peripatetic *onoma* and *rhēma,* as Plutarch does.

There are no signs that the Stoics made any attempts to develop a suitable terminology to apply the distinction between things signifying and things signified to such elements as negative and privative particles and conjunctions. The words commonly used to designate such elements, *morion* and *syndesmos,* suggest that they simply took over the terminology for linguistic expressions and left it to the reader to interpret it in the appropriate way.

5. THE STOIC *AXIŌMA*

As we saw in the foregoing chapter, an *axiōma* is a complete and independent *pragma* which is expressed in a speech act of asserting. The complete and independent *pragma* is the thought of an action or passion and its indispensable complements. In so far as this *pragma* is put into words it is a *lekton*; in so far as it is expressed in a speech act of asserting it is an *apophanton* or *axiōma,* an asserted thought-content. A *pragma* such as 'Plato liking Dion' can be expressed in different speech acts: for instance, in a yes-or-no question, 'Does Plato like Dion?', in a wish, 'May Plato like Dion', or in an assertion, 'Plato likes Dion'. On the other hand, the same type of speech act, say asserting, may be related to different *pragmata*; for I may assert many different things. Reflections of this kind must have led the Stoics to a distinction between the generic element of the *pragma* or *lekton* and the specific element of the speech act in which a certain thought is expressed.

As a rule, then, an *axiōma* is a thought-content which is in fact asserted. Nevertheless, the Stoics used the name *axiōma* also for the antecedent and consequent of a conditional, although as parts of the composite whole these are not actually asserted. This may be accounted for by the fact that *axiōma* originally meant that which is assumed or taken to be true. Or, as I suggested at the end of 4.2.5, the Stoics may have regarded the antecedent and consequent as potential *axiōmata,* just as they held that a privative assertion of the form 'Un(kind he is)' contains the potential *axiōma* 'Kind he is'. Such an assertable would lie somewhere between the neutral *pragma* or *lekton* and the factually asserted *axiōma*.

5.1. The *axiōma* as bearer of truth or falsity

5.1.1. According to SE, *PH* II, 81, and *AM* VII, 38, the Stoics distinguished between the truth (*hē alētheia*) and the true (*to alēthes*). For them the truth is a certain state of the principal part of the soul and as such a *sōma*; it is the systematic and integrated knowledge of true statements that is characteristic of the sage who cannot err. The true, on the other hand, is asomatic, since it is a *lekton* and an *axiōma*; it is not necessarily part of a coherent system of knowledge but may be found in the form of a single and isolated statement (*monoeides ti kai haploun*) so that even the fool may from time to time hit upon something true.

That the *axiōma* as the complete thought expressed in a speech act of asserting is the true or the false is confirmed by numerous passages (Cf. 4.2.5). In SE, *AM* VIII, 11, the Stoic doctrine that the true and the false are to be placed in the *sēmainomenon,* the thought expressed, is contrasted with two rival doctrines; some place the true and the false in the sound, others in the movement of thought. In discussing the thesis that the true and the false are to be placed in vocal utterances, which he ascribes to Epicurus[1] and Strato of Lampsacus, Sextus (*AM* VIII, 131) produces some arguments against this doctrine which may be of Stoic origin. The first of these begins with the observation that if the true resides in speech, it is either in significant or in non-significant speech. It is clear that it cannot reside in non-significant speech. But it cannot reside in significant speech either, for no sound as such is significant; otherwise all those who perceive the sounds, both Greeks and barbarians, ought also to apprehend the thought that is signified by the sound. This must mean that if a Greek and a barbarian hear the same utterance, only the Greek has the appropriate thought and therefore understands the utterance and knows whether that which is said is true or false. The barbarian, although he perceives the same sounds, cannot attach any meaning to them and *a fortiori* does not know whether that which is said is true or false. Consequently, the sounds are significant for some but not for others. What makes the difference is the thought that accompanies the sounds, and it must, for that reason, be the thought signified which is the true or the false. The second argument starts from the consideration that if the true resides in speech, it must reside in composite speech — for example, in 'Dion walks'. But a composite utterance never exists in its entirety, for when we utter 'Dion' we do not yet utter 'walks', and when we utter 'walks' the sound

---

[1] Cf. Plutarch, *Adversus Colotem* 1119 f: the Epicureans do not admit the existence of *lekta* or intervening thoughts signified, but leave only the sounds and the real objects.

'Dion' is no longer there (Cf. also *AM* VIII, 81). This difficulty, which is reminiscent of Aristotle, *Cat.* 5 a 34, is frequently discussed in medieval writings (Cf. 9.5.1 and 12.2.3).

One of the differences between the Aristotelian and Stoic conceptions of the bearers of truth and falsity is that Aristotle regards utterances that are used to make statements as at least one category of bearers of truth and falsity, whereas I have not found a single passage in Stoic writings where the *logos,* in the sense of a complex of significant sounds (DL VII, 56), is called true or false. SE, *PH* II, 138, makes a distinction between *logoi* which are true and *logoi* which are not true, but there he is speaking about conclusive arguments and such *logoi* are complexes of *axiōmata,* the *syllogismoi* that are mentioned among the complete *lekta* in DL VII, 63.

Another point that was strongly emphasized by the Stoics, probably against such a doctrine as was defended by Aristotle in the ninth chapter of *De interpretatione* (*SVF* II, 198), is that every *axiōma* is either true or false. Cicero (*De fato* 21) tells us that Chrysippus did his utmost to convince people of this thesis and in *SVF* II, 912, it is referred to as 'that much-discussed proposition' (*to polythrylēton touto*).

5.1.2. As far as we can judge from the remnants of their writings the Stoics seem to have paid most attention to truths and falsehoods that are expressed in speech, by means of a verbal act of making one's opinion known to others. For them the bearer of truth or falsity *par excellence* is the *axiōma.* If they attribute truth or falsehood to other subjects than the *axiōma,* they appear to regard this attribution as derivative and secondary in comparison with the central case. SE, *AM* VIII, 10, says that the Stoics held that such objects of perception (*aisthēta*) as are true are so only in an indirect way, by reference to the things thought (*noēta*) that are associated with them; and these things thought are asomatic *axiōmata.* Another instructive passage is SE, *AM* VII, 242, where some distinctions of presentations (*phantasiai*) are mentioned. First, some presentations give rise to belief, some give rise to disbelief, some to both, some to neither. The examples given make it clear that the presentations concerned are thoughts which can be the object of an act of assenting or dissenting; they are the accepted or rejected thought-contents which become *axiōmata* when they are expressed in words. Presentations which give rise to belief are such evident thoughts as that it is now day or that I am discoursing. Presentations which give rise to disbelief are those thoughts that make us decline to assent — for instance, 'If it is day, then the sun is not above the earth' or 'If it is dark, then it is day'. Presentations which give rise to both are, for example, presentations of *aporoi logoi,* perplexing arguments such as The

Hooded Man, The Bald Man, The Horned Man (Cf. *AM* VII, 418; DL VII, 82; *SVF* II, 286, 287). Presentations which give rise to neither are presentations of such thoughts as 'The stars are even in number', 'The stars are odd in number'. In this latter instance the thoughts are referred to as *pragmata*; the same word occurs in SE, *PH* II, 97, where the *pragmata* are divided into the evident and the non-evident, with partly the same examples as in *AM* VII, 242–243 (Cf. also SE, *PH* II, 42; DL VII, 49). It is obvious, I think, that what the Stoics meant when they defined the *lekton* as that which exists *kata logikēn phantasian* (Cf. 4.1.6) are exactly these *pragmata,* certain thoughts which present themselves in the mind and become *lekta* when they are expressed in words.

In a second division some convincing presentations are characterized as true, some as false, some as both true and false, and some as neither true nor false. True presentations are those about which it is possible to make a true affirmation (*katēgorian*), for instance 'It is day' or 'It is light' at the present moment (when it is day and light). False presentations are those about which it is possible to make a false affirmation, as that the oar under water is bent or that the porch is tapering. This explanation clearly suggests that what is basically true or false is the object of the verbal act of affirming. A somewhat similar emphasis on verbal acts of holding something true and their objects will be found in Abelard (Cf. 9.4.3).

5.1.3. Both presentations and *axiōmata* are proper objects of an act of assenting (*synkatathesis*). For presentations this is shown by such passages as *SVF* II, 70, 74, III, 63, 177, 548, and SE, *AM* VII, 151, 242, 417, VIII, 397. For *axiōmata* we have the evidence of *SVF* III, 171, where it is said that the *synkatatheseis* are acts of assenting to *axiōmata*; we may assume that the speech act of *axioun,* from which the *axiōma* got its name, is the verbal expression of a mental act of assenting. Occasionally a *synkatathesis* is called false (*SVF* III, 172, 548; SE, *AM* VII, 151), no doubt because it is an assent to a false presentation or *axiōma*.

The words *krisis* and *hypolēpsis,* with the verbs *krinein* and *hypolambanein,* are more or less equivalent to *synkatathesis* (*SVF* II, 992); they have the same neutral and generic sense of judging that something is the case. In *SVF* II, 994, falsity is attributed to an *hypolēpsis. A doxa,* on the other hand, is a kind of assent that is only weak and associated with the unconvincing and false. In SE, *AM* VII, 151, it is contrasted with two forms of assent that are by definition successful: *katalēpsis* or apprehension and *epistēmē* or knowledge. While a *doxa* is found only in fools, knowledge is the privilege of the wise; it is the unerring and firm apprehension which is unalterable by reasoning. An apprehension is intermediate between mere opinion and knowledge; it is assent to an evidently true presentation. Zeno (*SVF* I, 66) compared a presentation to an open hand, assent to a slight contraction of the fingers, apprehension to the making of a fist, and knowledge to firmly squeezing the fist with the other hand.

In so far as a *synkatathesis, krisis, hypolēpsis, doxa, katalēpsis,* or *epistēmē* is an act of assenting, judging, opining, apprehending, or knowing, it is in all probability asomatic. As we saw at the end of 4.1.6, however, there may be a shift of emphasis from the act or state considered on its own to the act or state as realized in a somatic subject. Just as Plutarch (*De communibus notitiis contra Stoicos* 1084 a) regards walking and dancing as bodies, he calls *synkatatheseis* bodies and even living beings, no doubt from the perspective of the body which is in that state. In the same way SE, *AM* VII, 38, considers all knowledge as the principal part of the soul in a particular state, meaning by knowledge the possession of a system of truths rather than a single act of apprehending something true (Cf. *SVF* III, 112).

Finally, it should be noted that most of the words that are used for acts or attitudes of holding something true may easily come to be used for the objects of those acts or attitudes as well. A word such as *hypolēpsis,* for instance, primarily stands for the act of judging that something is the case but it may also come to designate that which is taken to be true, the presentation or *axiōma.*

5.1.4. Besides being the fundamental bearers of truth and falsity the *axiōmata* are also the subjects of the modalities. In DL VII, 75, and *SVF* II, 182, *axiōmata* are said to be possible or impossible, necessary or not-necessary. Boethius (*SVF* II, 201) refers to such a Stoic division as a distinction between *enuntiationes,* but it is clear that he uses the Latin equivalent of the Aristotelian term *apophansis* for that which the Stoics called *axiōma.*

Furthermore, the *axiōmata* were regarded as the terms of certain logical relations. They stand to each other in the relation of contradiction (DL VII, 73; SE, *AM* VIII, 89) or in the relation of contrariety (*SVF* II, 175, 176). In *SVF* II, 173, it is explicitly stated that the whole consideration of contraries has to do with *pragmata* or things thought. *Axiōmata* are also the terms of the relation of following from (*akolouthein, hepesthai*) that exists between the consequent and the antecedent of a conditional or between the conclusion and the premisses of an argument (DL VII, 81; SE, *AM* VIII, 111; *SVF* II, 253, 283). As structural parts of a conditional *axiōmata* are called *hēgoumenon* and *lēgon,* or simply the first and the second. As premisses of an argument they are called *lēmmata,* things that are assumed to be true. The

second premiss is the *proslēpsis,* the additional assumption; and for the conclusion the Stoics used the name *epiphora* instead of the Aristotelian *symperasma* (*SVF* II, 236, 237).

5.2. Further characteristics of the *axiōma*

5.2.1. According to Dionysius of Halicarnassus (*SVF* II, 206 a) and DL VII,
76, one of the kinds of *axiōmata* that the Stoics distinguished were the
metapiptonta or changing *axiōmata*; they display a change or conversion
(*metaptōsis, antistrophē*) from true to false or from false to true. Furthermore, among the treatises ascribed to Chrysippus two are mentioned whose
titles contain the phrase *metapiptontes logoi,* presumably designating arguments in which some kind of change plays an essential part (DL VII, 195—
196).

SE, *PH* II, 231, contains what seems to be an example of a changing
argument. The Stoics declared that a sophism is a plausible argument cunning-
ly framed to induce acceptance of a conclusion that is false, or resembles
what is false, or is non-evident (*adēlos*) or otherwise unacceptable. As an
illustration of a sophism leading to a non-evident and unknowable conclusion
Sextus adduces a reduction to the non-evident which according to the Stoics
belongs to the genre of the changing arguments: 'It is not the case both that I
have propounded a proposition to you already (*prōton*) and that the stars are
not even in number; but I have propounded a proposition to you already;
therefore, the stars are even in number'. In *PH* II, 97, and *AM* VIII, 147, 149,
the statement that the stars are even in number is offered as an example of a
pragma that is altogether non-evident and cannot be ascertained at all, not
even by means of signs. It seems that the Stoics came close to considering
such statements as untrue. That we are nevertheless led to accept it as a
conclusion is brought about by the fact that a change occurs in the premisses.
At the beginning the first premiss is true because the first conjunct of the
negated conjunction is false. The first premiss may also be read as the conditional 'If I have propounded a proposition to you already, then the stars are
even in number'. After the first premiss has been put forward, however, 'I
have propounded a proposition to you already' is true and can therefore be
presented as the true affirmation of the antecedent of the first premiss. And
from the two true premisses the unacceptable conclusion then follows by
modus ponendo ponens. The double role of 'I have propounded a proposition
to you already' is of decisive importance for the plausibility of the reasoning:
as a false statement it makes the first premiss true, and as a true statement it

makes the second premiss true. That the argument must be rejected as a sophism can be shown in either of two ways. It may be objected that the two statements made by the utterance-type 'I have propounded a proposition to you already' are different, because they refer to different times, a time before the first utterance and a time before the second utterance (namely, the time of the first utterance itself). In this interpretation the second premiss does not really affirm the antecedent of the first premiss. But one may also argue that if 'The stars are even in number' is held to be untrue, the premisses cannot be true at the same time. If 'I have propounded a proposition to you already' is taken to be one and the same statement which is first false and then true, the first premiss cannot remain true once the second premiss has become true. The fact that the latter objection is put forward in the text makes it probable that the Stoics regarded 'I have propounded a proposition to you already', as used in this sophism, as one and the same *axiōma* with changing truth-values.

SVF II, 206, gives more examples of changing *axiōmata*. 'If Dion is alive, then Dion will be alive' is true as long as both the antecedent and the consequent are true. But, since Dion is not immortal, there will come a moment when the conditional becomes false, namely when the antecedent is still true but the consequent ceases to be true. As the time at which 'Dion will be alive' changes from true to false and thereby makes the whole conditional change from true to false is uncertain, the Stoics said that the change of such *axiōmata* takes place at an undetermined and indefinite time; they are *metapiptonta aperigraphōs*. As we know from the so-called Master Argument (*SVF* II, 283), Diodorus Cronus, of the Megarian school, held that everything that is past and true is necessary, defining the necessary as that which, being true, will not be false. While Chrysippus agreed with this Diodorean thesis, Cleanthes denied it, as is confirmed by Cicero (*De fato* 14)[2]. This must mean that Cleanthes considered *axiōmata* about the past as susceptible of changing truth-values. We also learn from Cicero (*De fato* 17, 20) that Diodorus

[2] In *De fato* 14, 17, 18, 20, 28, Cicero apparently uses the Latin words *commutari, commutatio, immutabile, immutabilitas, convertere* as equivalents of the Greek terms *metapiptein, metaptōsis, antistrophē,* and their derivatives. It is interesting to note that Walter Burleigh in his treatise *De insolubilibus,* which dates from the first years of the fourteenth century, uses the term *transcasus* in connection with a solution of a version of the paradox of the Liar and says that we have a *transcasus* when a *propositio* changes from truth to falsity or from falsity to truth (De Rijk 1966 b: 89). The same word, with the verb *transcadere,* already occurs in the so-called *Ars Meliduna,* probably written between 1154 and 1180, but there it is used in connection with Aristotle, *Topics* 157 b 11 (De Rijk 1967: I, 385).

regarded statements about the future as no less immutable than statements about the past; in neither case can there be a change from true to false. According to *SVF* II, 961, the Stoics rejected such a view. In their opinion an *axiōma* of the type 'There will be a sea-fight tomorrow' cannot be necessary, in the sense of being always true, since it remains no longer true once the sea-fight has taken place. This may mean that it then becomes false, as in the case of 'Dion will be alive'; but there is also the possibility that it becomes inapplicable.

For we know from *SVF* II, 202 a–b (Cf. also 624) that the Stoics held that some *axiōmata* can be destroyed (*phtheiresthai*). Chrysippus thought that he could refute the view that the impossible does not follow from the possible by means of the example 'If Dion is dead, then this (man) is dead'. As long as Dion can be pointed at, the conditional is true (since the contradictory of the consequent is incompatible with the antecedent). And the antecedent is possible, because it can become true that Dion is dead; but the consequent is impossible, because it can never become true. The reason why it can never become true is that the demonstrative *houtos* can be used to refer to something only when the referent exists and can be pointed at. As soon as Dion has died the *axiōma* 'This (man) is dead' therefore becomes inapplicable. The same holds of the example 'If it is night, then this is not day(light)', expressed at a moment when one can point at the existing daylight. In general, the Stoics seem to have regarded the definite *axiōmata* (Cf. 4.2.5), which contain a demonstrative and can thus become inapplicable, as destructible or perishable. In *SVF* II, 182, a distinction is mentioned between *axiōmata* that are *phtharta* and *axiōmata* that are *aphtharta*.

If 'There will be a sea-fight tomorrow' is paraphrased as 'There will be a sea-fight on the day after this day', in which 'this day' refers to the time of utterance, it is obvious that this *axiōma* too could be thought to become inapplicable. Because of the demonstrative reference to a definite day it can apply only as long as the referent is there. In that case, however, one would have to conclude that the *axiōma* already becomes inapplicable before the sea-fight has taken place, namely during the time when it would be appropriate to say 'There will be a sea-fight today'. Moreover, it is not easy to see how this hypothesis can be squared with the fact that the Stoics apparently did not appeal to their doctrine of destructible *axiōmata* in relation to 'I have propounded a proposition to you already' in the above-mentioned sophism, although 'tomorrow' and 'already' have relevant features in common. On the other hand, there are also difficulties for the view that the *axiōma* 'There will be a sea-fight tomorrow' becomes false after the sea-fight has taken place. One would think that someone who said 'There will be a sea-fight tomorrow'

after the event concerned would either say something which is utterly unintelligible or be referring to another day and another sea-fight, in which case
his statement might be true.

There are indications that the identity of an *axiōma* as the thought expressed in a speech act of asserting was not considered to be tied to a *logos* in
the sense of an utterance-token; a conditional such as 'If it is day, then it is
day' consists of the same *axiōma* repeated (DL VII, 68–69). On the other
hand, it is also highly improbable that the Stoics always took the identity of
an *axiōma* to be tied to a *logos* as an utterance-type in general. If utterance-
types such as 'Dion walks' or 'This (man) walks' are used to assert the walking
of different persons who happen to have the same name or can be referred to
by the same demonstrative pronoun, we may be sure that there are different
axiōmata. As a rule the *axiōma* seems to have been a rather definite thought
whose identity is not affected by the circumstance that the words in which it
is expressed can also be used to express other definite thoughts. This does not
mean, however, that there are no connections between the identity of the
axiōma and the way in which it is expressed. As we saw, the Stoics regarded
'Dion is dead' and 'This (man) is dead' as different *axiōmata*. A thought
which is expressed by means of a proper name or a common noun differs
from a thought which is expressed by means of a demonstrative. The identity
of the *axiōma* probably also depends upon the tense of the verb in the *logos*
which is used to express it. DL VII, 190, mentions two titles of writings by
Chrysippus which suggest a connection between *axiōmata* and the tenses of
the verb. And SE, *AM* VIII, 255, makes it likely that, for instance, 'He will
die', 'He is dying', and 'He has died' were considered to be different *axiōmata*, even when they are related to the same event. This is confirmed by the
facts that *axiōmata* about the future were regarded as one class of statements
that are susceptible of changing truth-values and that Cleanthes at least took
the view that *axiōmata* about the past are another class of statements that can
have changing truth-values.

The several data which we have surveyed, meagre and uncertain though
they are, appear to suggest the following conclusion. The *axiōma* is a definite
thought-content expressed in a speech act of asserting, of such a kind that the
same thought-content can be expressed by different utterance-tokens and
that the same utterance-type can express different definite thought-contents.
At the same time, the identity of the definite thought-content is determined
by certain features of the *logos* by which it is expressed: 'Dion walks' and
'This (man) walks' do not express the same *axiōma*, and similarly the *axiōmata* associated with 'Dion will die', 'Dion is dying', and 'Dion has died' are
different. All this is most naturally explained by remembering that for the

Stoics the *axiōma* was also the *sēmainomenon,* the particular meaning or thing meant, of the *logos* which is used to make a statement. This *sēmainomenon* is the *lekton* or *pragma,* the particular thought which precedes the words spoken and gives them a definite meaning. The identity of the *axiōma* is made dependent upon certain differences in the linguistic expression of it because the *axiōma* is regarded as the specific thought which constitutes the linguistic meaning of the spoken utterance.

As long as a thought expressed by means of a statement-making utterance is quite definite it is impossible that its truth-value changes; once true it remains true and once false it remains false as long as it is applicable. That the Stoics nevertheless acknowledged *axiōmata* with changing truth-values can be explained, I suggest, in the following way. An *axiōma* such as 'Dion will be alive' fails to specify the exact time at which Dion will be alive. If time-references are added, for instance 'Dion will be alive at t_1', 'Dion will be alive at t_2', it is clear that we get different *axiōmata* the first of which becomes inapplicable at and after t_1 and the second at and after t_2, while the first may be true as long as it is applicable and the second false. By identifying the *axiōma* primarily with the thought behind the words the Stoics had also to admit not fully specified thoughts as *axiōmata* and then they were led to hold that such *axiōmata* can undergo a change of truth-value. If they had required that an *axiōma* be a fully specified thought, they would have noticed that 'Dion will be alive' has to be supplemented by time-references and that then we may get different *axiōmata* upon which their doctrine of inapplicability can be brought to bear.

We do not know on what grounds Cleanthes founded his opinion that statements about the past can have changing truth-values. He may have thought of an example of the same sort as is found in the fourteenth century scholastic Pierre d'Ailly: 'Adam was every man' (*Adam fuit omnis homo*)[3]. In that case it would again be a thought which is left unspecified as to temporal reference and thereby leads one to believe that its truth-value can change. As soon as proper time-references are supplied it is seen that no such change can occur.

If the Stoics considered 'I have propounded a proposition to you already' in the above-mentioned sophism as one *axiōma* with changing truth-value, they may have come to this view by failing to make a clear distinction between the general meaning and the particular meaning of the *logos* concerned. Instead of paying attention to the fact that the particular meaning of 'already' (*prōton*) depends upon the moment of utterance and that conse-

---

[3] *Quaestiones super libros Sententiarum* I, q.11, art.1, D (Cf. 15.4.1).

quently the same utterance-type may be used to make two different definite statements, they apparently gave priority to the general meaning and thereby came to think that the same thought, left partially unspecified, changed from false to true.

5.2.2. Since Mates (1961: 19–26) compared the Stoic *lekton* to Frege's *Sinn* and the *axiōma* to Frege's *Gedanke,* several other influential authors have put forward the view that the *axiōma* is a kind of objective and public thought-content, quite different from subjective and private ideas or mental images. Bocheński (1962: 127) maintains that the *lekton* is not something which is dependent upon thought, a *conceptus subiectivus,* but rather a *conceptus obiectivus,* the Fregean *Sinn,* an independently existing object of thought. Popper (1968: 27–28) goes so far as to regard the *axiōmata* as the most important inhabitants of his third world, aligning the Stoics with Plato, Leibniz, Bolzano, and Frege. And even Kneale & Kneale (1962: 156), in their excellent survey of the Stoic doctrine of meaning and truth, hold that *axiōmata* exist in some sense whether we think of them or not. For this thesis, that *lekta* may exist which are neither expressed nor thought, they adduce two arguments. First, according to the Stoic theory of natural signs an *axiōma* which is a sign reveals another *axiōma* which is its significate; the latter must therefore exist in order to be revealed. Second, the remark made by Sextus (*PH* II, 83; cf. *AM* VII, 42) that, while truth is necessarily connected with knowledge, the true is not, implies that true *axiōmata* may exist although they are not known. Both arguments, however, are based on a mistaken interpretation of the texts.

Let us begin with the second argument. As we saw in 5.1.1, the Stoics regarded the truth as the systematic and integrated knowledge of true statements that is typical of the sage who cannot err. It is a certain state of the principal part of the soul and as such a *sōma* (Cf. also *SVF* III, 112). The true, on the other hand, is an asomatic *axiōma* which is not necessarily part of a coherent system of knowledge but may have the form of a single and isolated statement so that even the fool may sometimes assert something true. Now what Sextus says in *PH* II, 83, and *AM* VII, 42, is precisely that while there is always a connection between the truth and systematic knowledge in the sense of a certain state of mind, there is no such connection between the true and knowledge. If the fool expresses a true *axiōma,* he may be said to apprehend that something is the case, but he does not possess knowledge of the true in the strict sense in which knowledge can be ascribed only to the wise. From this it does not follow that *axiōmata* may exist although they are not known, in the sense that they may exist although no one is aware of them and expresses them in words. What does follow is that not all true *axiōmata* are part of a system of strict knowledge as possessed by the wise.

In order to see that the first argument is mistaken we have to look at the Stoic doctrine of proof (SE, *PH* II, 134–143, *AM* VIII, 300–315, 411–426). A proof is an argument which is conclusive and true (in the sense that its premisses are known to be true) and has a conclusion which is non-evident and established as true (*ekkalyptomenon*) through the power of the premisses. The verb *ekkalyptein* (literally 'to uncover, disclose, reveal') is a technical term which means that the true premisses of a valid argument establish the truth of a non-evident conclusion in such a way that one assents to the conclusion only on account of the logical force of the premisses. Proof is a kind of sign: the conjunction of the premisses is a sign of the truth of the conclusion (*AM* VIII, 277). And a sign is defined as an *axiōma* which is the antecedent in a sound conditional and serves to establish the truth of the consequent, a sound conditional being in this context a conditional which both begins with truth and ends in truth (*AM* VIII, 245). Furthermore, it is explicitly stated that the sign and that of which it is a sign must both be present. Let us now take an example: 'If this man is wounded in the heart, then he will die'. That this conditional, in which the two *axiōmata* 'This man is wounded in the heart' and 'He will die' are both present, is sound must presumably be deduced from a general conditional of the type 'If anyone is wounded in the heart, then he will die', of which it is an instantiation (Cf. Hay 1969: 151). We are supposed to know that the antecedent is true and by affirming the antecedent we can therefore establish the truth of the consequent, which is a non-evident *axiōma* and one to which we assent only on account of the logical force of the premisses. Now what the conjunction of the premisses, which is a sign of the conclusion, 'reveals' is of course not the existence of the *axiōma* which is the conclusion, but its truth. It is obvious that the *axiōma* which is the conclusion of the argument must exist, that is must be thought, in order to be demonstrated, since the sign and that of which it is a sign must be co-present. But this does not at all mean that this *axiōma* has an independent existence in a sort of Platonic third world where it is waiting to be discovered and expressed in speech.

Actually, there is not a shred of evidence for such Platonizing views. All the data available point in the opposite direction: that *lekta* in general and *axiōmata* in particular exist only in so far as they are thought and expressed in words. Every *lekton* must be expressed in words (*legesthai*), whence it acquired that name, as Sextus puts it (*AM* VIII, 80). Its existence is *noeisthai* and *legesthai*. And as ideas in the mind, as *nooumena, noēta, (en)noēmata*, the *lekta* and *axiōmata* should be interpreted not in some Platonic or Aristotelian sense but as something much more akin to the ideas of, for instance, classical British empiricism — as a kind of mental images which precede and accompany our words and give meaning to them. They are exactly that which the Fregeans say they are not.

6. LATER DEVELOPMENTS IN GREEK ANTIQUITY

6.1. Fusion of terminologies

When Plutarch (*Platonicae quaestiones* 1009 c) discusses, in connection with Plato, *Sophist* 262, the combination of linguistic expressions which is of such a nature that it can be called true or false, he shows himself fully aware of the existing differences in terminology. What Plato calls a *logos* others designate by the names *protasis* and *axiōma*; and the parts of the *logos* or *protasis*, the *onoma* and *rhēma*, are named *ptōsis* and *katēgorēma* by the later dialecticians. But the context makes it clear that Plutarch considers these terms only as different names for the same things. He apparently finds no difference worth mentioning between the Platonic *logos*, the Aristotelian *protasis*, and the Stoic *axiōma*.

Galen, in his *Institutio logica*, occasionally uses the word *apophansis* in a rather non-technical way (III, 1, XII, 5, XIII, 3; cf. also I, 5, and II, 1). As a rule he keeps to the term *protasis*, either in the sense of premiss (along with *lēmma* and *proslēpsis*) or in the sense of statement in general. As for *axiōma*, he makes a distinction between the Aristotelian use in the sense of axiom (I, 5, III, 2) and the Stoic use in which, according to him, it stands for all statement-making utterances (I, 5). Although he sometimes calls attention to the difference between the Peripatetic *protasis*-terminology and the Stoic *axiōma*-terminology (I, 5, III, 3, 4, XIV, 2), he never mentions any difference of denotation. For him both the Peripatetic *protaseis* and the Stoic *axiōmata* are *logoi*, utterances (III, 4, 5, IV, 5). He nowhere acknowledges the fundamental distinction which the Stoics drew between the *logos* and the *lekton* (as the thought expressed by means of the utterance) of which the *axiōma* is a species.

89

This gradual fusion of Aristotelian and Stoic terminologies[1], with the accompanying neglect of the differences in denotation, is strikingly confirmed by a passage in Clement of Alexandria (*Stromateis* VIII, 3, 8, 2–3): he who wants to prove things in a correct manner must pay due attention to the truth of the premisses and the logically valid connection between premisses and conclusion, but he need not care about the names, for it is indifferent whether he speaks of *axiōmata* or *protaseis* or *lēmmata*. That such subtle distinctions are of very little use for a Christian is implied by the second century apologist Athenagoras, who in his *Legatio pro Christianis* (ed. Migne 6, 912 B) throws doubt on the moral efficacy of the doctrines of the dialecticians who elucidate the nature of homonyms and synonyms, *katēgorēmata* and *axiōmata,* subject and predicate.

On the whole it is the typically Stoic doctrine which suffers most in this process of amalgamation. Within the Peripatetic school much care was given to the maintenance of a clearly defined terminology. Ammonius, for instance, makes a distinction between *logos, apophansis,* and *protasis* according to degrees of generality. Every *protasis* is an *apophansis* and every *apophansis* is a *logos.* Not every *logos,* however, is an *apophansis* but only that *logos* which can be said to be true or false. And not every *apophansis* is a *protasis.* Only the *apophansis* or *logos apophantikos* which is part of a syllogism can be called a *protasis,* whereas an *apophansis* can also occur as an isolated statement (*In Analytica priora,* ed. Wallies p. 15, 17; cf. also Alexander of Aphrodisias, *In Analytica priora,* ed. Wallies p. 10, 13).

6.2.   The perfection of sense

In the rest of this chapter I shall give a sketch of the way in which the themes of the perfection of sense and of the classification of kinds of speech were elaborated in the later period of Greek antiquity. As we have seen and as we shall see, both themes keep recurring in the discussions concerning the bearers of truth and falsity. For a proper understanding of the context in which our main subject was treated it is therefore necessary to trace the development of these topics in some detail.

6.2.1. Dionysius Thrax (*Ars grammatica* 11, ed. Uhlig p. 22, 4) offers two definitions, one of *lexis* ('word') and one of *logos* ('sentence'). A *lexis* is the smallest part of a well-ordered *logos.* In the *Scholia* on Dionysius Thrax (ed.

---

[1] Cf. also Plotinus, *Enneads* V, 5, 1, and V, 8, 6.

Hilgard p. 56, 16, p. 212, 2, p. 353, 8, p. 513, 13) it is pointed out that this definition is not quite complete. In order to exclude letters and syllables one should speak of the smallest part that signifies something thought (*noēton ti sēmainon*). In this connection the word *lekton* occurs twice (p. 352, 28, and p. 513, 36): *lexeis* in the strict sense are only those smallest parts which are associated with a thought expressed. If the scholiasts' interpretation is followed, there is a difference from the definition given by Diogenes of Babylon (Diogenes Laertius, *Vitae philosophorum*, VII, 56). For him a *lexis* is articulated sound, even if it has no significance.

Dionysius Thrax defines a *logos* as a combination of speech in prose that makes known a complete thought (*dianoian autotelē dēlousa*). Two things are worthy of note. First, the completeness which in Stoic texts is constantly ascribed to *pragmata* or *lekta* is here attributed to the *dianoia*, in the sense of the thought which is the product of the activity of the thinking faculty. It is understandable that Dionysius does not use the phrase *lekton autoteles*; it is already sufficiently obvious from the context that the complete thought is expressed in speech. On the other hand, he may have felt that the phrase *pragma autoteles* belonged too markedly to the technical vocabulary of one philosophical school and may therefore have preferred the less esoteric term *dianoia*. In the second place, his definition makes it impossible to speak of a *logos* if the combination of words is not accompanied by a complete thought. Consequently, when we find later authors speaking of both a perfect and an imperfect *logos*, in the sense of a *logos* which is associated with a complete thought and of a *logos* which is not, they must have another conception of *logos* in mind than the one put forward by Dionysius Thrax. They apparently adhere to Aristotle's definition, according to which a *logos* is a significant spoken sound some part of which is significant in separation, as an expression, not necessarily as an affirmation or negation (*De int.* 16 b 26).

In the *Scholia* on Dionysius Thrax several variants of the phrase *dianoian autotelē dēlousa* are found: *dianoēma, ennoia, noēma, nous* are used instead of *dianoia*; *entelēs* and *teleios* instead of *autotelēs*; and *apartizousa* and *sēmainousa* instead of *dēlousa*. The scholiasts point out that the definition of *logos* excludes metrical utterances. Some of them, therefore, propose a wider definition: for instance 'a correctly constructed combination of words expressing a complete thought' (p. 214, 5). Others offer a separate definition for the metrical utterance, which they call a *periodos*: 'a metrical combination of words expressing a complete thought' (p. 57, 8, p. 355, 23).

6.2.2. When discussing the phrase *ti perainei* in Plato, *Sophist* 262 d 4 (Cf. 2.2.3) we saw that Aristotle (*Rhetoric* 1409 b 9) says that a period must be

complete as regards *dianoia*. This connection between the period and a complete thought is further elaborated by Demetrius, who perhaps lived towards
the beginning of the Christian era and wrote a treatise on style (*Peri hermēneias*). According to Demetrius the period is a collection of members (*kōla*) or
phrases (*kommata*) rounded off skilfully to fit the thought to be expressed
(*eis tēn dianoian tēn hypokeimenēn apērtismenon*). Referring to Aristotle's
definition of the period, he explains that the very use of the word 'period'
implies that there has been a beginning at one point and will be an ending at
another and that we are hastening towards a definite goal as runners do when
they leave the starting-place (I, 10–11). The proper function of *kōla* is to
mark the conclusion of a thought (*dianoian apartizein*), either a whole
thought (*holēn dianoian*) or a whole part of a whole thought. Other expressions that are used to convey the idea of completeness are: *symperaioun,
syntelein, plēroun*; *echein peras, echein holoklērian* (I, 2–3). A *komma* is
defined as that which is less than a member. Some of them – for example,
'Know thyself' – are characterized by the fact that much thought is compres-
sed in a little space (*to en oligōi pollēn dianoian ēthroisthai*; I, 9). In later
treatises on rhetoric (for instance, *Rhetores Graeci* XIV, *Prolegomenon sylloge*, ed. H. Rabe p. 213) the period is defined as an intricate *logos* composed
of members and phrases, expressing a complete thought (*dianoian autotelē
dēlōn*).

Another field where the perfection of sense or the completeness of
thought plays a conspicuous role is the study of the art of punctuation.
Dionysius Thrax (*Ars grammatica* 4, ed. Uhlig p. 7, 5) says that there are
three marks of punctuation: the full stop or period (*teleia stigmē*), the colon
(*mesē stigmē*), and the comma (*hypostigmē*). The period is the sign of a
complete thought (*dianoias apērtismenēs*) and the comma is the sign of a
thought that is not yet complete but still has need of some addition (*dianoias
mēdepō apērtismenēs all' eti endeousēs*). In the *Scholia* on Dionysius Thrax
(ed. Hilgard p. 24, 9, p. 313, 1) we find more varied expressions to convey
the idea of such completeness and incompleteness of thought. *Enthymēma,
ennoia, noēma* occur along with *dianoia*. The verbs *legein, perainein, plēroun,
telein, teleioun* are employed to express the notion of being or making complete. And to the 'not yet'-vocabulary of incompleteness belong forms of
such verbs as *deisthai, (ek)kremasthai, (el)leipein, epizētein*, which express
the idea of standing in need of something, being suspended, being deficient,
missing something. The scholiasts also offer a practical criterion to decide
whether an expressed thought is complete or not: in the case of a complete
thought the utterance can be followed by silence and the hearer does not feel
any need to urge the speaker to go on, whereas in the case of an incomplete
thought the hearer will be inclined to ask for the rest.

6.2.3. In the passages we have discussed so far it is always the *dianoia* which is the subject of the qualifications that have to do with completeness and incompleteness. It is, however, a natural step to extend the characterization as complete or incomplete from the thought expressed to the expressions which signify the thought, especially when the *logos* is taken not in the sense defined by Dionysius Thrax, but rather in the Aristotelian sense of a group of words which is either a phrase or a full sentence. An interesting intermediate position is found in Apollonius Dyscolus (*De syntaxi,* ed. Uhlig p. 2, 8). He draws a parallel between the way in which a syllable is formed out of letters and a word is composed of syllables and the way in which the things thought (*noēta*) which are associated with the words are grouped together and arranged into a complete (*autotelēs*) *logos.* Although Apollonius generally uses the word *logos* in the sense of a significant complex of sounds — Priscian regularly translates it by the Latin word *oratio* — it is evident that for a Greek the transition from *logos* in the sense of a linguistic expression to *logos* as the thought-content behind the spoken words was a very easy one. As long as terms like *pragma, lekton, dianoia* are used for the expressed thought-content, it is quite feasible to maintain a contrast with the *logos* as the significant complex of sounds. But the natural tendency to transfer the character of completeness from the thought expressed to the linguistic expression is considerably strengthened when only the word *logos* is employed in contexts where both aspects of its meaning are at issue.

If *logos* is taken in the Aristotelian sense of a group of words, it may be either complete or incomplete. Apollonius speaks of a *logos* which is not concluded (*synkleietai*), but is incomplete (*(el)leipei*), missing (*epizētōn*) a necessary component (p. 17). In the *Scholia* on Dionysius Thrax such phrases as *autotelēs* or *teleios logos* frequently occur (ed. Hilgard p. 57, p. 211, p. 213, p. 214, p. 354, p. 355, p. 515, p. 516; cf. also Choeroboscus, ed. Hilgard p. 6, p. 7, p. 8, p. 17, p. 31, p. 32). That the completeness or incompleteness of the *logos* derives from the completeness or incompleteness of the thought expressed is often pointed out; a complete *logos* is a combination of words which expresses a complete *dianoia* (p. 354, 20).

6.2.4. In 3.2.2 we saw that there are several passages in Aristotle's *De interpretatione* where the incomplete and defective character of *onomata* and *rhēmata* is contrasted with the self-sufficiency of statement-making utterances which are either true or false. It was only to be expected that the later commentators would try to elucidate Aristotle's rather rudimentary remarks by means of the more elaborate ideas on this topic which had developed in the meantime. And this is exactly what indeed is found in Ammonius's commentary on *De interpretatione.* There the statement-making utterance which is true or false is called a *teleios* or *autotelēs logos* (ed. Busse pp. 27–28). Of such combinations as 'Philo's is' it is said that they cannot serve to state something true or false because they need to be supplemented by something in order to yield a complete thought (*pros to apartisai dianoian*; p. 43, 27). Besides the statement-making utterance, address, prayer, question, and command are mentioned as forms of speech which are self-sufficient and by themselves signify a complete thought (*apērtismenēs dianoias*; p. 64, 31). On p. 70, 25, the distinction 'perfect/imperfect' (*teleios/atelēs*) is explicitly connected with the Aristotelian definition of a *logos* as a significant sound which has a significant part. As a genus the *logos* comprises every group of words. This genus has two species, groups of words that express a complete thought and groups of words that express an incomplete thought (for instance, the definition of man as a two-footed land animal).

6.2.5. For Plato the *logos* was a certain combination of a *rhēma* with an *onoma.* Aristotle considered the *symplokē* of an *onoma* and a *rhēma* as the sign of a composition or separation of concepts which is susceptible of truth or falsity. And the Stoic *axiōma* was held to consist of a *katēgorēma,* expressed by means of a *rhēma,* and the thought which is associated with an *onoma* or *prosēgoria,* a proper name or a common noun. In all these cases it is a definite combination of an *onoma* and a *rhēma* or of their meanings which is regarded to be a necessary and sufficient condition of the production of a complete and independent bearer of truth or falsity. This theme of the indispensability of the noun and the verb in the process of forming a bearer of truth or falsity remains a much-discussed issue in the period of the epigones.

Plutarch (*Platonicae quaestiones* 1009 b – 1011 e) offers an extensive defence of Plato's thesis that the only essential parts of a *logos* are the *onoma* and the *rhēma.* Plato was right in not paying any attention to the other parts of speech, because they play an altogether secondary role. Apollonius Dyscolus (*De syntaxi,* ed. Uhlig p. 17, 1) takes as an example the sentence 'The same man, having slipped, fell down today' and shows that the utterance becomes defective when we leave out the noun or the verb, whereas all the other parts can be omitted without the *autoteleia* of the *logos* being affected. In the *Scholia* on Dionysius Thrax (ed. Hilgard p. 516, 28) the noun and the verb are compared to the brain and the heart in the human body, and the other elements of speech to such parts as a hand or a foot. Just as a man can live without a hand or a foot but not without brain or heart, so we can have a perfect utterance without the other parts of speech but not without a noun or a verb.

Sometimes the question was raised which of these two necessary ingredients of a complete utterance is the more important, the noun or the verb. An interesting answer is given in the *Scholia* on Dionysius Thrax (ed. Hilgard p. 400, 6)[2]. The writer rejects the view that the infinitive is prior to the indicative because the infinitive is the name of the *pragma* and the *pragmata* are naturally prior to the persons who act or suffer. On the contrary, the indicative is prior to the infinitive because a *pragma* is seen and known only through a person and exists only in so far as it belongs to a person. If we read 'body' instead of 'person', this is pure Stoic doctrine. The *sōmata*, signified by proper names or common nouns, form the actual reality and are therefore prior to the *pragmata* which are merely thought in connection with a body and can only be said to be true of a body (Cf. also p. 216, 8, where a somewhat different account is given).

Another problem lies in those utterances which appear to be complete but contain only a finite verb, for instance *peripatō* ('(I) walk'), *peripateis* ('(You) walk'), *hyei* ('(It) rains'). Some grammarians were of the opinion that, although such one-word-utterances are not a combination of words, as the definition which Dionysius Thrax gives of a *logos* requires, they should be counted as *logoi*, since they have a complete sense. There is no more reason to exclude them than to exclude the unit from the class of numbers because it is not a combination of units, or to refuse to admit a one-letter-syllable as a syllable because it is not a combination of a consonant and a vowel (*Scholia* on Dionysius Thrax, ed. Hilgard p. 57, 12). Such a view tends to give a certain priority to the verb as that part of speech that must always be present in order to get a complete *logos*. As a rule, however, utterances consisting of only one word seem to have been considered as elliptical. In the *Scholia* on Dionysius Thrax (ed. Hilgard p. 515, 13) it is said that a one-word-utterance which expresses a complete thought is regarded as complete because the thing (*ousia*) that performs or undergoes the action or passion is supplied from outside by the understanding. The same view is taken by Ammonius in his commentary on *De interpretatione* (ed. Busse p. 28, 11). The whole *logos*, which is true or false, always consists of a *rhēma* and an *onoma* which is supplied in thought, for instance *egō peripatō* ('I walk'), *sy peripateis* ('You walk'), *ho Zeus hyei* ('Zeus rains'). As Sextus Empiricus puts it, the man who says *peripatō* is virtually (*dynamei*) saying *egō peripatō* (*PH* I, 199). If it is objected that *egō* and *sy* are not *onomata* but pronouns, the answer is that in

---

[2] Cf. also p. 558, 21; *Anecdota Graeca*, ed. I. Bekker II, p. 881, 1–8; Apollonius Dyscolus, *De syntaxi*, ed. Uhlig p. 18, 5.

these cases the pronoun is taken as a noun (*Scholia* on Dionysius Thrax, ed. Hilgard p. 515, 33; Apollonius Dyscolus, *De syntaxi,* ed. Uhlig p. 17, 15).

It is evident that the importance assigned to the noun and the verb as the indispensable ingredients of a self-sufficient utterance that can be true or false has certain consequences for the treatment of the other elements of speech. It seems that the Peripatetics took the most radical attitude and refused to admit other parts of speech (*merē tou logou*) than nouns and verbs. In his commentary on *De interpretatione* (ed. Busse p. 12, 29) Ammonius says that it would be wrong to call conjunctions, articles, pronouns, and adverbs parts of speech, because no combination of these elements alone can yield a perfect utterance. This is confirmed by the *Scholia* on Dionysius Thrax (ed. Hilgard p. 515, 19), where we read that the Peripatetics recognized only two parts of speech, the noun and the verb. The other words are not parts of speech but are used only as means of binding the actual parts together, as a kind of glue. The noun and the verb may be compared to the sides, the rudder, and the sail of a ship, whereas the other words are more like the pitch, the tow, and the nails.

Others took a less extreme course: they admitted the other kinds of words as parts of speech but drew a borderline between the nouns and verbs, which are necessary components of a complete statement-making utterance, and the rest. Nouns and verbs are the parts of speech in the most proper and genuine sense, being as it were body and soul of the utterance (*Anecdota Graeca,* ed. I. Bekker II, p. 881, 2; cf. also *Scholia* on Dionysius Thrax, ed. Hilgard p. 216, 13). Apollonius Dyscolus (*De adverbiis,* ed. Schneider p. 121, 5) says that the noun and the verb are the most important (*thematikōtera*) parts of speech and that the other parts only serve to make them function in a ready way. Elsewhere (*De syntaxi,* ed. Uhlig p. 28, 6) he calls the noun and the verb the most vital (*empsychotata*) parts of speech; if the speaker does not make them known, he will cause the hearer to ask questions about them.

One of the criteria for drawing a distinction between two groups of parts of speech, then, is the contribution they make to the completeness of an utterance. Another criterion is reminiscent of what Aristotle (*De int.* 16 b 20) says about the difference between the copula and other verbs. As we saw in 3.2.2, verbs by themselves do not yet signify whether something is the case or not, but most of them have a meaning of their own in the sense that the speaker arrests his thought and the hearer pauses. The copula, on the other hand, is nothing by itself, but it additionally signifies some synthesis, which cannot be thought of without the components. This criterion – whether or not the word is accompanied by a thought which is relatively distinct and self-sufficient – is also applied by Plutarch (*Platonicae quaestiones* 1010 a), as we already noted in 4.1.4. The verbs 'beats' and 'is beaten' and the nouns 'Socrates' and 'Pythagoras' make us think of something; but if such words as *men, gar, peri* are pronounced in isolation, they are not associated with any distinct thought of either a *pragma* or a *sōma*. Unless they are uttered in combination with nouns and verbs, they are like empty noises; by themselves they signify nothing. In the same vein is the remark made by Apollonius Dyscolus (*De syntaxi,* ed. Uhlig p. 27, 10) that a conjunction does not signify anything by itself, without the matter (*hylē*) of words that signify in an independent way, just as binding material is useless if there are no objects which it binds together. In *De syntaxi* (ed. Uhlig p. 13, 1) he draws a parallel between words and sounds. Just as we can distinguish between vowels (which by themselves form a sound) and consonants (which cannot form a sound without a vowel), so we can distinguish between, on the one hand, verbs, nouns, pronouns, and some adverbs (for instance 'Very well') and, on the other hand, prepositions, articles, and conjunctions, which are more like consonants in so far as they have no meaning on their own but signify only together with the other parts of speech (*syssēmainein,* a term which is also used of conjunctions in *De coniunctionibus,* ed. Schneider p. 222, 12). As the completeness of an utterance is determined by the completeness of the thought expressed by it, it is not surprising that the two criteria lead to much the same result: nouns and verbs are the essential components of a complete utterance because they contribute those parts of the complete thought which can also be conceived of in isolation.

6.3. Kinds of speech

6.3.1. As we saw in 4.3, the Stoics had developed a rather detailed classification of complete *lekta*. In the Peripatetic school more or less the same question was discussed under the head of *eidē logou,* 'kinds of speech', no doubt as an elaboration of Aristotle's distinction between the *logos apophantikos* and prayer in *De int.* 17 a 1. Ammonius (*In De interpretatione,* ed. Busse p. 12, 6, and p. 64, 30) mentions, besides the statement-making utterance, four other kinds of speech that are self-sufficient and by themselves signify a complete thought: one used for addressing (*klētikos*), one for praying or wishing (*euktikos*), one for asking questions (*erōtēmatikos*), and one for giving commands (*prostaktikos*)[3]. Elsewhere in the same work (p. 5, 1; cf.

---

[3] Ioannes Doxopatres, an eleventh century commentator of Hermogenes's *Peri ideōn* (*Rhetores Graeci* XIV, *Prolegomenon sylloge,* ed. H. Rabe p. 421, 22) ascribes this divi-

also *Scholia in Aristotelem*, ed. C.A. Brandis p. 93 and p. 95) he says that this division is based upon a distinction between two sorts of functions of the soul, the cognitive (*gnōstikai*) and the appetitive (*zōtikai, orektikai*). The statement-making kind of speech belongs to the cognitive faculty of the soul because it conveys information about things we know or think we know; it is therefore true or false. According to Ammonius this kind of speech was also called *hermēneia*, the expression in words of knowledge in the mind, and that is the reason why Aristotle entitled his treatise *Peri hermēneias*. The other kinds of speech are connected with the appetitive functions of the soul. In all of them the speaker directs himself to a hearer who seems to be able to contribute to the satisfaction of his desires. He either elicits a verbal reaction from the hearer (in questions) or tries to get a thing, either the hearer himself (in addresses or calls) or some action on the part of the hearer, either from a superior (in prayers) or from an inferior (in commands).

The difficulty that such addresses as 'Hector!' are not *logoi* in the Aristotelian sense is solved by the introduction of two names: *klēsis* or *anaklēsis* for the address in general, even if it consists of one word, and *logos klētikos* specifically for those cases in which the address consists of more than one word. Both sorts of addresses can be combined with other kinds of speech, such as assertions and commands (*Ibidem* p. 44, 2, p. 60, 24). Utterances used for asking questions are divided into two types, the dialectical or yes-or-no question, and the *pysmatikē erōtēsis* (*Ibidem* p. 199, 26). The Peripatetics used *erōtēsis* and *logos erōtēmatikos* in a generic sense, whereas in Stoic terminology *erōtēma* is the name of the yes-or-no question, as one species besides the *pysma*.

6.3.2. There is evidence that among the many controversies between the Peripatetics and the Stoics there was one concerning the exact number of kinds of speech: the former preferred a canon of five, while the latter kept to a canon of ten. This difference is mentioned by Ammonius (*In Analytica priora*, ed. Wallies p. 2, 3, and p. 26, 31). In his commentary on *De interpretatione* (ed. Busse p. 2, 9; cf. *Scholia in Aristotelem*, ed. C.A. Brandis p. 93) he first gives some examples of the Peripatetic division into five species and then adds that the Stoics used partly different names for them: *axiōma* for the *logos apophantikos*, *aratikon* for the *logos euktikos*, and *prosagoreutikon* for the *logos klētikos*. Moreover, the Stoics had a list of ten species, including also the oath, the exhibition of a particular instance, the supposition, what is

sion to the philosophers and contrasts it with a quite different one made by the rhetoricians.

like an *axiōma,* and the question put to oneself in order to express doubt or despair (Cf. 4.3.2). According to the Peripatetics the first four of these additional species can be reduced to the *logos apophantikos,* since they are either true or false; an oath and what is like an *axiōma,* for instance, are to be considered as an *apophansis* to which an invocation of a god or an intensive particle has been added. The tenth item of the Stoic list can be regarded as a special sort of question, besides the two other sorts[4]. There are no signs whatever that those who tried to reduce the Stoic list were aware of the fundamental difference between the objects of the Stoic classification, namely *lekta,* and the objects of the Peripatetic classification, which were *logoi.* On the contrary, the very attempt at reduction shows that in their view that which was differently classified was generically the same, viz. speech utterances.

6.3.3. That there were different opinions about the point where to draw the line between utterances which can and utterances which cannot be said to be true or false is confirmed by Simplicius (*In Categorias,* ed. Kalbfleisch p. 406, 6). He reports that the second century Platonist Nicostratus criticized Aristotle's thesis in *Cat.* 13 b 2 that only in the case of affirmations and negations is it necessary always for one utterance to be true and the other one false. According to Nicostratus this equally applies to such oaths as 'By Athena, I have done it' and 'By Athena, I have not done it', and also to utterances which are used to express admiration or disapproval and their negations. Simplicius then adduces the Stoic view that only the *axiōma* is true or false and that in the case of an oath it is improper to speak of truth and falsehood, but that we should characterize the person who swears as either swearing faithfully (*euhorkein*) or forswearing himself (*epihorkein*). Similarly, utterances which express admiration or disapproval are not true or false but only resemble things which are true or false. Simplicius's own position is that the swearing formula as such ('By Athena') is neither true nor false, but that the statement with which it is combined is true or false; if it is true the speaker swears faithfully, if it is false he forswears himself. In the same way he distinguishes between the 'How' of 'How beautiful is Piraeus' and the statement 'Beautiful is Piraeus', which is either true or false.

It is clear from *SVF* I, 581, and II, 197, that there was no unanimity concerning the interpretation of oaths within the Stoic school itself. Clean-

---

[4] More or less the same information is given by the *Prolegomena in Hermogenis Peri staseōn, Rhetores Graeci* XIV, *Prolegomenon sylloge,* ed. H. Rabe p. 186, 17; cf. *Anecdota Graeca,* ed. I. Bekker III, pp. 1178–1179.

thes held that he who swears either swears faithfully (*euhorkein*) or forswears himself (*epihorkein*) at the time when he is swearing. When he has the
intention to act in accordance with the oath he swears faithfully; when he has
no such intention he forswears himself. Chrysippus, on the other hand, drew
distinctions between swearing truly (*alēthorkein*) and keeping one's oath
(*euhorkein*) and between swearing falsely (*pseudorkein*) and not keeping
one's oath (*epihorkein*). At the time of swearing the speaker always swears
either truly or falsely; for what he swears is either true or false, being an
axiōma (presumably because he gives the hearer to understand that he has the
intention to act in accordance with the oath). Only at the time when the
obligation becomes due can the person who has undertaken something be said
to keep or not to keep his oath, just as someone who makes a covenant can
be said to keep faith (*eusynthetein*) or to break the covenant (*asynthetein*)
only when the time mentioned in the agreement has arrived and not at the
time of making the covenant. In any case it is obvious that at the same time
as classification of kinds of speech was a much-discussed topic efforts were
being made to determine the specific character of particular speech acts.

6.3.4. A field where kindred problems were treated was the doctrine of the
figures of thought (*ta tēs dianoias schēmata*), which together with the theory
of the figures of speech (*ta tēs lexeōs schēmata*) was developed towards the
end of the first century B.C. The way in which the terms *dianoia* and *lexis* are
used in this connection should be carefully distinguished from the way Aristotle uses them in *Poetics* 1456 a 33 (Cf. 3.2.3). In particular the later figures
of speech have very little to do with the ways in which the meaning of a
phrase may be determined by the speaker's intonation, which Aristotle discussed under that head. Part of what Aristotle counts as manners of speaking
belongs rather to the later theory of the figures of thought, although the
point of view from which the material is investigated is different in the two
cases.

   According to Dionysius of Halicarnassus (*De compositione verborum* 8,
ed. Usener-Radermacher p. 32, 6) there is not one manner of expression for
all thoughts. Some thoughts are put into words in an attitude of making
known an opinion (*hōs apophainomenoi legomen*), others in an attitude of
inquiring, others in an attitude of praying, others in an attitude of enjoining,
others in an attitude of doubt and despair, others in an attitude of assuming,
and others again in some other attitudes (*allōs pōs schēmatizontes*). In accordance with these various attitudes we also try to vary the wording (*tēn
lexin --- schēmatizein*). Just as there are many ways of forming thoughts,
there are also many ways of expressing them in speech; they cannot be

comprehended summarily and perhaps they even are countless in number. At any rate it is a subject that stands in need of much discussion and deep reflection.

These remarks, which even in their formulation are strongly reminiscent of the Stoic characterization of complete *lekta*[5], were further systematized by Caecilius of Calacte, a contemporary and friend of Dionysius of Halicarnassus. He defines a figure of thought as a deviation from natural thought and insists that the figures of thought should be treated before the figures of speech, since the thought precedes the expression in words. Under the head of figures of thought he discusses (apart from aposiopesis and irony) yes-or-no questions, specific questions, and oaths (*Fragmenta,* ed. Ofenloch p. 33). Later rhetoricians added perplexity (*diaporēsis*), vexation (*aganaktēsis*), curse (*ara*), entreaty (*deēsis*), prayers (*euchai*), exhortation (*protropē*)[6].

6.3.5. Another subject which is closely connected with the classification of kinds of speech, either in the Peripatetic or in the Stoic sense, is the problem of distinguishing between various moods of the verb. In our oldest source, Dionysius Thrax (*Ars grammatica* 13, ed. Uhlig p. 47, 3), five moods (*enkliseis*) of the verb are listed: the indicative (*horistikē*), the imperative (*prostaktikē*), the optative (*euktikē*), the subjunctive (*hypotaktikē*), and the infinitive (*aparemphatos*). This division became more or less standard with Greek grammarians[7].

The word *enklisis* stands for a certain inclination of the soul, for a mental attitude adopted towards the action or passion indicated by the verb; but at the same time it is also used for the configuration of sound which conventionally expresses such an inclination or attitude. This conception of an *enklisis* as a particular state of mind causes difficulties in the case of the infinitive; being merely the name of the *pragma*, the infinitive differs from the other moods by the very absence of any form of showing one's mental attitude. That the infinitive was nevertheless counted as a mood was justified by the considera-

---

[5] It is also difficult to refrain from quoting Wittgenstein's words: 'But how many kinds of sentence are there? Say assertion, question, and command? – There are countless kinds: countless different kinds of use of what we call "symbols", "words", "sentences"' (*Philosophical Investigations* I, 23).

[6] Cf. *Rhetores Latini minores,* ed. Halm pp. 37–47. For a brief but excellent survey of the field see 'Longinus', *On the Sublime,* ed. D.A. Russell, Oxford, 1964, pp. 126–128.

[7] Cf. in particular *Scholia* on Dionysius Thrax, ed. Hilgard p. 245, p. 399, p. 558, p. 578; Apollonius Dyscolus, *De syntaxi,* ed. Uhlig p. 43, p. 320, p. 346, p. 350, p. 360, p. 374; Choeroboscus, ed. Hilgard pp. 4–9; Sophronius, ed. Hilgard, pp. 409–411.

tion that all the other moods can be developed from it and resolved into it: it is the generic name of the *pragma* of which the indicative, imperative, and optative are special cases. According to Apollonius Dyscolus (*De syntaxi*, ed. Uhlig p. 44) the activities of someone who utters the indicative 'Trypho walks', the optative 'May Trypho walk', and the imperative 'Let Trypho walk' can be described by means of the sentences 'He asserted that Trypho walked', 'He wished that Trypho would walk', and 'He ordered Trypho to walk'. In Greek these sentences contain a finite verb that makes explicit the speech act which is included in the mood, and an accusative and infinitive phrase. The infinitive is the name of the common *pragma,* and the finite verbs indicate the specific attitudes that are adopted towards that *pragma.* In contrast with such verbs as *graphō* ('(I) write'), which signify both a *pragma* and, in their endings, a certain attitude towards that *pragma,* there are also verbs – for instance, *boulomai* ('(I) want to') – which signify, in a lexical way, only a state of mind and need a complement in the form of an infinitive which indicates the *pragma* that is the object of that state of mind (*Ibidem* pp. 323–324). Such passages show that there was a clear awareness of a difference between the *pragma* in general, as the neutral action or passion of which the infinitive is the name, and the specific attitudes that can be adopted towards such a *pragma* in various speech acts. As we saw in 4.3.3, at least some of the Stoic definitions of complete *lekta* were c onstructed along the same lines, viz. out of the *pragma* or *lekton* as the generic element and a reference to a speech act as the specific difference.

   Although the details of the historical development remain obscure, it is safe to assume that the grammarians' differentiation of the five moods of the verb was at least partly inspired by the Peripatetic and Stoic classifications of kinds of speech. The names *prostaktikos* and *euktikos* are common to all three divisions; and the name *horistikos* is only a variation on the name *apophantikos* (Apollonius Dyscolus, *Ibidem* p. 346). We have seen that the Peripatetics and the Stoics actually classified different things: *logoi* and *lekta.* But there are many signs that the awareness of this difference gradually disappeared. The grammarians, again, took as their object of classification certain forms of the verb and the mental attitudes that are signified by those forms. But given the close connections between some of these mental attitudes associated with verbal forms and the *logoi* or *lekta* of the other classifications, it would not be surprising if the exact borderlines were not always immediately clear. That there was some uncertainty about the relation between the five moods and the five or ten kinds of speech is indeed confirmed by a passage in Choeroboscus (ed. Hilgard p. 232, 24). There we are told that the philosophers added to the five above-mentioned moods a self-hortatory (*hypothetikē*) mood and an interrogative (*erōtēmatikē*) mood. Choeroboscus adduces two reasons against admitting an interrogative mood. First, not only a verb but every word can be used in an interrogative way; this interrogative character can therefore hardly be a mood of the verb. Second, each mood has its own sounds (*idias phōnas*), but the interrogation which the philosophers want to add as a mood is not characterized by its own linguistic form, in the same way as the indicative mood and the other four have their own endings. This second objection is also valid against admitting a self-hortatory mood. In Greek self-hortations of the type 'Let us go' are expressed by means of the subjunctive mood; therefore they do not satisfy the condition that a mood should have its own sounds. Self-hortations are discussed also by Apollonius Dyscolus (*Ibidem* pp. 360–361). He does not agree with those who consider self-hortations as imperatives; in his view they compress two moods into one. As we cannot issue commands to ourselves but can only admonish ourselves, he thinks it more proper to distinguish between the genuine imperative mood and a self-hortatory mood, the former being characterized by its lack of a first person and the latter by its being restricted to the first person singular and plural. This shows that even among grammarians there was no unanimity concerning the number of the moods and the criteria of classifying them.

7. THE TRANSITION TO THE LATIN WEST

7.1. The Latinization of Stoic terminology

7.1.1. According to Aulus Gellius (*Noctes Atticae* XVI, 8, 2) Lucius Aelius Stilo Praeconinus, who lived about 150-70 B.C., had written a treatise entitled *Commentarius de proloquiis* which was about *axiōmata* and still existed in Gellius's time, apparently as the only one in Latin. From the same source we know that Varro, a pupil of Praeconinus, called *axiōmata* sometimes *profata* and sometimes *proloquia*; that he called them *proloquia* is confirmed by Apuleius (*Peri hermeneias*, ed. Thomas p. 176, 15). Gellius quotes the Greek definition of *axiōma*: *lekton autoteles apophanton hoson eph' hautōi*. He refrains from giving a literal translation, because in order to give one he would have to use crude and unfamiliar words which would offend his readers' ears, but he refers to a definition proposed by Varro in book XXIV of his *De lingua Latina*: *proloquium est sententia, in qua nihil desideratur*. A bit further on (XVI, 8, 8) he circumscribes that which the dialecticians call an *axiōma* as everything that is said with a full and complete thought associated with the words in such a way that it is necessarily either true or false (*quicquid ita dicitur plena atque perfecta verborum sententia, ut id necesse sit aut verum aut falsum esse*).

As for *sententia*, Varro (*De lingua Latina* VIII, 1) says that the third part of his work (books XIV—XXV) will treat of the question of how the words express a *sententia* when they are properly combined with each other. This is reminiscent of the way in which Dionysius Thrax had defined the *logos* as a combination of words expressing a complete *dianoia*. As a matter of fact, in the definition of the sentence (*oratio*) the Latin grammarians constantly translated *dianoia* by *sententia*. Diomedes says that it is a combination of words *consummans sententiam remque perfectam significans* (*Ars gramma-*

105

tica, ed. Keil p. 300, 16); Marius Victorinus has *consummans unam senten-tiam* (*Ars grammatica,* ed. Keil p. 5, 2); and Priscian has *sententiam perfectam demonstrans* (*Institutiones grammaticae,* ed. Hertz I, p. 53, 28). Also in the other contexts which we surveyed in 6.2.2 and 6.3.4 — the doctrine of the *periodos,* the art of punctuation, and the theory of the figures of thought — the Greek word *dianoia* is rendered by *sententia,* occasionally interchanged with *sensus*[1]. And in the definition which Dionysius Thrax (*Ars grammatica* 20, ed. Uhlig p. 86) gives of the conjunction, *syndeousa dianoian* is rendered in Latin by *connectens --- sententiam* (Cf. ed. Uhlig p. 87).

It is therefore safe to conclude that in Varro's (apparently incomplete or incompletely quoted) definition of *proloquium* the Latin phrase *sententia, in qua nihil desideratur* stands for the Greek phrase *dianoia autotelēs,* which was already used by Dionysius Thrax instead of the Stoic *lekton* or *pragma auto-teles.* In general all our evidence will be seen to show that the Latins consid-ered the word *sententia* as capable of doing duty for both *dianoia* and *lekton.* The typical character of the Stoic *lekton,* that it is not just a thought but a thought expressed in words, is almost always obvious from the contexts in which *sententia* occurs, just as it is obvious that *dianoia* means a thought expressed in words in the definition of a *logos* given by Dionysius Thrax. Moreover, the Latin word *sententia* itself commonly denotes a thought— content in so far as it is expressed in speech: the meaning of a word or a group of words, in particular a sentence. This connection between thought and speech in the meaning of *sententia* is so strong that already in classical Latin it occasionally comes to be used for a sentence as a meaningful unit of speech, for example by Cicero (*In M. Antonium oratio Philippica* XIII, 22). A *sententia* can be a thought expressed, a *lekton* or *dianoia,* but also a meaning-ful expression — somewhat in the same way as a *logos* can be both a linguistic expression and the thought behind it. The fact that the Romans chose this word *sententia* as the equivalent of *lekton* and *dianoia* thus undoubtedly contributed to the gradual disappearance of the difference between the Stoic terminology, which originally was concerned with thoughts expressed, and the Peripatetic terminology, which applied to utterances.

Turning now to the words *proloquium* and *profatum,* it is just as well first to have a look at the way in which Cicero rendered the Greek term *axiōma.*

---

[1] For the period see Cicero, *De oratore* III, 44, 175, and 49, 191; *Orator* 61, 208; Martianus Capella, *De nuptiis Philologiae et Mercurii,* ed. Dick p. 262, 1; Quintilian, *Institutio oratoria* IX, 4, 122. For the art of punctuation see *Grammatici Latini,* ed. Keil I, p. 437, 14, VI, p. 192, 8, VII, p. 324, 13. For the figures of thought see Quintilian, *Institutio oratoria* IX, 17, and *Rhetores Latini minores,* ed. Halm *passim.*

His first attempt at a translation is found in *Tusculanae disputationes* I, 7, 14, where he suggests *pronuntiatum*, adding that later he may use another term if he can find something better (Cf. also Gellius, *Noctes Atticae* XVI, 8, 8). The same word is still used by Augustine (*De magistro* 16, 2, 3, 5, and 20, 5), who refers to Cicero and elucidates the term by pointing out that it stands for a complete thought expressed (*plena sententia*), which can be either affirmed or denied. In another work (*Academica priora* (*Lucullus*) 29, 95) Cicero uses the verbs *enuntiare* and *effari* to form the paraphrase *quidquid enuntietur* and the term *effatum* for that which is either true or false. In *De fato* he employs *enuntiatio* (1, 20, 21, 27, 37, 38), *enuntiatum* (19, 28; cf. also Apuleius, *Peri hermeneias*, ed. Thomas p. 176, 15), and once *pronuntiatio* (26). Sometimes he leaves *axiōma* untranslated (21) or gives such paraphrases as *omne quod enuntietur* (21). According to Boethius (*Introductio ad syllogismos categoricos*, ed. Migne 64, 767 C) Cicero used also *proloquium* and *propositio* instead of *enuntiatio,* but in our texts there is no evidence confirming this (at least for *propositio* in the sense of *axiōma*)[2].

It is highly probable that all the verbs used in the attempts to translate *axiōma* – *proloqui* (*eloqui* is found in Cicero, *De fato* 38), *profari*, *effari*, *pronuntiare, enuntiare* – are to be considered as equivalents of the Greek verb *apophainesthai.* An *axiōma* is an *apophanton,* a thought expressed in a speech act of making known one's opinion. That *pronuntiare* was used to render *apophainesthai* is shown by Apuleius (*Peri hermeneias,* ed. Thomas p. 176, 13), who translates *logos apophantikos* by *oratic pronuntiabilis.* And in the works of Boethius *enuntiare* and its derivatives become the standard translation of *apophainesthai* and its derivatives. *Proloquium, profatum, effatum, pronuntiatum, pronuntiatio, enuntiatum, enuntiatio* can therefore, I submit, all be regarded as translations of the Greek term *apophanton* which was a synonym of *axiōma,* just as *apophainesthai* and *axioun* are practically synonymous in Stoic texts. Cicero uses *pronuntiatio* and *enuntiatio* in exactly the same sense as *pronuntiatum* and *enuntiatum;* what they designate is not the act of making known one's opinion or the utterance by means of which the act is performed, but that which is expressed in words, the true or false opinion. It is, however, clear that his choice of these words was one more factor which could easily further the fading away of the distinction between the Stoic *apophanton* and the Aristotelian *apophansis,* the latter of which Boethius will render by the same word *enuntiatio.*

---

[2] Cf. also *De differentiis topicis,* ed. Migne 64, 1174B: *haec* (*sc. propositio*) *et enuntiatio et proloquium nuncupatur.*

Seneca (*Epistula* 117, 13) tries to elucidate by means of an example the Stoic doctrine that *sapientia* is a body and a good but that *sapere,* being an asomatic predicate, is neither (Cf. 4.1.1). If I say 'Cato walks', then what I now express in words (*quod nunc loquor*) is not a body but something which is expressed in order to make a statement about a body (*enuntiativum quiddam de corpore*). This something is called by some *effatum,* by others *enuntiatum,* by others *dictum.* We have seen that both *effatum* and *enuntiatum* were used by Cicero in order to render *axiōma.* We know, moreover, from Apuleius (*Peri hermeneias,* ed. Thomas p. 176, 15) that *effatum* also occurred in the work of a certain Sergius. This must be Lucius Sergius Plautus, a Stoic philosopher of the first century, who is mentioned several times by Quintilian (*Institutio oratoria* II, 14, 2, VI, 6, 23, VIII, 3, 33) in connection with the translation of Greek terms into Latin[3]. The occurrence of *dictum* along with *effatum* and *enuntiatum* and as apparently synonymous with them makes it certain, in my opinion, that *dictum* too is intended here as an equivalent of *axiōma* or *apophanton.* This interpretation goes very well with the meaning of the Latin verb *dicere,* which is often used in the sense of *axioun* and *apophainesthai.* Seneca seems to express the idea of *lekton,* on the other hand, by means of the phrase *quod nunc loquor,* which indicates the generic element to which *enuntiativum* adds the specific difference. What is expressed by 'Cato walks' is a *lekton apophantikon* or *axiōma* and as such asomatic.

We have already touched upon the description of an *axiōma* given by Aulus Gellius: all that is said (*quicquid --- dicitur*) with a full and complete thought associated with the words (*plena atque perfecta verborum sententia*) in such a way that it is necessarily either true or false. If we ask ourselves what is the exact meaning of the verb *dicitur* in this sentence, three possibilities may come to mind: it is used in the sense of the Greek verb *propherein* ('to utter'), or in the sense of the Stoic technical term *legein* ('to express in words'), or in the sense of *apophainesthai.* The second and third candidates are implausible. The translation 'everything that is expressed' leads to an awkward redundancy, since that which is expressed must be a *sententia*; and the translation 'everything that is asserted' would suggest that things can also be asserted in such a way that they are not true or false. I think, therefore, that the interpretation 'all that is uttered with a full and complete thought associated with the (uttered) words' is the correct one. This would mean that the phrase *quicquid dicitur* cannot be regarded as a paraphrase of the Stoic term *lekton.* On the other hand, it also means that an *axiōma* is said to be an

---

[3] Cf. Pauly–Wissowa, *Realenzyklopaedie der klassischen Altertumswissenschaft, s.v.* SERGIUS, 37.

utterance, one which is associated with a complete thought and is either true or false. Perhaps Gellius just did not succeed in rendering adequately the Greek phrase *lekton autoteles* and ended up with something that is more reminiscent of a *logos,* in the sense of Dionysius Thrax, than of a *lekton.* It is also possible that he simply was not aware of any difference between a *logos* and a *lekton*; this would not be astonishing in view of the confusion we shall encounter in his contemporary Apuleius.

Furthermore, Gellius mentions some Latin names of compound *axiōmata*; *adiunctum* or *conexum* for the conditional, *coniunctum* or *copulatum* for the conjunction, and *disiunctum* for the disjunction. That these terms originally were adjectives associated with the Latin equivalents of *axiōma* is made probable by such a passage as V, 11, 8, where Gellius speaks of a *proloquium diiunctivum.*

7.1.2. The first four chapters of Augustine's *De dialectica* and the fourth book of Martianus Capella's *De nuptiis Philologiae et Mercurii,* which treats of dialectic[4], are also important for our subject. Both authors probably draw the main points of their exposition from the second book of Varro's lost *Disciplinarum libri IX,* which dealt with dialectic. Augustine (4) and Martianus (p. 155, 18) divide logic into four parts: *de loquendo, de eloquendo, de proloquendo,* and *de proloquiorum summa.* This division seems to be partly based upon Aristotle's distinction between things that are said involving combination and things that are said without combination (*Cat.* 1 a 16). The first part deals with simple expressions: that is, expressions which signify only one thing – for instance, 'man', 'horse', 'disputes', 'runs'. According to Martianus this part contained such subjects as the five predicables, definition, and the Aristotelian categories. The three other parts have to do with complex expressions, signifying more than one thing. Some of these expressions are such that they do not express a complete thought (*non comprehendunt* or *implent sententiam*); others are associated with a complete thought. Of the latter there are two species: those which cannot be called true or false and those which can. The first group was discussed under the head *de eloquendo,* a designation which covered also questions concerning noun and verb, and subject and predicate, presumably as parts of complete expressions (Martianus, p. 156, 13). The second group is divided by Augustine into two subclasses: *sententiae simplices,* such as 'Every man walks', and *sententiae coniunctae,* such as 'If he walks, then he moves'. Only the *sententiae simplices*

---

[4] Cited by page and line in the edition by A. Dick, Leipzig, 1925.

belong to the part *de proloquendo*, with such topics as quantity and quality, universality and particularity, affirmation and negation (Martianus p. 156, 19). The *sententiae coniunctae* have their place in the part *de proloquiorum summa*, which in general is concerned with reasoning. It is clear that a good deal of the division of complex expressions somehow stems from the Stoic distinctions between incomplete and complete *lekta*, between *axiōmata* and other complete *lekta*, and between simple and non-simple *axiōmata*, interwoven with Peripatetic threads.

This remarkable mixture of Aristotelian and Stoic ingredients has its counterpart in the way the word *sententia* is used. Let us begin with Augustine. What he classifies are linguistic expressions (*verba*). Now at all those places where he speaks of expressions which *comprehendunt* or *implent sententiam* it is natural to assume that what was uppermost in his mind was the *sententia* as the thought expressed, the *lekton* or *dianoia* (Once he uses the variant *implet sensum*). But he also uses the phrase *impletur sententia* for a *sententia* which is such that it cannot be affirmed or denied, although it *perficiat propositum animi* (2). This can be interpreted as 'Or we have a complete sentence of such a kind that, although it expresses something before the mind which is complete, it cannot be affirmed or denied'. Such an interpretation is corroborated, I think, by the fact that at the end of 2 and in 3 he continues his classification of linguistic expressions by speaking of *sententiae*. The truth of the matter is that the word *sententia* is ambiguous between 'thought expressed' and 'sentence expressing a thought'. When it is contrasted with words for linguistic expressions such as *verbum*, the sense of 'thought expressed' tends to dominate. When it is used without that contrast and in contexts where it is just as natural to think of the sentences as of the thoughts expressed by them, the meaning of 'sentence expressing a thought' may become more conspicuous. And even in those cases in which there is a contrast with *verbum* the difference between the two interpretations of such a saying as *sed coniunctorum verborum alia sunt, quae sententiam comprehendunt* (2) – namely, either 'But of the complex expressions there are some which express a complete thought' or 'But of the complex expressions there are some which form a complete sentence' – was much less marked for a Roman than the translations suggest. It is difficult to find an English word that has exactly the same ambiguity as the Latin word *sententia*. It is easier in Dutch, for example, where the word 'zin' has the meaning of both 'sense' and 'sentence'.

Another interesting point in Augustine's exposition is the way he uses *sententia* in 3. There he draws a distinction between *sententiae simplices* and *sententiae coniunctae*. On the one hand, this distinction is reminiscent of the

Stoic distinction between simple *axiōmata* and non-simple *axiōmata*. But there are also indications that it could stem from Peripatetic sources. In his commentary on *De interpretatione* (ed. Busse p. 3, 7) and also in his commentary on *Prior Analytics* (ed. Wallies, p. 17, 19) Ammonius, after giving the Peripatetic classification of kinds of speech and the Stoic deviations from it, points out that the statement-making utterance has two species, the categorical and the hypothetical. Aristotle dealt only with the categorical statement-making utterance because it is self-sufficient (*autoteles*) and useful for proofs. The hypothetical, however, is defective (*ellipes*), since he who says 'If it is day, then it is light' does not assert in an absolute way (*ou teleiōs apophainetai*) that it is light, but only that it is light if a certain condition is fulfilled, namely that it is day. In order to support the conclusion that it is light the hypothetical statement needs to be supplemented by the categorical statement 'It is day'. Now exactly the same point is made by Augustine at the end of 3. The premiss 'This man walks' is called a *simplex sententia*. The premiss 'If anyone walks, then he moves', however, is characterized as *aliam* (*sc. sententiam*), *quae aliquid expectat ad impletionem sententiae*. This can only mean, in my opinion, that the hypothetical statement is defective in the sense that it needs the categorical statement in order to yield the conclusion 'This man moves'. It is, therefore, highly probable that Augustine's *sententiae simplices* and *sententiae coniunctae* are the categorical and hypothetical species of the *logos apophantikos* mentioned later by Ammonius. This means that *sententia* here stands not only for a linguistic expression, for an utterance or a *logos*, but, more specifically, for a statement-making utterance. In other words, the way in which *sententia* is used is not only a faithful reflection of the vanishing awareness of the difference between Stoic and Peripatetic terminologies with regard to sentences and the thoughts expressed by them in general, but it also shows that its meaning could easily be narrowed to that of a sentence used for the special purpose of making a statement, of a *logos apophantikos* or of an *axiōma* in the sense in which the word *axiōma* had become practically synonymous with the phrase *logos apophantikos* or the word *protasis*. This is not surprising if one calls to mind that the Latin word *sententia* often designates a thought expressed in the sense of a judgment or an opinion about some factual question which as such is either true or false. Moreover, that *sententia* could have the same meaning as *axiōma* and *enuntiatio* is strikingly confirmed by a passage in the commentary on Terence written by the fourth century scholar Aelius Donatus[5]. In connection with

---

[5] And also by a passage in Arnobius's *Adversus nationes*, written shortly after 300; *proloquium* and *sententia* are practically synonymous in III, 44: *in unius proloquii finibus convenit vos stare nec per varias distractos repugnantesque sententias fidem ipsis rebus quas struitis derogare.*

Andria 45 and *Eunuchus* 175 Donatus remarks (ed. P. Wessner I, pp. 55–56, p. 303) that in older Latin the word *verbum* was sometimes used with the same meaning as *axiōma* and *sententia*. And an *axiōma*, according to him, is a *sententia* or *enuntiatio* that expresses a complete thought (*perfectam intellegentiam*) by means of one verb (and a noun). From the example of an *axiōma* given by Donatus (*has bene ut adsimules nuptias,* a kind of injunction) it is, however, clear that he is not speaking of statement-making sentences only, but of sentences in general, using the words *axiōma, sententia,* and *enuntiatio* in a rather loose way[6].

If we now look at Martianus Capella's exposition, especially pp. 186–189, we find that his use of *sententia* displays the same ambiguity between 'thought expressed' and 'sentence expressing a thought'. In such a phrase as *multa dici plena sententia* (p. 188, 7) the sense of things which are uttered with a complete thought in one's mind is predominant. In other passages where *sententiae* are said to consist of a noun and a verb (p. 187, 6), or where an imperative mood such as *curre* and an optative mood such as *utinam scribam* are characterized as *plenae sententiae* (p. 187, 9, 21), it is the sense of complete sentence that becomes more prominent. Martianus seems to use *sententia* only in the generic sense of a *dianoia* or that which expresses a complete *dianoia,* the sentence in general. For the species he has the words *proloquium* and *eloquium.* Judging from such remarks as that a *proloquium* consists of the nominative case of a noun and the third person of a verb (p. 186, 9), while a noun and a verb are explicitly defined as linguistic expressions (p. 184, 12), we must conclude that here too the original Stoic conception of complete *lekta* as thoughts expressed or meanings has been supplanted by a nearly exclusive concern with the linguistic expressions that signify the thoughts.

---

[6] How great the confusion finally became is also apparent from a rather strange distinction between *logos* and *dianoia* that occurs in the *Scholia* on Dionysius Thrax, ed. Hilgard p. 513, 17–22, and 27–31. There we are informed that a *logos* is composed of several *dianoiai,* a *dianoia* being a combination of words that expresses a complete thought (*noun apartizousa*). 'The sun is above the earth' is called a *dianoia,* whereas 'If the sun is above the earth, then it is day' is called a *logos.* The difference between a *dianoia* and a *logos* is that the *dianoia* does not include anything consequent (*akolouthon ti*), but forms a simple *axiōma,* for example 'Socrates sends', while the *logos* often introduces also the causes of the things, by means of many *dianoiai.* In a way, all this reminds one of Augustine's distinction between *sententiae simplices* and *sententiae coniunctae* and the Peripatetic distinction between categorical and hypothetical statements. It is, therefore, something of a surprise to learn immediately afterwards (p. 513, 27–31) that 'The sun is above the earth' is not a complete *dianoia,* but that only 'If the sun is above the earth, then it is day' conveys a complete thought,

Eloquia are those full sentences to which the question whether they are true or false does not apply. Martianus gives two examples, sentences in the imperative mood and in the optative mood. He adds that there are many more (p. 188, 2). This may mean that he had before him something like the Stoic classification of complete *lekta* rather than the Peripatetic list of kinds of speech, but it is also possible that he alludes to a much more extensive collection of the sort we shall meet with in Apuleius. Augustine (2) gives as examples of sentences that cannot be affirmed or denied those in which we give a command, or wish something, or utter a curse ('May the gods ruin him').

Proloquia are those full sentences which are susceptible of truth or falsity. Both Augustine (1) and Martianus (p. 185, 2) consider such utterances as *disputo* and *disputas* to be complete and either true or false; since the first or second person is supplied by the understanding, the condition that a *proloquium* should consist of a noun and a verb is fulfilled. The same applies to such forms as *pluit,* where everybody knows that it is a god who makes it rain. But utterances of the type represented by *disputat,* without a noun, cannot be said to be true or false. In order to be true or false they have to be supplemented by a noun in the nominative case or, in special constructions, by a noun in some other case (Martianus p. 186, 20). There are also *proloquia* that are called *dubia*; Martianus gives the example *ille disputat* (p. 186, 14) and points out that, although the person concerned either disputes or does not dispute and the *proloquium* is therefore true or false, we do not know which it is. This makes sense, I think, only if *ille* is taken in the same way as the Greek pronoun *ekeinos* is taken in an indefinite *axiōma* (Cf. 4.2.5). In Latin, however, it is more natural to use the pronoun *is* in such contexts, as is confirmed by Cicero (*De fato* 12 and 15): 'If one is born while the Dog Star is rising, then he (*is*) will not die in the sea'. Finally, it is worthy of note that according to Martianus (p. 188, 10) a *proloquium* such as *omnis homo animal est* does not cease to be true if the natural order of the noun and the verb is reversed: *animal est omnis homo* is a variant which does not change the truth-value. It is not made clear, however, whether in such a case there are two sentences or only one (Cf. 10.1.2).

The division of dialectic into four parts and the *sententia— proloquium— eloquium*—terminology are also found in the commentaries on Martianus Capella which were written by John the Scot, 'Dunchad', and Remigius of Auxerre in the ninth century[7]. Remigius (ed. Lutz II, p. 21, 16, and p. 47, 4) gives as the names of the four parts *locutio, elocutio, prolocutio* or *prolo-*

---

[7] Edited by C.E. Lutz, Cambridge, Mass., 1939; Lancaster, Pa., 1944; Leiden, 1962–1965.

quium, and *summa proloquiorum*. A *locutio* is defined as every part of speech that by itself signifies something, such as a noun and a verb. *Locutio* in this sense seems to be synonymous with *periermenia, interpretamentum*, and *interpretatio* (Cf. 8.2). It should be noted, however, that according to Boethius the word *locutio* was also used in a different sense, namely that of the Greek word *lexis* in so far as it designates any articulate sound, even if it has no meaning (Cf. Diogenes Laertius, *Vitae philosophorum* VII, 56); accordingly, Boethius distinguishes *locutio* from *interpretatio* (*In Peri hermeneias (II)*, ed. Meiser p. 8, 11). *Elocutio* and *prolocutio* are synonyms of *eloquium* and *proloquium*. The word *effamen*, which occurs in Martianus (p. 150, 17), apparently as a variant of *effatum*, is explained by John the Scot (ed. Lutz p. 81, p. 88) as a synonym of *oratio*, comprising *propositiones, assumptiones,* and *conclusiones*; and by Remigius as a synonym of *proloquium* and *pronuntiatio* (ed. Lutz II, p. 9, 14). In connection with the word *axioma*, which occurs in Martianus (p. 151, 2), apparently with the same meaning as *primordia fandi* ('the principles of speaking'), John the Scot remarks that *axioma* literally means *dignitas* (a translation already found in Priscian, *Institutiones grammaticae*, ed. Hertz II, p. 214, 20), an *axioma* being a *proloquium dignum*; he explains this meaning by pointing out that no *eloquium* can rival the *proloquium* (ed. Lutz p. 81, p. 89). Remigius, on the other hand, regards *axiomata* not as *proloquia* in general, but as *summae pronuntiationes* or axioms (ed. Lutz II, p. 10, 7). That the word *axioma* had become rather enigmatic is clear from 'Dunchad', who declares that *Axiomas* is the name of the first teacher of dialectic (ed. Lutz p. 15). That *proloquium* had completely lost its sense of a thought expressed is evident from Remigius, who speaks of the *sententiam pronuntiationis sive proloquii* (ed. Lutz II, p. 10, 11).

At the end of the tenth century Notker the German still uses the terms *proloquium* and *eloquium*, for instance in the preface to the German text of *De interpretatione* (*Die Schriften Notkers und seiner Schule*, ed. P. Piper I, p. 499). For him a *proloquium* is the same as an *enuntiatio* or *propositio* (*Ibidem* p. 510). The same applies to the treatises which are found in the *Codex Brusselensis* edited by Piper, *Ibidem* p. XIII ff. There *sententia* frequently occurs in the sense in which it is used by Martianus Capella and *proloquium* is explicitly identified with *propositio* (*sciendum autem propositiones et proloquia unum atque idem significare*; p. LXIII, 7). *Eloquia* are said to be composite expressions having a complete sense (*usque ad plenum intellectum*); *proloquia* too have a complete sense (*habent plenum intellectum*), but they signify something true or false (p. LXI, 2, 14). One of the last medieval traces of *proloquium* is found in Garlandus Compotista's *Dialectica*, probably written around 1040: *propositio vero enuntiativa et proloquium et sumptum nuncupatur* (ed. De Rijk p. 87, 3).

7.1.3. The upshot of our examination of the available evidence appears to be that the terms *sententia, proloquium,* and *eloquium* are characteristic of the Stoic tradition in the Latin West. It may be assumed that they were introduced originally to convey that which was expressed in Greek by the terms *lekton* or *dianoia* and *axiōma* and by the different terms that designated other complete *lekta* than the *axiōma.*

But almost from the beginning they seem to have suffered from a certain ambiguity between two senses, that of the thought expressed and that of the linguistic expression indicating the thought, no doubt due to their occurrence in contexts which are typical of the increasing fusion of Stoic and Peripatetic doctrines. The result of this process of amalgamation was that *sententia, proloquium,* and *eloquium* gradually lost their original meanings and became synonymous with Peripatetic terms which finally ousted them altogether. The choice of *sententia* as a translation of the Greek words *dianoia* and, perhaps indirectly, *lekton* tended to facilitate this development. *Sententia* could mean not only the thought expressed but also the sentence expressing the thought or, in terms characteristic of Dionysius Thrax, not only the *dianoia* but also the *logos.* Thus it could serve as a sort of bridge between the Stoic and Peripatetic idioms. Moreover, it was closely associated with acts and attitudes of holding something true so that occasionally it even came to be used for a statement or statement-making utterance. *Proloquium* had a good many rivals — *dictum, effamen, effatum, enuntiatio, enuntiatum, quiddam enuntiativum, profatum, pronuntiatio, pronuntiatum* — but on the whole it appears to have been the favourite rendering of the word *axiōma.* But it shared the fate of its Greek equivalent; first its meaning became indistinguishable from that of such Peripatetic terms as *enuntiatio* and *propositio,* and then it was supplanted by them. *Eloquium* is peculiar in not having a counterpart in Greek. As far as we know, the Stoics did not coin one word to designate those complete *lekta* which are not *axiōmata*; neither did the Peripatetics have a single designation for those *logoi* that are not used for making a statement. Originally *eloquium* may have meant those complete thoughts which cannot be said to be true or false, but in our sources it is equally applicable to the sentences which express such thoughts. It disappears together with its associate *proloquium.*

There can be little doubt that *sententia* is in the first place a translation of *dianoia*; only in so far as *dianoia* was a synonym of *lekton* could the word *sententia* be regarded as a rendering of *lekton* as well. It is, therefore, natural to ask if there are any indications that a separate Latinization was sought for *lekton* as such. I have already suggested that the phrase *quod nunc loquor* in Seneca (*Epistula* 117, 13) looks like an attempt to render the Greek word *lekton* or some equivalent phrase (The word *dictum* there certainly has the sense of that which is asserted and thus cannot be considered for this role). Another passage which deserves our attention is Augustine, *De dialectica* 5, where a distinction is made between *verbum, dicibile, dictio,* and *res.* The understanding of this distinction is facilitated, I think, by comparing it to *De quantitate animae* 32 (ed. Migne 32, 1071-1072). There we find a distinction between *sonus, intellectus* or *notio, nomen,* and *res.* A *nomen* consists of sound and signification; the sound is that which pertains to the ears, the signification is that which pertains to the mind. The *intellectus* or *notio* is the thought which the speaker has in his mind even before he expresses it by means of a word. Once it has been expressed by a word the hearer comes to have the same thought as the speaker wanted to convey. It is clear that the *intellectus* or *notio* is a thought which can but need not be expressed in speech; it can be in the mind without being expressed. Now *De dialectica* 5 bears a striking similarity to this passage, although it is somewhat complicated by the fact that Augustine simultaneously tries to elucidate a distinction between 'mention' and 'use'. For him a *verbum* is a linguistic expression which is used to refer to itself and a *dictio* is a linguistic expression used to refer to something else. But apart from this complicating factor, we may, I believe, identify the *dictio* with the *nomen* and the *dicibile* with the *intellectus* or *notio*. The *dicibile* is a thought which exists in the mind even before it is put into words (*ante vocem*); it is something that is capable of being expressed. In itself this may just as well be understood in an Aristotelian as in a Stoic way[8]. What Augustine apparently means by *intellectus, notio,* and *dicibile* is the *noēma* as a mere thought that may be expressed or not, but at any rate precedes the expression in words. Now if the interpretation that was given of the Stoic *lekton* in Chapter 4 is correct, what

---

[8] The third chapter of the treatise *Categoriae decem* (ed. Migne 32, 1422) which has been attributed to Augustine contains a discussion of the question of the actual subject of Aristotle's *Categories*. In that connection a distinction is drawn between the *res* and the images in the mind (which in Greek are called *sēmainomena* or *phantasiai*) and the words used to express those images. If the terms *sēmainomena* and *phantasiai* are from Themistius, to whose authority the writer here appeals, it is quite probable that this fourth century expositor used the Stoic distinction between sounds, mental images, and things in the outside world to elucidate Aristotle's distinction between spoken sounds, affections of the soul, and actual things in the first chapter of *De interpretatione*. Aristotle's characterization of the affections of the soul as likenesses of the actual things no doubt made it easy to regard them as mental images and thus to identify them with the Stoic *phantasiai*. It may also be remarked that John of Salisbury, who mentions Augustine's *dictio–dicibile–res–* distinction in his *Metalogicon* III, 5, takes it without hesitation as drawn from Aristotle.

Augustine intends by *dicibile* cannot be the Stoic *lekton*. The Stoics used the term *lekton* only for a thought that is in fact expressed in words - that is, as a synonym of *sēmainomenon* - and never for a thought that can be expressed in words but is as a matter of fact not (yet) so expressed. They had, however, another term, *ekphorikon,* of which Ammonius says (*SVF* II, 236) that the Stoics used it to designate that which the Peripatetics called *noēma. Ekphorikon* means exactly what Augustine seems to have in mind: that which is capable of being expressed. And *dicibile* would be a very adequate translation of this Greek word *ekphorikon* as used by the Stoics.

The hypothesis that *dicibile* is a translation of *ekphorikon* would be weakened if one could provide strong evidence that the usual rendering of the Stoic term *lekton* was *dicibile*. As a matter of fact, there are, as far as I know, two indications that *lekton* was translated in Latin by *dicibile*. In the *Corpus glossariorum Latinorum* (ed. G. Loewe & G. Goetz II, p. 48, 41) we find: *dicibile lekton.* The isolated character of this note makes it impossible to decide whether *lekton* is here meant in the technical sense of the Stoa. The Greek word has several other meanings, just as does the Latin translation, which covers only one aspect of these meanings, the potential side. The second place is in the Latin translation of Ammonius's commentary on *De interpretatione,* made by William of Moerbeke in 1268[9]. Ammonius says there that the Stoics assumed something between the Aristotelian *noēma* and *pragma* which they called *lekton* (*SVF* II, 168). William renders *lekton* by *dicibile,* no doubt wrongly, since what the Stoics wanted to introduce as an intermediate entity is not something that can be expressed but the thought in so far as it actually has been expressed[10].

There are, however, other passages which show that *lekton* was also translated by *dictum* or *dictio.* Isidore of Seville (*Etymologiae* II, 22) and Alcuin (*De dialectica,* ed. Migne 101, 953 A) explain the word *dialectica* by the fact that what it designates is concerned with *dicta* (*in ea de dictis disputatur*) and both add: *nam lekton dictio dicitur.* The same explanation is found in a fragment of an anonymous commentary on Porphyry probably dating from the second quarter of the twelfth century and quoted by De Rijk (1967: I, 165); there *lekton* is declared to mean the same as *dictum* and *sermo.* In these

[9] Ed. G. Verbeke, Louvain–Paris, 1961, p. 32, 34.
[10] In De Rijk (1967: II, 218, 4–7), in a passage from the *Tractatus Anagnini* dating from about 1200, a distinction between *significantia* and *significata* is mentioned. There are two kinds of *significata*: the *dicibile* as that which is signified by a combination of words (*oratione*) and the *praedicabile* as that which is signified by a word (*dictione*). Nothing, however, points towards a connection with *lekton.* Elsewhere (I, p. 470) *dicibile* is declared to be synonymous with *praedicabile.*

texts *lekton* is apparently taken as that which is uttered, a word, or speech in general. There is no doubt that the Greek word could have this meaning too; Ammonius even mistakenly held that the Stoics called the sounds by the name of *lekta* (*SVF* II, 236). In this connection it should also be mentioned that Boethius (*In Categorias,* ed. Migne 64, 286 B) uses *dictum,* along with *sermo,* to render the Greek word *logos* as it occurs in *Cat.* 14 b 15 ff.

I do not think that this evidence is of such a natuie that it forces us to consider Augustine's term *dicibile* as the translation of the Stoic term *lekton.* It is, of course, possible that Augustine, or his source, was confused about the exact meaning of the Stoic term. But we should not be too rash in assuming such a misunderstanding as long as there is another interpretation that is at least as plausible.

7.2.   The first appearance of the term *propositio*

7.2.1.   Of the authors with whom we have been concerned in 7.1 Cicero uses the word *propositio* in the sense of the major premiss which together with the *assumptio* (the added premiss) and the *complexio* (the conclusion) forms an *argumentatio* (*De inventione* I, 34, 58). Galen (*Institutio logica* VII, 1) shows that in Greek the word *protasis* could designate the first premiss, in contrast with the added premiss or *proslēpsis.* In the same vein Gellius (*Noctes Atticae* II, 7, 21) says that the statement 'What the father commands is either good or bad' is not a sound *propositio.* In another passage (V, 11, 8) a similar statement, the disjunction 'You will marry either a beautiful woman or an ugly one', is called the first *protasis.* This makes it likely that *propositio,* like *protasis,* could have the meaning of premiss in general but that in contexts such as II, 7, 21, this meaning was easily narrowed to that of first premiss. *Propositio* in the sense of first premiss is also found in Martianus Capella (p. 202, 18, p. 203, 7, p. 204, 8). It seems to have been a competitor of *sumptum,* the literal translation of the Stoic *lēmma.* Besides, *propositio* is used by Martianus as the translation of the rhetorical term *prothesis,* the statement of the case which precedes the actual argumentation (p. 249, 5, p. 272, 2, p. 275, 13, 16, p. 276, 5, p. 281, 9, p. 282, 1). Already in the *Rhetorica ad Herennium,* written *c.* 86–82 B.C., we find the definition: *propositio est, per quam ostendimus summatim, quid sit quod probari volumus* (II, 18, 28). Further, Augustine (*Contra Academicos* III, 13) speaks of all those *propositiones* the truth of which dialectic has taught him, apparently meaning non-simple statements that can serve as first premisses and from which, if a second premiss is added, a conclusion can be drawn. He also uses the paraphrase *quae per conexionem --- proposui* and *quae per repugnantiam vel disiunctionem a me sunt enuntiata* for examples that can be identified as complex *axiōmata*. The context makes it probable, however, that they are given the name *propositiones* in view of their function as first premisses in arguments.

In general, we may conclude that those authors who are representative of the Stoic tradition in logic use the word *propositio,* if at all, only in other senses than the one that is going to be predominantly associated with it in works which bear the marks of a more Peripatetic orientation.

7.2.2. At the beginning of the treatise on logic that has been transmitted under the title *Peri hermeneias* and is usually attributed to the second century writer Apuleius two terms are introduced which henceforward will become of overwhelming importance for our subject: *oratio* and *propositio.* The author first gives a remarkably long list of species of *oratio* which, apart from the familiar commanding, enjoining, and wishing, also contains such items as vowing, showing anger, hatred, or envy, favouring, pitying, admiring, despising, objurgating, repenting, deploring, causing pleasure or fear, and several kinds of stylistic devices in which the orator excels, such as maximizing and minimizing things. This exuberant enumeration seems to be inspired by rhetorical sources more than by the sober classifications of the Stoics and Peripatetics. Some items are clearly reminiscent of Aristotle (*Poetics* 1456 a 36) who, as we saw in 3.2.3, says that the thought (*dianoia*) of the characters in a play is shown in their efforts to arouse such emotions as pity, fear, anger, and to maximize or minimize things. This was, however, only the core of much more extensive lists which came to circulate under the head of *schēmata dianoias.* Quintilian (*Institutio oratoria* IX, 22) complains that especially Greek authors included far too much in the category of the figures of thought, in particular practically all the emotions. According to him showing anger, grief, pity, fear, confidence, contempt, advising, threatening, asking questions, and excusing oneself are not figures of thought at all. How great the confusion eventually became is shown by Isidore of Seville (*Etymologiae* II, 21, 13), who mentions under the head of *sententiarum multae species* almost every type of utterance that can be conceived of from one point of view or another.

Of all these many species of *oratio* only one is declared to be important for logic, the *oratio pronuntiabilis,* which is characterized as comprising a complete thought (*absolutam sententiam comprehendens*) and as the only species which is susceptible of truth and falsity. The fact that the condition of completeness of thought is brought up only in connection with the *oratio pronuntiabilis* need not mean, as Sullivan (1967: 18) holds, that the other kinds of speech do not have a complete sense. It is more plausible to assume that the author takes *oratio pronuntiabilis,* which must be a translation of *logos apophantikos,* as designating an utterance that shares with other full utterances the generic character of expressing a complete thought and that, as a statement-making utterance, is differentiated from the rest by the circumstance that it is either true or false.

According to Apuleius this statement-making kind of utterance had various names. Sergius called it *effatum,* Varro *proloquium,* Cicero *enuntiatum,* the Greeks sometimes *protasis* and sometimes *axiōma.* This remark about Greek usage is quite typical of the period in which the distinction between Stoic and Peripatetic terminologies had practically vanished. Now while Varro, Cicero, and Sergius translated *axiōma,* Apuleius tries to translate *protasis* and suggests as literal equivalents *protensio* ('proposal') and *rogamentum* ('problem'). In fact, however, he is going to use the more familiar word *propositio.* Although *protensio* is nearest to *protasis* in etymological structure, it apparently was too uncommon to prove attractive; as a matter of fact, it occurs only at this place[11]. *Rogamentum* is occasionally used in the rest of the text, but it did not really take root; there are no traces of it elsewhere. Both words are nonetheless interesting in so far as they throw some light upon the meaning Apuleius attached to the word *propositio.* As is confirmed by his exposition in Chapter 7, for him this word was still vividly associated with the original Aristotelian sense of a question that is put to an opponent in a debate. If someone propounds the question 'Is every honourable thing good?', then this question is a *propositio*; and if the opponent gives his assent, the *propositio* becomes an *acceptio,* without the questioning, and this *acceptio* too is commonly called a *propositio*: 'Every honourable thing is good'. *Acceptio* is no doubt the equivalent of the Greek word *lēpsis* which is used already by Aristotle in contrast with *erōtēsis* (*Prior Analytics* 24 a 23). Although Apuleius sometimes sets it in opposition to *propositio,* this latter word is his usual term for that which the opponent concedes. A *propositio,* then, is a question or problem put forward in a debate which becomes a premiss when the opponent assents to it. As such it may be contrasted with the conclusion, as is the case at the beginning of Chapter 2, but in so far as *propositio* is the name of every *oratio pronuntiabilis* the conclusion too is

---

[11] Much later it occurs in the Latin translation of Ammonius's commentary on *De interpretatione* (ed. G. Verbeke, Louvain–Paris, 1961, p. 3, 31): *protentiones, id est propositiones.*

called a *propositio.* Even the word *rogamentum* occurs in the characterization of the conclusion as an *illativum rogamentum* (Ch. 7).

All our data point to the conclusion that the long history of the word *propositio* as a technical term for the statement-making utterance had its beginning in the work of Apuleius or whoever wrote the treatise *Peri hermeneias.* As the author himself remarks, the term was already in use; we saw that in particular it could designate the first premiss of an argument. But henceforth it also has a more general meaning, although even with that meaning it will for a very long time retain certain traits which are reminiscent of its origin in the domain of dialectical debates. Finally, it is worth mentioning that the term *enuntiatio* does not occur in *Peri hermeneias.*

The bearer of truth or falsity, according to Apuleius, is the *oratio pronuntiabilis* or *propositio,* the utterance which is used to make a statement. In this respect he is a typical representative of the Peripatetic tradition. At the beginning of Chapter 4 Plato (*Theaetetus* 206 d) is adduced as an authority for the opinion that a *propositio* consists at least of a noun and a verb. Therefore some consider the noun and the verb as the only parts of speech, since by themselves they are sufficient to yield a *perfecta oratio,* an utterance that expresses a complete thought (*quod abunde sententiam comprehendant*). Adverbs, pronouns, participles, conjunctions, and kindred elements which the grammarians enumerate are no more parts of speech than the curved poops are parts of ships; they are more like the nails, the pitch, and the glue. This too, as we noticed in 6.2.5, is a characteristically Peripatetic point of view. Further, in the utterance 'Apuleius discourses' the noun is said to be the subject-part and the verb the predicate-part. It is not necessary, however, that the subject consists of just one noun and the predicate of just the verb: each part may be stretched out into more than one word, as in the utterance 'The Platonic philosopher of Madaura uses speech', *eadem vi manente.* Sullivan (1967:22) suggests that this phrase could be understood as indicating that the two utterances have the same meaning and that therefore a *propositio* should be distinguished from the complete meaning or *absoluta sententia* which it expresses. Now the latter part of this suggestion may be true, but I do not think that the interpretation of the phrase *eadem vi manente* from which Sullivan wants to derive it is correct. In my opinion, this phrase does not indicate that the meaning of the two utterances remains the same, but rather that the functions of the two parts, the subject and the predicate, remain the same whether they are formed by one word or by more words. *Vi* has to be combined with *utramvis partem* and refers to the functions which these two parts have in the utterance[12]. This interpretation is con-

---

[12]   For the same meaning of *vis* in a similar context see Boethius, *Introductio ad*

firmed, I believe, by a passage in Martianus Capella (p. 188, 13), where the sentence *Cicero disputat* is extended into the sentence *Cicero Romanus in Tusculano prudenter et copiose cum Catone disputat.* It is obvious that in this case the meanings of the two sentences are quite different; nevertheless the function of the extended subject and the function of the extended predicate remain exactly the same. In the *Codex Brusselensis* (ed. Piper, *Die Schriften Notkers und seiner Schule* I, p. XIV) the same sentence *Cicero disputat* is extended in various ways, no doubt as a sort of exercise in assigning the added words to the main parts, the subject and the predicate, whose functions remain the same through all the variations.

syllogismos categoricos, ed. Migne 64, 769 A, B, where the verb *est* in *Socrates est* is said to have a double function (*vi gemina fungitur*), namely that of predicate and that of a sign of quality; and where the phrase *eadem vis permanet* occurs in connection with the *termini* as the subject and the predicate of a statement.

8. BOETHIUS AND THE BEGINNING OF THE MIDDLE AGES

8.1. Boethius

The central figure in the borderland between the ancient and the medieval conceptions of the bearers of truth and falsity is undoubtedly Boethius. As his logical works — translations, commentaries, and treatises[1] — were a constant source of inspiration for practically all medieval writers on dialectic, he is more important for the further history of our theme than any of the authors discussed in the foregoing chapter.

8.1.1. In order to explain the title of Aristotle's treatise *Peri hermēneias* Boethius points out that by an *interpretatio* (*hermēneia*) is meant any linguistic expression that by itself signifies something (*vox significativa per se ipsam aliquid significans*; *In P. herm. (I)* p. 32, 11; cf. *In P. herm. (II)* p. 8). These expressions are either simple or composite, and the composite *interpretationes* are either imperfect or perfect.

Boethius identifies the simple *interpretationes* with verbs and nouns — among which he includes also participles, pronouns, adverbs, and some interjections — and contrasts them with conjunctions and prepositions, which by themselves do not signify anything but designate something only in combination with other words and are, therefore, not *interpretationes*. While the

---

[1] The following abbreviations will be used. For the two commentaries on Aristotle's *De interpretatione*: *In P. herm. (I)* and *In P. herm. (II)*, cited by page and line in the edition by C. Meiser, Leipzig, 1877–1880. For the commentaries on Aristotle's *Categories* and Cicero's *Topica*: *In Cat.* and *In Top. C.* For the treatises *Introductio ad syllogismos categoricos, De syllogismo categorico, De hypotheticis syllogismis, De differentiis topicis*: *Intr., De syll. cat., De hyp. syll., De diff. top.* All these are cited by column and section in Migne, *Patrologia Latina*, vol. 64.

grammarians distinguish eight parts of speech (*orationis partes*), the philosophers consider as parts of speech only those expressions which have a full
signification (*quidquid plenam significationem tenet*), namely the verb and
the noun, with which participles, adverbs, pronouns, and conventional interjections may be aligned. Conjunctions and prepositions, on the other hand,
are not parts of speech for philosophers but merely means of holding the
actual parts together, comparable to a chariot's reins and strips of leather (*In
P. herm. (II)* p. 14, 28; *Intr.* 766 A–C; *De syll. cat.* 796 D). The copula *est* or
non est is said to signify or designate the quality of a statement, just as the
words *omnis, nullus,* and *quidam* signify the quantity (*Intr.* 769 A–B). As the
signs of quality and of quantity are distinguished from the *termini,* which are
the nouns and the verbs serving as subjects and predicates, their signification
must be of the same kind as the signification of conjunctions and prepositions: they signify only in combination with *interpretationes.* Boethius does
not yet have a technical term for all those words which are not *interpretationes.* That such a technical term already existed is shown by a remark of his
contemporary Priscian (*Institutiones grammaticae,* ed. Hertz I, p. 54, 5): according to the dialecticians there are only two parts of speech, the noun and
the verb, since they alone make a combination of words complete even if it
consists of nothing else; the other parts they called *synkatēgorēmata,* that is
consignificantia. There can be no doubt that the dialecticians are the Peripatetics; we saw (6.2.5 and 7.2.2) that they constantly took the view that there
are only two parts of speech. That the dialecticians cannot be the Stoics is
clear from the next line, in which Priscian says that according to the Stoics
there are five parts of speech. As to the meaning of the Greek term *synkatēgorēmata,* it is advisable, I think, to follow Priscian's explanation, namely that
it literally means things which co-signify. There is good evidence that *katē-
gorein* was used in the sense of indicating, revealing, signifying, and *katēgorēma* in the sense of indication or sign. It is therefore plausible to assume that
synkatēgorein could be a synonym of such verbs as *prossēmainein* (Cf.
3.2.2)[2] and *syssēmainein* (Cf. 6.2.5). It is from this passage in Priscian's
grammar that the technical terms *syncategorema* and *consignificans,* which
often occur in medieval writings, originate.

The class of the simple *interpretationes* is coextensive with the class of
those expressions that are said without combination and signify one of the
categories (Cf. Aristotle, *Cat.* 1 b 25). Composite *interpretationes,* on the
other hand, are combinations of nouns and verbs. They are the Aristotelian

---

[2] In his translation of *De interpretatione* Boethius uses the verb *consignificare* to
render *prossēmainein.*

logoi, significant spoken sounds some part of which is significant in separation. Boethius uses the word *oratio* in the sense of such an Aristotelian *logos* and can thus make a distinction between *orationes imperfectae* and *orationes perfectae.* That this distinction could not be taken for granted but had to be justified is apparent from *In P. herm (II)* p. 80, 28, and especially p. 87, 30, where we are informed that Syrianus, the fifth century Neoplatonist and commentator on Aristotle, denied the existence of *orationes imperfectae* on the curious ground that an imperfect thing cannot have parts; consequently, when Aristotle says that an *oratio* is a significant sound some part of which is significant in separation, he can mean only an *oratio perfecta.* Another source of uncertainty was the definition of a *logos* or *oratio* given by Dionysius Thrax and taken over by most grammarians. It is remarkable, for instance, that Priscian defines an *oratio* as a well-ordered combination of words expressing a complete thought (*ordinatio dictionum congrua, sententiam perfectam demonstrans; Institutiones grammaticae,* ed. Hertz I, p. 53, 28), but that elsewhere (II, p. 109, 9, p. 111, 4, p. 116, 5, p. 149, 15) he nevertheless speaks of a *plena* or *perfecta oratio* and the *perfectio orationis,* as if there could be incomplete *orationes* as well.

In any case, Boethius holds that the composite *interpretationes,* the *orationes,* can be divided into two groups: those from which that which is said (*id quod dicitur*) can be fully understood and those where the meaning of the words is pendent and unsettled (*pendet ac titubat*) and the hearer still expects something, for example 'Socrates with Plato' (*In P. herm. (II)* p. 9,1). Boethius employs the words *sententia, sensus,* and *intellectus* for the thought or meaning which is expressed by an *oratio* and is complete or incomplete in the primary sense. As far as I see, he never uses *sententia* for the linguistic expression; it always means the thought expressed in contrast with the words expressing it. As he puts it in *In P. herm. (I)* p. 70: words are conventional instruments to make known (*prodere, proferre, demonstrare*) one's thoughts (*sensa, sententias*).

8.1.2. In passing, I want to call attention to the interesting distinction between an *argumentum* and an *argumentatio* which is mentioned by Boethius in *In Top. C.* 1048 A and *De diff. top.* 1174 C. Cicero (*Topica* 8) had defined an *argumentum* as a *ratio, quae rei dubiae faciat fidem,* a reasoning proving something that is questioned (Cf. also *De inventione* I, 29 and 40). An *argumentatio,* on the other hand, is characterized as the unfolding (*explicatio*) of an *argumentum* in words (*Partitiones oratoriae* 45)[3]. In general Boethius calls

---

[3] Cf. also *De inventione* I, 74; Chirius Fortunatianus, *Ars rhetorica, Rhetores Latini*

the *argumentum* the *vis sententiae ratioque ea quae clauditur oratione,* the *virtus, vis, mens,* or *sententia* of the *argumentatio* (In *In Top. C.* 1053 B–D four meanings of the terms *argumentum* and *argumentatio* are distinguished). All these explanations imply that the *argumentum* is the thought or meaning which is associated with the *argumentatio.*

It would take us too far afield to examine in detail the complicated history of the logical and rhetorical theory of proof in order to find a satisfactory answer to the question where exactly this distinction had its origins. I confine myself to drawing attention to the problem and offering some suggestions that may prove useful for its solution. One might think of the distinction between refutations dependent on language and refutations outside language made by Aristotle in *Sophistici elenchi,* or of the distinction between arguments directed against the expression (*pros tounoma*) and arguments directed against the thought expressed (*pros tēn dianoian*) which is mentioned but rejected by Aristotle (*Ibidem* 170 b 12)[4]. Another passage that may be relevant is *Posterior Analytics* 76 b 24, where it is said that demonstration does not address itself to the spoken word (*ton exō logon*) but to the discourse in the soul (*ton en tēi psychēi* or *esō logon*); one can always object to the former, but not always to the latter[5]. There are also indications, however, that there could have been some influence from the Stoic theory of proof (Cf. 5.2.2). Martianus Capella (p. 132, 29) and Boethius (*In Top. C.* 1132 A) say that in a conditional syllogism the first premiss, which is a conditional statement, contains both the *argumentum,* in the antecedent, and the *quaestio,* in the consequent. If we affirm the antecedent in a second premiss, that is if we add the *argumentum,* we can draw the *quaestio* as a conclusion from the two premisses and thereby prove it. Now the *argumentum* is here exactly what the Stoics called a *sēmeion,* an *axiōma* which is the antecedent in a sound conditional and serves to establish the truth of the consequent, which must be a non-evident (*adēlon*) *axiōma.* And a *sēmeion,* being an *axiōma,* is of course a thought expressed by the words that convey the reasoning. In the light of this striking resemblance it even becomes probable that the definition of the *argumentum* as a *ratio, quae rei dubiae faciat fidem* stems from the Stoic definition of a proof (*apodeixis*) as a *logos --- epiphoran ekkalyptōn*

---

minores, ed. Halm p. 115, p. 118; Q. Fabius Laurentius Victorinus, *Explanationes in Ciceronis Rhetoricam, Rhetores Latini minores,* ed. Halm p. 240; Martianus Capella, p. 278, 10.

[4] Cf. the commentary on *Sophistici elenchi* which is ascribed to Alexander of Aphrodisias, ed. Wallies p. 5, 8, and pp. 78–79.

[5] Cf. Themistius, *In Analytica posteriora,* ed. Wallies p. 23, 22, and John Philoponus, *In Analytica posteriora,* ed. Wallies pp. 130–131.

adēlon, a reasoning that establishes the truth of a non-evident conclusion (Cf. for instance Sextus Empiricus, *AM* VIII, 314). Given the fact that the Stoics used their term *pragma* in connection with evident and non-evident thought-contents (Sextus Empiricus, *PH* II, 97, and *AM* VIII, 141), I would not be surprised if *res dubia* is a translation of *adēlon pragma.*

8.1.3. As we saw in 2.4, the thought which precedes overt speech and gives meaning and content to its sounds is often characterized by Plato in terms that are borrowed from the field of spoken language. For him thinking is a dialogue of the mind with itself and a judgment is a *logos* pronounced silently to oneself. Although Aristotle had developed a terminology for mental acts and attitudes of holding something true and their objects which is less dependent upon the sphere of spoken language, he too occasionally indulges in a 'lingualization' of these mental phenomena: in *Posterior Analytics* 76 b 24—27 the spoken word is contrasted with the discourse in the soul or the interior word. More or less the same distinction between a *logos* that resides in the mind (*endiathetos*) and a *logos* that is uttered by means of the vocal organs (*prophorikos*) is found in the Stoa (Cf. 4.4.2).

It is not surprising that this conception of a generic *logos* which has a mental and an oral species came to be applied also to the first chapter of *De interpretatione.* As Aristotle makes there a distinction between three levels — the affections of the soul, the spoken sounds, and the written marks — the dichotomy of the *logos* easily became a trichotomy. As a matter of fact, we have the testimony of Boethius (*In P. herm. (II)* p. 29, 16, p. 30, 3, p. 42, 15) that the Peripatetics held that there are three *orationes,* one consisting of thoughts (*intellectus*), one consisting of sounds (*vox*), and one consisting of letters (*litterae*). And that accordingly there are also three kinds of parts of the *oratio,* namely nouns and verbs that are written, nouns and verbs that are uttered by the vocal organs, and nouns and verbs that are thought in silence. *Ibidem* p. 36, 10, Porphyry is mentioned as one of those who held this view. In his extant commentary on Aristotle's *Categories* there is a place where a distinction between the *logos endiathetos* and the *logos prophorikos* is drawn (ed. Busse p. 64, 25; cf. also p. 101, 24, and p. 106, 35). What he said in his lost commentary on *De interpretatione* can perhaps be gathered from some passages in Ammonius's commentary on that treatise. In connection with *De int.* 16 a 3—9 Ammonius points out that the *logos* and its parts, the noun and the verb, can be considered in three ways: in so far as they are in the soul as simple thoughts and as the so-called *logos* that resides in the mind (*endiathetos*), or in so far as they are uttered, or in so far as they are written (ed. Busse p. 22, 12, p. 23, 10). A distinction between the *logos endiathetos* and the *logos prophorikos* is made also on p. 256, 28, and p. 272, 11. While in the first passage William of Moerbeke translates *logos endiathetos* by *orationem --- endiatheton, id est intus dispositam,* in the two latter passages he chooses the phrase *oratio mentalis* as the Latin equivalent[6].

Boethius himself follows this Peripatetic line. He does not yet have a fixed term for the discourse of the soul. It is characterized as the *oratio* which can be put together in thought (*quae cogitatione conecti (possit)* or *quae coniungeretur in animo; In P. herm. (II)* p. 29, 19, p. 30, 5), as the *oratio* which the thought of the mind unfolds (*quam mentis evolveret intellectus;* p. 36, 12), or as the *oratio* which consists of thoughts (*quae in intellectibus est;* p. 42, 16). Once he uses the phrase *cogitabiles orationes* (p. 44, 26). In all probability it was much more natural for a Greek to use *logos* in the twofold sense of inward speech and spoken or written speech than it was for a Roman to use *oratio* in the same way; while *logos* included in its varied spectrum of meanings both an interior and an exterior aspect, with rather easy transitions between the two, the Latin word *oratio* covered only the exterior aspect, in particular spoken language.

8.1.4. At several places Boethius gives a division of kinds of complete speech. In *In P. herm. (II)* p. 95, 8, he says that there are various divisions but that he will adhere to the Peripatetic division into five species, although many authors hold that there are more than five and some even think that there are countless sorts (*innumeras --- differentias*)[7]. The Peripatetic division is already found in the treatise *Categoriae decem* which has been transmitted among Augustine's works. There (ed. Migne 32, 1425–1426) the Greek terms are rendered in Latin as (*sermo*) *imperativus, optativus, interrogativus, vocativus,* and *pronuntiativus.* The author remarks that the first four kinds are sometimes elliptical and non-composite (*suspensa sunt atque simplicia*) and therefore only half-complete (*semiplena*). We do not understand what they are unless the last kind, speech in which something is affirmed or denied, is added. This may be a confused way of stressing the importance of the statement-making kind of speech for logic; in contrast with the other kinds it is always true or false, since a predicate is affirmed or denied of a subject.

If we compare the several divisions given by Boethius (*De syll. cat.* 797 B; *In P. herm. (I)* p. 35, p. 71; *In P. herm. (II)* p. 9, p. 95; *Intr.* 767 B), we find that the statement-making utterance, which Boethius calls *oratio enuntiativa,*

---

[6] Ed. G. Verbeke, Louvain-Paris, 1961, p. 41, 85, p. 455, 74, p. 478, 4.

[7] Cf. Ammonius, *In De interpretatione,* ed. Busse p. 65, 13, who in this connection refers to Plato, *Philebus* 17 a.

the imperative utterance, and the vocative utterance (which once, in *Intr.*
767 B, is called *oratio invocativa*) constantly recur. As a rule they are comple-
mented by the interrogative utterance and the optative utterance, which is
usually called *oratio deprecativa*, in the sense of a prayer. The interrogative
utterance is omitted in one passage (*In P. herm. (I)* p. 71), where a distinction
is made between an *oratio optativa*, for wishing, and an *oratio deprecativa*, for
praying. It is worth noting that the example of the *oratio optativa* there,
utinam tibi istam mentem di immortales duint ('May the immortal gods put
that thought into your mind'; Cicero, *In Catilinam* I, 9, 22) contains the old
optative form *duint* which may be the reason why it is mentioned separately.

The Peripatetic division of complete utterances into five species also occurs in Alcuin (*De dialectica,* ed. Migne 101, 974), where it is ascribed to the
dialecticians, and in Garlandus Compotista (*Dialectica,* ed. De Rijk p. 42, 11).

8.1.5. At the same time the Latin grammarians were concerned with the
proper classification of the moods of the verb. The term *modus* occurs for the
first time in Quintilian (*Institutio oratoria* I, 5, 41) along with *status* and
qualitas. All three words are probably translations of the Greek term *diathe-
sis,* which according to a scholiast on Dionysius Thrax (ed. Hilgard p. 578,
18) was used originally for both the moods and the voices of the verb. The
literal translation of *enklisis* is rather *inclinatio*; Priscian, for instance, defines
the *modi* as the *diversae inclinationes animi, varios eius affectus demon-
strantes* (*Institutiones grammaticae,* ed. Hertz I, p. 421, 16). This surely is a
very curious definition: the moods are said to be the diverse inclinations of
the soul and at the same time to signify its various affections. The confusion
is no doubt due to the fact that *enklisis* was used for the inclinations of the
soul as well as for the verbal forms expressing them (Cf. 6.3.5).

Priscian distinguishes five moods: the indicative (also called *definitivus*[8]),
the imperative, the optative, the subjunctive, and the infinitive (*infinitus*).
Eventually this division became more or less standard; but it was far from
unchallenged. Quintilian already mentions divisions of six and eight moods.
According to Martianus Capella (p. 135, 6) the number of moods distinguished ranged from five to ten. One of the few who went as far as ten was
Marius Victorinus (*Ars grammatica,* ed. Keil p. 199, 17), who gives the following enumeration: indicative (*lego*), imperative (*lege*), promissive (*legam*),
optative (*utinam legerem*), conjunctive (*cum legam*), concessive (*legerim*),

---

[8] Other grammarians use the names *finitivus* and *pronuntiativus*; for the subjunctive
we also find *iunctivus, adiunctivus, coniunctivus, dubitativus*; for the infinitive, besides
infinitivus, perpetuus.

infinitive (*legere*), impersonal (*legitur*), gerund (*legendo*), and hortatory mood (*legat*); to which by some the interrogative (*percunctativus*) mood was added (*legisne?*). Occasionally a *participialis modus* is mentioned (Diomedes, *Ars grammatica,* ed. Keil p. 342, 3); sometimes the conjunctive and the subjunctive were differentiated (Martianus Capella, p. 135, 12).

Some passages are instructive regarding the arguments which played a role in accepting or rejecting a certain mood. From *Grammatici Latini,* ed. Keil IV, p. 412, 6, and p. 503, 29, we learn, for instance, that those who refused to admit the promissive mood did so on the ground that it is nothing but the future tense of the indicative mood. Its defenders replied that the indicative mood cannot have a future tense, since we can only indicate things which we know and the future is unknown. To this it was objected by the opponents that a mood cannot be restricted to just one tense; which objection the defenders countered by pointing out that it is quite natural that the promissive mood always occurs in the future tense, since promises can be made only for the future. Against admission of an impersonal mood it was urged that no expression can be in more than one mood at the same time and that therefore impersonal expressions, which must be in the indicative, imperative, or subjunctive mood, are not to be regarded as a separate mood (*Ibidem* p. 412, 12). In discussing the imperative Priscian (*Institutiones grammaticae,* ed. Hertz II, p. 236, 24) rejects the view that imperatives have a first person singular; for nobody can give orders to himself. But he admits imperatives in the first person plural, such as 'Let us start the battle'. According to Priscian the Greeks called such expressions *hypothetika,* which he translates by *hortativa,* and held that they should be distinguished from the imperative proper because they are commonly directed to equals, whereas imperatives are directed by superiors to inferiors. In Priscian's opinion the latter thesis is simply false, since we often use the imperative mood in praying to the gods; he does not see any reason to distinguish between imperatives and hortatives as, for instance, Apollonius Dyscolus did (Cf. 6.3.5).

The difficulty of maintaining a clear difference between classifications of kinds of speech as they were attempted by the philosophers and classifications of moods as they were made by the grammarians on the basis of formal characteristics of the verb is strikingly illustrated by Martianus Capella, who adheres to the standard division into five moods of the verb (p. 135, 6). When he comes to giving examples of *eloquia,* which are kinds of sentences or of sentence-meanings (*sententiae*), he cites expressions which he characterizes as imperative and optative moods (p. 187, 9, 21). The lack of an adequate terminology which unmistakably separates the two fields remained a constant source of confusion.

8.1.6. The one kind of perfect speech which, being susceptible of truth or falsity, has importance for the logician is the statement-making utterance, the *logos apophantikos,* called *oratio pronuntiabilis* by Apuleius, *sermo pronuntiativus* by the author of the *Categoriae decem,* and *oratio enuntiativa* by Boethius. Besides the phrase *oratio enuntiativa* Boethius commonly uses the words *enuntiatio* and *propositio.* In his translations *enuntiatio* consistently stands for the Greek word *apophansis* (just as *enuntiare* stands for *apophainesthai*) and *propositio* for *protasis.* While it is natural that, for instance, in his commentary on *De interpretatione* the term *enuntiatio* is more frequent than *propositio,* on the whole Boethius treats the two words as synonymous for many purposes. Such combinations as *enuntiationes vel propositiones* and *in enuntiationibus propositionibusque (In P. herm. (I)* p. 33, 17, and p. 66, 8) are characteristic. For him the Stoics, too, in their books about *axiōmata,* dealt with the statement-making utterance and its parts; the only difference is that they treated both simple and composite utterances, while Aristotle confined himself to the non-composite ones *(In P. herm. (II)* p. 9, 26). No wonder then that he considers *proloquium* as a synonym of *enuntiatio* and *propositio (De diff. top.* 1174 B; cf. *Intr.* 767 C), though he never uses this word himself. The fact that Cicero had employed *enuntiatio* as one of his renderings of the Greek term *axiōma* (Cf. 7.1.1) no doubt facilitated this assimilation.

On the other hand, there are also some differences between *propositio* and *enuntiatio. Propositio* has at least three nuances of meaning which *enuntiatio* does not have or has in a markedly less degree. In the first place, *propositio,* or *propositum,* is said to be the Latin term for a dialectical question, in the sense of a *protasis* as described by Aristotle *(Topics* 101 b 28): 'Is pleasure the chief good?', 'Should one take a wife?' (*De diff. top.* 1177 C). This kind of *propositio* is not a *propositio* in the sense of an utterance which is either true or false; it has the same content as a true or false *propositio* but adds to this content an attitude of doubting and can thus be called a *dubitabilis propositio,* (the content of) a true or false *propositio* which has been turned into a question. What Boethius apparently intends to convey in this passage could be put rather simply as follows. 'Is pleasure the chief good?' is a question and 'Pleasure is the chief good' is an assertion; what they have in common is the content 'Pleasure being the chief good', and what is different are the attitudes of questioning and asserting which have this common content for their object. The same things can be said about a question and about an assertion in so far as they have a common content. But his exposition is complicated by the fact that he does not clearly isolate the common content as such and that he uses the word *propositio* both in the sense of a propounded question and in the sense of a statement-making utterance. How puzzling this could be for logicians who were not acquainted with the history of the word *propositio* will be seen in the case of Garlandus Compotista (Cf. 8.2).

Although the meaning of premiss in general is not very prominent, it can be concluded from such passages as *De diff. top.* 1174 C and 1177 C that a distinction was made between a *propositio* as such (*enuntiata simpliciter*) and a *propositio* in the narrower sense of a statement that is adduced to prove a conclusion (*aliud probans*). On the other hand, especially in *De syllogismis hypotheticis* the word *propositio* frequently occurs with the sense of the first premiss, as a synonym of *sumptum* and in contrast with the words for the added premiss and the conclusion. At the beginning of the second book Boethius states that every syllogism is a texture of *propositiones,* of which the first is called *propositio* or *sumptum,* the second *assumptio,* and the third *conclusio.*

According to *De diff. top.* 1174 C an *enuntiatio,* whether it is uttered for its own sake or is adduced to prove something else, is a *propositio*; if it is questioned, it is a *quaestio*; and if it is the object of proof, it is a *conclusio.* In a way, therefore, a *propositio, quaestio,* and *conclusio* are the same, but their different names reflect the diverse roles they play in arguments.

8.1.7. In so far as an *enuntiatio* or *propositio* is an *oratio enuntiativa* it can be defined by means of the genus *oratio perfecta* and the specific difference indicating that the complete utterance is used for making known an opinion. At all the places where Boethius divides the *oratio perfecta* into five species he adds that the *oratio enuntiativa,* in contrast with the other four species, is characterized by the fact that it contains the true or the false or that the true and the false are found in it. This somewhat circuitous manner of speaking no doubt reflects such passages as *De int.* 16 a 10 and 17 a 3, where Aristotle says that falsity and truth have to do with combination and separation and that not every utterance is a statement-making utterance, but only those in which there is truth or falsity. Elsewhere (*In Cat.* 181 A, 199 B; *In Top. C.* 1130 D) Boethius straightforwardly declares that statement-making utterances are either true or false.

Together with these characterizations of an *enuntiatio* or *propositio* as the kind of complete speech that is used to make known an opinion and therefore contains the true or the false or is true or false, we find the definition *propositio est oratio verum falsumve significans,* or some variant of it. As this definition has been extremely influential in medieval times, it is worthwhile to ask ourselves what its exact meaning and origins are.

In 3.2.2 we discussed some passages in which Aristotle stresses the incomplete nature or 'not yet'-character of nouns and verbs when not used in a certain combination. 'Goat-stag' signifies something but not, as yet, anything true or false; 'Philo's is' does not yet say anything true or false; a verb uttered by itself does not yet signify whether something is the case or not, just as the word *anthrōpos* signifies something, but not that something is the case or not. Measured against the *logos apophantikos*, certain expressions are defective. If we formulate this insight in a more positive manner, we get the following. A person who utters a sentence in order to make a statement may be said to express his opinion (*apophainesthai*) that something is the case or is not the case; or to signify (*sēmainein*) something, namely an opinion, that is either true or false; or to say something true or false (*alētheuein* or *pseudesthai*; cf. also *Metaphysics* 1011 b 28). Replacing *apophainesthai*, which preferably has a person for its subject, by such equivalent verbs as *sēmainein* or *dēloun*, we can say the same of the utterance that is used for making a statement, taking over Aristotle's vocabulary: it expresses the opinion (*sēmainein*) that something is the case or is not the case, or it signifies (*sēmainein*) something, namely an opinion, that is either true or false, or it says something true or false (*alētheuein* or *pseudesthai*; with an utterance as subject these verbs easily get the sense of being true or false).

Whereas Aristotle uses the phrase 'to signify something true or false' only once and then in a 'not yet'-sense (*De int.* 16 a 18), Ammonius makes a rather frequent use of it in his commentary on *De interpretatione*, not only in connection with 16 a 18 but also in commenting upon 16 b 22, and in a positive as well as in a negative way, usually with a linguistic expression as subject but once or twice with a person as subject (ed. Busse p. 56, 2 and 25–26; in the latter passage *legein* is used alongside *sēmainein*). The same is true of Boethius. He translates *De int.* 16 a 18 as '*hircocervus' enim significat aliquid, sed nondum verum vel falsum*, using *significare* as the equivalent of the Greek verb *sēmainein* as he generally does. Commenting upon 16 a 10, he says that an expression which sets forth a true or false thought itself signifies something true or false (*veri falsique retinet significationem*); and that a negation is something that signifies a truth or a falsehood (*In P. herm. (I)* p. 42, 24, and p. 43, 11). A *propositio* is then defined as an *oratio verum falsumve significans* (*De diff. top.* 1174 B and 1177 C). Further, in connection with *De int.* 16 a 15, he states that 'man' and 'white', uttered in isolation, do not designate anything true or false (*nihil tamen neque verum neque falsum designant*; *In P. herm. (I)* p. 43, 25). The phrase *in enuntiationibus propositionibusque* is explained as *in veri falsique scilicet designatione* (*In P. Herm. (I)* p. 66, 9). And in *In Top. C.* 1048 D and 1054 A a *propositio* is defined as an *oratio verum falsumve designans*. In *Intr.* 767 B–C the *enuntiatio* is contrasted with the other kinds of perfect speech in so far as it signifies that something is the case or is not the case and is an *oratio* in which truth and falsity can be found; therefore it is defined as the *enuntiatio* (*oratio??*) *quae verum falsumve denuntiat*. In *De syll. cat.* 795 D Boethius points out that every noun in combination with the verb *est* indicates something which is either true or false (*aut verum aut falsum demonstrat*). Elsewhere (*In P. herm. (I)* p. 66, 21) he uses the verb *monstrare*: the copula *est* can indicate something true and something false in a statement-making utterance (*verum falsumque in enuntiatione monstrare*), by bringing about a composition. In the same passage the phrase *in veri falsique enuntiatione* occurs twice, apparently with the same meaning as *in veri falsique designatione*; in *In P. herm. (II)* p. 44, 16, we are said to entertain sometimes simple thoughts *sine veri vel falsi enuntiatione*.

Thus we see that the verbs *significare, designare, denuntiare, demonstrare, monstrare, enuntiare* – to which we might perhaps add such verbs as *dicere* (Cf. *In Top. C.* 1130 D) and *proponere* (Cf. *Intr.* 767 C) – could readily be construed with an object-expression indicating that which is true or false. Used with a person as subject, they (like *apophainesthai, sēmainein, dēloun*, and *legein* in Greek) mean that someone makes known his opinion that something is the case or is not the case and consequently asserts something that is either true or false. With the possible exception of *enuntiare*, which seems to share the predilection for a personal subject typical of *apophainesthai*, those verbs can also be used of a linguistic utterance; by expressing the opinion that something is the case or is not the case the words make known something that is either true or false. The definition of the *enuntiatio* or *propositio* as an utterance which signifies something true or false reflects the fact that in Aristotle's view it is the thought or belief that something is the case which is true or false in the primary sense. As Boethius puts it, truth and falsity are not in things but in thoughts and opinions and secondarily (*post haec*) in words and utterances (*In Cat.* 181 B; cf. also such a passage as *In P. herm. (I)* p. 42, 1). Only in so far as it expresses a true or false belief can the utterance itself be said to contain the true or the false or to be true or false.

At first sight there is a certain similarity between the Boethian definition and Stoic views. The *propositio* as an utterance which signifies something true or false resembles a *logos* which expresses a true or false *axiōma* as the *lekton* or *sēmainomenon* or the associated *pragma*. But this *prima facie* similarity should not make us overlook important points of difference. In the first place, *significare* and its variants as they are used in the Boethian contexts have a narrower meaning than the Stoic terms *legein* and *sēmainein*: they designate the expression of a true or false belief, while the Stoic terms have the wider sense of expressing any thought whatever, not only in connection with the speech act of asserting but also in connection with various other speech acts. The Boethian *significatum* is more like an *apophanton,* which from a generic point of view is a *lekton* or *sēmainomenon,* a thought expressed, but differs from other *lekta* or *sēmainomena* by the fact that it is a thought expressed in a speech act of asserting. In the second place, the Stoics considered the *axiōma* as a complex of mental images in so far as it is expressed in words, whereas Boethius explicitly rejects the view that the *intellectus* or affections of the soul are *imaginationes* or *phantasiai,* quoting with approval Aristotle, *De anima* 432 a 10–14 (*In P. herm. (II)* p. 27, 25; cf. 3.4.1). For Boethius, as for the Peripatetics in general, such terms as *intellectus, sensus, sententia* stand for the Aristotelian *noēmata* which are held to be different from mental images. Finally, in the Peripatetic tradition the utterance which is used for making a statement is considered to be true or false according as it expresses a true or false opinion, while the Stoics apparently did not recognize the *logos* as a proper subject of truth and falsity.

8.2. Between Boethius and Abelard

In 7.1 we followed the ups and downs of Stoic terminology in the Latin West until it finally succumbed to the Peripatetic tradition. This tradition was most strongly represented by the works of Apuleius and Boethius, which became the main source of inspiration for the scanty writings on logic in the early Middle Ages. As these writings offer scarcely anything new regarding the topic with which we are concerned, I shall confine myself to a few incidental remarks.

In his *Institutiones* II, 11, Cassiodorus gives a brief survey of the contents of *De interpretatione,* recommending to his monks the commentary in six books that had been written by Boethius and apparently was available in the library of Vivarium. He defines an *enuntiativa oratio* as a significant sound about whether something is or is not the case, no doubt following Boethius's translation of *De int.* 17 a 23. From the same source he adds the definitions of an affirmation and a negation that occur in 17 a 25 (*enuntiatio alicuius de aliquo* and *alicuius ab aliquo*).

Isidore of Seville, in turn, partially copies Cassiodorus. The only point of interest in the paragraph he devotes to *De interpretatione* (*Etymologiae* II, 27) is the occurrence of the word *interpretamentum.* He explains the title *Perihermenias* by pointing out that the two parts of speech, the noun and the verb, interpret everything that the mind has conceived in order to express it; for every utterance is an interpreter of that which the mind has conceived (*conceptae rei mentis interpres est*). This explanation, which is already found in Boethius (*In P. herm. (I)* p. 32, 8; cf. 8.1.1), is typical of a translation theory of meaning: thinking is regarded as a kind of mental language which has to be translated into spoken or written language[9]. According to Boethius the term *interpretatio* (the Greek *hermēneia*) designates every significant sound that by itself signifies something, in particular nouns and verbs and combinations of them. Isidore takes *perihermenia* as a noun having the same meaning as *interpretamentum* which, as the Latin equivalent of *hermēneuma*, is no doubt only a variant of *interpretatio*. Out of *perihermeniae* or *interpretamenta,* namely out of nouns and verbs and combinations of them, syllogisms are formed. The word *interpretamentum* is also found in Remigius of Auxerre's commentary on Martianus Capella (ed. Lutz II, p. 47, 3): *incipit nunc de periermeniis, id est de interpretamentis, tractare* (Cf. 7.1.2).

Alcuin (*De dialectica,* ed. Migne 101, 964 D and 974 C) defines the *enuntiatio* as an *oratio verum aut falsum significans* or *veri vel falsi significativa.* There is no reason to believe that Alcuin made any difference between these two formulas, but we shall see that later logicians, for instance Paul of Venice, distinguished between a linguistic expression that actually signifies something true or false and a linguistic expression that is capable of signifying something true or false, and considered a *propositio* as a linguistic expression in the latter sense (Cf. 15.5.1).

Passing over in silence Abbo of Fleury's *Syllogismorum categoricorum et hypotheticorum enodatio,* which is nothing but an elucidation of Boethius's treatises on categorical and hypothetical syllogisms, I finally want to call attention to some points in the *Dialectica* which was written by Garlandus Compotista shortly before 1040[10]. Garlandus divides expressions into simple and composite (*vox incomplexa* and *complexa*) and the composite expressions into perfect and imperfect. He distinguishes five kinds of perfect speech and defines the *enuntiativa oratio* as speech in which something is stated of something or is denied of something (ed. De Rijk p. 42, 17). Elsewhere (ed. De Rijk p. 86, 25) the Boethian definition of the *propositio* as *oratio verum vel falsum significans* is given. In discussing questions (ed. De Rijk p. 89, 11) Garlandus mentions the definition of a question as a *propositio* which is made the object of doubt and uncertainty (*adducta in dubitationem et ambigui-*

---

[9] Cf. Maximus Confessor, *Opuscula theologica et polemica,* ed. Migne 91, 21 A, where the *logos prophorikos* is called the messenger of thought (*angelos noēmatos*).

[10] Edited by L.M. De Rijk, Assen, 1959.

tatem; cf. Boethius, *De diff. top.* 1174 B, and 8.1.6) and then asks himself what the term *propositio* means in that definition. The first possibility he considers is that the word *propositio* has a double meaning and can also stand for something signifying that which is neither true nor false, for example 'whether the heaven is revolving'. He suggests that in this case a question is called a *propositio* because it is as it were a *proculpositio,* something that is placed outside the actual syllogism (*procul a syllogismo ponitur*) as that for the sake of which the syllogism is formed. Another possibility is that the word *propositio* has to be taken as standing for the genus *oratio.* Lastly, it is also conceivable that *propositio* is used in its ordinary sense of an utterance signifying something true or false; then the phrase *propositio adducta in dubitationem vel ambiguitatem* means the same as *dubitabilis propositio,* designating, at the cost of a contradiction *in adiecto,* a statement that is made into a question. In this connection Garlandus also draws an interesting distinction between two kinds of *quaestio.* What he has said about the puzzling use of *propositio* applies only to the definition of a *quaestio per quam quaeritur,* an expression that is formally marked by some sign of interrogation, for instance *utrum caelum sit volubile.* If, on the other hand, we have to do with a *quaestio de qua quaeritur,* a *propositio* about which it is doubted whether it is true or false and which is not formally marked by some sign of interrogation, such as *caelum est volubile,* then there is no difficulty in calling such a *quaestio* a *propositio* in the straightforward sense of an utterance that signifies something true or false.

9. ABELARD

Although Abelard draws the material for his studies on logic from such traditional sources as Boethius in the field of dialectic and Priscian in the field of grammar, many of his reflections are so fresh and original that in the history of the problems concerning the bearers of truth and falsity he belongs among the few pioneers who really broke new ground and contributed insights which were a lasting source of inspiration for later generations. The following survey is based upon his glosses on Porphyry's introduction to the *Categories* and Aristotle's *Categories* and *De interpretatione*, which are found in the so-called *Logica ingredientibus*[1], and upon his systematic treatise *Dialectica*[2].

9.1. The signification of thoughts and the signification of things

9.1.1. Abelard defines a word (*dictio*) as a sound significant by convention none of whose parts is significant in separation (*D* 147, 21). Some words, namely nouns and verbs, have a definite signification by themselves; other words, namely conjunctions and prepositions, have an indefinite signification by themselves (*D* 117, 26). The definite signification of nouns and verbs, which for certain purposes include also pronouns, adverbs, conventional interjections, and participles (*D* 121, 8, 18; *G* 334, 23), is twofold: they signify

---

[1] Edited by B. Geyer, *Peter Abaelards philosophische Schriften, Beiträge zur Geschichte der Philosophie und Theologie des Mittelalters* XXI, 1–3, Münster, 1919–1927; I shall refer to this work by means of the letter *G*, followed by page and line.

[2] Edited by L.M. De Rijk, Assen, 1956 (revised edition 1970); I shall refer to this work by means of the letter *D*, followed by page and line.

thoughts (*intellectus*) and they signify things (*res*). Thoughts are the affections of the soul or the *noēmata* of which Aristotle speaks in the first chapter
of *De interpretatione*; Abelard interprets an *intellectus* as an act of attending
to the nature or a property of a thing which is either present to the senses or
put before the mind by means of a mental image (*G* 20, 30; *G* 312, 36; *G*
328, 18). In connection with a thought the verb *significare* either has the
same meaning as *exprimere* or *manifestare intellectum* — the speaker or the
word he uses expresses the speaker's act of thinking — or, more often, it has
the same meaning as *constituere*[3] or *generare intellectum*: the speaker or the
word he uses produces a certain act of thinking in the hearer's mind (*G* 307,
30). For this meaning of *significare* I shall commonly use the phrase 'to
produce a thought'. Further, nouns and verbs signify things; for this kind of
signifying Abelard uses, apart from *significare,* such verbs as *appellare, demonstrare, denotare, designare,* and *nominare.* For this meaning of *significare* I
shall employ the phrase 'to denote a thing'. Although for several reasons
Abelard regards the signification of thoughts as more important, in the context of his reflections on *De interpretatione,* than the signification of things
(*G* 308, 19), there is some difference between his conception of the signification of nouns and verbs and Aristotle's. For the latter nouns and verbs primarily signify thoughts; they can only be said to signify things because of the
fact that the thoughts which they signify are the likenesses of things. In
Abelard, on the other hand, this difference between the directness of the
signification of thoughts and the indirect character of the signification of
things is less prominent; both significations are treated, so to speak, on the
same level.

9.1.2. That conjunctions and prepositions have an indefinite signification is
the view defended by Abelard in his *Dialectica* (118—120). When, for instance, the preposition *de* and the conjunction *et* are uttered in isolation,
they have a signification which is vague and undetermined: the hearer's mind
is kept in suspense about that to which they are to be attached. Only when
the open places by which they are accompanied have been filled is their
imperfect and indefinite signification rendered precise and definite. In the
case of *homo et lapis*, for example, the general signification of *et*, namely that
certain things are conjoined, has been made specific by the meanings of the

---

[3] Abelard (*D* 112, 6; *G* 308, 11; *G* 357, 29) and others connect the phrase *constituere intellectum* with Aristotle, *De int.* 16 b 21: *histēsi --- tēn dianoian* had been
translated by Boethius as *constituit --- intellectum.* They apparently took *intellectum* as
referring to the hearer's thought.

two nouns: we now know that we are dealing with the conjunction of a man and a stone. In the glosses on *De interpretatione,* however, Abelard objects that this view makes it impossible to draw a clear distinction between, on the one hand, conjunctions and prepositions and, on the other hand, nouns and verbs; for the latter, too, can be said to have a signification which is not precise until they are combined with other words (*G* 337, 41). He therefore prefers to say that conjunctions and prepositions when uttered by themselves have no signification at all; they signify only in combination with other words (*consignificant*), but in that case they contribute a clearly distinguishable part to the meaning of the whole. It is necessary to hold that they have a signification of their own when they are used in combination with other words, since otherwise they cannot be differentiated from letters and syllables.

Whichever of the two views one adopts, there is a problem about the *intellectus* and the *res* which are produced and denoted by conjunctions and prepositions. If those words have a signification, either in isolation or only in combination with other words, they must produce some thought; and they can produce a thought only if there is a thing or a mental image of a thing to which the thought is directed (*G* 338, 41). According to Abelard some authors held that words with an indefinite signification produce a thought but do not denote a thing, in the same way as *propositiones* (*D* 119, 3). But it is hard to see how they could produce a thought if there is nothing to which the thought is related. Some grammarians tried to solve this difficulty by suggesting that prepositions denote the thing which is denoted by the noun to which the preposition is attached; but in that case the denotation of the noun would be superfluous. Abelard's own view is that conjunctions and prepositions denote a certain characteristic (*proprietas*) with regard to the thing that is denoted by the adjoining nouns or verbs. In the combination *in domo,* for instance, the preposition *in* denotes the characteristic of the house that consists in its containing something; and the conjunction *ergo,* placed between statements, denotes the characteristic that consists in the circumstance that the premisses prove the conclusion and the conclusion is proved by the premisses. Abelard finds it difficult, however, to state clearly the thought which belongs to each preposition and conjunction; it is as hard, he says, as stating explicitly the thought that belongs to utterances that are not used for the purpose of making a statement, such as 'Come to me' (*D* 118, 29).

The copulas *est* and *non est* get a separate treatment. They neither produce a thought nor denote anything, but they contribute to the affirmative or negative import of a *propositio* (*ad vim affirmationis* or *ad vim negationis proficit*) by causing the mind to combine or separate the things thought of (the *intellecta* or *intellectae res*; cf. *D* 154, 25–27). In understanding a *propo-*

sitio the mind performs three acts: it thinks of each of the two parts, the subject and the predicate, and it combines or separates the things thought of. Although the act of combining or separating the things thought of is not itself an *intellectus,* it nevertheless is part of the thought produced by the whole *propositio* (*G* 339, 20). Similarly, the conjunctions *si* and *non si* have no signification, but they unite or separate significant sounds by inclining the mind to a certain mode of conceiving (*animum inclinant ad quendam concipiendi modum*; cf. also *G* 329, 29).

The same expression *modus concipiendi* is used in connection with the difference between a finite verb such as *currit* and a noun such as *cursus.* The verb and the noun denote the same thing, running, but the different mode of conceiving it causes a difference in the thought produced (*diversus modus concipiendi variat intellectum*). The distinction between parts of speech pertains to a difference in thought produced rather than to a difference of denotation (*G* 308, 25).

In *D* 124, 11, a distinction is made between the principal signification of a noun and its accidental significations, which have to do with the modes of signifying. The difference between singular and plural is said to be a difference of accidental signification. Differences in case and gender, on the other hand, are not related to any difference in signification, but only to the position which nouns can occupy in constructions (Cf. *G* 364, 2). Similarly, such pairs as *comedere/vesci* ('to eat') and *carere/non habere* ('to lack') have the same signification but they play different roles in constructions (*D* 125, 33; *G* 369, 27). The same is true of such forms as *curro, curris, currit, curritur.* They all have the same signification but the ways in which they are completed into a full *propositio* by the addition of such pronouns as *ego, tu, ille, a me, a te, ab illo* are different. In other words, differences in person are not connected with any difference in signification, whereas differences in number, tense, and mood are differences in (accidental) signification (*G* 138, 31).

9.1.3. In contrast with a word, which signifies only as a whole and not by means of significant parts, an *oratio* is defined as a sound significant by convention one of whose parts is significant in separation (*D* 146, 35; *G* 363, 25); or, more briefly, as a *competens dictionum coniunctio,* a properly ordered combination of words (*D* 147, 28). Combinations of words which are formed according to the rules of syntax always produce a composite thought (*intellectus compositus*), made up of the thoughts produced by the parts (*G* 308, 36; *G* 370, 9). These parts are primarily nouns and verbs which produce a simple thought (*intellectus simplex*). The difference between a simple and a composite thought may be illustrated by means of the word *homo* and the phrase *animal rationale mortale* (*G* 325, 19). If I hear the word *homo*, I attend to the various elements of the concept man in a single act of the understanding; whereas in hearing the phrase *animal rationale mortale* I attend to the same ingredients by three acts of the understanding. Moreover, in the first case I grasp a whole of which the parts are already conjoined or disjoined, while in the second case I have to conjoin or disjoin the parts myself. In both cases, however, there is one thought; for a composite thought too is one thought, since it consists in one operation of conjoining or disjoining things. The whole thought is thus composed of the three acts of thinking of the three ingredients of the concept man and of an act of conjoining these three *intellectus simplices* in a certain manner. Similarly, there are three acts in the process of understanding such a phrase as *homo rudibilis* ('braying man'): two acts of attending to man and attending to braying and an act of conjoining them. While the first two acts are simple thoughts, the act of conjoining the things thought of is not itself an *intellectus*. It is nonetheless an integral part of the composite thought as a whole, for otherwise it would be incomprehensible how two thoughts, each of which has application when taken separately, form a composite thought which has no application; it must be the conjoining that makes the difference (*G* 330, 2).

Although the combination *homo rudibilis* is given as an example of a noun-phrase which is formed by joining an adjective to a substantive, it might also be taken as an instance of a construction that expresses an inherence (*inhaerentia*), in the same way as *homo currens* and *homo albus* may be understood as expressing the inherence of running or whiteness in a man (*inhaerentia cursus vel albedinis ad hominem*; *D* 149, 8). In that case *homo* is the subject-term and *rudibilis, currens, albus* are the predicate-terms; together the two terms form an *oratio* which differs from a *propositio* only by the fact that the inherence is not yet affirmed or denied. As long as there is no finite verb, the thought produced by such phrases is a composite thought consisting of two simple thoughts, one for the subject and one for the predicate, and an act of uniting the things thought of in the manner that is typical of inherence, without any affirmation or negation. I shall call the thought produced by such phrases the composite thought of mere inherence.

Concerning these (imperfect) *orationes* which produce composite thoughts of mere inherence, by far the most important for our purposes, let us further ask to what extent they can be said to have a signification of things. Among words the signification or denotation of things is restricted to nouns and verbs and other words that can play the role of subject-term or predicate-term, namely pronouns, adverbs, and participles. Apart from words which have a definite signification there are, however, also *orationes* that can play the role of subject-term or predicate-term, for instance *animal rationale mortale* or *animal risibile*. Such phrases have the same twofold signification as the words to which they are comparable; they produce a composite thought and denote a certain thing (*G* 365, 17). Actually, we should distinguish between two kinds of thoughts produced by words and phrases which have a definite signification. The simple thoughts associated with nouns and verbs and their functional equivalents may be either sound (*sanus*) or empty (*cassus*); they are sound when they are related to existing things and they are empty when they have no actual object, as is the case with the thoughts produced by such words as *chimaera* and *hircocervus* ('goat-stag'). The same applies to the composite thoughts associated with phrases; some are sound and some, for example the composite thought produced by *homo rudibilis,* are devoid of an object (*G* 326, 30; *G* 330, 2).

Now it is clear that an *oratio* which produces a composite thought of mere inherence can be said to denote things only in so far as its principal parts, the subject-term and the predicate-term which are either words or functionally equivalent phrases, denote things; but there is no separate thing denoted by the *oratio* itself, in so far as it is a certain combination of the terms. We shall see that this is a point of fundamental importance for Abelard's doctrine of the bearers of truth and falsity.

9.2.   Complete utterances and the statement-making utterance

9.2.1. Although the composite thought of mere inherence which is produced by phrases of the type *homo currens, homo albus* has a certain degree of completeness in so far as the subject and the predicate and the connection between them are put before the mind in an unmistakable way, it is still true that such phrases are not made to stand on their own. When spoken in isolation, they make the hearer wait for something more; he knows that in the construction of the words he has heard so far there is an open place which still has to be filled (*G* 373, 1). What is needed to bring these imperfect *orationes* to completeness and perfection is a finite verb. In order to get a full statement-making utterance, for instance, it is not enough to utter a combination of words that produces a composite thought of mere inherence; one must also assert that this inherence holds or is as a matter of fact the case. It is remarkable − though no doubt a coincidence − that Abelard (*D* 149, 11) describes this necessary addition of the assertive force in a way that is strongly reminiscent of what Plato (*Sophist* 262 d 2) says about the peculiar activity of *legein.* It is not enough to combine man and running or man and whiteness in a certain manner, but the completeness of the statement-making utterance requires that one says or states that the one inheres in the other, has inhered in the other, or will inhere in the other; and that can be done only by means of a finite verb in the indicative mood, for example by adding *est* to *homo currens* or *homo albus.*

The assertive force which has to be added to an inherence in order to get a proper statement is characterized by such verbs as *dicere, enuntiare, exprimere, loqui, pronuntiare, proponere, significare, affirmare,* and *negare,* usually with a linguistic expression – an *oratio enuntiativa, enuntiatio, propositio, affirmatio,* or *negatio* – as the subject. The fact that a combination of words is a statement-making utterance, an *oratio perfecta* which is an *oratio enuntiativa,* Abelard often expresses by saying that such a combination *implet (complet) sensum (sententiam, intellectum) propositionis (G* 137, 30; *G* 339, 39; *G* 357, 20; *G* 388, 25; *G* 491, 8). This phrase, with its variants, means that the *propositio,* as one of the complete utterances, has a signification of its own, which I shall call the mental counterpart of the *propositio.* It is that which later came to be called the *propositio mentalis.* Abelard does not use this name; indeed, he hardly mentions the doctrine of the three kinds of *oratio* which we found in Boethius (Cf. 8.1.3). He occasionally refers to it (*D* 66, 18, where the phrase *intellectualis oratio* occurs; *G* 324, 29), but he never characterizes the mental correlate of a *propositio* as being in its turn a *propositio* of a peculiar kind, namely a mental *propositio*[4]. This mental counterpart of the *propositio* is not the composite thought of mere inherence which is typical of an incomplete *oratio,* but rather the composite thought of an inherence in which the combination or separation is held to be true. It is the *componens intellectus* which is expressed or produced by an affirmative statement-making utterance or the *dividens intellectus* which is expressed or produced by a negative statement-making utterance (*G* 331, 31); in other words, an *intellectus compositus affirmativus* or *negativus* (*G* 358, 7). It should be noted that Abelard does not have special terms for the acts of assenting or dissenting which are the mental counterparts of the acts of affirming or denying; he either uses such verbs as *componere* and *dividere* with the added

---

[4] In those glosses on *De interpretatione* which have been edited by L. Minio-Paluello (*Twelfth Century Logic* II, Rome, 1958) Abelard points out that Aristotle in 23 a 32 means by the spoken sounds (*ea quae sunt in voce*) the *propositiones* and by the things in the mind (*ea quae sunt in anima*) their *intellectus* (p. 87, 22). He also gives *intellectus* as an equivalent of *opinio,* which is the translation of the Greek word *doxa* (p. 87, 5, 7). In commenting upon *Cat.* 4 a 22 he also uses *intellectus* rather than *opinio* for the word *doxa* in the Greek text (*D* 53, 11; *G* 161, 5).

nuance of assenting and dissenting or makes do with indirect devices in terms of the verbal acts of affirming and denying.

On the one hand, Abelard draws a clear distinction between the imperfect sense of such phrases as *homo currens* and the perfect sense of such complete utterances as *homo currit* (*D* 148, 19): the difference lies in the assertive force which *homo currens* lacks and which makes *homo currit* into a statement-making utterance. On the other hand, there are also passages where he insists that the phrases *Socrates currens* and *Socratem currere* and the complete utterance *Socrates currit* have one and the same *intellectus* (*G* 327, 1; *G* 369, 32; *G* 373, 1; *G* 375, 32). This seeming contradiction is due to the fact that he uses the term *intellectus* both for the composite thought of mere inherence and for the affirmative or negative composite thought produced by a *propositio*. The composite thought of an inherence, which is mainly determined by the thoughts produced by the subject-term and the predicate-term and an act of conjoining or disjoining the parts, is common to the phrases *Socrates currens, Socratem currere,* and the utterance *Socrates currit.* The latter has an *intellectus* which is typical of a *propositio* not because of some additional *intellectus* but because of the affirmative or negative way of conceiving the inherence. Just as the phrase *homo rudibilis* produces a composite thought consisting of two acts of attending to things and an act of conjoining the things thought of in a certain manner (*G* 330, 2), the utterance *Socrates currens est* produces a composite thought consisting of the two acts of attending to Socrates and attending to running and an act of thinking of the one as actually inhering in the other. The latter act is not itself an *intellectus,* an act of attending to things, but is nevertheless an essential part of the whole composite thought produced by the *propositio* (*G* 339, 30; *G* 359, 2). In the same way the utterance 'If Socrates is a pearl, then he is a stone' produces a composite thought consisting of the composite thoughts produced by the antecedent and the consequent and a particular mode of conceiving these thoughts which is contributed by the word *si*; the word *si* as such, however, does not produce a separate thought but inclines the mind to a certain mode of conceiving (*G* 340, 2). We might say that the three expressions *homo albus* as a nominal phrase, *homo albus* as a phrase indicating a mere inherence, and *homo albus est* as a statement-making utterance share the two acts of attending to man and attending to whiteness, while the differences in the composite thoughts which they produce are wholly due to acts of the understanding which are not themselves *intellectus* in the narrow sense of acts of attending to a thing but rather modes of conceiving.

Whether there is a difference in *intellectus* between *Socrates currens* and *Socrates currit* depends, therefore, on the point of view one takes. If one looks only at the acts of attending to certain things and at the act of conceiving the one as inhering in the other, there is no difference; if one takes into account the whole way of conceiving that is produced in the hearer's mind, then the composite thought associated with the *propositio* has an additional feature in comparison with the composite thought of mere inherence: the finite verb of the *propositio* causes the hearer to consider the inherence as being the case in the outside world.

9.2.2. The statement-making utterance is not the only kind of *oratio perfecta*. Abelard (*D* 151, 6) considers as complete also the utterances by means of which we ask a question (*oratio interrogativa*), pray (*deprecativa*), give an order (*imperativa*), or express a wish (*desiderativa*), to which perhaps the utterance by means of which we address or call somebody (*vocativa*) can be added, although it lacks a finite verb and has other peculiarities (*G* 373, 36). He also mentions expressions of admiration (*admirativa*) and hortative or dehortative utterances such as 'Let us (not) fight', and suggests that there may be many more (*G* 375, 21). In the case of the standard complete utterances which are not declarative, no less than in the case of a statement-making utterance, there is always an inherence; but this inherence is presented according to various mental attitudes (*secundum varios affectus animi demonstratur*; *D* 149, 21). The inherence of coming-to-me in a certain person is, for example, presented according to an attitude of commanding or wishing in the utterances 'Come to me' and 'O, that he would come to me'. There is a common core of mere inherence which is made into different complete utterances by the addition of one of several mental attitudes. Just as there is not a full statement-making utterance unless the speaker asserts that the predicate inheres in the subject, there is not a full utterance of some other kind if the speaker does not make it understood that he, for instance, commands or wishes the predicate to inhere in the subject.

In general there is a close connection between the kind of complete utterance and the mood of the verb. Abelard even uses the name *affectus animi* for the moods of the verb (*G* 139, 16) as well as for the mental attitudes expressed by them (Cf. 6.3.5 and 8.1.5). The mood of the verb is not, however, the sole criterion for determining the character of a complete utterance. In a question it is not the mood of the finite verb that distinguishes it from a statement, but rather the formal feature that Abelard vaguely describes as the *modus proponendi qui interrogationem constituit*, the typical mode of presenting the common content which forms a question (*D* 152, 14). For wishing something it is not enough to use the appropriate mood of the verb, but one has to add such words as *utinam, libenter, vellem* as necessary complements

(*G* 375, 6). It is also possible that one and the same mood is used for different purposes: *festinet amica* ('Let my girl-friend hurry') may be a commanding, praying, or wishing utterance according to the mental attitude that predominates (*D* 152, 17; *G* 374, 1). And *non occides,* the indicative mood of the future tense of the verb *occidere* ('to kill'), may be used to issue a universal command; if it were taken in an affirmative way, it would often be found to be false (*D* 152, 23). Finally, utterances containing an optative verb (a verb in the subjunctive mood) sometimes have the force of a statement-making utterance (*D* 149, 26; *G* 374, 31); otherwise we could not validly argue 'If you had been here, you would have seen him (*si fuisses hic, vidisses eum*); but you were here (*sed fuisti hic*); therefore, you saw him (*quare vidisti eum*)'.

We saw that, according to Abelard, a full statement-making utterance is the sign of a *sensus* or *intellectus propositionis,* the mental counterpart of the *propositio* which is the act of believing that something is or is not the case. Now the question may be raised whether the other complete utterances too are signs of some mental counterpart which is expressed by the speaker and produced in the hearer. Abelard's answer to this question is as follows (*G* 327, 27; *G* 374, 21; cf. also *D* 118, 30). If one utters the sentence 'O, that the king might come' (*utinam rex veniret*), the composite thought produced in the hearer, the *intellectus* of that sentence, is the same as that produced by the sentence 'I wish that the king would come' (*volo regem venire* or *opto, ut rex veniat*). If one utters the sentence 'Help me, Peter' (*adesto, Petre*), either as a command or as a prayer, the *intellectus* is the same as that of the sentence 'I order you to help me' (*praecipio, ut adsis mihi*) or of the sentence 'I pray you to help me' (*deprecor, ut adsis mihi*). The utterance 'Peter!' (*o Petre*) produces the same mental counterpart as the sentence 'I call you, Peter'. And the question 'Did Socrates come?' produces the same thought as the sentence 'I ask you if Socrates came'. Similarly, the one-word-utterances *papae* and *heu* produce the same thought as *ego admiror* ('I admire (it)') and *ego doleo* ('I feel grief (at it)'), although in the first two cases the thought is non-composite and in the second two cases the thought is composite.

This means that in spite of the differences in force of the vocal utterances, namely between the non-declarative utterance and the statement-making utterance which in each case corresponds to it, there is no difference between the mental counterparts of the non-declarative utterance and the corresponding statement-making utterance. The composite thought produced in the hearer's mind by each of the several non-declarative utterances is the mental counterpart of the *propositio* that may take its place. Two points are worthy of note. In the first place, Abelard considers such sentences as 'I wish that the king would come', 'I order (pray) you to help me', 'I ask you if Socrates came' as statement-making utterances; he does not regard them as wishes, commands, prayers, or questions with an explicit speech-act-indicating device, but as statements (*enuntiationes, propositiones*) which are either true or false. In the second place, although he reduces the mental counterparts of non-declarative utterances to the mental counterparts of the corresponding statement-making utterances, namely in each case to an act of believing that the speaker has a certain mental attitude concerning something, he does not go as far as, for instance, Paul of Venice who, as we shall see later (Cf. 15.5.1), reduces all non-declarative vocal utterances to statement-making vocal utterances, on the ground that there is no difference in the mental counterparts, all of which are indicative *propositiones mentales*. Abelard, on the other hand, does recognize a difference between, for example, an *oratio desiderativa* and the corresponding *oratio enuntiativa* on the level of the vocal utterances or, as one might be inclined to say, on the level of the surface-structure. He explicitly states that the criterion for deciding whether an utterance is an *enuntiatio* or *propositio* is not the *intellectus* but the *modus enuntiandi* or *pronuntiandi* (*G* 327, 40; *G* 374, 28). If the criterion were the *intellectus,* we would be forced to regard wishes, commands, prayers, and questions as *enuntiationes* or *propositiones,* for their *intellectus* are exactly the same as those of the corresponding statement-making utterances. Abelard, however, does not make the mental counterpart the decisive criterion, but rather the verbal mode of expressing and producing the mental counterpart, as in general he pays more attention to the verbal than to the mental side of acts and attitudes of holding something true.

9.2.3. As far as the signification of thoughts is concerned, we may conclude that there is a special sort of composite thought which is produced in the hearer's mind by complete utterances; although it should not be overlooked that this thought is of the same nature for all kinds of complete utterances and that its hard core consists of those acts of attending to things which are associated with the nouns and the verbs that are the subject-term and the predicate-term in the inherence-construction underlying the complete utterance. While Abelard thus recognizes to a certain extent that a special thought corresponds to a *propositio,* namely an act of believing that one thing inheres in another thing, he is most emphatic in denying that a *propositio* signifies its own thing. The *propositio* as a whole has no thing which it denotes (*nullam rem subiectam habet*; *D* 119, 5; cf. *G* 261, 13; *G* 393, 28). On the other hand, he insists that in uttering *propositiones* we are concerned with the things that are denoted by their parts, the nouns and the verbs, and not with the *proposi-*

tiones themselves or the thoughts which are produced by them. Statement-making utterances are about the things designated by their parts and not about the words or the thoughts (*D* 119, 5; *D* 147, 9; *D* 154, 20; *D* 156, 22; *D* 287, 36). This thesis, that in uttering *propositiones* we are concerned with things and that the *propositiones* are about things (*agere de rebus*), is defended by means of several arguments (*D* 154, 30). If the *propositiones* were about acts of thinking, a conditional such as *si est homo, est animal* would not be true, since it is quite possible that the thought associated with the antecedent is present without the thought associated with the consequent being present. The same applies if *propositiones* are taken to be about the words uttered: the conditional would be false, since it may happen that the antecedent is uttered without the consequent being uttered. In both cases, moreover, we would have to give names to the utterances or thoughts about which we are going to speak; but then the antecedent and the consequent would become names and it is impossible to form a conditional out of two names.

9.3. The *dictum* as that which is asserted

9.3.1. In Abelard's time there were at least two theories about the signification of complete utterances, in particular statement-making utterances, which restricted this signification to one or both of the types of signification which we have considered so far, the signification of thoughts and the signification of things (*G* 365, 21). One of them held that a *propositio* signifies only a composite thought. The other maintained the view that a *propositio* also signifies the things themselves which are signified by its parts; not however, as in the case of the parts, one by one, but all at once. The utterance *homo est animal* not only produces a composite thought but also denotes man and animal as a whole (*totaliter*) in such a state (*in hoc habitu*) that the one is the other; the negation *homo non est animal* denotes the same things in such a state that the one is not the other; while the conditional *si est homo, est animal* again denotes the same things but in such a state that if the one exists, the other exists.

Against the first theory Abelard adduces arguments of somewhat the same kind as those against the view that *propositiones* are about the thoughts they produce. In a necessarily true conditional the necessity cannot lie in the thought produced, since that is a transitory act (*G* 366, 5). Moreover, it would be false to assert that the thought of the antecedent cannot occur without the thought of the consequent (*G* 367, 2). And if the composite thought is taken as a thought of mere inherence, there would be no difference between *Socrates currens* and *Socrates currit* (G 366, 41).

Among the arguments which Abelard puts forward against the second theory — that the *propositio* also denotes the things as a totality of a certain kind — are the following. Such conditionals as 'If it is a rose, then it is a flower', 'If he is a man, then he is an animal' are necessarily true even if the things concerned do not exist (D 160, 15; D 264, 38; D 282, 5; G 366, 8). Similarly, a negation can be true of non-existent things (G 30, 3; G 366, 27; G 368, 3). And a modal statement such as 'It is possible that Socrates exists' can be true at a time when Socrates does not exist (D 160, 21). But even if one takes an affirmative statement of a very special kind, for instance 'Socrates is Socrates', which cannot be true unless Socrates exists and which is about one thing, it is still not correct to say that the *propositio* as such denotes Socrates. For there is an essential difference between a name and a *propositio*: the name 'Socrates' does indeed denote Socrates, but it does not say that he is Socrates and cannot be true or false, whereas the *propositio*, on the other hand, says something about Socrates but does not name him (D 157, 23; G 366, 30). Moreover, if the signification of a *propositio* were the denotation of things, there would be no contradiction between an affirmative and a negative statement, since they denote exactly the same things (G 367, 36).

9.3.2. As we have seen, Abelard's own view was that a *propositio* as such does not denote anything, although it is about things and not about words or thoughts. A *propositio*, rather, is a sign of a composite thought of a special sort, namely of an act of believing that one thing inheres in another thing. But apart from the signification of things, which *propositiones* do not have, and the signification of thoughts, which they do have, there is still a third kind of signification. We noticed that *significare* is one of the verbs which Abelard uses to characterize the assertive force that has to be added to an inherence in order to get a proper statement. Along with *dicere, enuntiare, proponere, affirmare,* and *negare* the verb *significare* then stands for a third kind of signification which is precisely that which makes a *propositio* a complete utterance and at the same time distinguishes it from other species of complete utterances. Just as a person who uses an appropriate combination of words may be said to make known his opinion and to indicate, declare, or assert that something is the case, in the sense of the Greek verbs *apophaines-thai, sēmainein, dēloun, legein,* so the utterance itself may be characterized as making known the speaker's opinion and indicating, declaring, or asserting that something is or is not the case. Now Abelard shows that it is exactly this aspect of the *propositio* which is neglected by the other theories, in particular the theory that restricts the signification of the *propositio* to a composite act of thinking. A *propositio* produces a composite thought about the things which are denoted by its principal parts, but it also asserts that something is or is not the case. Apart from the things denoted by the nouns and the verbs and the composite thought produced by the utterance about these things, there is therefore also a third element, namely that which is asserted. This third kind of *significatum* is often designated by such phrases as *quod propositio dicit* (D 157, 18), *ea quae dicunt affirmatio et negatio et proponunt* (G 275, 4), *id quod (propositio) proponit et dicit* (G 365, 35); in the glosses Abelard also frequently refers to it by the one word *dictum*, which is, however, conspicuously absent from his *Dialectica.*

Abelard's view can be regarded, I think, as the natural outcome of the development that I have tried to sketch in 8.1.7. The most remarkable differences from Boethius are that Abelard more exclusively stresses the purely verbal side of acts and attitudes of holding something true, whereas the mental side — the act of assenting which corresponds to the assertive force on the verbal level and especially the thought-content which is its object — remains in the background; and secondly, that this prominence of the verbal side finds expression in a special terminology, particularly in the word *dictum*. After what has been said about the difference between the Boethian *significatum* and the Stoic *lekton* at the end of 8.1.7 it is hardly necessary to add that the Abelardian term *dictum* has nothing to do with the Stoic term *lekton*. If one insists on comparing it to Stoic terminology, it should be aligned with such words as *apophanton* or *axiōma*, and with the term *dictum* as it is mentioned by Seneca (*Epistula* 117, 13; cf. 7.1.1); although even then one should keep track of the differences.

It is only natural that Abelard specified the *dictum* also as the inherence in so far as it is asserted. What we propound as true in a *propositio* is that something inheres in another thing, has inhered in it, or will inhere in it (D 149, 18); an *oratio enuntiativa* affirms or denies the predicate of the subject (D 151, 9); *propositiones* declare that something is, or is not, something else, they assert how the things are connected, whether the one belongs to the other or not (D 160, 28, 31, 35). All this is reminiscent of *De int.* 17 a 21, 25. Elsewhere (G 374, 26) he characterizes that which a *propositio* propounds as true as *esse vel non esse*, that (it) is or is not the case, no doubt thinking of such passages as *De int.* 16 b 22, 29 (where Boethius translates the Greek verb *sēmainein* by *significare*); occasionally he speaks of the *essentia* which a *propositio* asserts (D 205, 25). He also says, in accordance with *De int.* 17 a 23, that a *propositio* asserts that something is or is not (D 160, 28; G 491, 9); this is also expressed by the phrase *essentia rei ut a proposi-*

tione designata (*D* 372, 8). Finally, in connection with *Cat.* 12 b 6, he points out that Aristotle means by that which underlies an affirmation or negation (Cf. 3.3.3) the *dictum* of the *propositio*, that which underlies the affirmation or negation as the thing signified (*orationum significata* or *tamquam earum significationes*: *D* 390, 20; *suppositum eis tamquam significatum*: *G* 275, 15).

9.3.3. I have already drawn attention to Abelard's rejection of the view that the *propositio* as such denotes a thing or a complex of things. *A fortiori,* if we take *significare* in the sense of *dicere,* that which is asserted or the *dictum* cannot be considered as a thing. Abelard never tires of emphasizing this point: a *dictum* is not a *res,* an *essentia* (in this context the word *essentia* is a synonym of *res*), or *aliquid* (*D* 160, 23, 29, 34; *G* 261, 13; *G* 287, 5; *G* 365, 37; *G* 366, 26, 39; *G* 367, 13; *G* 369, 38). As we noted before, Abelard is fully awake to the difference between names and *propositiones.* In much the same way as Plato distinguished between the *onomazein*-level and the *legein*-level (Cf. 2.2) he carefully separates naming expressions whose function consists in denoting the things which can be subject or predicate from *propositiones* whose function consists not in naming anything, but in saying that something is or is not the case: their signification is *in dicendo,* not *in nominando* (*D* 150, 22; cf. *D* 160, 23; *D* 157, 17; *G* 366, 33). Naming expressions and statement-making utterances are two entirely different categories, each with its own way of signifying and its own type of significate. The circumstance that in both cases the verb *significare* is used should not lead us to identify these categories.

In his glosses (especially *G* 389—393 and 489—493; cf. also *G* 361, 26, and 369, 37) Abelard offers a very ingenious antidote against confusing the *dictum* with a thing. He starts from impersonal constructions of the type *evenit* (*accidit, contingit*) *Socratem legere librum* ('It happens (to be the case) that Socrates is reading a book'), in which a purely impersonal verb is combined with an accusative and infinitive phrase as a complement. That in such constructions the complement has the force of a verb, and not of a noun, is shown by the fact that it contains a subject and an object. In these cases we can no more properly say *quid evenit?* or *aliquid evenit* or *nihil evenit* ('What is happening?', 'Something is happening', 'Nothing is happening') than we can react to such purely impersonal expressions as *ventum est ad ecclesiam* or *curritur* by saying *aliquid ventum est* or *quid curritur?, aliquid curritur, nihil curritur.* The words *quid, aliquid, nihil* belong to a category whose members are not fit to be combined with purely impersonal verbs. What we should say is 'What happens to be the case?', 'Something happens to be the case', 'Nothing happens to be the case'. Now Abelard maintains that such expressions as *possibile, impossibile, necessarium, verum, falsum, bonum, malum, honestum, utile est* can be treated in an analogous way, as purely impersonal expressions of the same kind as *evenit, accidit, contingit.* The sentence *bonum est Socratem legere librum* may be interpreted as *evenit aliquid boni esse propter hoc quod Socrates legit librum* ('It happens (to be the case) that there is some good on account of the fact that Socrates is reading a book'). Just as it would be ungrammatical to ask, in connection with *taedet me legere* ('It irks me to read'), *quid taedet me?* instead of *quid facere taedet me?,* it would be wrong to ask the question *quid evenit?* in connection with the above-mentioned sentence; the proper question is *quid esse evenit?* Similarly the sentence *possibile est Socratem legere* should be interpreted as *potest contingere, ut Socrates legat,* and the proper question to be asked is not *quid est possibile?* but rather *quid potest contingere?* For Abelard the words *quid, aliquid, nihil* belong to the same category as naming expressions of the type 'The table', 'The horse'. And his point is, approximately, that the question 'What happens?' cannot properly be answered by 'The table' or 'The horse' but only by such expressions as 'The table collapses' or 'The horse stumbles'; what we actually mean is 'What happens to be the case?'.

The *dictum* of a *propositio* will usually be rendered by an accusative and infinitive phrase in such sentences as *verum est Socratem legere librum.* Abelard clearly recognizes the strong temptation to construe the complement of *verum est* as a sort of naming expression which requires a thing as its denotatum. By assimilating the phrase *verum est* to the purely impersonal verb *evenit* he tries to counter this tendency. In the case of *evenit* it is obvious that its proper complement is not a naming expression but some verb-phrase which indicates what kind of happening takes place. It is only one step from *evenit* to *verum est,* from 'It happens to be the case' to 'It is true', and it is *via* this resemblance that Abelard attempts to transfer the insight which is so easily gained in relation to constructions with *evenit* to the same constructions with *verum est.* By directing the eye to the similarities with the *evenit*-case he hopes to restrain the inclination to interpret the sentence *verum est Socratem legere librum* along the same lines as the sentence *verum est hoc dictum.*

Abelard draws the consequence that it would be wrong to say that the *dictum* of a *propositio* is nothing (*nihil*). In so speaking one would commit the same mistake as in saying *contingit nil,* a mistake which consists in combining two words that belong to categories which are grammatically unfit to go together. If one wants to make the point that a *dictum* is not a thing, it is therefore preferable to express oneself by means of the negative sentence *non est aliquid* (*G* 369, 37).

9.3.4. The impersonal interpretation of such sentences as *verum est Socratem legere librum* is found only in the glosses. Already there, however, Abelard also offers an alternative view. If we use the expression *hoc dictum* as the name of that which is asserted by a statement-making utterance, there can be no doubt that the sentence *verum est hoc dictum* is a personal construction, syntactically similar to sentences of the type *dulce est hoc vinum* (*G* 370, 11; *G* 392, 32). Now Abelard appeals to the authority of Priscian, who says that *bonum est legere* has the same meaning as *bona est lectio* (*Institutiones grammaticae,* ed. Hertz II, p.226, 21), in order to establish the point that an infinitive need not always be taken in the full verbal force which it has in impersonal constructions, but that it can also have the function of a noun and as such occur in a personal construction (*G* 391, 22; *G* 490, 27; *G* 491, 18). Abelard is willing to admit this nominal interpretation of the infinitive even in cases where it is combined with a subject-term in the accusative case: *me legere* can be taken in the sense of *mea lectio* and so become part of the personal construction *bonum est me legere,* just as *mea lectio* is part of the personal construction *bona est mea lectio* (*G* 392, 31). Only when the verbal force is predominant, which may be shown by such features as the addition of a grammatical object, Abelard clearly prefers an impersonal interpretation of infinitive-constructions; in other cases we may make our choice between the impersonal and the personal reading.

There is no such choice in the *Dialectica,* for the simple reason that in that work Abelard nowhere even mentions the impersonal interpretation. In the only passage where he explicitly deals with the present problem (*D* 149, 37) he unreservedly defends a kind of nominal interpretation of such accusative and infinitive phrases as *Socratem currere.* There he discusses the objection that the definition of a *propositio* as an *oratio verum vel falsum significans* applies to *Socratem currere* as well as to *Socrates currit*; for both expressions signify something that is either true or false. Abelard's answer to this objection is that in *verum est Socratem currere* the part *Socratem currere* is not an *oratio* in the same sense as it would be if it occurred in isolation, but rather a sort of name (*quasi nomen*) of that which is asserted by the *propositio,* just as *homo* and *homo albus* are names of a man. If it were not a name, it could not be combined, by means of the verb *est,* with the predicate-term *verum.* Even the expression *Socrates currit* would have to be understood as a name, and not as a *propositio,* if it were made the subject in a sentence of the type *Socrates currit verum est* (a construction, by the way, which is declared to be ungrammatical in *G* 369, 31). Once the nominal character of the phrase *Socratem currere* has been clearly recognized, it is obvious that it does not have the same signification as the statement *Socrates currit,* since the typical signification of a *propositio* consists in saying that something is the case and not in naming. In other words, the makers of the objection are not aware of a crucial ambiguity in the verb *significare*.

This conception of an accusative and infinitive phrase of the type *Socratem currere* as the designation of the *dictum* – or, in the terminology of later logicians, the *appellatio dicti* – is not without its difficulties. Although Abelard compares the accusative and infinitive phrase to such names as *homo* and *homo albus,* it is evident that there is, along with the similarities, at least one remarkable difference, namely that the denotatum of *Socratem currere* is not a thing; that is no doubt the reason why Abelard is careful to speak of a *quasi nomen* (as he speaks in G 367, 12 of the *dicta* as the *quasi res propositionum,* immediately adding that they are not at all things in the ordinary sense). At best we can say that the denotatum is an *aliquid* in a rather loose sense of the word, in so far as it is used for both existing and non-existing things, in the way Aristotle (*De int.* 16 a 17) says that the word 'goat-stag' signifies something (*aliquid significare*; D 137, 16; cf. G 396, 28). We shall see that this point was a source of endless dicussions in the times after Abelard.

In the second place, Abelard holds the view that it is a necessary condition of the truth of an affirmative categorical statement that the things about which the statement is made exist (D 176, 21; D 279, 18; G 366, 30). This seems to have the awkward consequence that the statement *verum est Socratem currere* cannot be true, since *Socratem currere* does not denote an existing thing. As a way out Abelard suggests, rather hesitatingly, that such a statement be taken in a naming sense (*in sensu nuncupativo*; G 361, 19). This means that, just as *chimaera est chimaera* is interpreted as *chimaera vocatur chimaera* ('A chimaera is called by the name "chimaera" '), the sentence *verum est Socratem non esse* should be read as saying that the *dictum* of the statement *Socrates non est* is called by the name 'true' or 'something true'. But Abelard immediately adds that it is certainly more convenient to take it in an impersonal sense.

9.4.   The bearers of truth and falsity

9.4.1. According to Abelard the qualifications 'true' and 'false' may be applied in three different ways: to *propositiones,* to the mental counterparts of *propositiones,* and to the *dicta* (D 154, 4; D 204, 30; G 492, 9). If we call a *propositio* true or false, we always do so in a derivative sense. The Boethian definition of a *propositio* as an *oratio* signifying something true or false is susceptible of a twofold interpretation: 'signifying something true or false' either means the same as 'saying something that is the case in reality or is not the case in reality' or as 'producing a mental counterpart which is true or false' (*D* 156, 27; cf. however *G* 327, 18). Accordingly, a *propositio* is true if its *dictum* is true or if its mental counterpart is true, and false in the contrary cases.

The mental counterpart of a *propositio* is always a composite thought of a special kind: it is an act of conceiving that one thing inheres in another thing (*D* 154, 10). Such a thought is true if it is an act of thinking of what is or is not the case that it is or is not the case, of what has been or has not been the case that it has been or has not been the case, or of what will or will not be the case that it will or will not be the case (*G* 328, 20); or, more briefly, an *intellectus* is true or false according as it is an attitude (*habitus*) concerning that which is, or is not, the case in reality (*D* 154, 7). Especially in the glosses the borderline between a composite thought of mere inherence and the mental counterpart of a *propositio* is never a very sharp one, not nearly so sharp as that between an incomplete *oratio* and a complete *oratio enuntiativa,* where the element of asserting makes all the difference. The fact that Abelard does not have a clear terminology for the act of assenting or dissenting which is the mental correlate of the act of saying or asserting which is performed by means of a finite verb in the indicative mood leads him to suggest that not only the mental counterparts of *propositiones* can be true or false but perhaps (*fortasse*) also the composite thoughts produced by certain incomplete *orationes* such as *homo currens,* since there is no difference in *intellectus* between *homo currens* and *homo currit* (*G* 326, 39). This confusion is facilitated by his use of the word *opinio* as a synonym of *intellectus* even in cases where a non-composite thought is meant, for example the thought produced by the word 'man' (*G* 326, 34). Nevertheless, it may be assumed that on the whole Abelard means by a true or false *intellectus* the mental counterpart of a *propositio,* of an utterance which asserts that something is the case or is not the case. The lack of an adequate terminology for the act of assenting or dissenting which corresponds to the verbal act of asserting may also be part of the explanation of the very strange fact that Abelard never even mentions a mental counterpart of the *dictum.* One would expect that in the same way as a verbal act of asserting yields something that is asserted, a *dictum,* the mental counterpart of the *propositio* – the act of believing that something is the case – would yield something that is believed, an *opinatum* or *creditum.* As he frequently stresses the act-character of the *intellectus,* it is not plausible to assume that he consciously uses such terms as *intellectus* or *opinio* in a double sense: that of the act of believing that something is the case and that of the state of affairs believed to be the case. We can only conclude that he apparently did not feel the need to elaborate the mental analogues of the act of *dicere* and its product, the *dictum*, which play so prominent a part in the verbal sphere.

9.4.2. At the end of 9.3.2 we already noted that, in connection with *Cat.* 12 b 6, Abelard identifies that which Aristotle characterizes as underlying an affirmation or negation with the *dictum* of a *propositio*. In the same passage (12 b 15) Aristotle calls that which underlies an affirmation or negation a *pragma*. This place, together with *Cat.* 14 b 20 (Cf. 3.3.3), leads Abelard to the view that his *dictum* is the same as the Aristotelian *pragma* or *res* (*G* 367, 20): the *dicta* are the *quasi res propositionum,* a kind of *res,* in the sense of the Aristotelian *pragma,* but not of course things in the ordinary sense of the word (*G* 367, 12). Other expressions which Abelard occasionally uses for this kind of *res* are *rerum essentia* (*D* 155, 34; elsewhere he uses this phrase for a thing in the ordinary sense, for example *D* 160, 29), *rerum existentia* (*D* 155, 35; *D* 156, 29; *D* 157, 14), and *eventus rerum* (*D* 211, 5, 29, 32; *D* 221, 4) or simply *eventus* (*G* 423, 13, 26). In all these cases we might speak of the asserted or alleged state of affairs.

That a *dictum* is true or false may now be clarified in one of the following ways. We may say that the *dictum* that Socrates runs is true if it is really the case that Socrates runs (*ita est in re quod Socrates currit*), if that which the *propositio* says is really the case, or if it is really as the *propositio* says (*D* 154, 13; *D* 372, 4). But it is also possible to follow the Aristotelian formula *toi gar einai to pragma ē mē* (*Cat.* 14 b 21), which is translated into Latin as *in eo enim quod res est aut non est* (*G* 367, 21), and simply say that the *dictum* is true if the *res* or the asserted state of affairs is the case and false if it is not. Thus Abelard explains the meaning of 'true' and 'false' as applied to a *dictum* by pointing out that these words are the names of an *existentia rei* or a *non-existentia rei* (*D* 154, 11; *D* 204, 37, and 205, 3): they indicate that the *res* or the asserted state of affairs exists or is the case or does not exist. In the same way he formulates the following rule for conditionals of the type 'If every man is an animal, then every man is a body': 'If some state of affairs expressed by the antecedent exists, then it is necessary that some state of affairs expressed by the consequent exists' (*existente aliqua antecedenti rerum essentia necesse est existere quamlibet rerum existentiam consequentem ad ipsam*; *D*155, 34). Further, it is worthy of note that, in connection with *Cat.* 14 a 9, he says with regard to two contrary *dicta* such as the *dictum* that Socrates is well and the *dictum* that Socrates is ill that it will not be possible that the one is the case when the other is the case (*G* 284, 1). The Greek *einai* is here translated as *contingere; res contingit* (Cf. *G* 367, 35) is of course a proper construction if *res* is taken in the Aristotelian sense of an asserted state of affairs which happens to be the case.

In spite of his good intentions Abelard's terminology made it rather difficult to distinguish between a thing which exists and an asserted state of affairs which is in fact the case. This is clear from such passages as *D* 205, 20. There he points out that by *Socratem esse hominem verum est* we mean that what the utterance *Socrates est homo* asserts is one of the number of states of affairs which are the case (*una est de numero existentium rerum*). But he immediately adds that even then the *dictum* is not a *res existens,* meaning that it is not an ordinary thing and does not exist in the same way as things exist. Similarly, his terminology is apt to obscure the difference between a state of affairs as asserted and a state of affairs as it exists independently of any utterances concerning it. Although he is aware of the fact that it often happens that a state of affairs is the case (*contingit rem esse*) without there being a *propositio* which asserts that it is the case (*D* 371, 34; *G* 291, 28) and although he distinguishes between the things themselves which happen (*res ipsas quae eveniunt*) and the *eventus* as the state of affairs asserted by a *propositio* (*G* 423, 3, 13, 25), the circumstance that he sometimes uses the same word in more than one sense easily leads to confusion or to difficulties of interpretation. A striking example is the phrase *essentia rei.* This is used – as a synonym of *substantia rei* – for reality outside language (*G* 60, 24, 32), but equally for the state of affairs in so far as it is asserted by a *propositio* (*D* 372, 8), as a variant of *rerum essentia,* which in its turn is also used for a thing in the ordinary sense (*D* 160, 29).

According to Abelard we call *propositiones* true or false or opposed to each other because of the fact that their *dicta* are true or false or opposed to each other (*G* 367, 13; cf. *D* 221, 3). In this connection he appeals to *Cat.* 14 b 20, where it is said that the *pragma* or *res* seems in some way the cause of the truth of the *propositio.* But if the *pragma* or *res* is identified with the *dictum* and the *dictum* is not a thing, how then can the *pragma* or *res* be a cause? Abelard is aware of this difficulty (*G* 293, 21; *G* 368, 40; cf. also *G* 20, 9) and tries to meet it by giving examples of cases in which some sort of causal influence is ascribed to various kinds of nonentities: a man is hanged because of a theft committed in the past, or a man dies because he does not eat, or victory may be said to be the (final) cause of a war.

In the same way as *propositiones* are called true or false because their *dicta* are true or false, they are called necessary or possible because their *dicta* are necessary or possible (*G* 367, 13). In dealing with modal statements Abelard distinguishes between an interpretation *de re* and an interpretation *de sensu* (*G* 489, 1). If we take a modal statement *de sensu,* it is interpreted as being about the *dictum* of a *propositio*; in that case it can be understood either in an impersonal sense or in a personal sense. For us the main point is that *sensus* in this context is apparently a synonym of *significatum* or *dictum*; the *totius propositionis sensus* (*G* 489, 25) as that which the *propositio* asserts is different from the *intellectus totius propositionis* (*G* 339, 31), the act of thinking produced by a *propositio*, for which Abelard frequently uses the phrase *sensus propositionis* too, especially in the expression *implere sensum propositionis* (Cf. 9.2.1).

As we saw in 8.1.2, Boethius had drawn a distinction between an *argumentum* and an *argumentatio*: an *argumentum* is a reasoning proving something that is questioned and an *argumentatio* is the verbal expression of an *argumentum*. Abelard restricts the term *argumentum* to the premisses of a proof and says that this word is the name both of the *propositiones* and of their significations (*D* 459, 26). According to him these significations are not, as some have held, the mental counterparts produced by the *propositiones*, but rather the *dicta* of the *propositiones*. For some *argumenta* are said to be necessary and it is hard to see how the transitory acts of thinking which are associated with a *propositio* can be necessary.

9.4.3. Surveying the data which we have gathered about the *dictum* we find, on the one hand, that Abelard leaves no doubt concerning its indispensability and importance. It is not enough to assume that every *propositio* produces a composite act of thinking that something is the case; it also has another signification, namely that which it asserts. And that which the *propositio* asserts is true or false in the fundamental sense; it is also that which is primarily necessary or possible and that which can serve as a term in logical relations. If the *propositio* itself is called true or false, necessary or possible, or if *propositiones* are said to stand in certain logical relations to each other, these characterizations are always derivative and secondary; what is the cause of the truth or falsity of a *propositio* is its *dictum*. On the other hand, notwithstanding these impressive functions, the ontological status of the *dictum* is far from clear. Negatively, we may be sure that it is not a thing in the sense that it can be classified in one or another of Aristotle's categories. Neither does it seem to be some sort of thought-content. Although Abelard admits acts of thinking that something is the case, he never speaks of any contents of such acts, of *opinata* or *credita* which, as states of affairs believed, might be materially identical with states of affairs asserted. In a more positive sense, one may be tempted to identify the *dicta* of true statements with the states of affairs which are actually the case in reality. But even if this would prove a correct interpretation of Abelard's view, we are still confronted with the *dicta* of false statements, which are not among the features of the world outside language. As a matter of fact, Abelard leaves his readers in the same state of puzzlement concerning *dicta* as he leaves them in concerning the cause of the imposition of a general word. Although he states that the noun 'man' is predicable of many individuals because of the fact that they are all alike in being a man, he nevertheless maintains that this state of being a man is not a thing of any kind (*G* 19, 21).

If we compare Abelard's conception of the bearers of truth and falsity to the Aristotelian view as it was summarized in 3.6, the most striking difference is found to lie in what we might call the autonomy of the Abelardian *dictum*. Whereas Aristotle gives a definite priority to the *doxa* as the thought-content believed and clearly regards that which is asserted, in so far as he considers it at all, as a thought-content or belief expressed in words, Abelard pays hardly any attention to the content of the composite act of thinking which is associated with a *propositio* and certainly does not make it the primary bearer of truth and falsity of which the *dictum* would be only a special case, namely the thought-content made known by verbal means. He simply leaves the *dictum* without any counterpart in the mental sphere and thereby lends it an independence which is absolutely foreign to Aristotle's conception and even to Stoic doctrine, according to which the *axiōma* is a special kind of *lekton,* a thought or complex of mental images expressed in a verbal act of asserting that something is the case.

9.5. Problems of sameness and difference

9.5.1. Abelard holds that both the *propositio* and the *intellectus* which it produces as its mental counterpart are transitory acts performed by a particular person at a particular place and time (*G* 366, 3, 6). This view is explicitly defended in connection with *Cat.* 4 a 22 (*D* 53, 11; *G* 161, 5; cf. 3.5.2). Concentrating mainly on the *propositio,* Abelard maintains that one cannot make sense of the objection that the same utterance, for example 'Socrates is seated', seems to be both true and false, unless the utterance is taken in the not unusual acceptation of those who call different utterances the same utterance on account of a similarity in form (*D* 54, 15; cf. also *D* 71, 10). This notion of an utterance-type is, however, mentioned only to be rejected. Abelard is certain that an utterance is of such a nature that the utterance which is produced while Socrates is sitting cannot be the same as the utterance which is produced after he has risen. He agrees with Aristotle's saying in *Cat.* 5 a 34 that an utterance, once it has been produced, can no longer be recaptured.

In connection with *Cat.* 4 b 32 he brings up the question how it is possible that utterances such as 'Socrates is seated' or 'Man is an animal', whose parts are never all present at the same time, yet have a signification in the sense that they produce one definite thought in the hearer's mind (*D* 68, 25; *G* 175, 10; cf. 5.1.1). Abelard's answer is that such an utterance is supposed to signify only at the moment when all its parts have been uttered. The difficulty that in this case we would be forced to attribute the signification to something which is not there any more he solves by interpreting 'The utterance signifies' along the same lines as 'A chimaera is conceivable'. Just as the latter sentence should be understood as saying that somebody has, or is able to have, the thought of a chimaera, so that nothing is ascribed to the non-existent chimaera, in the same way the sentence 'The utterance signifies' should be interpreted as saying that because of the utterance there exists now a thought in somebody's mind (Cf. also *D* 553, 20). This kind of discussion at any rate proves that the *propositio* was taken as an utterance-token. And as an utterance-token it can have only one truth-value; a *propositio* is too short-lived to admit of any change of truth-value.

9.5.2. Abelard mentions a case in which one and the same utterance-token may produce different thoughts in different hearers (*D* 54, 5). If I say 'Peter runs', one hearer may associate the proper name with one individual and another hearer may associate it with a different individual; in the one case the thought produced may be true and in the other case the thought produced may be false. Abelard does not give us any clue as to what the *dictum* of such a *propositio* is; probably it is that which the speaker intends to assert rather than that which the hearers take him to assert. This example is symptomatic of a serious shortcoming in Abelard's treatment of *dicta*: he apparently assumes that we can simply read off from the words of the *propositio* what it says or asserts. Although, of course, the intention of the speaker (which in Abelard's terminology must be the composite act of thinking that something is the case which the speaker expresses by means of the *propositio*) is very often decisive for the answer to the question what exactly the *propositio* asserts in a given case, he hardly discusses this connection between the precise nature of the *dictum* and the speaker's intention or, for that matter, factors of context and situation. We can guess that the *dictum* of such pairs of utterances as *Socrates currit* and *Socrates currens est, volo regem venire* and *opto, ut rex veniat* (*G* 327, 30, and 374, 23), *careo cappa* and *non habeo cappam* (*G* 369, 30), or *Socratem possibile est esse episcopum* and *Socrates possibiliter est episcopus* (*D* 191, 15) is the same because of the fact that the associated acts of thinking are the same. But given Abelard's view that acts of thinking are particular and fugitive, this must mean that they are the same in so far as they have the same content; and it is about this thought-content that we hear practically nothing. In general Abelard leaves us in the dark about the pertinent question when there is one *dictum* instead of two or when there are two *dicta* instead of one.

This shortage of information about the conditions of identity and difference of *dicta* makes it also impossible to give a satisfactory answer to the question when the truth-value of one and the same *dictum* remains constant and when there may occur a change of truth-values. On the one hand, Abelard recognizes necessary *consequentiae* which are true from eternity; 'If there is a man, then there is an animal', for instance, says something that has never begun to be true and will never cease to be true. On the other hand, since affirmative categorical statements cannot be true unless the things talked about exist, the truth of such *propositiones*, or rather of their *dicta*, begins and ends together with those things (*D* 279, 13). This may mean that the *dictum* of such utterance-types as 'Socrates is a man' is false when a *propositio* of that type is uttered before the birth of Socrates, true when it is uttered during his life, and false again when it is uttered after his death.

10. THE DOCTRINE OF THE *DICTUM* IN THE CENTURY AFTER ABELARD

In this chapter I shall consider some treatises on logic which contain views about the signification of the *propositio* that are closely akin to the theory developed by Abelard. The treatises discussed date from the period between the middle of the twelfth century and the beginning of the thirteenth century and have recently been edited for the first time by L. M. De Rijk. In general I shall refer to De Rijk's edition without specifying the individual treatises concerned[1]. An exception, however, will be made for the so-called *Ars Meliduna,* a most interesting text which was probably written between 1154 and 1180 by a French master who belonged to the school of Melun and taught at Paris, on the Mont Sainte Geneviève[2].

10.1. The statement-making utterance

10.1.1. The treatises with which we are concerned follow traditional lines in defining the *propositio* or statement-making utterance as a kind of *oratio perfecta.* An *oratio* is a complex of sounds significant by convention some part of which is significant in separation. The distinction between an incomplete and a complete *oratio* is made according to different criteria. A group of words is a complete utterance if it produces a perfect thought in the hearer's

---

[1] These references are made by page and line in the second part of *Logica modernorum,* Vol. II, Assen, 1967.

[2] Large excerpts from the *Ars Meliduna* are given in the first part of *Logica modernorum,* Vol. II, Assen, 1967, pp. 292–390. They will be referred to by means of the abbreviation *AM,* followed by page. Other references to the first part will be marked by the Arabic figure for one, followed by page.

mind (17, 21; 79, 7; 113, 24); a complete utterance can be used as an independent unit of speech (151, 26; 181, 26; cf. 17, 17); it consists of a noun and a verb (17, 10; 382, 3; 419, 15); it always contains a finite verb (358, 29); it cannot serve as a subject or as a predicate (185, 5). In one passage (467, 21) a complete utterance is defined as a group of words in which there is neither too much nor too little, a definition which is reminiscent of the Stoic definitions by means of the verb *apartizein* that were mentioned at the end of 4.2.3.

As to the classification of kinds of complete utterances, we usually find the Boethian division into five species (18, 12; 79, 10; 113, 27; 151, 28; 181, 31; 467, 25). But it is noteworthy that we also meet with passages in which the division of the kinds of speech is obviously confused with the classification of the moods of the verb: the *oratio interrogativa* is omitted and to the *oratio indicativa, imperativa, deprecativa,* and *optativa* an *oratio coniunctiva* is added (358, 30), and even an *oratio infinitiva* (419, 19). This confusion of kinds of speech and utterances in different moods of the verb was continued by such influential authors as William of Sherwood and Peter of Spain in the thirteenth century, and this fact no doubt contributed to the eventual atrophy of such philosophical inquiry into the nature and classification of kinds of speech as there had been in the past.

10.1.2.   The usual designation for the statement-making utterance is *propositio.* Occasionally this term is also used for the first premiss (98, 15) or for premiss in general, in which case it is explained as *pro alio positio,* as something assumed in order to get the conclusion (1, p. 452). In the sense of a statement-making utterance the *propositio* is sometimes defined as an *enuntiatio alicuius de aliquo vel alicuius ab aliquo* (119, 5) or as that which can be propounded in a disputation with the purpose of proving it or proving something else by means of it (123, 1). But most frequently it is elucidated by the Boethian definition *oratio verum vel falsum significans.* As we saw in 9.3.4, one may be tempted to apply this definition to the phrase *Socratem currere* as well as to the statement *Socrates currit.* This temptation is harmless as long as one realizes that the meaning of *significans* used in connection with the phrase *Socratem currere* is different from its meaning in connection with the statement *Socrates currit*: as Abelard points out (*Dialectica* 150, 13), the phrase is a kind of name of the *dictum,* while the statement asserts the *dictum.* In order to eliminate this ambiguity of *significans* some authors proposed to add to it in the definition of the *propositio* the qualification *indicando* or *cum indicatione,* thereby making it equivalent to *oratio verum vel falsum indicans,* understood in the sense of a combination of words asserting, by means of the indicative mood of the verb, something which is either true or false (382, 8; 468, 13; 485, 25; cf. *AM* 320 and 359). According to one of these authors Boethius did not feel any need to add such a qualification because he took *oratio* in the narrow sense of a complete utterance (468, 19), an explanation which is no doubt wrong.

Actually, it even seems wrong to tie the activity of asserting in such an exclusive way to the indicative mood; it would be preferable to say, with Abelard, that *significare* here just means the same as *indicare,* in the sense of *dicere, enuntiare, proponere,* and to admit that an utterance occasionally asserts that something is the case even though it contains a verb in a mood other than the indicative. The examples of such utterances given by Abelard are sentences of the type 'If you had been here, then my brother would not have died' and 'I would rather eat than fast' (*mallem comedere quam ieiunare*; *Glosses* 374, 36, and 375, 4; cf. 9.2.2). In contrast with Abelard, the author of the *Ars Meliduna* is of the opinion that such utterances as *ego vellem habere centum marcas* ('I would like to have a hundred pounds'; *AM* 320−321) are never statement-making utterances, but rather wishes, just as *utinam haberem centum marcas*. Master Alberic of Paris went even farther and evidently considered the indicative *ego volo legere* ('I wish to read') as a wish rather than as a statement, although he admits that it can sometimes be uttered to signify something true (19, 10). As for conditionals in the subjunctive mood, the author of the *Ars Meliduna* holds that the antecedent and consequent are not *propositiones,* but expressions doing duty for *propositiones* (*aliqua loco propositionum sumpta*; *AM* 321); the same view was taken by Alberic of Paris (De Rijk 1966 a: 14). In this connection it is also noteworthy that the author of the *Ars Meliduna* is aware of a difference in assertive force between *propositiones* uttered by themselves and *propositiones* in so far as they are part of compound statements. Uttered by itself, a categorical *propositio* both signifies an inherence and says that the predicate inheres in the subject (*significat et enuntiat*); as part of a compound statement, however, it only signifies an inherence (*tantum significat*), without saying that it is so (*AM* 342).

Further, the definition of a *propositio* as an *oratio verum vel falsum significans* is said not to apply to an ambiguous utterance (*multiplex propositio*). For an ambiguous utterance does not assert something which is either true or false, but it can be interpreted as asserting at least two things, either both true or both false or one true and one false (19, 15). The word *propositio* is here apparently used in a broad sense, in which it may stand for an ambiguous utterance, as well as in a narrower sense, either for an utterance-type in so far as it is used to make one definite statement or, more likely, for an unambiguous utterance-token. The same author discusses also *propositiones* of the type *ego disputo, tu disputas,* in which the subject is a demonstrative or personal pronoun or, as we might say, an indexical word. One might be inclined to call them *propositiones* in the sense of the definition, because at one time they assert something true and at another time something false. But the author points out that they signify nothing if they are uttered without reference to a thing present (*absque demonstratione rei praesentis*) or if one sees them written somewhere. By themselves, without context or situation, they are not sufficient to assert something, although they are capable of being used to make a statement which is either true or false (19, 19).

At the end of 7.1.2 we saw that according to Martianus Capella a *proloquium* such as *omnis homo animal est* does not cease to be true if the order of the noun and the verb, or rather of the subject-term and the predicate-term, is reversed, so that we get *animal est omnis homo*; and we noted that Martianus does not make it quite clear whether in such cases there are two sentences or only one. Now it is remarkable that the author of the *Ars Meliduna,* in discussing the effects of transposition, states that *necesse est deum esse* and *deum necesse est esse, Socrates aliquem hominem videt* and *Socrates videt aliquem hominem, a Socrate curritur* and *curritur a Socrate* are in each case the same *propositio* (*AM* 352). This is the more remarkable, because elsewhere (*AM* 338) he says that *homo albus* and *albus homo* are not the same terms. Moreover, he explicitly maintains that in cases in which one transposes the *propositiones* which are the disjuncts of a disjunction or the conjuncts, one affirmative and one negative, of a conjunction, the disjunctive and conjunctive *propositiones* and that which they assert do not remain the same, although they are logically equivalent (*AM* 348). With regard to the above-mentioned pairs one would rather expect that each time there are two *propositiones* which mean the same, in the spirit of Aristotle, *De int.* 20 b 1 (Cf. 3.4.2). Perhaps this is just what the author means by *eadem propositio.* At any rate there does not seem to be any reason to assume that the author uses *eadem propositio* in the sense of the same mental *propositio*. In the treatises with which we are concerned the topic of the threefold *oratio* is hardly mentioned. In a few passages a distinction is made, in connection with the enthymeme, between a *propositio* which is actually uttered and a *propositio* which exists only in the mind. The enthymeme itself is explained as an *argumentatio mentalis* (363, 15; 488, 3).

10.2. That which is asserted

10.2.1. That which is asserted by a *propositio* is commonly referred to by the terms *dictum* and *significatum,* in the sense in which they are used by Abelard, but also by a term which is not found in Abelard's writings, namely *enuntiabile.* On the one hand, there is evidence that the three terms were regarded as synonyms; it is explicitly stated that the *dictum* or *significatum* of a *propositio* and the *enuntiabile* are the same (152, 6; 208, 16). On the other hand, there are also indications that at least originally the term *enuntiabile* had a meaning that was slightly different from that of the two other words. The author of the *Ars Meliduna* identifies *enuntiabilia* with *propositionum significata,* but at the same time he points out that they are so called because they are either in fact asserted or capable of being asserted. He is still quite clearly aware of the nuance of potentiality in the meaning of *enuntiabile;* an *enuntiabile* may be true even if there happens to be no language in which to express it (*AM* 357, 362, 384).

As far as I know, the oldest treatise in which the word *enuntiabile* occurs as a more or less technical term is Adam of Balsham's *Ars disserendi,* which dates from 1132[3]. The author, who taught logic in Paris, deals primarily with question (*interrogatio*) and statement (*enuntiatio*); the *enuntiatio* is defined as *veri vel falsi dictio ut ad disserendum,* the assertion of something which is either true or false with the purpose of starting a disputation (ed. Minio-Paluello p. 8, 21). Now Adam introduced the term *interrogabile* for that which is capable of being asked, even if it is not actually asked (ed. Minio-Paluello p. 92, 18). Although unfortunately the part in which he discusses the *enuntiatio* is lost, the passages in which the term *enuntiabile* occurs in the extant text give the impression that the *enuntiabile* stands in the same relation to the *enuntiatio* as the *interrogabile* to the *interrogatio.* We may, therefore, surmise, that Adam, who seems to have been rather fond of words ending in *-bile,* coined the word *enuntiabile* as a technical term with the meaning of that which is assertable; that those schools which used the Abelardian terms *dictum* and *significatum* gradually came to adopt Adam's term as well, while perhaps the school of the *Parvipontani,* to which Adam belonged, added the Abelardian terms to its vocabulary; and that in this process the nuance of potentiality in the meaning of *enuntiabile* was often lost.

The author of the *Tractatus Anagnini* (218, 4) draws a distinction between *significantia* and *significata* and divides the *significata* into the *dicibile,* which is signified by an *oratio,* and the *praedicabile,* which is signified by a

---

[3] Edited by L. Minio-Paluello, *Twelfth Century Logic* I, Rome, 1956.

word. He does not discuss the *dicibile,* so that it remains obscure what exactly he means by it. As he is speaking of an *oratio* in general and as he elsewhere uses the word *dictum* in the normal sense of that which is asserted by a *propositio,* it is certainly not evident that he uses *dicibile* as a synonym of *dictum* or *enuntiabile.* There are only two further places where *dicibile* is found. In the *Ars Meliduna (AM* 361) it is stated that it sometimes happens that someone says what Socrates is; thus it can be said what Socrates is, and so it is a *dicibile* and therefore an *enuntiabile.* Elsewhere (1, p. 470) *dicibile* is used as a synonym of *praedicabile;* the predicate can be said of many subjects. From these meagre data we may perhaps conclude that even if *dicibile* was occasionally used as a synonym of *enuntiabile,* it never became a technical term on the same footing as *enuntiabile, dictum,* and *significatum.*

In one passage (485, 30) the *enuntiabile* or *dictum* is defined as the *sententia complexa* which is signified both by a *propositio* of the type *Socrates currit* and by a designation of the type *Socratem currere,* in the first case with assertive force, in the second without assertive force. A little further on (487, 1) the author who gives this definition explains the word *ratio* which occurs in the phrase *ratio rei dubiae faciens fidem* (Cf. 8.1.2 and the end of 9.4.2) as the *sententia complexa* which is signified by the *propositiones* that serve as premisses in proving a conclusion. Although he uses also the word *argumentatio* for the *ratio rei dubiae faciens fidem,* it is clear that he is actually speaking of the *argumentum* which, according to him, is the *virtus* and *sententia* expressed by the premisses, while the *argumentatio* in the proper sense is the compound utterance consisting of the premisses and the conclusion. It is obvious from the context that the word *sententia,* together with *virtus* and *vis,* stems from the passages in Boethius where the difference between *argumentatio* and *argumentum* is discussed. We saw that Abelard identified the *argumentum* with the *dicta* of the premisses. In our treatises too the *argumentum* is connected with the *dictum* in various ways (164, 13; 193, 10; *AM* 375). It is, therefore, plausible to assume that in the *ratio-*passage *sententia* is taken in the same sense as *dictum* or *enuntiabile,* as a thought-content which is asserted; and that this thought-content is called complex because the *argumentum* usually consists of the *dicta* of more than one premiss. In that case it has to be supposed that the author confuses that which is asserted by a *propositio* in general with the complex thought-content which constitutes an *argumentum.*

10.2.2. It is not surprising that after the mainly negative answer that Abelard had given to the question of what a *dictum* actually is, the discussion about this point did not come to an end. The author of the *Ars Meliduna*

(*AM* 357) subjects the issue to a thorough examination and starts with giving three opinions which he rejects. The first theory holds that *enuntiabilia* are acts of thinking produced by the words of a *propositio* (*intellectus per voces conceptos*). Such an act of thinking is a *proprietas animae*, a particular state of the soul, and as such a something (*aliquid*). Against this psychologistic view the author adduces the following objections. Every falsehood, being an act of thinking, would be a something. Further, it is not clear with which of infinitely many particular acts of thinking such an *enuntiabile* as *Socratem esse hominem* should be identified. If we suppose that the designation of the *enuntiabile* stands for any one of the infinitely many acts of thinking, then the statement *Socratem esse hominem est verum* will be indefinite and therefore not the contradictory of *Socratem esse hominem non est verum*. Moreover, when all men are asleep, nothing will be true, not even that all men are asleep or that God exists; for if there are no acts of thinking, there will be no *enuntiabilia* and thus no truths. That God exists will frequently begin and cease to be true, according as the acts of thinking come and go. Finally, the act of thinking produced by the words *Socrates est homo* is composite; it consists of three partial acts of thinking. Now if the composite act is true, it is either true in each of its parts (*totus*) or not. But it cannot be said to be true in each of its parts, since the act of thinking produced by a single word is not something true; therefore it is not true in its totality and consequently should not be accepted in its totality.

According to the second theory, which is reminiscent of Aristotle's view in *Metaphysics* 1051 b 1, a true *enuntiabile* such as *Socratem esse album* is nothing but the circumstance that the property of being white belongs to Socrates, while a false *enuntiabile* such as *Socratem esse asinum* is nothing but the circumstance that the property of being an ass does not belong to Socrates. A truth is the *compositio* of the predicate with the subject, a falsehood is the *divisio* of the one from the other. As every *divisio* is a state (*proprietas*), this theory too would have the consequence that a falsehood is a something. Furthermore, it may be asked in which subject or subjects such a *compositio* or *divisio* is, whether in the terms or in their significates or in the person who asserts the *enuntiabile*. Whichever of these possibilities is chosen, in each case we are confronted with an absurdity, namely that terms or their significates or the persons who assert the *enuntiabile* are something true or false; for a subject can always be denominated after the characteristics which it possesses.

After mentioning a third opinion according to which 'the true' and 'the false' are only elements in certain manners of speaking, without any correlate in reality, the author comes to the view preferred by his teacher and presumably by himself. *Enuntiabilia* are neither substances nor qualities but they have a peculiar being of their own (*habent suum esse per se*); they are grasped only by reason and thinking and are inaccessible to the senses. The author ascribes to *enuntiabilia* practically the same kind of being as he had assigned to universals (*AM* 307–308): universals are not in the sensible things, but they are a kind of abstract entities which are thought in connection with sensible things and in which sensible things participate. More or less the same view about *enuntiabilia* is found in the *Ars Burana* (208, 16): an *enuntiabile*, which we can grasp only by thought, is called an *extrapraedicamentale*, not because it does not belong to any category at all, but because it belongs to a category which is not one of the ten distinguished by Aristotle, but forms a separate category of *enuntiabilia*. The author of the *Ars Meliduna* adds an interesting remark about the phrase *audiri verum*. Strictly speaking, only a *propositio* by means of which something true or false is asserted, and not that which is asserted itself, can be heard; on the other hand, only the *enuntiabile*, not the *propositio* connected with it, can be asserted. In accordance with this difference of category, the question whether there is only one *propositio* heard or more than one cannot be answered by taking account of the number of the *enuntiabilia* asserted: if one person hears the words *Tullius est candidus* and the other the words *Marcus est albus*, they have heard different *propositiones* (in spite of the fact that they have understood one and the same *enuntiabile*). As the author puts it: *non secundum pluralitatem vel singularitatem enuntiabilium attenditur singularitas auditorum vel pluralitas*. He has grasped at least one side of the difference in arithmetics between utterances and things asserted: the criteria for counting *propositiones* are different from the criteria for counting *enuntiabilia*.

The author of the *Ars Meliduna* concludes his survey of the opinions concerning the ontological status of the *enuntiabile* with a rather pessimistic reflection. Although it has become more or less clear what *enuntiabilia* are not, their actual nature is hard to ascertain. Only things that are accessible to the senses can be fully known; in the case of such abstract entities as *enuntiabilia* we have no sure means of deciding which of the many views about their nature is correct. His skepticism leads him to say that even if *enuntiabilia* became visible and were all exposed to view, nobody could answer the question which of them is the *enuntiabile* that God exists.

10.2.3. The passage (486, 4) in which it is stated that truth and falsity are in the *enuntiabile* as in their subject and in the *propositio* as in a sign (of the *enuntiabile*) seems to be representative of the general view about the bearers of truth and falsity. *Dicta, significata, enuntiabilia* are the bearers of truth and falsity in the primary sense, while *propositiones* are true or false only in so far as they are used to assert something true or false; although it should be noted that in one passage of the *Ars Meliduna* (*AM* 361) a true or false *enuntiabile* is characterized as that which is signified by a true or false *propositio*. Apart from *enuntiabilia* and *propositiones*, the *intellectus* or acts of thinking produced by statement-making utterances are bearers of truth and falsity (*AM* 384); they are, however, mentioned only once or twice.

Although *dicta* or *enuntiabilia*, being the fundamental bearers of truth and falsity, are no doubt also the actual terms in logical relations, in practice logic is done mainly by means of *propositiones*. In the *Tractatus Anagnini* (236, 24) an interesting distinction is drawn between several ways of formulating logical laws. The law of the conversion of negative universal statements, for example, may be expressed in the following manners: 'No man is a stone; therefore no stone is a man' (*loquendo de rebus*); or 'The *propositio* "No man is a stone" is true; therefore the *propositio* "No stone is a man" is true' (*loquendo de propositionibus*); or 'It is true that no man is a stone; therefore it is true that no stone is a man' (*loquendo de dicto*).

Enuntiabilia are also the fundamental bearers of the modalities (209, 3). It is noteworthy that in the *Dialectica Monacensis* (478, 27) a distinction is drawn between the expressions *verum* and *falsum* on the one hand and the expressions *possibile, impossibile, necessarium, contingens* on the other. Although a *propositio* such as *Socratem currere est verum* has a superficial similarity to *Socratem currere est possibile*, in reality it is not a modal statement at all. Unlike what is found in the case of a genuine modal statement, there is no substantial difference between *Socrates currit* and *Socratem currere verum est*; the latter says neither less nor more than the former.

Just as there are true and false, possible, impossible, and necessary *enuntiabilia*, there are also those about the present, those about the past, and those about the future (209, 1). This must mean that at least some logicians regarded the things asserted by such utterances as 'Caesar will be killed', 'Caesar is killed', and 'Caesar was killed' as different *enuntiabilia*. In the next chapter we shall see that this point became a cause of heated debate in theological circles.

Finally, I want to call attention to a passage in the *Ars Meliduna* (*AM* 362–363) where the *enuntiabilia* or *dicta* of so-called *propositiones implicitae* are discussed. A *propositio* is called *implicita* if it contains, in addition to its principal signification, the content of another *propositio*; for example, *Socrates est aliquid quod currit* ('Socrates is something that runs') includes *aliquid currit* ('Something runs'). One might also say that a *propositio implicita* can be resolved into two *propositiones*; *aliquis homo qui desiit esse, non est* ('Some man who has ceased to exist does not exist'), for instance, can be resolved into *aliquis homo desiit esse* and *ipse non est* (Cf. *AM* 354; 1, p. 34; 159, 24; 268, 31). As the author of the *Ars Meliduna* remarks, it would be better to call the embedding or containing sentence *implicans* and the embedded or contained sentence *implicita*. Now it is contended that the *enuntiabile* or *dictum* of a containing *propositio* becomes nugatory (*nugatorium*) if the contained *propositio* ceases to be true. *Socratem diligere filium suum*, the *dictum* belonging to the containing sentence *Socrates diligit filium suum* ('Socrates loves his son'), becomes nugatory when Socrates ceases to have a son. It is clear from the context that 'nugatory' means the same as 'neither-true-nor-false'. If the sentence 'Socrates loves his son' is uttered at a moment when Socrates has no son, the *dictum* is neither true nor false, but simply incongruous. There are, therefore, *enuntiabilia* which, according to the circumstances in which they are asserted (*iuxta rei variationem*), can repeatedly begin and cease to be either-true-or-false. Apparently, the *enuntiabile* is here taken as belonging to the utterance-type; the sentence as such is supposed to assert something, but that which is asserted by the sentence as such does not have a definite truth-value unless certain presuppositions are fulfilled. Only if the situation is such that the thing asserted by the sentence in general fits into it does the *enuntiabile* come to have a definite truth-value; otherwise it does not make contact with features of reality which are capable of rendering it either true or false.

10.3.   The designation of that which is asserted

As we saw in 9.3.4, one of the ways in which Abelard interpreted such a statement as *verum est Socratem currere* was to consider the phrase *Socratem currere* as a kind of name of that which is asserted by the utterance *Socrates currit*. This view (*Dialectica* 150, 13) was generally taken over by the authors of the treatises we are now discussing. They call phrases of the type *Socratem currere* the *appellatio dicti* ('the designation of that which is asserted') and regard them as a kind of proper name (*quasi proprium nomen*; 209, 8) standing for the *dictum* as 'Socrates' stands for the philosopher of that name. The *appellatio dicti* can be derived from a *propositio* according to certain recipes: by turning the *propositio* into an accusative and infinitive phrase or by prefixing the word *quod* ('that') to it, either leaving the verb in the indicative or changing the indicative into the subjunctive (152, 9; 209, 24; 485, 32; *AM* 361; 1, p. 457).

According to a remarkable passage in the *Ars Burana* (210, 24) there are not only designations of particular *enuntiabilia,* with approximately the force of proper names, but also designations of classes of *enuntiabilia,* with the function of common names (*appellativorum nominum*). Just as the proper name is derived from the *propositio,* the general designations are derived from questions. From every direct question an indirect question may be formed: from *quis homo currit?* ('Which man runs?'), for example, *quis homo currat* ('(It is asked) which man runs') or from *estne Socrates homo?* ('Is Socrates a man?') *an sit Socrates homo* ('(It is asked) if Socrates is a man'). Now the indirect specific question of the type *quis homo sit albus* is said to be the common name of all those *enuntiabilia* each of which forms a true answer to the direct question *quis homo est albus?* Among the members of this desig-nated class are such *enuntiabilia* as *Socratem esse album, Platonem esse al-bum,* and *Ciceronem esse album.* It follows that the statement *quis homo sit albus enuntiatur* ('It is said which man is white') is indefinite (just like *homo iustus est*). In contrast with an indirect specific question, which is the com-mon name of only those *enuntiabilia* that are true answers to the corre-sponding direct question, an indirect yes-or-no question is the common name of both the true and the false answers. *An Socrates sit homo,* for instance, is the general designation of a class of *enuntiabilia* of which not only *Socratem esse hominem* but also *Socratem non esse hominem* is a member.

At the same time, such phrases as *quis homo sit albus* and *an Socrates sit homo* can be regarded as a kind of proper name of the *interrogabile* that is signified by such *interrogativae orationes* as *quis homo est albus?* and *estne Socrates homo?,* in the same way as *Socratem esse album* is a kind of proper name of the *enuntiabile* that is signified by the *enuntiativa oratio* of the form *Socrates est albus.* In 10.2.1 we saw that Adam of Balsham had introduced the notion of the *interrogabile* as the content of an *interrogatio* and the notion of an *enuntiabile* as the content of an *enuntiatio*; it was, therefore, only natural to parallel the designation of the *enuntiabile* with a designation of the *interrogabile.* The phrase *quis homo sit albus,* then, plays a double part: it is the proper name of the *interrogabile* belonging to the question *quis homo est albus?* and it is the common name of the *enuntiabilia* of those *propositiones* which give a true answer to that question. It should be noted that the author of the *Ars Meliduna* rejects the distinction between *enuntia-bilia* and *interrogabilia*; for him every *enuntiabile* is an *interrogabile* (*AM* 361).

The conception of the phrase *quis homo sit albus* as the common name of a class of *enuntiabilia* is probably based upon the following consideration. The true answers to the question *quis homo est albus?* can be seen as the things asserted by means of such *propositiones* as *Socrates est albus, Plato est albus, Cicero est albus.* If someone utters one of these *propositiones* in answer to the question, we can characterize this event by saying *enuntiatur (dicitur, scitur) Socratem esse album* ('It is asserted (stated, known) by somebody that Socrates is white'). In every case in which a true answer is given we can also say *enuntiatur (dicitur, scitur) quis homo sit albus* ('It is asserted (stated, known) which man is white' or, in other words, 'Somebody gives or knows the correct answer to the question which man is white'). The specific *enuntiabilia* or *dicta* or *scita* which are the complements of the verbal forms *enuntiatur, dicitur, scitur* in the separate cases can all be considered instances of the general characterization 'that which is stated or known as the correct answer to the question *quis homo sit albus*'. Because in Latin for every case in which *enuntiatur (dicitur, scitur)* is followed by a different true answer exactly the same verb can be followed by the phrase *quis homo sit albus* (a construction, it should be noted, which seems to be rejected as ungrammatical by the author of the *Ars Meliduna*; *AM* 361), it is a natural step to regard the phrase *quis homo sit albus* as a kind of name of all the different *enuntiabilia* for which it can be substituted.

11. PRELIMINARIES TO THE FOURTEENTH CENTURY DEBATE

The best known treatises on logic from the thirteenth century — William of Sherwood's *Introductiones in logicam,* Peter of Spain's *Summulae logicales,* Roger Bacon's *Summulae dialectices,* the commentaries on *De interpretatione* by Albert the Great and Thomas Aquinas — however interesting they may be from other points of view, contain very little news concerning the topic of the bearers of truth and falsity. Outside the narrow bounds of logic, however, there were some developments which are both remarkable in themselves and worthy of attention in connection with the further history of our theme in the fourteenth century. Partly, these developments were prompted by the efforts to find a solution for certain difficulties regarding such theological matters as the object of faith and the immutability of God's knowledge. This field was explored for the first time by Chenu in two very instructive articles (1934 and 1936). It will be my first concern in this chapter. Next, I shall deal with some terminological questions, one related to certain meanings of the word *iudicium* and one related to some new aspects of the so-called inner speech.

11.1. The object of faith

11.1.1. In his exegesis of the gospel according to St. John 10, 8 (*In Johannis Evangelium tractatus* XLV, 9, ed. Migne 35, 1722) Augustine points out that before the coming of Christ our fathers believed that he would be born of a virgin, would suffer, would rise from the grave, and would ascend to heaven, whereas those who live after the coming of Christ believe that he was born of a virgin, suffered, rose from the grave, and ascended to heaven. Notwithstand-

177

ing these differences in the tenses of the verbs, however, that which is believed is the same for all believers: *tempora variata sunt, non fides*. The same
point is made in *De nuptiis et concupiscentia* II, 11 (ed. Migne 44, 450):
although what is believed about Christ is worded in different ways by those
who express their belief before and after his coming, the content remains
exactly the same.

It is to this doctrine of Augustine that Peter Lombard appeals in his gloss
on St. Paul's second epistle to the Corinthians 13 (*habentes autem eundem
spiritum fidei*; ed. Migne 192, 33), followed by an anonymous author of the
end of the twelfth century whose *Quaestiones in epistulas Pauli* have been
transmitted under the name of Hugh of Saint Victor (ed. Migne 175,
546–547). Hugh of Saint Victor himself had discussed Augustine's doctrine
in his *De sacramentis* I, 10, 6–7 (ed. Migne 176, 335–336, 340). It is evident
from these passages that, on the one hand, there was agreement concerning
the sameness of that which was believed by the *antiqui* and that which was or
is believed by the *moderni*. On the other hand, it seemed questionable whether such expressions as *Christum nasciturum esse* and *Christum natum esse*
which appear to mean clearly different things could be held to contain the
identical content of the article of faith. The problem, then, was how to
explain the identity of the articles of faith in spite of the apparent differences
in the way they are expressed.

11.1.2. One answer to the question of what the article of faith actually is
came to be called the *res* theory (*articulus est res*). There are three variants of
this theory. The weakest variant holds that the *antiqui* and the *moderni* can
be said to have the same belief because their faith is about the same things[1].
The second version, which is found in Prevostin of Cremona's *Summa theologica* (Cf. Chenu 1934: 131), identifies the articles of faith with the *res* or
eventus – for instance, Christ's birth, passion, resurrection, and ascension.
The word *eventus,* used by Prevostin as a synonym of *res,* together with the
examples given, suggests that the things with which the articles of faith are
identified are the actual events or the facts as they belong to the objective
world. Now one might expect that the things taken in this sense have a
certain complexity, the complexity typical of events and facts in contrast
with things in a stricter sense of the word. But in the third variant of the *res*
theory the *res* is considered rather as an *incomplexum,* as something that in

---

[1] This view was held by Robert of Melun in his *Quaestiones de divina pagina,* by the
anonymous author of the *Quaestiones in epistulas Pauli,* and by Geoffrey of Poitiers in
his *Summa theologica*; the relevant texts are quoted by Chenu (1934: 129, 130, 131).

any case does not have the complexity of the *enuntiabile* which is regarded as the object of faith by rival theories. In their commentaries on Peter Lombard's *Sentences* III, Dist. 24, Bonaventure (art. 1, q. 3) and Peter of Tarantasia (art. 3) mention some arguments which the defenders of the *res* or *incomplexum* as the object of faith put forward. In the first place, as the articles of faith are the truth about God and God is absolutely simple, the object of faith cannot be complex. This is confirmed by the fact that the Apostles' Creed begins with the sentence *credo in deum omnipotentem.* Secondly, the faith of the believers who live in this world has the same object as the future vision which they will enjoy in heaven. The object of that vision, which is a simple intuition of the highest light, is certainly not complex; therefore the object of faith must be an *incomplexum.* Thirdly, the theological virtues of faith, hope, and charity have the same object; but the object of hope and charity is something which is not complex; therefore the object of faith is an *incomplexum* too. Fourthly, according to Aristotle, *De anima* 430 b 1, a *complexio intellectuum* is connected with time. But the articles of faith cannot be determined by time; otherwise very few people would have believed that Christ was suffering, since only very few knew about it at the time when it took place. Therefore, the articles of faith are *incomplexa.* Finally, faith is about the things themselves rather than about the *enuntiabilia,* since the truth of things is the cause of the truth of *enuntiabilia.*

Against the theory that the articles of faith are *res* or *incomplexa* arguments of the following kind are mentioned by Bonaventure and Peter of Tarantasia. Believing is thinking with assent (*cogitare cum assensione*); now the proper object of assent is an *enuntiabile* or *complexum*; therefore the object of faith is not an *incomplexum* but a *complexum.* Next, we believe something because it is true and we disbelieve something because it is false; but truth and falsity have to do with combining (*complexio*); therefore the object of the act of believing is a *complexum* or *enuntiabile.* The same conclusion follows from an examination of the opposite phenomenon of error and also from the consideration that faith is intermediate between opinion and knowledge, each of which is certainly related to *complexa.* Further, if the object of faith were a *res* or *incomplexum,* for instance the coming of Christ, there would be no difference between those who believe that the incarnation has taken place already and the heretics who believe that it is still to take place. The time of the advent makes an essential difference for the article of faith; and a *res* theory cannot do justice to this temporal aspect.

11.1.3. The arguments which are adduced against the *res* theory are at the same time reasons for adopting a *complexum* theory or *enuntiabile* theory.

Only once a third theory is mentioned. Prevostin of Cremona (Chenu 1934: 131) informs us that some identified the articles of faith with the acts of believing, with *credere nativitatem* and *credere passionem.* In that case, Prevostin remarks, there would be as many articles of faith as there are particular acts of believing; moreover, we could not say that someone believes an article of faith, because then we would have to say *iste credit credere passionem,* which is nonsense.

One of the first authors in whose works we find an *enuntiabile* theory is Peter of Poitiers. In his commentary on the *Sentences,* written about 1170 (III, 21, ed. Migne 211, 1089–1090, 1093), he says that we can indicate the articles of faith by means of such *dicta propositionum* as *Christum esse natum* and *Christum esse passum*; Abraham believed the same things but in different words, namely *Christum esse nasciturum* and *Christum esse passurum.* Appealing to Augustine he adds that there are not three kinds of faith, one about the present, one about the past, and one about the future, but that the faith of the *antiqui* and of the *moderni* is exactly the same. As we saw in 10.2.3, some logicians distinguished three sorts of *dicta* or *enuntiabilia,* those about the past, those about the present, and those about the future. If, then, the articles of faith are the *enuntiabilia* which contain different tenses of the verb and are therefore different, how can the identity of faith be explained? Several solutions to this problem were proposed.

According to Prevostin of Cremona (Chenu 1934: 131) some held that the article of faith consists of a disjunction of three different *enuntiabilia,* for example *Christum esse natum, vel nasci, vel nasciturum esse.*

Another kind of solution was suggested by the so-called *nominales.* John of Salisbury (*Metalogicon* III, 2) informs us that Bernard of Chartres defended the thesis that such words as *albedo, albet,* and *album* have a common principal signification, although they differ in *consignificatio* in so far as they belong to different word-classes. They all stand for the same quality of being white, but in different ways[2]. From other sources, for instance Bonaventure in his commentary on the *Sentences* (I, Dist. 41, art. 2, q. 2; cf. also Chenu 1936: 11 ff.), we know that in the same way it was held that *albus, alba, album,* though being different in sound and having different modes of signifying, yet form one and the same *nomen,* since they have the same principal signification. In general, the diversity of the inflected forms pertains only to differences in accidental signification; there is a constant nucleus, the *nomen*

---

[2] Cf. what Abelard says about *currit* and *cursus* : 9.1.2. Garlandus Compotista states that all the categories (*praedicamenta*) can have the same signification, but in different ways (*Dialectica*, ed. De Rijk p. 18, 6–7).

as such, which remains the same through all inflexions[3]. From this doctrine of the unity of the *nomen* the adherents of this theory were called *nominales*. Now the *nominales* applied their doctrine to the problem of the diversity of the *enuntiabilia* and the identity of the article of faith in the following way. An anonymous author of *Quaestiones*, writing around 1220 (Chenu 1936: 13), says that just as *albus, alba, album* are different sounds (*voces*) but one *nomen*, so *Christum esse passurum* and *Christum esse passum* are different *enuntiabilia* but one and the same article of faith. He adds that time according to its substance (*secundum suam substantiam*) belongs to the being of the article and that time according to its differences belongs to the being of the *enuntiabile*; that is the reason why the *enuntiabilia* vary while the article of faith remains the same. To this point we shall return in a moment. According to William of Auxerre (*Summa aurea in quattuor libros Sententiarum* III, tr. 2, cap. 2, q. 2) the *nominales* rejected the argument that, since the *enuntiabilia* have changed and the *enuntiabilia* are the articles of faith, the articles of faith have changed. In their opinion this is a fallacy of accident; its invalidity is clear from the analogous reasoning 'This adjectival name *albus* is this sound *albus*; but it is another sound than the sound *alba*; therefore it is another adjectival name'.

While the anonymous author of the *Quaestiones* makes a distinction between the different *enuntiabilia* and the identical article of faith, it is clear from the passages where, for instance, Bonaventure[4] and Thomas Aquinas[5] discuss the theory of the *nominales* that the actual doctrine was that there is only one *enuntiabile*, just as there is only one *nomen*. As the same term *enuntiabile* is used both for the different forms and for that which remains constant, it is rather difficult to state this doctrine in an unambiguous way. I shall use the term 'inflexion of an *enuntiabile*' for the varying forms. Just as the unity of the *nomen* is determined by the identical principal signification, the unity of the *enuntiabile* (*unitas enuntiabilis*) is determined, not by the sounds or the modes of signifying, but by the unity of the thing signified (*unitas rei significatae*). Three inflexions of an *enuntiabile* such as *Socratem cucurrisse, Socratem currere,* and *Socratem fore cursurum,* pronounced at different times, form one and the same *enuntiabile* because they signify the same *res* taking place at a certain time. A distinction was drawn between the

---

[3] Cf. Abelard, *Dialectica* 124–125, and also De Rijk (1967: I, 293 and 311–312).

[4] *In I Sententiarum,* Dist. 41, art. 2, q. 2, and *In III Sententiarum,* Dist. 24, art. 1, q. 3.

[5] *Quodlibeta* 4, art. 17; *In I Sententiarum,* Dist. 41, q. 1, art. 5; *Summa theologiae* I, q. 14, art. 15.

tempus significatum and the *tempus consignificatum.* The *tempus significatum* is the absolute time of the event, the *mensura rei.* This moment at which the event takes place may first lie in the future, then become present, and finally belong to the past. The *tempus consignificatum* is the relative time indicated by the tenses of the verb. Differences of *tempus consignificatum* connected with the various inflexions of an *enuntiabile* do not cause a change in the *enuntiabile* itself. On the contrary, one might say that such differences are necessary to maintain the identity of the *enuntiabile* in so far as it signifies one event taking place at a definite time. If I say today 'Socrates is running' and repeat the same words tomorrow, the *tempus significatum* will be different, and this difference brings it about that the *enuntiabile* is not the same in both cases, since the particular action referred to is not the same.

If one takes *enuntiabile* in the sense just set forth, it is obvious that an *enuntiabile* cannot have changing truth-values; once true, it is always true, and once false, it is always false. As it signifies a particular event individuated by a definite *tempus significatum,* an absolute time to which all the inflexions of the *enuntiabile* remain related by the *tempus consignificatum,* it is exactly what is needed to explain the identity of the article of faith through the different ways of expressing it according to the various positions in time occupied by the believers.

There are indications that not all those who accepted the spirit of the solution of the *nominales* were prepared to take over their somewhat cumbersome terminology. We already saw that the anonymous author of *Quaestiones* is careful to distinguish between the varying *enuntiabilia,* with their different tenses, and the one article of faith. The same distinction is kept up by his contemporary Richard Fishacre in the commentary on the *Sentences,* written towards the middle of the thirteenth century (Chenu 1934: 135–136). Fishacre also agrees with the author of *Quaestiones* that time according to its essence belongs to the article and time according to its differences to the *enuntiabile.* Although *Christum esse natum in a, Christum esse nasciturum in a,* and *Christum nasci in a* are three *enuntiabilia* because of the differences in time indicated by the tenses of the verb, they are the same article of faith. For the article of faith is not the *enuntiabile* but rather the truth that remains the same through the variations of the *enuntiabilia,* which in spite of the different tenses are all three about exactly the same absolute time, namely *a.* It seems clear that both authors mean by the time according to its substance or essence the absolute date of the event concerned, which individuates the article of faith as such, and by the time according to its differences the *tempus consignificatum,* which is typical of the indexical tenses of the verb in the *enuntiabilia.*

Other than purely terminological objections were brought against the doctrine of the strict *nominales*. From Bonaventure[6] and Thomas Aquinas[7] we learn that the thesis that *Christum nasci, Christum esse nasciturum,* and *Christum esse natum* are the same *enuntiabile* because all three signify the same *res,* namely the *nativitas Christi,* was rejected on the following grounds. First of all, the doctrine is incompatible with what Aristotle says in *Cat.* 4 a 22: the same utterance may be true at one moment and false at another (Cf. 3.5.2). Next, although for the grammarian *albus, alba, album* may be one *nomen,* for the logician who considers the *nomen* as a significant sound they are three different *nomina.* Moreover, it is incorrect to say that an *enuntiabile* signifies a *res*; it rather signifies a *modus se habendi* (Cf. Abelard, *Dialectica* 160, 35), and this signified state of things is different according as the verb is in the present, past, or future tense. It is also wrong to hold that, for instance, a verb in the present tense signifies different present things at different times. Just as the noun 'man' has exactly the same signification when it is used to refer to Peter and when it is used to refer to Paul, so a verb in the present tense has exactly the same signification whether it is uttered today or tomorrow; it signifies the present in general. Similarly, an *enuntiabile* such as *te esse nasciturum* remains the same at whatever time it is uttered; consequently, the same *enuntiabile* which was formerly true is now false. It should be noted that here an *enuntiabile* is taken not only as an expression – a point to which I shall return in 11.2.2 – but as an expression-type, with a constant general meaning.

Bonaventure, who adduces the above-mentioned arguments against the theory of the *nominales,* adheres to the conception that the object of faith is a *complexum* or *enuntiabile.* But it is evident that he had to find another solution for the problem concerning the identity of the article of faith and the diversity of the *enuntiabilia* than the one suggested by the *nominales.* Both he[8] and Peter of Tarantasia[9] distinguish two kinds of *complexa* or *enuntiabilia.* An act of believing may be related to its object in an implicit way or in an explicit way. The object of implicit faith is a *dictum* that is neutral and indifferent to all time (*commune et indifferens ad omne tempus*) or, as Peter puts it, an *enuntiabile* which is indeterminate as to differences of time. Examples of such indeterminate *enuntiabilia* are *Christum incarnari, Christum incarnandum fuisse, Christum fuisse passurum.* In the first phrase

[6] *In I Sententiarum,* Dist. 41, art. 2, q. 2.
[7] *Summa theologiae* I, q. 14, art. 15.
[8] *In III Sententiarum,* Dist. 24, art. 1, q. 3.
[9] *In III Sententiarum,* Dist. 24, art. 3.

the infinitive *incarnari* was probably understood as the tenseless present. The other infinitives must have been chosen because in Latin they are used to render the consequent of a counterfactual conditional in indirect speech in such a way that there is no difference between the present and the past: *Christum fuisse passurum* may mean either 'that Christ would suffer' or 'that Christ would have suffered'. Explicit faith, on the other hand, concerns a *complexum* in so far as it is characterized by a definite specification of time and is thus a determinate *enuntiabile*, for instance *Christum incarnatum esse* or *resurrectionem futuram esse*. Such variations in the tense of the verb are, however, quite accidental to the essence of faith; they are simply consequences of the contingent position which the believer occupies in the course of time. The substance of faith does not depend upon these superficial changes and may therefore be best expressed by means of a tenseless *enuntiabile*.

A few decades earlier William of Auxerre (*Summa aurea in quattuor libros Sententiarum* III, tr. 2, cap. 2, q. 2) had offered a more pragmatistic solution. He rejects the *res* theory on the ground that such verbs as *credere* and *scire* cannot properly be combined with a designation of a thing – *iste scit domum suam* ('He knows that his house'; cf. in French 'Il sait sa maison') is simply not a well-formed expression – but require a *complexum* as their complement. On the other hand, he insists that if the articles of faith are identified with the *complexa* or *enuntiabilia*, there is an essential difference between, for example, *Christum passurum esse* and *Christum passum esse*, since the time signified by the verb belongs to the essence of the *enuntiabile* and therefore of the article of faith. What he denies, however, is that there is a difference *formaliter* or *effective* or *finaliter*. The essentially different articles of faith are the same from a formal point of view because they display the same goodness of God which is the form or perfection of the articles; and they are the same from the viewpoint of effectiveness and finality because the thought of God's goodness arouses the same fear and love of God in all those who accept the articles of faith.

Finally, Bonaventure (*In III Sententiarum*, Dist. 24, art. 1, q. 3) mentions another variant of the *enuntiabile* theory according to which the article of faith can be said to be the same in spite of the different *enuntiabilia* because there is one immutable truth on account of which all the *enuntiabilia* are assented to. As Bonaventure points out, this view has the awkward consequence that just as there is only one immutable truth which is made the unique reason for assenting to an *enuntiabile*, so there will be only one article of faith.

11.1.4. Apart from theories which are either variants of a *res* doctrine or versions of an *enuntiabile* doctrine, there were also compromises and mixtures. According to Martin of Cremona[10] the article of faith consists both in the *res* itself and in the true *dicta* put forward about it, both in Christ's passion and in a true *enuntiabile* such as *Christum esse passum*. Albert the Great[11] favours a *res* theory, but as he is convinced that it is of the nature of the article of faith to have a certain *complexio,* he rejects the view that it is an *incomplexum* and regards it rather as a *res complexa ordinata ad omne tempus*. Philip of Greve[12] draws a distinction between what can be said about the object of faith from the standpoint of the believer (*ex parte credentis*) and what can be said about it from the standpoint of that which is believed (*ex parte crediti*). Human knowledge is necessarily connected with a *complexio,* with combination and separation, and also with determinations of time; its object is therefore a true *complexum*. But the *complexio* and the determinations of time are only accidental to the article of faith as such; in its own nature it is an *incomplexum* and in future life it will be grasped immediately without any *complexio* or qualification of time. Practically the same view is defended by Thomas Aquinas[13], who adds that given the different points from which the object of faith can be considered, *ex parte ipsius rei creditae* and *ex parte credentis,* both the *res* theory and the *enuntiabile* theory may claim relative truth (*secundum aliquid utrumque est verum*).

11.2.   The immutability of God's knowledge

11.2.1. Since the second theological problem, concerning the immutability of God's knowledge, is closely akin to the problem regarding the object of faith, I shall be rather brief about it. Peter Lombard (*Sentences* I, Dist. 41) mentions the following objection against the doctrine that if God knows something at a certain time, he has always known it and will always know it. God has formerly known that this man would be born; but he does not know now that this man will be born; therefore he has known something which he does not know now. Similarly, he has known that the world would be crea-

---

[10] In his *Quaestiones theologiae,* written towards 1200; for the relevant text cf. Chenu (1934: 130–131).

[11] *In III Sententiarum,* Dist. 24, art. 5, and *Liber de sacrificio missae,* tr. 2, cap. 10, art. 12.

[12] In his *Summa quaestionum theologicarum,* written towards 1228; for the relevant texts cf. Chenu (1934: 133–134).

[13] *Summa theologiae* II, 2, q. 1, art. 2; cf. also *De veritate,* q. 14, art. 12, and *In III Sententiarum,* Dist. 24, q. 1, art. 1.

ted, but he does not know now that the world will be created. Peter's answer to this objection is that at present God knows exactly the same about this man's birth and the creation of the world as he knew about them before they took place, but that this knowledge has to be expressed by means of different words at different times. To speak about the same event we often have to vary our words; just as we refer to the same day by using the adverb *cras* ('tomorrow') when it is still to come, by using the adverb *hodie* ('today') when it has arrived, and by using the adverb *heri* ('yesterday') when it is gone. Peter is fully aware that the tenses of the verb have the same indexical character as some adverbs of time: *iste potest legere hodie* ('He is able to read today') and *iste potuit legere heri* ('He was able to read yesterday') may have the same sense (*eundem faciunt sensum*) in so far as they convey the same information. If we use the same tense of the verb and the same adverb at different times, saying for instance *iste potest legere hodie* both today and tomorrow, we assert different things (*Ibidem,* Dist. 44)[14]. Peter concludes that in the same way as the *antiqui* who believed that Christ would be born and the *moderni* who believe that he was born have the same faith in spite of the differences in the wording, God who knew, before the creation of the world, that the world would be created and who now knows that it has been created has exactly the same knowledge about the creation of the world.

Although Peter Lombard does not mention the *nominales,* his solution leads to the same result as theirs and was as a matter of fact usually identified with it. The main point of this solution is that both with regard to the identity of the article of faith and with regard to the immutability of God's knowledge we have to assume something that, once true, is always true (*semel verum, semper verum*). As we learn from Alexander Neckam (*De naturis rerum*, cap. 173, ed. Wright p. 303; cf. p. 290), dialecticians of his time defended the thesis that one and the same *enuntiabile* has been always true or has been always false. This thesis was apparently borrowed by some of the theologians who wrestled with the problem of how to reconcile the stability of certain truths with the changing ways in which they were expressed. If there is something, an *enuntiabile* as the *nominales* conceived of it, which unifies the diversity through comprehending all those expressions which are related to the same objective event, this comprehensive unit will possess the

---

[14] Peter of Poitiers (*In I Sententiarum* 14, ed. Migne 211, 849), no doubt echoing these passages in Peter Lombard, says that the tenses of the verb vary but that the article of faith and the *significatio* remain the same; one and the same truth may be expressed by different *propositiones,* with different words and tenses of the verb; on the other hand, the same *propositio,* uttered at different times, may express different things.

required characteristic of having a constant truth-value. And then we can say that once such a unit is known by God, it is always known by him.

As we noted before, the theory of the *nominales* was rejected by Bonaventure and Thomas Aquinas. Both of them are prepared to concede that the thesis that God now knows everything he knew before is false in so far as it is related to *enuntiabilia*. But that does not mean that God's knowledge is variable; for he does not know *enuntiabilia* in the way we know them, by composition and division[15].

11.2.2. Coming from the relatively clear-cut notions of *significatum, dictum,* and *enuntiabile* in Abelard and in the treatises on logic which were written between 1150 and 1225 one is bound to be somewhat puzzled by the terminology that is used in the discussions of the problems concerning the object of faith and the immutability of God's knowledge. In the *res* theory pride of place is given to the *creditum* as the *res credita* or *significata* — for instance, Christ's passion. As both the articles of faith and that which God knows are obviously truths, it is very easy to mix up that which is believed or asserted and, on the other hand, the facts that belong to the objective world and make the beliefs and assertions true. Once the step has been made from the believed or asserted contents to the facts in the world, it is again easy to confuse facts and events; from the fact that Christ suffered one moves to the actual event of his suffering. And as the event is referred to as a *res,* there is a strong temptation to characterize the event in terms appropriate to things. In their zeal to emphasize that which is signified against the signifying expressions the defenders of the *res* theory were apt to overlook the possibility of differences between that which is believed or asserted and the facts, between the facts and the actual events, and between events and things. At the same time they did not sufficiently realize that differences in the manner of knowing — for instance, between direct apprehension and knowledge by way of composition and division — and differences in the manner of verbal expression — for instance, between using such noun-phrases as *passio Christi* and using phrases of the type *Christum passum esse* — do not necessarily reflect differences in the ontological status of that which is known or indicated. It was too rashly assumed that an incomplex way of knowing or a way of verbal expression in which no predication is involved is always related to an intended object that is an *incomplexum* or *res.* The word *incomplexum* itself, moreover, is dangerously ambiguous. It may refer to a linguistic expression that is not an *oratio,* and it was apparently also used for things that are not complex.

[15] Cf. Thomas Aquinas, *Summa theologiae* I, q. 14, art. 15.

In the *enuntiabile* theory, on the other hand, there is an unmistakable tendency to consider the *dictum* and the *enuntiabile* as significant expressions rather than as that which is signified. By stressing the contrast with the *res significata* the adherents of the *enuntiabile* theory came to use the terms *dictum* and *enuntiabile* as synonyms of *complexum* and as standing for an accusative and infinitive phrase, an *oratio infinitiva*, which takes the place of an *enuntiatio* or *propositio* after verbs of knowing and believing. This is quite clear in the case of the *nominales*. Just as the *nomen* may be considered as the class of all inflected forms that have the same principal significate and is therefore itself a kind of signifying unit, so the comprehensive *enuntiabile* may be regarded as the class of all 'inflexions' that are related to the same *res significata* and is therefore itself a kind of signifying unit. And the *enuntiabilia* which are inflexions of the comprehensive *enuntiabile* are explicitly called *voces*. This is confirmed by the objections which Bonaventure adduces against the *unitas enuntiabilis* of the *nominales*: for him an *enuntiabile* is an *oratio* that can be first true and then false; it does not signify a *res* but a *modus se habendi*; an *enuntiabile* with a verb in the present tense does not signify different present things at different times but the present in general. There can be no doubt that for Bonaventure the *enuntiabile* was an *oratio infinitiva* in the sense of an expression-type. From there it was only one step to identifying the *enuntiabile* with the *enuntiatio* or *propositio*. Albert the Great speaks of a *propositio vel enuntiabile*[16]. Thomas Aquinas does not distinguish between an *enuntiabile* and an *enuntiatio*; in the same way as a *propositio* or *enuntiatio* can be a thought or an utterance, an *enuntiabile* can exist both in the mind (*in intellectu*) and as a spoken utterance (*in voce*)[17].

That *dictum* and *complexum* are used for significant expressions is not surprising in the light of what we shall find later. In the fourteenth century *complexum* is practically a synonym of *propositio* and *enuntiatio*. And in that period *dictum* hardly ever has the sense of that which is asserted; it commonly stands for an accusative and infinitive phrase. But as for *enuntiabile*, we shall see that Gregory of Rimini uses it again with much the same meaning as it had in the treatises on logic discussed in the foregoing chapter (Cf. 14.1.3).

One would have expected that both parties in the theological controversy could have reached some agreement by concentrating upon an enlarged conception of the *significatum, dictum,* or *enuntiabile* in the original sense, that is to say an asserted (believed, known) content which is not tied to an

---

[16] *In I Sententiarum,* Dist. 41, art. 6.
[17] *Summa theologiae* I, q. 16, art. 7.

expression with a definite tense of the verb, but rather remains the same through the varying ways in which, according to the changing positions in time, it is formulated by means of different tenses of the verb. What we actually find is a movement away from the intermediate thought-content towards either of two extremes: the *significatum* as the *res significata* or *credita,* the event itself interpreted as an *incomplexum* or *res*; or, on the other side, the *dictum-enuntiabile* as the signifying expression, namely an accusative and infinitive phrase or a statement-making utterance.

11.3.   Some relevant meanings of the word *iudicium*

Hitherto there has been little need to concern ourselves with the term *iudicium* ('judgment'). Up to the thirteenth century it does not play any conspicuous part in the discussions about the bearers of truth and falsity. But now it is time to call attention to some uses of the word that are connected with the problems we are examining. I shall begin with the contrast between *inventio* and *iudicium.*

11.3.1. According to Quintilian (*Institutio oratoria* III, 3, 5) some teachers of rhetoric added to the five traditional parts of their discipline – invention, arrangement, style, memorization, and delivery – a sixth branch, which was closely connected with invention and pertained to the critical examination of its products. This valuation was called *krisis* in Greek and *iudicium* in Latin. One of those who thus combined invention and critical judgment was Cicero. And it was Cicero too who transferred the pair *inventio/iudicium* from rhetoric to logic. In his *Topica* (2, 6–7) he says that a proper theory of disputation has two parts, invention and judgment. Aristotle initiated research in both fields, whereas the Stoics concentrated upon the art of judging and neglected the art of inventing. Cicero himself wants to give priority to the art of inventing and deals with it in the *Topica.*

This passage in Cicero is twice commented upon by Boethius: rather briefly in his commentary on Porphyry's introduction to the *Categories* (ed. Migne 64, 73 B), more extensively in his commentary on Cicero's *Topica* (ed. Migne 64, 1044 C). Boethius divides logic into three parts: *definitio, partitio,* and *collectio.* The third part deals with reasonings, necessary, probable, and sophistical. All three parts presuppose invention; but once the definitions, divisions, and reasonings have been discovered, they must be subjected to a critical examination in order to judge the correctness of the definitions and divisions and, in the case of a *collectio,* to discern the nature of the constituent statements and the exact way in which they are combined. In general, the heuristic phase of invention must be followed by the criticism and justification of the *iudicium*.

This doctrine of the two aspects of the theory of disputation, discovery and critical judgment, is frequently touched upon in medieval texts on logic. But it does not gain real importance until the period of the renaissance when the dialecticians, following Cicero, retighten the connections between logic and rhetoric.

11.3.2. Another nuance in the meaning of the word *iudicium,* of more direct relevance to the further history of our subject, is connected with a distinction between two ways of knowing that had already been made by Aristotle. At several places[18] he refers to a difference between the direct apprehension of non-composite objects of knowledge and a way of knowing that consists in making up a composite whole out of concepts. As Garceau shows in his excellent monograph (1968: 107 ff.), this distinction was elaborated by the Arabian philosopher Avicenna. In the Latin translation of his *Logica* we find the terms *imaginatio* and *credulitas,* meaning the same as the terms *formatio* and *fides* which occur in the Latin translation of the commentary on *De anima* composed by Averroës. It is not improbable that the Arabic terms of which these Latin words are the translations originated as the equivalents of the Stoic expressions *phantasia* and *synkatathesis.* According to Avicenna the pair *imaginatio/credulitas* indicates the difference between an act of pure comprehension which consists in putting something before the mind and, on the other hand, an act of believing that something is the case in reality (*credere ita esse*). Similar remarks are found in Algazel's *Logica,* which was translated into Latin by Dominic Gundisalvi in the first half of the twelfth century, and in *De divisione philosophiae* written by Dominic himself. In the Latin translation of Averroës' commentary on *De anima* the word *actio* is used for the apprehending and the assenting of the mind; Albert the Great speaks of *actus*; John de la Rochelle uses the word *operatio,* which then becomes the common term in Thomas Aquinas (For details cf. Garceau 1968: 103–104).

Now the important point is that Peter of Spain, in his commentary on *De anima* 430 a 6, uses for the second operation of the mind, the *compositio intellectuum,* not only the terms *credulitas* and *fides,* but also the word *iudicium.* For Peter of Spain a *iudicium* is an activity of the mind that combines concepts in a certain way, sees the conformity of this combination with reality, and consequently assents to it (Cf. Garceau 1968: 112–116).

---

[18] *De anima* 430 a 6; *Metaphysics* 1027 b 20, 1051 b 2, 1065 a 22; *De int.* 16 a 10.

This use of the word *iudicium* for the second operation of the mind was facilitated by the circumstance that some authors had already employed it as one member of the pair *receptio/iudicium* in connection with sense-perception. In his *De anima* William of Auvergne distinguishes two factors in sense-perception: the reception of a sensible form in the sense-organ and a mental act of judging or interpreting what it is. Garceau (1968: 72) thinks it likely that this conception goes back to Nemesius of Emesa's *De natura hominis* which was written around 400 and shows traces of Neoplatonic influence. Peter of Spain too uses the terms *receptio* and *iudicium*, but in contrast with William of Auvergne he does not restrict them to sense-perception; *iudicium* comes to stand for the active element in knowledge in general, adapted to the Aristotelian psychology. This modification may be due to the influence of Arabian philosophers; the pair *receptio/iudicium* occurs rather frequently in the Latin translation of Averroës' commentary on *De anima* (Cf. Garceau 1968: 93).

Thomas Aquinas frequently speaks of a trichotomy of the operations of the mind. I refer only to the first lines of his commentary on *De interpretatione* where he distinguishes between the operation which is called *indivisibilium intelligentia* and the operation that consists in an act of compounding or separating, and then adds a third operation in which the mind reasons and proceeds from the known to the unknown. This articulation is already suggested by Aristotle in such passages as the beginning of the *Prior Analytics* where *protasis*, *horos* ('term'), and *syllogismos* are mentioned in order to indicate the chief points of interest. Following these lines, Abelard says that logic is concerned with *dictiones*, *propositiones*, and *argumentationes*; the first are treated in Aristotle's *Categories* and partly in his *De interpretatione*, where the properties of *propositiones* are also discussed, while his *Topics* and *Analytics* deal with reasonings (*Glosses*, ed. Geyer p. 2, 8, and p. 111, 5). Now for the second of the three operations of the mind Thomas Aquinas, probably influenced by Peter of Spain, uses the words *iudicium* and *iudicare*[19], along with such terms as *compositio/divisio*, *credulitas*, and *fides*. He emphasizes that there can be no truth or falsity unless the mind judges that something is the case.

Finally, I shall merely mention that there is one place in William of Sherwood's *Introductiones in logicam* (ed. Grabmann p. 35, 18) where it looks as if the word *iudicium* were used in the same sense as *enuntiatio* or *propositio*. William says there that it is not necessary to take account of indefinite

[19] *De veritate*, q. 1, art. 3; *Summa theologiae* I, q. 16, art. 2; *In I Peri hermeneias* 3, 31; *In VI Metaphysicorum* 4, 1236; cf. Garceau (1968: 144).

statements, *quia simile est iudicium indefinite et particulariter* (the manuscript has *particulare*; cf. Kretzmann 1966: 30). If the adverbs *indefinite* and *particulariter* are the correct readings, this may perhaps be translated as 'because the act of judging is similar whether it is expressed in an indefinite or in a particular way'. It seems most plausible to assume that *iudicium* has here the same meaning as is found in the writings of Peter of Spain and Thomas Aquinas. It is not until later, however, that a judgment in this sense is called an *enuntiatio,* more specifically a mental one. According to Gregory of Rimini, for instance, *iudicare* is *enuntiare mentaliter quod sic est* [20].

11.4.   The inner word

11.4.1. The Peripatetic doctrine of the threefold *oratio,* which we discussed in 8.1.3, although not unknown to Abelard and the logicians of the following generations, does not at all occupy a prominent place in their works. Before it was brought to the fore again by the logicians of the fourteenth century, it had been reinforced by a similar doctrine which I shall try to outline in this paragraph. As we noted in 7.1.3, Augustine, in his *De dialectica* 5, draws a distinction among *verbum, dicibile, dictio,* and *res,* a distinction that may be paralleled with the distinction among *sonus, intellectus* or *notio, nomen,* and *res* which he makes in *De quantitate animae* 32 (ed. Migne 32, 1071–1072). In both cases the complex of sounds, the *verbum* or *sonus,* is contrasted with the thought which the speaker has in his mind before he expresses it in language. Now it is remarkable that in Augustine's works the word *verbum* gradually underwent a change of meaning that finally brought it to a sense which is diametrically opposed to the one it has in *De dialectica.* I shall illustrate the result of this process, which is chiefly due to the influence of certain metaphysical and theological speculations about the *logos,* by means of some passages in his treatise *De trinitate,* especially IX, 7, and XV, 10–12, 21, to which later authors usually appeal.

Augustine refers there to a knowledge of things which we generate by a kind of inner speech and retain in our mind as an inner word. This inner word which we say in our heart is soundless and does not belong to Greek or Latin or any other particular language. When we speak to others we make use of vocal sounds or some other material signs in order to produce in the hearer's mind the same inner word as remains in our own mind. Letters have been invented for communication with persons who are absent; they are signs of

[20] *In I Sententiarum, Prologus,* q. 1, art. 3.

sounds, which in their turn are signs of what we think and know. Further, Augustine draws a clear distinction between the *verbum* as a *locutio cordis* which does not belong to any particular language but is a universal cognition and, on the other hand, the mental images of the words by which our knowledge is expressed. We can silently think of the sounds which we are wont to utter and hear; the mental images that we thus produce are as diverse from particular language to particular language as the spoken words which they represent.

A most interesting passage is found in a sermon which Augustine preached in honour of St. John the Baptist and in which he tries to explain the difference between *vox* and *verbum* to his congregation (*Sermo* 288, ed. Migne 38, 1304–1306). There he uses the word *verbum* in at least two different senses. Twice he says that a *verbum* that does not signify anything is not called a *verbum*. In this somewhat strange way he contrasts the *verbum* with a *vox* which may be a mere sound (*informis quidam sonus*); the *verbum* is always a significant sound and apparently the same as what he elsewhere calls a *nomen* or *dictio,* for instance *homo, pecus, deus, mundus.* These significant sounds are used to carry the speaker's thought, the *verbum* in the second sense, to the hearer's mind. The inner word, which is also referred to as *sententia quaedam,* does not belong to any particular language but remains exactly the same whether it is conveyed by the different sounds of Latin, Greek, Punic, Hebrew, Egyptian, or Indian.

Thus the inner word, contrasted with the spoken word and its written mark or mental image, developed into one of the central notions of Augustine's philosophy and theology. Moreover, this doctrine of the *verbum* as the inner word has had an immense influence on medieval thinkers. I shall confine myself to giving some examples[21].

11.4.2. Anselm of Canterbury (*Monologion* 10, ed. Migne 158, 158) differentiates the following varieties of speech. I can refer to man by using the spoken sound *homo*; I can also use the noun by thinking it in silence; further, I can form a mental image of man; or I can conceive of the universal essence of man, as a mortal rational animal. In other words, I can speak of a thing by uttering sensible signs or by inwardly making images of those signs or by saying the things themselves in my mind (*res ipsas --- intus in nostra mente*

---

[21] One of the topics in which the doctrine of the inner word plays a crucial part but which must be passed over here is the question whether angels can converse with each other (*utrum unus angelus loquatur alteri*), a steadfast item of the theologians' repertoire and a source of much ingenuity.

dicendo), either by forming images of them or by the understanding of reason (*rationis intellectu*). The act of contemplating the exemplary forms of things is a mental or rational locution. Before the artist makes his work of art, for instance, he first says it in his mind by a mental conception (*prius illud intra se dicit mentis conceptione*).

The comparison with the artist also occurs in Thomas Aquinas (*De veritate*, q. 4, art. 1–2). Just as in the case of the artist we have to consider the conceived work of art, a model of it, and the finished product, so in someone who speaks there is a threefold word (*triplex verbum*). First, there is the word that is conceived by the mind, a word spoken in the heart without vocal sounds; next comes the model of the exterior word, an interior word that is an image of the sounds; and finally the exterior word, the *verbum vocis*, is uttered. In *Summa theologiae* I, q. 34, art. 1, Thomas Aquinas, in connection with the same trichotomy, refers not only to Augustine, *De trinitate* XV, 10, but also to John of Damascus, *De fide orthodoxa* I, 13 (ed. Migne 94, 857).

It should be noted that, according to Thomas Aquinas, the exterior word does not signify the act of understanding (*ipsum intellegere*). What is signified by the spoken word is rather the product of that act, that in which the operation of the mind comes to an end, the *ipsum intellectum*. As there are different operations of the mind, that which is understood may be either the concept of something that is signifiable by a single word (*significabilis per vocem incomplexam*), as is the case when the intellect forms the quiddities of things, or the thought of something that is signifiable only by a complex of words (*per vocem complexam*), as is the case when the intellect combines or divides (*De veritate*, q. 4, art. 2).

Besides the threefold division of the word in the sense of Augustine and John of Damascus, Thomas Aquinas also acknowledges the Peripatetic trichotomy. In his commentary on *De interpretatione* (1, 2), for example, he points out that nouns and verbs and combinations of nouns and verbs have a threefold way of being (*tripliciter habent esse*); they are conceived by the mind or uttered by means of vocal sounds or written by means of letters. Although he uses the phrase *verbum mentale* in the Augustinian sense (*Summa theologiae* II, 1, q. 93, art. 1), he does not speak of an *oratio mentalis* in connection with the Peripatetic trichotomy. At those places where *oratio mentalis* (*interior, mentis*) occurs, in contrast with *oratio exterior* or *vocalis,* it stands for interior or mental prayer (*Summa theologiae* II, 2, q. 83, art. 12; III, q. 21, art. 3).

12. THE *COMPLEXUM* THEORY OF OCKHAM AND HOLKOT

In the years between 1320 and 1335 we witness a revival of the debate between adherents of a *complexum* theory and defenders of some kind of *res* doctrine, centring less around narrowly theological issues than in the period we discussed in 11.1−2 and having as its chief scene the university of Oxford. I shall devote this chapter to the *complexum* theory as it was elaborated by William of Ockham and Robert Holkot.

12.1. William of Ockham

The works of Ockham which contain most information with regard to our theme are his commentary on Peter Lombard's *Sentences,* composed towards 1320, and the *Quodlibeta septem* and the *Summa totius logicae,* both written before 1327[1].

12.1.1. Ockham (*SL* I, 2, p. 10) points out that the word *terminus* can be used in three different senses. In the first place, a term may be contrasted with an *oratio* or combination of signs; in this sense every *incomplexum* is a term. Further, a *terminus* may be anything that serves as the subject or predicate of a categorical statement or determines that subject or predicate, as for instance the copula does. In this sense even a *propositio* may be a

---

[1] I shall refer to the commentary on the *Sentences* (Lugduni, 1495) by means of the letter *S*; to its *Prologus* by means of the letters *SP*, followed by the page of the edition by G. Gal, St. Bonaventure, N.Y., 1967. *Summa totius logicae* will be abbreviated as *SL*, followed by part, chapter, and page in the edition by Ph. Boehner, St. Bonaventure, N.Y., 1951−1954. *Quodlibeta septem* (Strassburg, 1491, reprinted Louvain, 1962) will be abbreviated as *Q*.

terminus, like *homo est animal* in *'homo est animal' est propositio vera.* In a
stricter sense, finally, the word *terminus* is used to indicate that which can be
the subject or predicate of a *propositio* in a signifying function (*significative
sumptum*). In *'legit' est verbum* the subject is not taken in its signifying
function but rather mentioned and is therefore not a *terminus* in this third
sense.

In so far as *termini* are *incomplexa,* they may be divided into categorematic and syncategorematic terms (*SL* 1, 4, p. 15). Categorematic terms have
a distinct and definite signification, whereas syncategorematic terms do
not signify by themselves but only make a categorematic term to which they
are added stand for something in a certain way (*determinato modo*) or dis-
charge some other function in connection with a categorematic term. Of both
the categorematic and syncategorematic terms there are three kinds: the written term (*terminus scriptus*), the spoken term (*terminus prolatus*), and the
conceived term (*terminus conceptus*). While Ockham appeals to the doctrine
of threefold speech which is found in Boethius, he also identifies the conceived terms with those mental words of which Augustine in *De trinitate* XV
says that they do not belong to any particular language. This is symptomatic
of a gradual coalition of the Boethian and Augustinian divisions.

Categorematic mental terms — that is, such affections of the soul as concepts or 'intentions' — are natural signs of things and are contrasted with
spoken and written terms as conventional signs of the same things. Ockham's
view is thus different from what we find in the first chapter of Aristotle's *De
interpretatione,* namely that the written terms are conventional signs of the
spoken terms and the spoken terms symbols of the affections of the soul,
which latter alone are directly related to things. Ockham agrees in this respect
with Duns Scotus, who had already stated that what is signified by the
spoken sound is a thing rather than a concept[2]; he assumes that there is a
direct relation between written or spoken terms and things as well as between
mental terms and things, one difference being that in the first case the relation is that of conventional signification and in the second case that of
natural signification. The other difference, which restores something of the
Aristotelian hierarchy, is that the written term is a secondary conventional
sign of a thing compared to the spoken term which is the primary conventional sign of the thing and that the spoken term, in its turn, is secondary and
subordinate to the mental term (Cf. *SL* 1, 12, p. 39).

Further, it is important that of the several possible interpretations of the

---

[2] In his commentary on the *Sentences,* the so-called *Opus Oxoniense,* I, Dist. 27,
q. 3, 19.

'intention' of the mind which is the mental term Ockham eventually came to prefer the theory that it is the act of understanding itself, the *ipsa intellectio* or *actus intellegendi* (*S* I, Dist. 2, q. 8; *SL* I, 12, p. 39). Whereas Thomas Aquinas, for instance, as we saw in 11.4.2, explicitly states that the mental word is not the act of understanding but rather its final product, Ockham thinks that there is no need to introduce, apart from the acts of understanding and the things towards which they are directed, yet a third element, a distinct product of the act. Just as for Abelard the *intellectus* is a mere act of attending (Cf. 9.1.1), for Ockham the mental word or term is an act of apprehending which, together with the act of judging, belongs to the main operations of the human mind. This rejection of any intermediate entity between the act of understanding and the things to which it is related is one of the most characteristic features of Ockham's doctrine.

12.1.2. In the same way as there are written, spoken, and mental terms, which are categorematic or syncategorematic *incomplexa,* there are three kinds of *complexa* of which those terms are parts, namely written, spoken, and mental *propositiones.* Although the word *complexum* as such has a wider meaning than *propositio,* it is commonly used by Ockham as a synonym of *propositio* or as standing for the *oratio infinitiva* which takes the place of a *propositio* in indirect speech. This is the same usage as we found in the theological disputes of the thirteenth century where *complexum* and *enuntiabile* or *enuntiatio* were often employed interchangeably (Cf. 11.2.2). One of the rare occasions on which Ockham uses the term *enuntiabile* is precisely in a passage dealing with the question whether God could know more than he knows (*S* I, Dist. 39).

The *propositio* which is only conceived in the mind, now regularly called *propositio mentalis,* consists of categorematic and syncategorematic mental terms, of relatively independent acts of understanding or meaning things and of at least one act of integrating those acts. This act of integrating is in the first instance a particular kind of apprehension, namely the formation of a *complexum* by compounding or dividing (*Q* V, 6). This *formatio* is the act of conceiving the identity or non-identity of that which is meant by the act of understanding which is called the subject-term and that which is meant by the act of understanding which is called the predicate-term (*Q* III, 5). It is an act of apprehending things in a determinate way, the determinate way being contributed by the syncategorematic act of meaning. This act of purely conceiving that things are in a certain way (*ita esse*), the *formatio* in the sense of Averroës' commentary on *De anima* (Cf. 11.3.2) – to which Ockham refers (*SP*, p. 21) – may be supplemented by an act of assenting, a *fides, iudicium,* or *actus iudicativus.*

Of such acts of assenting there are two kinds. Especially in *Q* III, 6, where Ockham discusses the old question whether the object of the act of assenting and more particularly the object of faith is an *incomplexum* or *complexum*, he makes the following distinction (Cf. also *Q* IV, 17, and *Q* V, 6). On the one hand, there is an act of assenting or believing which consists solely in judging that something is the case, for instance that man is an animal. Although this act of judging naturally involves the formation of a *complexum*, this *complexum* as such is not apprehended. All that is apprehended are the things themselves, in the determinate way that is typical of the formation of a *complexum*. The act of assenting has for its object the apprehended things, the *res extra*, and not the *complexum*, for that is not apprehended. But though the act of assenting has for its object the things themselves and is thus about them, the things themselves are not that to which we assent. Such combinations as *assentio lapidi* ('I assent to a stone') or *scio lapidem* ('I know that a stone') are simply not well-formed. What is assented to is rather that a stone is heavy, the *ita esse* which is the composition or division characteristic of the formation of a *complexum*. Strictly speaking, it is even wrong to say that something (*aliquid*) is assented to or known; for this way of expressing oneself suggests that such things as stones are assented to or known. Nothing is believed, in the sense that no thing is believed. To the adherents of an *incomplexum* theory who adduce such arguments as that God is the object of the future vision and must therefore be the object of faith too, or that we say 'I believe in God the father' and not 'I believe in the *complexum* "God is the father" ', Ockham replies that they are right only in so far as they mean that God is the object of the acts of assenting which belong to the first kind, or that such acts of assenting are about God himself.

But there is also a second kind of acts of assenting, namely those which involve a separate apprehension of the formed *complexum* itself. To this category of judgments belong the cases in which we do not simply and directly judge about things through the formation of a *complexum* which remains purely instrumental, but rather are explicitly concerned with the truth of the *complexum*. In the context of verification and scientific proof the *complexum* itself becomes the object of examination. Apart from the apprehension which is the formation of the *complexum* and consists in apprehending the things in a determinate way, we also perform in such situations a separate act of apprehending the *complexum formatum*; and it is then this *complexum formatum*, and not the thing in the outside world, that is the object of assenting or dissenting, of doubting, believing, and knowing (Cf. also *SP* pp. 202–203). It is always this context of discursive reasoning and scientific proof, a context in which the question of truth or falsity is prominent, that Ockham has in mind when he defends the thesis that the object of judgment or assent, of belief and knowledge is the *complexum* or *propositio*.

Ockham, then, distinguishes between two kinds of apprehension and between two kinds of assent (*Q* V, 6). One kind of apprehension is the formation of a *propositio*, an act of apprehending things in a compounding or separating way. The other kind of apprehension is the act of apprehending the *propositio* or *complexum* already formed. One kind of assent is the act of judging that something is the case without any apprehension of the *complexum* itself; its object is the thing about which the act of judging that something is the case is performed, while that which is judged or assented to is not that thing but rather that something is the case. The other kind of assent has for its object the *complexum* formed and apprehended and consists in an act of judging that the *complexum* is true; here both the object of the act of assenting, as that which the act of assenting is about, and that which is assented to are the *complexum*. Ockham emphasizes that the act of assenting in both cases is different from the apprehension which is the formation of the *propositio* as well as from the apprehension of the *complexum* already formed.

Further, it should be noted that both on the level of apprehension and on the level of assent there are only acts. Whether the *propositio mentalis* is a neutral composition or division, without assent or dissent, or a full-grown judgment, there exists nothing but acts and things towards which the acts are directed. Just as in the case of a mental term there is, according to Ockham, no need to posit a separate product of the act of understanding or meaning, there is no reason to assume the existence of a distinct product yielded by a mental *propositio*. There is only a natural signification, an act of thinking that something is the case, but no detachable significate or thought-content. One might say that for Ockham an act of thinking that something is the case cannot be split into an act of thinking and a content thought, but that the complement is more like an internal accusative or an adverbial modification of the act.

12.1.3. It may be assumed that *propositiones* display the same hierarchy as the terms of which they consist: written *propositiones* are secondary conventional signs compared to spoken *propositiones* and the latter are secondary and subordinate to the mental *propositiones* as natural signs. Although the spoken utterance is not a conventional sign of that which goes on in the mind but rather directly of a state of things in the world, it discharges its signifying function in subordination to the mental acts of apprehending and judging which always precede it (*SL* I, 12, p. 39). What we think and mean in our minds determines the way in which the spoken utterance functions as a conventional sign. Since Ockham thus maintains a clear dependence of the signification of spoken utterances upon the corresponding mental acts, it becomes as important for him as for those who follow the orthodox Aristotelian conception to raise the question of exactly how the vocal and the mental terms are related and in particular whether each difference in the spoken *propositio* is matched by a difference in the mental *propositio*. This question is discussed at some length in *SL* I, 3, pp. 11–14, and in *Q* V, 8.

As to the traditional word-classes, Ockham holds that there are mental as well as spoken nouns, verbs, adverbs, conjunctions, and prepositions. There is no need, however, to assume mental participles. Since a verb and a participle of that verb combined with *est* – for instance, *Socrates currit* and *Socrates currens est* – always seem to be equivalent in signification, we cannot appeal to an indispensability for signification or expression (*necessitas significationis* or *expressionis*) in order to justify a distinction between a mental verb and a mental participle. As in the case of synonyms generally, the difference in the spoken utterances is due simply to stylistic or other accidental motives. Ockham suggests that the same may apply to pronouns, probably because their work can always be done by nouns.

Of the different forms that a noun can take those which determine differences in case and number have their parallels in the mental sphere, since these differences are relevant to the question whether the *propositio* is true or false. Of two *propositiones* having parts which differ in case or number one may be true and the other false (Here Ockham's position is at variance with the view defended by Abelard, *Dialectica* 125, 11, namely that differences of case do not alter the signification). Gender and form, on the other hand, have no correlates in the mental *propositio*. In order to decide whether a *propositio* is true or false one need not pay any attention to the gender of the subject-term or the predicate-term. With respect to signification and verification it is indifferent whether, for example, the masculine word *lapis* or the feminine word *petra* is used to refer to a stone, though the choice of the one or the other affects such inessential matters as agreement. Neither is it important whether the form (*figura*; in Greek *schēma*) of a word is simple or compound. As to the degrees of comparison, finally, the question whether they also belong to the mental sphere is left open in *SL* I, 3, p. 13, but answered in the affirmative in *Q* V, 8, on the ground that *homo est albus, homo est albior,* and *homo est albissimus* may have different truth-values.

According to Ockham the mood, tense, voice, and person of verbs are common to spoken language and mental language, while the different conjugations and the form (*figura*) are peculiar to spoken and written language.

Here too he applies the criterion of the indispensability of some form for signifying or expressing something and of the possibility of a difference in truth-value. In the same vein he discusses the question whether or not the distinction between concrete and abstract nouns is common to spoken and mental language (*SL* I, 6, pp. 18–21; *Q* V, 9).

From these considerations it follows that such a phenomenon as ambiguity must be restricted to spoken and written language. The very notion of ambiguity implies that the same vocal form is or can be used in subordination to different acts of meaning; as these acts of meaning are precisely the mental terms, these mental terms themselves cannot properly be called ambiguous (*SL* I, 13, p. 41). It is also obvious that mental speech will not contain any synonyms. If all that can be signified by synonymous words can be satisfactorily expressed by one of them, it is unnecessary to posit more than one concept corresponding to the many synonyms. One might say that one of the uses to which Ockham and others put the notion of mental speech was to convey their insight that sometimes diversity on the level of spoken or written language is irrelevant to meaning and verification and can therefore be reduced to unity on the semantic level of thought and that, conversely,· sometimes sameness of spoken or written expression neutralizes important distinctions with respect to meaning and verification and has therefore to be replaced by diversity on the semantic level of thought. This awareness of irrelevant diversity and deceptive sameness led them to realize that expressions of spoken or written language and mental acts of meaning differ in their arithmetics (Cf. 10.2.2).

12.1.4. For Ockham the only bearers of truth and falsity are the *complexa* or *propositiones*. A *propositio* is true if the things signified are in such a state as is signified by the *propositio,* and false if they are not. A *propositio* has categorematic parts which signify things and at least one syncategorematic part which makes the categorematic parts signify in a determinate way; the whole *propositio* then signifies things in a determinate way or in a certain manner of being. The *propositio* as a whole has no other significate than what is signified by the categorematic terms; but in comparison with the isolated categorematic terms it adds an adverbial element, namely the way in which the signified things are connected. If the things indicated by the categorematic terms exist in the manner contributed by the syncategorematic part, then the *propositio* is true; if they do not, it is false (*est ita vel non est ita a parte significati, sicut denotatur per propositionem, quae est signum*)[3]. Strict-

---

[3] *Expositio aurea et admodum utilis super artem veterem* (Bononiae, 1496, reprinted

ly speaking, Ockham has no room for a *significatum propositionis,* neither when this phrase is taken in the sense of a distinct thought-content nor when it is taken in the sense of a state of affairs in the world. In the world there are only things and things are signified by categorematic terms; what the *propositio* adds is a way of being, an *ita* or *sic,* which is not a separate thing but rather a mode in which things exist.

The *complexa* or *propositiones* which are the bearers of truth and falsity are as a rule particular acts of thinking, speaking, or writing. There are indications that Ockham attributed a certain duration to such acts. In connection with *Cat.* 4 a 22 he states that the same *oratio* may be first true and then false (*SL* I, 43, p. 119). Elsewhere [4] he asks us to suppose that someone thinks that such a *propositio* as 'Socrates is seated' is true although it is false, because Socrates is standing, and that while that act remains in his mind that *propositio* becomes true. His remark that one and the same *propositio* may be first believed and then known (*Q* V, 6) points in the same direction. That the borderline between a *propositio* in the token-sense and a *propositio* in the type-sense was rather vague is further shown by *SL* II, 9, p. 247, where he defines a necessary *propositio* as one which, if it is formed, cannot be false but is each time true (Cf. *SL* III, II, 5).

Truth and falsity are not qualities inhering in *propositiones* as, for instance, whiteness and blackness inhere in things. They are nothing but the true or false *propositio* itself. If they were taken to be inhering qualities, it would follow that changes in the world which alter the truth-value of a *propositio* cause a real change in the *propositio* itself. There would be different qualities in the mind of someone who thinks 'This moves' according as something in the outside world moves or does not move. And the written statement *musca volat* would undergo real changes according as the fly is or is not flying (*SL* I, 43, p. 119; *Q* V, 24).

In the context of verification and scientific proof the *complexum* or *propositio* which then as a rule will be the conclusion is simultaneously the immediate object of knowledge and that which is known. Ockham draws a distinction between the *subiectum scientiae,* which is the subject of the conclusion, and the *obiectum scientiae,* which is the conclusion itself (*SP* p. 266).

Farnborough Hants, 1964), in the prooemium to the commentary on *De interpretatione.* For similar formulas in which the words *sic* or *ita* and *sicut* have the same crucial position cf. *Ibidem,* in the commentary on the *Categories,* cap. 9.

[4] *Tractatus de praedestinatione et de praescientia dei et de futuris contingentibus,* q. 2, art. 3, F (Cf. Adams & Kretzmann 1969: 60).

12.2.   Robert Holkot

A more radical version of the *complexum* theory than the one put forward by Ockham was defended by Robert Holkot, in his commentary on the *Sentences*, composed between 1330 and 1332, in the first of his *Sex articuli*, written in 1332, and in a quodlibetal dispute on the question whether God is able to know more than he knows, also written in 1332[5].

12.2.1.   According to Holkot (*Q* 306) the act of understanding or apprehending is an act of using a likeness (*similitudo*)[6] of a thing in order to attend to the thing to which the likeness is related or would be related if such a thing existed. The act of apprehending, however, is not something distinct from the likeness, but the likeness or image itself used in a certain way (Cf. *Q* 39). Next, the act of compounding or dividing consists in a composite act of using different images standing for one thing or using the same image twice and of inserting a concept that corresponds to the word *est,* adding, for division, the syncategorematic concept that corresponds to the word *non.* The act of compounding or dividing is an act of the mind in which it produces images of things or uses images already produced in a certain arrangement; this act is the mental *propositio* or *complexum* which according to Aristotle consists of concepts or natural significations and which Holkot explicitly identifies with the inner word as it had been characterized by Augustine and Anselm (*SA,* E). Although Holkot does not give any details about the exact way in which mental, spoken, and written *propositiones* are related, it is obvious that the mental *propositio* as an act of natural signification is prior, both in time and in importance, to the spoken and written *propositiones* as acts of conventional signification. This mental *propositio* in the proper sense should not be confused with the *propositio* that consists of mental images of the spoken sounds or written marks (*SA,* E).

Acts of compounding or dividing may, according to the circumstances in which they are performed, be characterized as acts of believing, opining, assenting, knowing, of erring, doubting, or questioning. If we speak of an act of knowing, for example, it is implied that the person who forms the *proposi-*

---

[5] I shall refer to the commentary on the *Sentences* (Lugduni, 1510, reprinted Frankfurt, 1967) by means of the letter *S*; to the first of the *Sex articuli* (Lugduni, 1510) by the letters *SA* ; and to *Quodlibeta* I, 6, by means of the letter *Q*, followed by the line of the edition by Courtenay (1971).

[6] Also called *conceptus, species, imago, idolum, intellectus, intentio, verbum mentale, cognitio, intellectio, passio animae.*

tio is certain that it is so in reality as is indicated by the *propositio*. The same *propositio* can also be formed with a feeling of uncertainty, in which case it is an act of doubting. It even may happen that the same *propositio* is first doubted and later known; in that case doubt has become knowledge (*Q* 354). Further, Holkot holds that the doubted *propositio* itself is nothing but the act of doubting, the known *propositio* nothing but the act of knowing, the believed *propositio* nothing but the act of believing, and the *propositio* in which one errs nothing but the act of erring. For the thesis that the act of knowing and that which is known are the same (*idem est scientia et scitum*; *Q* 42) he appeals to Aristotle[7]. This means that if we say, for instance, 'Socrates knows that the stone is heavy' there is no need to assume that, apart from the mental act performed by Socrates and the things in the outside world, there is still a third entity, namely that which is known. That which we are tempted to regard as an intermediate entity between the act and the things in the outside world is simply the act of compounding or dividing performed in a certain frame of mind. The phrase 'that the stone is heavy' (*lapidem esse gravem*), we might say, is not the name of a separate entity, the thing known, but rather the *propositio* 'The stone is heavy' (*lapis est gravis*) itself in the guise required when it is preceded by a verb of knowing.

The distinction which Ockham had drawn between the formation of a *complexum* without any apprehension of the *complexum* itself and such a formation with an apprehension of the *complexum* formed is made by Holkot in a slightly different way. According to him a *complexum* such as the conclusion of a demonstration is always apprehended when it is formed. But it may be apprehended *pro rebus,* in a direct relation to the things in the world, or *pro se,* as something considered in itself. Holkot refers in this connection to Aristotle, *De memoria et reminiscentia* 450 b 24, where it is pointed out that a *phantasma* in the mind can be taken as a picture of something else or as an entity in its own right (*S* 1, q. 2)[8].

Holkot, then, holds a *complexum* theory in the sense that the object of doubt, opinion, belief, or knowledge, as that which is doubted, opined, believed, or known in the context of verification and scientific proof, is identical with the *complexum* or *propositio* formed and apprehended. This *complexum* or *propositio*, primarily mental and secondarily vocal and written, is also the sole bearer of truth and falsity. Holkot adduces practically the same arguments as Ockham in order to show that truth and falsity are not qualities

---

[7] Cf. *De anima* 430 a 3, 431 a 1, 431 b 17; *Metaphysics* 1072 b 21, 1075 a 1.
[8] Cf. also Ockham, *In I Sent.,* Dist. 2, q. 4.

distinct from the *propositiones* and inhering in them as accidents in a substance, but rather the true or false *propositio* itself (*S* II, q. 2, art. 4; *SA*, D).

12.2.2. Although the main lines of Holkot's view are very similar to Ockham's position, it is clear from *Q* I, 6, that Holkot disagreed with Ockham concerning the question whether God is able to know more than he knows. In his commentary on the *Sentences* (I, Dist. 39, q. 1) Ockham had maintained that in the strict sense of 'to know' (*scire*), the sense in which we can be said to know only something that is true, God can know something that he does not know, but cannot know more than he knows. The first thesis is illustrated by means of such a *propositio* as *ego sum Romae* ('I am in Rome'); this is now false but may be true at some time in the future. Consequently, it is not known by God at the present moment but it may be known by him at some future time. Therefore, God is able to know something which he does not know now. The second thesis is supported by the argument that all truths are known by God, and that the number of truths is always the same; therefore, God always knows the same number of truths. The premiss that the number of truths is always the same is based upon the consideration that of two contradictory statements always one is true; here Ockham apparently assumes that the number of statements is constant.

Against this Holkot argues that Ockham, if he wants to adhere to the principles of his own doctrine, should concede three things, namely that God can know more than he knows, that he can know less than he knows, and that the statement 'Nothing is known by God' is possible (*Q* 129–133). That God can know more than he knows is evident from the fact that to all the truths which exist at a certain moment one can be added which has never been true before and is therefore known by God for the first time at the moment when it is added; similarly, if one of the truths that have existed so far is destroyed, God's knowledge is diminished by one true *propositio*. Personally I am able to make God know more truths by thinking or saying many things which are true and also to make him know less truths by, for instance, burning one of my books or going to sleep (*Q* 226–232). As to the statement 'Nothing is known by God', its possibility follows from the consideration that only a *complexum* is true and that every *complexum* is a created thing (*creatura*); since it is possible that there are no created things, it is also possible that there are no true *complexa* for God to know.

Holkot further refuses to accept the theses that of two contradictory statements always one is true and the other false and that there is always an equal number of truths. According to him they contradict what Ockham himself states elsewhere, namely that only the *complexum* is true and that everything that is true exists (*omne verum est ens*). A *propositio* which is not actually formed cannot be true or false. Consequently, such logical rules as 'Some *propositio* is true, therefore its contradictory is false', 'The antecedent is true, therefore the consequent is true', 'The premisses are true and the syllogistic form is valid, therefore the conclusion is true', 'The consequent is false, therefore the antecedent is false too' apply only to those cases in which the *propositiones* concerned really exist. Without this presupposition of existence the rules do not hold, for it is quite conceivable that, for example, the true statement 'You run' is the only statement in existence, and then it does not follow that its contradictory is false, since that contradictory has not been formulated. Holkot explicitly rejects the view of those who held that a *propositio* can be true whether it exists or not, because a *propositio* is true when it is so as is signified by it or would be signified by it if it existed.

Moreover, it may happen that a thousand true *propositiones* contradict one false *propositio*. For suppose that 'Socrates runs' is written at one thousand places and that 'Socrates does not run' is written at only one place. Then, if it is actually the case that Socrates runs, one thousand true *propositiones* contradict one false *propositio*. As soon as Socrates stops running, however, one thousand *propositiones* become false and exactly one becomes true. There are therefore 999 true *propositiones* less than before and consequently God's knowledge is diminished by 999 truths (*Q* 166–179).

Holkot, then, does not share Ockham's presupposition that the total number of *propositiones* is constant. According to him there is a varying number of *propositiones* in the sense of particular acts of thinking, saying, or writing that something is the case. On the one hand, Holkot strongly emphasizes the token-character of the *propositio*; one thousand inscriptions of the form 'Socrates runs' are one thousand different *propositiones*. On the other hand, he attributes a certain duration to the acts, enough at least to allow of a change in truth-value. In this connection it should not be overlooked, however, that it is very easy, especially in the case of writing, to mix up the act itself, which is rather short-lived, and the product of the act, which may be much more durable. This emphasis on the token-character of the *propositio*, together with the corollary that a *propositio* must be actually formulated in order to be capable of being called true or false, leads Holkot to reject the thesis that there are always as many truths as falsehoods. It is quite possible that a true statement is not matched with any actually existing contradictory which is false (or conversely) and also that the numbers of the contradicting *propositiones* which do actually exist are as widely different as in the case of one thousand true ones contradicting a single false one.

12.2.3. In *S* II, q. 2, art. 4, Holkot discusses the traditional problem whether a spoken utterance, being never given as a whole, can be called true or false. His answer is similar to the one offered by Abelard (Cf. 9.5.1) and by Ockham who had treated the same question in *Quodlibeta* III, 11. We should consider a spoken utterance, which is by nature a succession of discrete sounds, as if it were a *res permanens*, something that is given in its entirety. This can be done at the last moment of the act of uttering, when the hearer still remembers what has preceded the final sound. Although in fact the spoken utterance never exists in its totality, we can imagine what it would signify and what would be its truth-value if it were given all at once.

In the same passage Holkot mentions the following difficulty. If we compare such *propositiones* as *aliquis homo est Socrates et ille est Plato* and *aliquis homo disputat et ille est Plato*, we may find that the conjunct *ille est Plato* is false in the first conjunction and true in the second. In that case we would have to conclude that *ille est Plato* is both true and false. Holkot concedes that in the case of *propositiones* whose subject-term or predicate-term is a proper name or a demonstrative or anaphoric pronoun it may happen that of two *propositiones* which are completely similar in sound (*omnino similes in voce*) one is true and the other false. In our example this is so because the pronoun *ille* once refers to Socrates and once to Plato. But all this does not mean that one and the same *propositio* is both true and false. Holkot apparently agrees with Abelard (Cf. 9.5.1) and with the author of the *Introductiones Montanae minores* who refused to call the utterance-types *ego disputo* and *tu disputas* by the name of *propositio* (Cf. 10.1.2) in considering as a *propositio* in the strict sense not a class of utterances which are similar in form but only a particular utterance which is used to make one definite statement.

A similar difficulty is brought up immediately afterwards. Suppose that somewhere the words *ego sum Robertus* are written. All those who read this *propositio* and whose name is not *Robertus* will read something that is false. But if it is read by someone whose name happens to be *Robertus*, he will say something that is true. The same written *propositio* will be false when read by some and true when read by others; therefore it will be both true and false. In his answer Holkot contends that the inscription *ego sum Robertus* is neither true nor false, since the written mark *ego* does not signify anything but the spoken sound *ego*, which in its turn signifies the person who utters the sound. All one can say is that the inscription represents a true spoken *propositio* when it is read by someone with that name and a false spoken *propositio* when it is read by someone who is not called by that name; but the written words themselves are neither true nor false. Holkot adds that this solution depends upon the special character of the written demonstrative pronoun. Three points are worthy of note here. In the first place, at least in the case of a written *propositio* that contains a demonstrative pronoun Holkot seems to adhere to the orthodox Aristotelian view that the written marks signify the spoken sounds; in this respect he apparently disagrees with Ockham. Further, it is strange that he does not mention the most natural interpretation of the written words *ego sum Robertus,* namely that the pronoun *ego* refers to the person who wrote the words, however difficult it may sometimes be to iden-tify that person. Finally, one has the impression that exactly the same point could have been made without introducing a written *propositio.* Considera-tion of the spoken utterance-type *ego sum Robertus* leads to the same diffi-culty, namely that the utterance-type is sometimes true and sometimes false and therefore both true and false. The only advantage of introducing the written *propositio* is that it becomes easier to keep the utterance-type before one's mind when it is written down and so remains available for reference. In that case, of course, it is indeed only a representation of the spoken utter-ance-type. What Holkot intended to convey may then after all not be very different from the line taken by the author of the *Introductiones Montanae minores*, that utterance-types of the form *ego sum Robertus* are neither true nor false and therefore not *propositiones* in any strict sense.

12.2.4. It may be concluded, I think, that the *complexum* theory as it was put forward by Ockham and, in its most radical form, by Holkot is at least partly an elaboration of the various *complexum* theories that were developed in the theological disputes of the previous century. This is clearly shown by the fact that the same arguments occur in both contexts. Moreover, even the specific form in which the *complexum* theory appears in the writings of Ockham and Holkot, namely as the view that the primary objects of assent and knowledge and the primary bearers of truth and falsity are particular acts of thinking that something is the case (with the corollary that act and content somehow coincide), has parallels in the past. The act-variant of the *com-plexum* theory is strongly reminiscent of the view that *enuntiabilia* are acts of thinking, which is mentioned and rejected by the author of the *Ars Meliduna* (Cf. 10.2.2). Several of the objections adduced against the older doctrine would hardly need any adaptation if one wished to oppose the theory pro-pounded in Holkot's writings. And there is also a striking resemblance be-tween the position of Ockham and Holkot and the theory mentioned by Prevostin of Cremona according to which the articles of faith are identical with the acts of believing (Cf. 11.1.3).

13. SOME REIST OPPONENTS OF OCKHAM AND HOLKOT

The *complexum* theory of Ockham and Holkot was not without its rivals. In this chapter I shall call attention to three contemporary thinkers, Chatton, Crathorn, and Burleigh, who are alike in opposing the one-sided emphasis on the sign typical of Ockham and Holkot and in concentrating instead upon the significate as something distinct from the sign. As the *res significata* or thing signified plays a predominant part in their theories or in what others regarded as their theories, they may be called reists, although it will be evident from what follows that this name should be handled cautiously. As we noted in 9.3.1, a reist doctrine was already mentioned by Abelard. Some of his contemporaries held the view that a *propositio* signifies, apart from a composite thought, the things themselves which are signified by its parts. A *propositio* of the form *homo est animal* signifies as a whole (*totaliter*) simultaneously man and animal in such a state that the one is the other. In 10.2.2 we saw, moreover, that the author of the *Ars Meliduna* refers to a conception of the *enuntiabile* according to which a true *enuntiabile* such as *Socratem esse album* is nothing but the circumstance that the property of being white actually belongs to Socrates, while the false one *Socratem esse asinum* is nothing but the circumstance that the property of being an ass does not belong to Socrates. This conception, which identifies the *enuntiabile* or the significate of a *propositio* with a *compositio* or *divisio* in the outside world, may perhaps also be included among the reist theories. Finally, a *res* theory or *incomplexum* theory was advanced by the theologians in connection with the problem of the identity of the article of faith. That which is believed was regarded as a *res* or an *eventus* — for example, Christ's birth or Christ's passion or Christ's resurrection (Cf. 11.1.2). Just as the *complexum* theory of Ockham and Holkot is clearly connected with the similar doctrines which were set forth in the theological disputes of the thirteenth century, the reist theories

which will be discussed in this chapter, notably those of Chatton and Crathorn, show points of contact with the *res* doctrine that had been propounded as an alternative answer to the problem concerning the identity of the
article of faith.

13.1.   Walter of Chatton

13.1.1. Walter of Chatton lectured on the *Sentences* at Oxford in 1322–
1323. The first question from the *Prologus* to his commentary has been
edited by Maria Elena Reina[1]; especially the first article is important for our
subject. In that article Chatton defends the view that a *propositio* is a complex apprehension or cognition that consists in a composition or division and
has for its object a thing (or more than one thing – presumably when the
subject-term refers to a plurality of things) which actually exists outside the
mind or in the mind, or would exist outside the mind or in the mind if it
existed. The thing signified by the *propositio* as a whole is the same thing as is
successively signified by the subject-term, the copula, and the predicate-term,
each of which is a specific cognition of that same object. This *propositio*,
which is formed in the mind but not necessarily apprehended by it, causes the
act of assenting or dissenting. The object of assent, however, is not the
propositio but the thing signified by the mental *propositio*. Chatton rejects
Ockham's thesis that the object of assent is the apprehended *propositio*, and
also the doctrine – which had recently been put forward by Peter Aureole in
the third book of his commentary on the *Sentences* – that the act of believing or knowing is identical with the article of faith or the conclusion of a
demonstration. It should be noted that in the last of the seven arguments
which Chatton adduces for his view he points out that those who regard the
article of faith as the immediate object of the act of believing have to concede
that the faith of the *antiqui* was different from that of the *moderni*.

13.1.2. The passages in Holkot's writings where Chatton's doctrine is discussed are *In I Sententiarum*, q.2[2], and *Quodlibeta* I, 6, ed. Courtenay
11–34. It is possible that *In II Sententiarum*, q.2, art.4, where Holkot rejects
the theory that the truth of a *propositio* is the thing signified by it, is also

---

[1] In *Rivista critica di storia della filosofia* 25 (1970), 48–74 and 290–314.

[2] In the edition Lugduni, J. Cleyn, 1510, the doctrine is wrongly attributed to
Ockham (*tenet Ocham*). Cf. Moody (1964: 66) and Schepers (1972: 127, n. 94).

directed against Chatton; but his name is not mentioned there. In *In I Sent.*, q.2, Holkot summarizes Chatton's arguments for the thesis that the object of knowledge, opinion, belief and, in general, assent is not the *complexum* itself but rather the thing signified by the *complexum* or by the parts of the *propositio*. In the first place, proving something does not require apprehension and explicit awareness of the conclusion or the premises as such; therefore, assent is given with respect to the thing and not with respect to the sign. Secondly, since the *propositio* is compounded of cognitions of a thing in the outside world, it also causes an act of assenting to the thing in the outside world. Thirdly, a mental *propositio* and a thing in the outside world are distinct cognoscibles; therefore, one assents to them by different acts of assenting. This is confirmed by the consideration that only God exists from eternity and that there have not always been *propositiones* or *complexa*. Nevertheless we must suppose that, given that you are not seated now, God once gave his assent to your not being seated (*quod tu non sedes*). Fourthly, one assents primarily to a thing, since it is decided whether a *propositio* is true or false according as the thing is or is not (*in eo quod res est vel non est*); one has, therefore, first to find out whether the thing is such as the *propositio* denotes and only then (in case it is) does one assent to the *propositio* itself. Finally, if the *complexum* theory were right, every act of assenting or knowing would be an act directed back upon itself (*actus reflexus*).

In *Quodlibeta* I, 6, Holkot further specifies the thing signified by the *complexum* by pointing out that, according to Chatton, the act of believing the *propositio* 'God is three and one' has for its object God himself and that the act of knowing 'Man is an animal' has for its object man. He then goes on to state the following objections against Chatton's position. What is known must be true; but the thing signified by a conclusion cannot be said to be true. Further, in the case of such true *propositiones* as 'Man is not an ass' it is not clear what the thing signified by the *propositio* is; for the *propositio* signifies both man and ass. Moreover, if the truth of a *propositio* were the thing itself which is signified by the parts of the *propositio,* the things in the outside world (being truths or falsehoods) would be contradictory. And then it would follow that a thing is its own contradictory, since every thing signified by 'Socrates exists' is signified also by 'Socrates does not exist'. But one might just as well draw the conclusion that, the things signified being the same, if the one is true, the other is true too. This argument shows a certain resemblance to an argument about contradictory statements adduced in *In II Sent.,* q. 2, art. 4. Finally, Holkot calls attention to the fact that something which is first doubted may later be believed or known; as that which is doubted is certainly a *complexum*, that which is believed or known must be a *complexum* too.

Before making a few comments upon Chatton's doctrine and Holkot's criticism I shall outline the view defended by Crathorn.

13.2. William of Crathorn

It has been conclusively shown by Schepers (1970) that the opponent to whom Holkot in the first of his *Sex articuli* refers as *quidam socius reverendus* is William of Crathorn, a fellow Dominican who had lectured on the *Sentences* at Oxford in 1330–1332 and had vehemently attacked Holkot in his first lecture on the Bible in the summer of 1332. Thanks to a second article by Schepers (1972), in which several extracts from Crathorn's commentary on the *Sentences* have been made available, we now also have some reliable information about Crathorn's view from a primary source.

13.2.1. From the passages in Crathorn's commentary on the *Sentences* that have been made accessible by Schepers (1972) we learn that for Crathorn the *verbum mentale* of which Augustine said that it belongs to no particular language is a natural sign of things, either as a sense-impression or as a mental image. But he refuses to call every such *verbum mentale* a mental term. Mental terms are only those *verba mentalia* which are likenesses of spoken or written words. Mental terms are not natural signs of the things outside language but rather, like the spoken or written words of which they are images, conventional signs of the things outside language. Accordingly, Crathorn recognizes three kinds of *propositiones*: the spoken *propositio* and the written *propositio*, both signifying in a conventional way, and a mental *propositio* which is a likeness of either a spoken utterance or written marks and belongs to the same particular language as the spoken or written *propositio* of which it is a sense-impression or mental image. The point where Crathorn most conspicuously differs from Ockham and Holkot is his refusal to apply the names *terminus mentalis* and *propositio mentalis* to acts of apprehending and of thinking that something is the case which do not belong to any particular language and signify things in a natural way. For Crathorn the semantic relation between *termini* or *propositiones* and the things outside language is always of a conventional nature.

Further, Crathorn rejects the thesis that everything that is known, either by scientific proof or by direct insight, is a mental or vocal *propositio*. What is known is rather that which is signified by the *propositio*, the *totale significatum* which is different from the *propositio* itself which is a conventional sign. He supports his view by arguments of the following kind. If someone knows that every compound is liable to disintegrate, the cause of that which he knows is the fact that the compound is made up of contraries (*compositio ex contrariis*). But nobody will consider this fact as the cause of the *propositio* 'Every compound is liable to disintegrate' (*omne mixtum est corruptibile*). It is rather the cause of that which is denoted or imported by the *propositio*. Moreover, two persons who do not share any mental or vocal *propositio*, for example an Englishman and a Greek, may know one and the same thing, for instance, that there will be an eclipse of the sun on a certain day.

Consequently, Crathorn rejects the statement that a *propositio* of the form 'There will be an eclipse of the sun' is knowable or known. What is known or can be known is that of which the *propositio* is a conventional sign. One of the reasons why we use *propositiones* as signs is that we are often unable to show the known things themselves to others to whom we want to communicate what we know. But it would be wrong to confuse the signs with the significates. Another distinction which should be kept in mind according to Crathorn is that between judging that a whole is larger than its parts and judging that the *complexum* 'A whole is larger than its parts' is true. One may form the first judgment without forming the second. Only if a *propositio* is actually conceived or uttered or written and is in fact a conventional sign for somebody can it be called true or false. Crathorn agrees with Ockham and Holkot that the truth or falsehood of a *propositio* is nothing but the true or false *propositio* itself.

13.2.2. The information from Crathorn's commentary on the *Sentences* can be supplemented by what Holkot tells us about his opponent's views in the first of the *Sex articuli*. There it is said that in his attempt to refute the thesis that the object of knowledge, belief, or opinion is a *complexum* and not a thing outside the mind signified by the term or terms of such a *propositio* Crathorn used the following arguments. Someone who has been born deaf and blind can know, believe, or opine such things as that a fire is warm or that Socrates is a good man. What he knows, believes, or opines cannot be a *propositio* because he has never seen or heard a written or spoken *propositio* and consequently cannot form any mental images of spoken words or written marks. The same applies to a new-born baby; it knows or believes that milk has a pleasant taste even though it cannot yet form any mental *propositio*. Further, although a lamb does not form any *complexum*, it immediately believes that the wolf is its enemy. Similarly, when a raven is building its nest it judges that a twig lies better in this way than in that way or that one twig lies better than another, without forming any *complexum*. The last argument that Crathorn adduces against the *complexum* theory is one that clearly comes from the theological dispute concerning the article of faith. The Jews believe that the incarnation of Christ is still to come, while Christians believe that it is already past; now that of which the Jews believe that it is still to come and of which the Christians believe that it belongs to the past is certainly not a *propositio*.

It is obvious that the controversy between Crathorn and the adherents of the *complexum* theory is at least partly terminological. Accordingly, Holkot points out that Crathorn's arguments are largely based on his gratuitous assumption that there is only one kind of mental *propositio,* namely a mental image of a spoken or written *propositio.* As soon as one allows that there are also mental *propositiones* in the sense of Aristotle, Augustine, and Anselm, that is, mental *propositiones* that consist of concepts or natural significations of things, his objections lose much of their force. In that case it can be replied that someone who has been born deaf and blind is still able to form a mental *propositio* in the primary sense and that what he knows or believes is that mental *propositio.* As for the new-born baby, the lamb, and the raven, Holkot maintains that they form *propositiones imaginatae,* presumably consisting of mental images of things; in this connection he appeals to Aristotle, *Metaphysics* 980 b 21, where animals are said to possess a certain degree of sagacity.

Among the arguments which Holkot originally had brought forward against Crathorn there are three which he also adduced against Chatton in *Quodlibeta* I, 6 (ed. Courtenay 18–34; cf. 13.1.2). That only that which is true can be known and that a thing signified by a *propositio* cannot be said to be true. That it cannot be decided which thing is signified by the *propositio* 'Man is not an ass'; with the addition that if it is answered that both man and ass are signified, one thing has to be simultaneously an ass and a man, since according to his opponents the significate of a *propositio* is one thing. And that from the fact that something which was first doubted can later be believed or known and that only a *complexum* can be doubted it follows that what is believed or known must be a *complexum* too.

To the first argument Crathorn replied by denying that a thing signified by a *propositio* cannot be true. According to him it follows from the Boethian definition of a *propositio* as a combination of words which signifies something true or false that the significate of a *propositio* is true or false. And as the significate is distinct from the *propositio,* it may happen that the significate is true and is believed or known without any *propositio* being true or being believed or known. When pressed by Holkot to specify the thing signified in particular cases, Crathorn answered that the significate of *Caesar est* is the existence of Caesar (*existentia Caesaris*) or the connection of Caesar with the present moment (*copulatio Caesaris ad instans praesens*); that the significate of *Caesar non est* is the non-existence of Caesar or the non-connection of Caesar with the present moment; that the significate of *Caesar fuit* is the pastness of Caesar (*praeteritio Caesaris*); that the significate of *Antichristus erit* is the futurity of the Antichrist (*futuritio Antichristi*) or the connection of the Antichrist with the future; and that the significate of *homo non est asinus* is the essential or local separation of man and ass (*distinctio essentialis vel localis hominis et asini*).

Since the futurity of the Antichrist, for instance, is certainly not a thing in any straightforward sense, Crathorn seems to have been forced to concede that the significate of *Antichristus erit* is nothing. In Holkot's eyes this admission is equivalent to a *reductio ad absurdum* of the whole doctrine, since for him everything that is true and known must be something that exists. As he points out in *Quodlibeta* I, 6 (ed. Courtenay 81–101), however, that which is known, believed, or opined cannot be a thing signified because such expressions as *scio lapidem* ('I know that a stone') or *credo deum* ('I believe that God') are ungrammatical. There are only two exceptions to the rule that only a *complexum* of the form *quod lapis est durus* or *deum esse trinum et unum* can be true and the object of knowledge. In the first place, God is true, being the one true knowledge that is equivalent and prior to every true *complexum*. In the second place, it sometimes happens that by a convention a certain object is made the equivalent of a *complexum,* for example a hoop at the entrance of an inn signifying that there is wine in the cellar. In such a case it may be said that the hoop is true. But apart from these exceptions, it is only an actually existing *complexum* that can be called true or the object of knowledge, belief, and opinion.

In his further criticism of Crathorn's doctrine Holkot steadfastly tries to interpret the thing signified in as literal a sense as possible, preferably as a substance or accident indicated by a categorematic term. Operating from this base he has no difficulty in showing that even if there are such things corresponding to the categorematic parts of a *propositio,* the consequences of the *res* view are disastrous. If, for example, we suppose that the significate of a *propositio* is one thing, the significate of the two contradictory statements *deus est* and *deus non est* will be the same; since the significate of a true *propositio* is true, the two contradictory *propositiones* will both have a true significate and will therefore both be true. Moreover, if the significate of a *propositio* is exclusively determined by the categorematic parts, all the *propositiones* which are represented in the square of opposition will have the same significate, since their difference depends entirely upon syncategorematic signs of quality and quantity. From the thesis that what is known or believed is the significate of the *propositio* it further follows that the same thing will be simultaneously known and doubted by the same person and even that everything that is known by him will not be known by him. The first consequence is established in this way. Suppose that 'Tullius' and 'Marcus' are two names for the same man, that you believe that the man concerned has only the name 'Tullius', and that you see him running. If somebody now propounds to you the *propositio* 'Tullius runs', you will agree that it is true; but if he says 'Marcus runs', you will not know whether that is true. Yet the significate is the same, and therefore exactly the same thing will simultaneously be known and doubted. The proof of the second consequence is as follows. Let us call all the *propositiones* in Latin that you know *A,* all the equivalent *propositiones* in Greek *B* (but you do not know Greek), and all the significates of two equivalent *propositiones C.* Now some *A* is known by you; therefore some *C* is known by you; but then also some *B* is known by you. On the other hand, some *B* is not known by you; therefore some *C* is not known by you. Consequently, some *C* is simultaneously known by you and not known by you. This argument may be compared to the one which Holkot uses in *Quodlibeta* I, 6 (ed. Courtenay 241–252) to refute the thesis 'I know that it is so in reality as is signified by a certain *propositio*; therefore I know that this *propositio* is true'. Let us suppose, he says there, that I know some *propositio* in Latin; that means that I know that it is so as is signified by it. Let it further be supposed that a *propositio* in Greek which is exactly equivalent to it is written on a wall and that I know no Greek. Now the *propositio* in Greek is obviously true and I know that it is so in reality as is signified by it; nevertheless it is certain that I do not know that the Greek *propositio* is true, since I do not even know whether the Greek characters have a meaning or not. I may therefore know that it is so as is signified by some *propositio* and at the same time doubt whether this *propositio* is true or not. Holkot cites this counterexample against those who maintain that God already knows a new written statement, because he formerly knew another statement which is equivalent to it or because he formerly knew that it is so in reality as is signified by the new written statement. It is plausible, I think, that one of those he has in mind is Crathorn and that in using such phrases as 'I know that it is so in reality as is signified by the *propositio*' he is taking over the idiom of the upholders of the view that the object of knowledge is the significate of the *propositio.* The move that he attributes to his opponents, namely that God knows the new written statement because he already knows its significate by means of an equivalent statement, is exactly similar to the move that some *B* is known by you, since some *C* is known by you by means of some *A* which is equivalent to *B.* It is doubtful, however, whether this version does justice to what Crathorn actually held. As we noted in 13.2.1,

Crathorn denied that a *propositio* can be called knowable or known and it is therefore unlikely that he would have agreed with Holkot's presentation in which *propositiones* are said to be known.

13.2.3. From Holkot's polemics with Crathorn and Chatton it is clear that he treats them very much alike and hardly allows for any difference between their views. He takes it for granted that the only thing they can mean by the significate of a *propositio* is the substances or accidents which are referred to by the categorematic terms occurring as parts of the *propositio*. And his criticism is consistently adapted to this interpretation. Now the question may be raised whether Holkot is right in so assimilating the doctrines of Chatton and Crathorn. And this question actually comes down to asking whether the presentation that Holkot offers of each doctrine is trustworthy.

As for Chatton, we have no reason to doubt that he considered the object of assent as the *res significata per complexum*, since these words often occur in his own writings. But what may be questioned is whether Holkot gives the whole truth when he states that according to Chatton the object of believing *deus est trinus et unus* is God and the object of knowing *homo est animal* man. When he sums up the arguments which Chatton put forward against the *complexum* theory (*In I Sent.*, q. 2), he reports him as saying that God assented to your not being seated (*quod tu non sedes*) and that before giving one's assent to the *propositio* one has to see that the thing is so (*quod res sic se habeat*) as the *complexum* indicates. From these remarks it may be concluded that for Chatton the *res* is not just a thing denoted by a categorematic term occurring in the *propositio*, but that thing as being in a certain state; in other words, not just God or man but God as being three and one and man as being an animal. Only such an interpretation, in which the thing signified is determined by the syncategorematic as well as the categorematic terms occurring in the *propositio*, can make sense of the fact that Chatton appeals to the Aristotelian formula 'according as the thing is or is not' (*in eo quod res est vel non est*). It is not the existence of God and of man which makes the above-mentioned statements true but rather the existence of God as three and one and the existence of man as an animal, or God's being three and one and man's being an animal. This interpretation, moreover, is in complete harmony with what Abelard says about the *res* theorists of his time, namely that they held that a *propositio* of the form *homo est animal* signifies as a whole simultaneously man and animal in such a state that the one is the other. And we shall see that this kind of interpretation is also found in later writers, for instance André de Neufchâteau (Cf. 15.3). In all probability Chatton drew no clear distinction between such phrases as 'man in so far as he is an animal' (*homo ens animal*) and 'man's being an animal' or 'that man is an animal' (*hominem esse animal*). When he ascribed truth and falsity to the thing signified by the *propositio* as a whole and made this thing the object of assent, he must have shifted his attention from, for example, *tu non sedens* ('you not being seated') to *quod tu non sedes* ('that you are not seated' or 'your not being seated'). At any rate it is practically certain that Holkot made his task far too easy by concentrating on the thing signified by categorematic terms and refusing to see the essential contribution of the syncategorematic terms.

In the case of Crathorn it is very striking that the phrase *res significata per propositionem* which Holkot constantly uses along with *significatum propositionis* nowhere occurs in the excerpts from Crathorn's commentary on the *Sentences* which Schepers (1972) has published. There we find such expressions as *totum* or *totale significatum propositionis* or *id quod per propositionem significatur* (*denotatur, exprimitur, importatur*), but never *res significata*. In stating the truth-conditions of a *propositio* Crathorn, appealing to the Aristotelian formula *in eo quod res est vel non est*, says that a *propositio* is true when something is or is not as is signified by the *propositio*. The significate of the *propositio* seems to be a *sic esse* or *ita esse* which may be expressed by such phrases as 'that there can be an eclipse of the sun' or 'that every compound is liable to disintegrate'. But according to Holkot Crathorn also used such noun-phrases as *existentia Caesaris, non-existentia Caesaris, praeteritio Caesaris,* and *futuritio Antichristi,* probably as equivalents of 'that Caesar exists, does not exist, has existed' and 'that the Antichrist will exist'. This usage, together with the fact that *significatum* may easily — and often harmlessly — be paraphrased as *res significata,* offered Holkot the opportunity to treat Crathorn's significate as intended as a thing in the sense of a substance or accident denoted by a categorematic term. In fact, however, it seems much more likely that Crathorn's position lies somewhere on the line which connects Abelard and Gregory of Rimini (whom I shall consider in the next chapter). That he was even more vulnerable to criticisms founded upon a one-sided *res* interpretation than these two is partly due to the fact that he apparently also used noun-phrases to refer to the significate. He may have done so under the influence of the theologians who spoke of the *nativitas, passio, resurrectio,* and *ascensio Christi* as the things signified by the utterances containing the articles of faith. Just as the theologians wavered among things, events, facts, and the contents of belief and assertion (Cf. 11.2.2), Crathorn himself may not always have been sure of the exact borderlines between these possibilities and may in this way have facilitated such extreme interpretations as the one forced on him by Holkot. After all, Holkot's onslaught could hardly have been acceptable to his audience if there had been no foothold at all for his interpretation.

The difference between the *res* theory which Abelard mentions and his own position may be summarized by saying that for the reists the significate of a *propositio* is a *res sic se habens,* a thing in a certain state, while for Abelard it is a *quidam rerum modus habendi se,* a certain state of things. The same difference is probably intended by Bonaventure when he points out that the *enuntiabile* signifies a *modus se habendi* rather than a thing (*In I Sent.,* Dist. 41, art. 2, q. 2). Now it is a plausible hypothesis, I think, that Chatton's *res significata per complexum* comes nearest to a *res sic se habens,* for example *homo ens animal,* whereas Crathorn's *significatum propositionis* is more like a *rerum modus habendi se,* for instance *hominem esse animal* or *quod homo est animal.* As both of them were primarily concerned to stress that which is signified in contrast with the signifying *propositio* or *complexum,* they tended to be somewhat careless about the internal differentiations that may be called for on the side of that which is signified, for instance between things as they are denoted by categorematic terms, things as being in a certain state, events or states as they are part of the world, facts, and contents of belief and assertion. The circumstance that their theory and the terminology in which it was expressed was not unambiguously fixed to exactly one point on this more or less continuous line, made it easy for Holkot to push both of them to the extreme where the significate is the thing in the sense of a substance or accident denoted by a categorematic term.

13.3. Walter Burleigh

13.3.1. In *Quodlibeta* III, 5, William of Ockham discusses the question whether a mental *propositio* is made up of things or of concepts. According to him those who considered things as the constituents of mental *propositiones* tried to establish their point by indicating that the mind is able to combine that which it understands with something else and that the mind understands things; therefore the mind is able to compound things which thus become the subject and the predicate of a mental *propositio*. Moreover, the truth of an affirmative statement requires the identity of its subject and predicate. As the sounds and the concepts which serve as subject and predicate in the vocal and conceived *propositio* are not the same, what is identical must be the things themselves which are therefore capable of being the subject and the predicate of a *propositio*. Ockham adduces no less than eight arguments against this view that there is a *propositio* consisting of actual things. If it were true, we could, for example, form a *propositio* out of an intellective soul and a body; such a *propositio* would then be a man. Or it would be possible to say about such a *propositio* as 'The dog eats the bread' that the subject eats the predicate.

There can be little doubt that Ockham's attack is aimed at Walter Burleigh. In the prooemium to his commentary on the *Categories*[3] — of which the final version may be dated around 1337 — Burleigh defends a view like the one described by Ockham, with the only difference that Burleigh speaks of a separate *propositio in re* rather than of a mental *propositio* consisting of actual things.

At the very beginning of his commentary on the *Categories* Burleigh makes mention of a disagreement in opinion between, on the one side, Boethius and Simplicius and, on the other side, the Arabian philosophers Avicenna and Averroës. While the former held that Aristotle's treatise is about words, according to the latter it is primarily about things. Burleigh agrees with the Arabian thinkers. In his opinion the interpretation that the *Categories* is about words leads to the absurd consequence that all the categories, being sounds, would belong to the one category of quality, since a spoken sound is a sensible quality (Cf. *In Categorias* 2 a 4). Moreover, he is convinced that several passages in Aristotle's *Categories* and *De interpretatione* clearly point to a *res* interpretation. In *Cat.* 1 a 16 it is stated that of things that are said some involve combination (*complexio*) while others are said without combination. Boethius and Simplicius interpret the phrase 'of things that are said' (*eorum quae dicuntur*) in the sense of significant sounds that are uttered. Averroës, on the other hand, maintains that Aristotle is speaking of the things that are signified by words or combinations of words. Burleigh himself adopts an intermediate position, holding that *complexa* and *incomplexa* are found both on the level of signifying expressions and on the level of the things signified (Cf. *In Categorias* 1 a 16). Next, in *Cat.* 1 a 20 Aristotle declares that of the existing things some are said of a subject but are not in any subject; for example, man is said of a subject, the individual man, but is not in any subject. According to Burleigh this means that the *moderni* who believe that nothing but a sound or a concept can be universal are wrong; for in that case every universal would be in a subject. If it is true that there are universals that are not in any subject, there must be universals outside the mind, since otherwise, if they were in the mind, they would be in a subject (Cf. *In Categorias* 1 a 20). Furthermore, Burleigh calls attention to *De int.* 16 b 7, 10, and 17 a 37. In the first passage Aristotle points out that a verb is always a sign of things said of something else; what is predicated and also that of

---

[3] In *Super artem veterem Porphyrii et Aristotelis,* Venetiis, 1497, reprinted Frankfurt, 1967.

which it is predicated are therefore things. In the second passage it is stated that of actual things some are universal and others particular; so it must sometimes be of a universal that one asserts that something holds or does not hold, sometimes of a particular thing (Cf. *In De interpretatione* 16 b 7 and 17 a 37).

Elaborating these data Burleigh maintains that, since the mind is able to compound things with each other by asserting that they are the same and to separate one thing from another by asserting that they are not the same and since a *propositio* is nothing but this compounding or separating activity of the mind, things can be part of a *propositio,* as subject or predicate. Apart from written, vocal, and mental *propositiones,* there are therefore also *propositiones* compounded of things outside the mind, so-called *propositiones in re.* Such a *propositio in re* is the adequate (*adaequatum*) and ultimate (*ultimum* or *ultimatum*) significate of the mental *propositio* which consists of concepts. If the written marks are the signs of a vocal utterance and the vocal utterance signifies a mental *propositio*, the mental *propositio* cannot again signify something that signifies, for this would lead to an infinite regress. Since the mental *propositio* itself is not the ultimate significate in the sense of something that is signified and does not signify something else, we must assume that the process of signifying comes to an end in an *aggregatum, compositum,* or *complexum* of things. This complex significate is different from the things signified by the subject and the predicate of the vocal or mental *propositio.* Burleigh explicitly rejects the view that, for instance, *homo est lapis* ultimately signifies only man and stone. In that case there would be no difference between *homo est lapis* and the phrase *homo lapis* and both would be false. He even refuses to accept the modified thesis that both expressions mean the same with respect to things but in a different way.

Another consideration by which Burleigh supports the assumption of a *propositio in re* is that questions are about things and not about concepts. Since questions become conclusions, according to Aristotle, *Posterior Analytics* 89 b 23, the conclusions must be about things too. Burleigh rather unashamedly exploits the ambiguity of the Latin phrase *de rebus* which can mean both 'about things' and 'out of things' and concludes that the *propositiones* which correspond to questions are not only about things but made out of things. Similarly, it is argued against those who hold that the conclusion of a scientific proof is a vocal or mental *propositio* that from this view it follows that all that is known by scientific proof are sounds and concepts. Since this consequence is palpably false with respect to such sciences about things as physics and metaphysics, there must be *propositiones* which are not composed of sounds or concepts but of the things themselves. Only in this way, moreover, can it be explained that our knowledge about the natural world is the same as the knowledge Aristotle had about it. Although the vocal utterances and the acts of conceiving may be different, the things have remained the same; these things are therefore what scientific conclusions are about and that of which they are composed.

Every *propositio* contains a material element and a formal element. In a *propositio in re* the things which serve as subject and predicate are the matter and the copula which consists in the compounding or separating activity of the mind is the form. A *propositio in re* is therefore partly in the mind and partly outside the mind. Burleigh then raises the question how something that exists in the mind and something that exists outside the mind can form a unity. Oddly enough, however, he does not give an answer to this question but offers an answer that rather fits another question, namely how it can be explained that the things which are the subject and the predicate of a *propositio in re* become a unity of some kind. Burleigh distinguishes between real composition, for instance the construction of a house out of stones and wood, and intellectual composition in which the mind combines a subject with a predicate. The product of such an intellectual composition is an *ens copulatum*. In order to elucidate this notion Burleigh draws a parallel with sense-perception. When an act of attending unites the seeing in the eye and the visible object outside the eye so that we can speak of an object seen, there is an *ens copulatum* consisting of the object and the act of seeing. Neither the act of attending nor the intellectual composition are said to be part of the *ens copulatum* which they produce. The intellectual composition is an act of coupling the subject-thing with the predicate-thing and the result of this act is a new entity, the *ens copulatum* or the subject-coupled- with-the-predicate.

This confusion of two questions betrays, I believe, a further confusion which vitiates Burleigh's notion of a *propositio in re*. On the one hand, he is concerned to emphasize, against the *moderni,* that a *propositio* is about things outside the mind, both universal and particular. This insight leads him, *via* the ambiguity of the phrase *de rebus,* to posit a *propositio in re* as something that consists of a formal ingredient, the compounding or separating activity of the mind, and a material ingredient, the actual things of which the identity or non-identity is asserted. It is this *propositio in re* that is interpreted by Ockham as a mental *propositio* that is made up of things rather than of concepts. On the other hand, Burleigh also takes the *propositio in re* as the product of the intellectual composition by which the mind couples the subject-thing with the predicate-thing, which product is an *ens copulatum,* the identity or non-identity of two things. While the first *propositio in re,* on account of its formal component, still shares something of the signifying character of the mental, vocal, and written *propositiones,* the second *propositio in re,* the *ens copulatum,* is precisely what is needed as the ultimate significate: what is believed or asserted is the identity or non-identity of two things. It is this *ens copulatum* that Burleigh identifies with the *res* in the Aristotelian formula *in eo quod res est vel non est* (*In Categorias* 14 b 12). If the *res,* namely the alleged identity or non-identity of the subject-thing and the predicate-thing, exists or is part of the world, then it is so as the mental *propositio* signifies and this *propositio* is therefore true; if the *res* does not exist, the mental *propositio* is false. In the prooemium to his commentary on the *Categories* Burleigh expresses the same view by saying that in the case of a true *propositio* the actual identity or non-identity of two things corresponds to the copula that exists in the mind, whereas in the case of a false *propositio* only the things exist in reality but not their alleged identity or non-identity. In other words, the ultimate and adequate significate of a *propositio* as a whole is an existing thing or a state of affairs that is actually the case if the *propositio* is true, and a non-existing thing or a state of affairs that is not the case in reality if the *propositio* is false. What exists in both cases is the things in so far as they are the significates of the categorematic concepts of the mental *propositio.* It should be noted that Burleigh apparently does not hold that corresponding to a false affirmative *propositio* there is a non-identity of the things concerned and that corresponding to a false negative *propositio* there is an identity of the things concerned.

By introducing his hybrid *propositio in re* Burleigh is able to account for the way in which both true and false *propositiones* signify. In the case of true *propositiones* the significate is the actual *complexum* as it belongs to the world of facts, the circumstance that one thing is identical or non-identical with another thing. In the case of false *propositiones* he can avoid embarrassing questions about the nature of a non-existent state of affairs by falling back upon the version of a *propositio in re* according to which it is an activity of the mind that compounds or separates things by judging that they are the same or not the same. This latter version of a *propositio in re* is involved in true as well as in false beliefs or assertions. Burleigh introduces it in order to counter the *complexum* theory of the *moderni* and to stress the fact that beliefs and assertions are about things outside the mind rather than about words and concepts. When we believe or assert something false, we claim the identity or non-identity of universal or particular things. But in fact we succeed only in referring to the things; in the world no identity or non-identity corresponds to the mental copula and this absence renders the belief or the assertion false. When we believe or assert something true, we equally claim the identity or non-identity of things, but now the things are as a matter of fact identical or non-identical and we therefore succeed in referring not only to the things but also to a state of those things corresponding to our claim. So there is always a *propositio in re* or *complexum* of things in the sense of a judgment about things, but there is not always a *propositio in re* or *complexum* of things in the sense of an actual state of affairs which makes the judgment about the things true. The significate of the *propositio* as such turns out to be not an intermediate entity between the act of judging that something is the case and a feature of the actual world but rather something that coincides with either the one or the other.

13.3.2. In connection with *Cat.* 14 b 12 Burleigh tries to refute the thesis of the *moderni* that a *propositio* cannot be true or false if it is not actually formed, and in particular that from God's existence it does not follow that 'God exists' is true and that from the falsity of a *propositio* it does not follow that its contradictory is true. As we saw in 12.2.2, such a view had been defended by Holkot in *Quodlibeta* I, 6. Burleigh argues that if this view were correct, it would be impossible for a debater to get involved in a contradiction. For given that the affirmative statement and the negative statement do not exist at the same time, the first is not true when the second is false and the second is not false when the first is true. Moreover, every disputation becomes pointless, since the respondent cannot react to the *propositiones* that are propounded by his opponent. He cannot do so before the opponent has formulated his thesis because at that time he does not yet know what the thesis is; neither can he answer at the same time because then they would have to talk simultaneously; and when the opponent has formulated his thesis, the respondent cannot give any answer to it because it does not exist any longer and is therefore neither true nor false. If it is said that the respondent reacts to a *propositio* that he conceives in his own mind, it can be replied that in that case he would not react to the thesis propounded by the opponent but only to his own *propositio*. Finally, if a *propositio* is not true unless it exists, such logical rules as 'The antecedent is true, therefore the consequent is true' lose their validity.

More positively, Burleigh points out that, in the first place, a *propositio* that has been formulated but does not actually exist any longer can still be remembered. In general, it often happens that something which does not exist in the actual world has a signification and makes the mind think of something, for instance in dreams. But apart from this the mind can also understand a *propositio* which is abstracted from particular utterances, just as it can think of a lion or an elephant in general without conceiving of a particular lion or elephant. In connection with *De int.* 17 a 37 Burleigh states that the word *homo* uttered by me and the word *homo* uttered by you have something in common, a universal nature that exists in both particular utterances and is distinguishable from them. In the same way the mind can understand a *propositio*, for instance *deus est*, which is the universal nature common to both the particular expression *deus est* uttered by me and the similar particular expression *deus est* uttered by you. Even if one is not willing to concede that such a universal exists outside the mind, it cannot be doubted that it can be the object of the understanding. Burleigh believes that in a disputation both the respondent and the opponent have this kind of universal before their mind and that by means of this universal it can be explained that a debater contradicts himself, because the universal is something that remains the same throughout the debate and can be first conceded and then denied.

Accordingly, he distinguishes between two kinds of *propositio in mente.* On the one hand, there is a *propositio* which has an *esse subiective in mente,* being in the soul as a quality in a subject; this mental *propositio* consists of acts of understanding and is itself a particular act of thinking that something is the case. On the other hand, there is a *propositio* that has an *esse obiective in intellectu,* being the object of the understanding; it is a universal grasped by the mind, distinct from the particular *propositiones* from which it is abstracted but still signifying something true or false. The same distinction between being in the mind subjectively and being in the mind objectively is made by Holkot (*Quodlibeta* I, 6, ed. Courtenay 279–292) in connection with Aristotle's remark that the true and the false are in the soul (*Metaphysics* 1027 b 25). For Holkot the only mental *propositio* is an *intentio existens subiective in intellectu,* a particular act of thinking which is a real quality of the mind. Although Holkot recognizes *propositiones* which are images of spoken or written statements, his system has no room for the abstract entity which Burleigh introduces as the common element of particular *propositiones* and which may perhaps be interpreted as an intensional variety of the utterance-type in so far as it is used to make one definite statement.

14. THE THEORY OF THE *COMPLEXE SIGNIFICABILE*

In the theológical disputes concerning the identity of the article of faith and the immutability of God's knowledge and in the ensuing debates about the object of assent that took place in the third and fourth decade of the fourteenth century the contestants can be regarded as belonging to either of two camps. One is made up of those who emphasize the role of the sign, both natural and conventional, the other of those who stress the importance of the significate or the thing signified. Although there are no doubt considerable differences in the ways these positions were worked out in detail, the general picture is one of a controversy between two parties, the defenders of that which signifies against the defenders of that which is signified. This situation was changed when a third theory succeeded in establishing itself between the *complexum* theory and a *res* theory in a narrower sense. This theory of the *complexe significabile,* of that which can be signified only in a complex way, was most forcibly championed by the Augustinian monk Gregory of Rimini, in the commentary on the *Sentences* which he completed shortly before 1345 in Paris[1].

14.1. Gregory of Rimini

14.1.1. Appealing to Augustine and Anselm, Gregory (*Prologus,* q.1, art.3) distinguishes, apart from the written and vocal *propositio,* two kinds of mental *propositio.* One kind consists of mental images of vocal (or written) *propositiones;* such mental *propositiones* belong to a particular language and are as

---

[1] *Super primo et secundo Sententiarum,* Venetiis, 1522, reprinted St. Bonaventure, N.Y., 1955.

diverse as the vocal utterances of which they are the likenesses. The other kind is formed by the mental *propositiones* in the proper sense which do not belong to any particular language and are the natural signs that precede the written marks, the vocal sounds, or the mental images. The latter three conventionally signify the same as the mental *propositio* in the proper sense but in a secondary and subordinate way. That the difference between this conception (which we also found in Ockham) and the orthodox Aristotelian view was rather small is clear from *In II Sent.,* Dist. 9–10, q.2, art.1, where Gregory says that the secondary sign which signifies the same in subordination to the primary sign is therefore in a sense (*quodammodo*) the sign of the primary sign.

Of the mental *propositio* in the proper sense there are again two sorts: acts of assenting and acts of knowing. Acts of assenting are mere acts of believing or thinking that something is the case; one mentally says and judges (*enuntiat mente et iudicat*) that it is so or is not so, but one does not have direct or mediate knowledge about the matter judged. The other kind of mental *propositiones* in the proper sense consists of acts that are not only acts of assenting but also of knowing (*notitia, scientia, cognitio*). The written and the vocal *propositio* and the conceived *propositio* as a mental image are neither acts of assenting nor of knowing. On the other hand, the mental *propositio* in the proper sense is never a neutral act of compounding or separating, without assent or dissent. Gregory discusses at some length the question whether the mental *propositio* in the proper sense is made up of partial acts of knowing of which one is the subject and the other the predicate or is rather one undivided act. On several grounds he thinks it more reasonable to assume that it is not composite. When we nevertheless are inclined to speak of the subject and the predicate of such a mental *propositio,* this can be explained by the fact that it is equivalent in signification to vocal or written *propositiones* which are indeed compounded of parts or by the fact that, according to Aristotle (*Metaphysics* 1027 b 20), it is the sign of a composition or division in the outside world.

Strictly speaking, a scientific proof consists of acts of knowing (*notitiae*). Written or spoken syllogisms or syllogisms formed by means of mental images of written marks or spoken sounds are proofs only in a secondary sense, in so far as their conventional signification is subordinate to a mental syllogism in the proper sense. From this it follows that the conclusion of a proper mental demonstration is an act of assenting and at the same time an act of knowing that it is so as the conclusion signifies. According to Gregory the conclusion is simultaneously an act of naturally signifying or mentally saying that something is the case (*actus enuntiandi*), an act of believing or assenting that it is so (*actus credendi seu assentiendi*), and an act of knowing that it is so (*actus cognoscendi*). This identity of the acts of mentally saying, assenting, and knowing in the conclusion of a scientific proof is defended in detail against those who argued that the act of mentally saying is different from the acts of assenting and of knowing or that the act of assenting is different from the act of knowing. It may, for example, be pointed out that the mind can form a *propositio* without knowing that it is so as it says or even without any assent. Gregory's answer is that this may be true for mental *propositiones* in the secondary sense which may be conceived without being accompanied by an act of assenting, but that such a *propositio* is never a conclusion in the strict sense, since that is always an act of knowing. Another counterexample that was adduced is the case of somebody who sees a stick which is partly under water and then forms the *propositio* 'That stick is broken', to which he assents. That this *propositio* cannot be the act of assenting is clear from the fact that if the same person later becomes convinced that the stick is not really broken, he still has the same *propositio* in his mind but no longer assents to it. Gregory replies that in such circumstances there are two mental *propositiones* in the proper sense, one act of assenting and one act of dissenting. What remains the same must be a mental *propositio* in the secondary sense, which is neither an act of assenting nor of dissenting. The same applies to the case of a believer and an unbeliever who form *propositiones* of the same kind, while the first assents to the *propositio* that he forms and the second withholds his assent from one which is exactly similar. According to Gregory the *propositiones* that are exactly similar must be mental images of spoken utterances or written marks; as for a mental *propositio* in the strict sense, there is one in the believer's mind in so far as he performs an act of assenting but none in the unbeliever's mind.

14.1.2. In *Prologus*, q.l, art.l, Gregory raises the question of what exactly the object of theology is, and in that connection he discusses the more general problem of the nature of the object of knowledge that is acquired by scientific proof. He first mentions Ockham's doctrine that the object of knowledge is the conclusion itself, quoting the distinction between *subiectum scientiae* and *obiectum scientiae* (touched upon at the end of 12.1.4) and a number of arguments that Ockham adduced in support of his theory. Gregory rejects the *complexum* theory on the following grounds. If the object of knowledge acquired by scientific proof were the conclusion itself, then it would follow that someone who has knowledge by means of a demonstration actually apprehends the conclusion. But in fact this is very seldom the case. Usually someone who proves something draws the conclusion without explicitly apprehending it and reflecting upon it. In the normal case what is known is not the conclusion as an apprehended *complexum* or *propositio* but rather that which the conclusion signifies, namely that it is so and so. Gregory admits that besides this first kind of knowing (*primum scire*) that something is the case there is also a second kind (*secundum scire*), namely knowing that a certain *propositio* is true. But even then it is not the *propositio* itself that is known, but what we know is rather that it is true.

In this connection Gregory introduces three important distinctions. In the first place, there is a difference between the circumstance that it is so or is not so (*sic esse vel non sic esse*) and the circumstance that the *propositio* which states that it is so or is not so is true; this is clear from Aristotle, *Cat.* 14 b 10. A second distinction which should not be overlooked and which also goes back to Aristotle (*Cat.* 12 b 6) is that between the circumstance that it is so and the *propositio* which states that it is so. Thirdly, we should distinguish between a *propositio* and the circumstance that it is true (*ipsam esse veram*). For otherwise it would have to be conceded that in apprehending a *propositio* we also apprehend that it is true. Moreover, it may happen that the same *propositio* is successively true and false. On the base of these distinctions it can be established that the *propositio* is not the object of knowledge. We know either that it is so or is not so or that the *propositio* which states that it is so or is not so is true. But in the light of the second and the third distinction it is evident that the *propositio* is different from both the circumstance that it is so and the circumstance that the *propositio* is true. Therefore, what we know cannot be the *propositio*.

Gregory also rejects the view that the object of knowledge acquired by scientific proof is a thing in the outside world (*res extra*). According to Aristotle (*Nicomachean Ethics* 1139 b 19; *Posterior Analytics* 75 b 21) that which is really known cannot be contingent in the sense that it might be otherwise than it is. But every thing except God is contingent and not necessary. Thus all those sciences which are about other things than God would have a contingent object, which is incompatible with what Aristotle says. Further, Gregory raises two objections against the *res* theory that are similar to Holkot's criticism of that view. If the thing were the object of knowledge, it would equally be the object of opinion, belief, and error and the same person could at the same time know, believe, and opine the same thing and even err about it. Moreover, it would follow that the faithful have a right to believe just as firmly in the devil as in God, since they correctly believe that God is almighty and that the devil is not.

14.1.3. Having eliminated both the view that the object of knowledge is the *propositio* or *complexum* and the view that it is a thing in the outside world, Gregory concludes that the only remaining candidate is that which is signified by the conclusion as a whole. In his opinion, what is known and assented to or believed is that of which the mental *propositio* in the proper sense is a natural sign and of which the vocal and the written *propositio* and the mental images of the spoken sounds or written marks are conventional signs. Apart from obvious paraphrases, Gregory commonly uses for his favourite the name *significatum,* often accompanied by the qualifications *totale* and *adaequatum.* As we saw in 13.2.3, the phrase *totum* or *totale significatum* was already employed by Crathorn. For its meaning we may compare what Abelard (*Glosses,* ed. Geyer p. 365, 27) says about the *res* theorists of his time: they contrasted the way in which the categorematic parts of a *propositio* signify, namely *singillatim* ('one by one'), with the way in which the *propositio* itself signifies, namely *totaliter* ('as a whole'). The word *adaequatum,* which we already met with in discussing Burleigh's theory (Cf. 13.3.1), conveys the same idea of a significate that exactly fits the *propositio* as a whole.

Gregory also frequently uses the word *enuntiabile,* in the old sense in which for many purposes it is synonymous with *significatum.* Even in such ' passages as *In I Sent.,* Dist.39, q.1, art.2, where the traditional problem of the immutability of God's knowledge is discussed, Gregory carefully distinguishes between the *enuntiabile* and the *enuntiatio.* He says, for example, that the *enuntiabile* of the *enuntiatio* 'The word became flesh' was false before the incarnation of Christ, just as the *enuntiatio* itself, if it had been formed, would have been false.

In addition to the familiar terms *significatum* and *enuntiabile,* we further find the phrase (*tantum*) *complexe significabile* for that which is signified by a *propositio.* In classical Latin the word *significabilis* had the sense of 'having meaning, significant'. Varro (*De lingua Latina* VI, 7, 52), for instance, expresses the fact that man utters significant sounds by *homo significabilem ore mittit vocem.* In a passive sense it was probably used for the first time by Augustine, *De magistro* 8, 4: there he proposes to call those things which can be signified and are not signs by the name of *significabilia,* just as the things that can be seen are named *visibilia.* In this passive sense the word became connected with the passage in Aristotle's *Categories* (1 a 16) where it is stated that of things that are said some involve combination while others are said without combination. As we noted in 11.4.2, Thomas Aquinas (*De veritate,* q.4, art.2) considered that which is understood by the mind as either something that is signifiable by a single word (*significabilis per vocem incomplexam*) or as something that is signifiable by a combination of words (*per vocem complexam*). Especially from *In I Sent.,* Dist.28, q.1, art.2, it is clear that

Gregory of Rimini's use of the phrase *complexe significabile* has to be put into this context. He there makes a sharp distinction between single words which signify entities as they are divided into the different categories and *complexa* in the narrow sense of combinations of words that signify that it is so or is not so. While the categories are entities that can be signified by single words and cannot be signified by *complexa* in the narrow sense of affirmations or negations and thus are *incomplexe significabilia,* that which is affirmed or denied must be regarded as *tantum complexe significabile,* as something that can be signified only by a *complexum* in the narrow sense and never by a single word or by a combination of words that lacks affirmative or negative force.

As for the word *dictum,* Gregory (*In I Sent.,* Dist. 42–44, q.2, art.1) points out that the verb *dicere* can be taken in two senses. On the one hand, saying is the same as uttering or forming something said (*dictum proferre vel formare*); in this sense one may say something without signifying anything. On the other hand, saying is the same as signifying something by means of something said (*per dictum aliquid significare*); what is signified in this way might also be signified without uttering any words. In the first sense of *dicere* the word *dictum* may be a synonym of *enuntiatio.* As we noted in 7.1.3, Boethius (*In Categorias,* ed. Migne 64, 286 B) already used *dictum,* along with *sermo,* to render the Greek word *logos.* In the second sense of *dicere* the same word *dictum* would in many contexts be synonymous with *enuntiabile, significatum,* and *significabile.* It is this meaning of *dictum* that was brought into prominence by Abelard and the logicians whose works were discussed in Chapter 10. In all probability the same kind of ambiguity as is found in *dicere* and *dictum* also explains the fact that the word *enuntiabile* could be taken as a synonym of *enuntiatio, propositio,* and *complexum* (Cf. 11.2.2) and at the same time as a synonym of *significatum* and *significabile.* Some understood *enuntiare* and *enuntiabile* in the sense of uttering words and the words uttered, others in the sense of asserting something and the thing asserted or assertable. Gregory of Rimini clearly adheres to the meaning of *enuntiabile* as the significate of a *propositio* or that which is signifiable by a *propositio,* while on the other hand he does not use the word *dictum* in that sense but prefers to take it as indicating the words uttered. This striking difference with Abelard and the logicians who employed *significatum, enuntiabile,* and *dictum* practically interchangeably is not so strange as it may seem at first sight. After all, besides undoubtable similarities, there are also considerable divergences between Abelard's doctrine and Gregory's position. Whereas for Abelard the vocal utterance and its assertive force are always in the centre of his inquiries, for Gregory the spoken *propositio* is secondary and subordinate to the act of assenting which is the mental *propositio* in the proper sense. According to *Prologus,* q.1, art.3, this act of assenting is nothing but an act of judging that it is so, and this judgment is an act of mentally saying that it is so (*enuntiare mentaliter quod sic est*). Since Gregory avoids the verb *dicere* for this act of mentally saying that it is so, and since the spoken *propositio* in itself, without a preceding act of assenting, has no assertive force whatever, he simply has no use for the term *dictum* in Abelard's sense.

14.1.4. Gregory is aware that he can expect at least three objections against his view (*Prologus,* q.1, art.1). In the first place, it may be argued that the significate of a *propositio* as a whole is either something (*aliquid*) or nothing (*nihil*). If it is nothing, then nothing is the object of knowledge and consequently the sciences will have no object, contrary to what Gregory himself holds. If the significate is something, then it is either something that exists in the mind or something that exists outside the mind. The latter possibility is excluded by Gregory's arguments against the *res* theory. In the first case that which exists in the mind is either an *incomplexum* or a *complexum*. As it cannot be an *incomplexum,* it must be a *complexum*; but this assumption is incompatible with Gregory's rejection of the *complexum* theory. Therefore, the significate of a *propositio* as a whole is neither something nor nothing, which is absurd.

In his answer to this first objection Gregory distinguishes three nuances of meaning in such words as *aliquid, res,* and *ens.* In their widest sense these words may stand for everything that is signifiable in an incomplex way, by a single word, or in a complex way, by a combination of words, both truly and falsely. According to Gregory Aristotle uses the word *res* (*pragma*) in this wide sense when he calls the significate of contradictory *propositiones* the underlying things (*Cat.* 12 b 15) and when he states that a combination of words is called true or false according as the thing is or is not (*Cat.* 14 b 21). In the latter case it cannot be Aristotle's intention to say that 'Man is an ass' is false because no man exists or no ass exists or that 'Man is white' is true because man exists or whiteness exists or both exist together; what he means by *res* are the significates of those *propositiones* as a whole, namely that man is an ass and that man is white (*hominem esse album*). Next, there is a somewhat narrower sense in which *aliquid, res,* and *ens* are used to indicate everything that is signifiable in an incomplex way or in a complex way, but only truly, by means of a true statement. In this sense what is signifiable by a false statement is not something but rather a nonentity (*non ens*). For this second meaning Gregory can refer to Aristotle, *Metaphysics* 1017 a 31 and 1027 b 18, and *Posterior Analytics* 71 b 25. Finally, in the strictest acceptation the three words stand only for existing entities. Everything that does not exist as an actual substance or accident is then nothing.

In the light of this threefold distinction Gregory is now able to point out that a significate of a *propositio* as a whole is something in the first sense and often also in the second sense, but never in the third sense. That man is an animal is not something in the sense of an existing substance or accident; all one can say is that it is the same as that man is a living substance possessed of senses and reason. On the other hand, from the fact that the significate that someone has procreated is something different from the significate that some-one has been born it does not follow that those significates are something in the narrow sense of an existing entity (*In I Sent.,* Dist.28, q.1, art.2). It is no doubt possible to move from 'The significate is not something' to 'The signif-icate is nothing' and then to conclude that nothing is the object of knowl-edge. But such an inference is valid only in so far as 'nothing' means the same as 'not a thing in the third sense'. It certainly does not follow that the sciences have no object at all. It should be noted that everything Gregory says about such phrases as *hominem esse animal* applies to them only in so far as they are used in a signifying function (*significative* or *personaliter*). If the phrase *hominem esse animal* merely refers to itself, in a way that was called *materialiter* or *simpliciter,* its significate is of course something in the third sense, namely a complex of sounds (*In I Sent.,* Dist.28, q.1, art.2).

A second objection against Gregory's doctrine is similar to an argument that he himself had advanced against the *res* theory. The objects of knowl-edge must be necessary and eternal. But everything except God is contingent; therefore, the significate of a *propositio* is contingent too and cannot be the object of knowledge. Gregory replies that by the necessary and eternal ob-jects of knowledge we do not intend things in the sense of existing substances or accidents; for all such things are indeed contingent. That the objects of knowledge are necessary and eternal means rather that what is known cannot be otherwise than it is and is always so.

Finally, it may be objected that Gregory's view is inconsistent with his rejection of the *res* theory. For the *propositio* 'God exists' signifies that God exists (*deum esse*) and this significate that God exists which is the object of knowledge and assent is nothing but God himself, since even if we think away everything else God still exists. But then it follows that there is at least one thing outside the mind that is the object of knowledge and this consequence contradicts Gregory's thesis that the object of knowledge is never a thing in the outside world. This objection which will be endlessly repeated in the future is countered by Gregory in two steps. In the first place, he denies that from the fact that if everything else is taken away God still exists it follows that God is the same as that God exists. For one might just as well reason 'If everything but man is taken away, then man does not exist (presumably because in that case God would not exist), therefore man is the same as that man does not exist', which reasoning is invalid, since the antecedent is true and the consequent is false. In the second place, Gregory is prepared to concede that the significate that God exists is not something other than God, in the sense of being an entity other than God. But nevertheless it is not God, since it is not an entity at all.

14.1.5. Gregory opposes the thesis of the defenders of the *complexum* theory that only the true is known and that only a *propositio* is true by maintaining that not only the *enuntiationes* themselves are called true and false but also their *enuntiabilia* or adequate significates, albeit in a different sense. He supports this view by the authority of Aristotle who states that the things underlying an affirmation and a negation are opposed to one another as are the affirmation and negation (*Cat.* 12 b 10; cf. 13 a 37 and 13 b 27). According to a first interpretation offered by Gregory the *enuntiabilia* are not the fundamental bearers of truth and falsity but have these attributes only by a kind of extrinsic denomination (*quadam extrinseca denominatione*), namely in a way that is derived from true or false *enuntiationes*. An *enuntiabile* is called false if the corresponding *enuntiatio* is false or would be false if it existed; and it is true if the corresponding *enuntiatio* is true or would be true if it were formed. Thus that man is not an ass is true and that man is an ass is false even if no created *enuntiatio* exists. In this context the potential element in the meaning of *enuntiabile* is prominent again: what is statable by a true statement is true and what is statable by a false statement is false. Analogously, an *enuntiabile* is necessary, contingent, possible, or impossible according as the corresponding *enuntiatio* is or would be necessary, contingent, possible, or impossible (*In I Sent.*, Dist.39, q.1. art.2).

This interpretation has the unattractive consequence that such an *enuntiabile* as that no creature exists would not be a possible truth (*verum possibile*), presumably because as often as the statement 'No creature exists' is formed it must be invariably false. It is therefore better to assume that the truth of *enuntiabilia* is grounded in the uncreated truth which is the true judgment of all *enuntiabilia*, namely God. Then we can say with Augustine (*Soliloquia* II, 2, ed. Migne 32, 886) and Anselm (*Monologion* 18, ed. Migne 158, 168) that before the creation of the world it was true that it would exist (*mundum fore*) and that if the world would perish it would be true that the world had perished (*mundum interisse*). But even then the awkward question arises what to say about false *enuntiabilia*: there is no first falsehood in which the false statables can be grounded. Gregory suggests two ways out. Either we may restrict the word 'false' to *enuntiationes* and characterize contradictory *enuntiabilia* by saying that one is true and that the other is not true. Or we might apply the word 'false' to *enuntiabilia* in such a way that it does not mean that the statable is false because it is signified by a false sign but that it rather indicates that the statable is false because it is not signified by that which is the sign of all truth.

A third way of elucidating the manner in which *enuntiabilia* are true is to say that an affirmative statable is true because it is so in reality and that a negative statable is true because it is not so in reality. For example, that man is an animal is true because man is an animal and that man is not an ass is true because man is not an ass.

The first interpretation of the truth and falsity of *enuntiabilia* according to which *enuntiationes* are true and false in the primary sense and *enuntiabilia* only in a derivative way is not easily brought into harmony with what Gregory elsewhere says about the object of opinion, belief, and knowledge. There cannot be the slightest doubt that for him that which is known or believed is primarily the significate of a *propositio,* while the *propositio* itself can be said to be known or believed only in a way that is at best secondary. In discussing the question what can be the subject of the attribute 'known in itself' (*per se notum*; *In I Sent.,* Dist.2, q.1, art.1) Gregory states that in fact certain *propositiones* as well as their significates are said to be known immediately. He has no objection against this established usage as long as it is realized that, strictly speaking, it is improper, since only the significate is known in itself. But in a loose sense we may say that a *propositio* is known in itself if we mean by such a manner of speaking no more than that what it signifies is immediately known.

In any case it is clear that for Gregory the bearers of truth and falsity are not only actually existing *propositiones* and the significates of actually existing *propositiones* but also states of affairs that are capable of being signified by true or false created *propositiones* even if these corresponding *propositiones* do not in fact exist. According to the second interpretation, however, the true *enuntiabilia* are always actually signified by God as the uncreated sign of all truth.

From what Gregory says about the way in which *propositiones* signify it is evident that one and the same *enuntiabile* can be the significate of different particular acts of signifying, either of a natural kind, in the case of a mental *propositio* in the proper sense, or of a conventional kind, in the case of a written and spoken *propositio* and a *propositio* that is the mental image of written marks or spoken sounds. There is a realm of statables which exist in their own peculiar way and remain identical through the varying acts by which they are known, believed, or asserted by different persons at different times and places. Concerning the factors by which their identity is determined we get no more information than that differences in the tenses of the verb yield different *enuntiabilia*, namely past, present, and future ones. From this it follows that the truth-value of an *enuntiabile* may change. It is possible that at a certain moment an *enuntiabile* which was not true in the past becomes true and that an *enuntiabile* which was true in the past becomes false. The *enuntiabile*, for instance, that corresponds to the statement 'The word became flesh' was false before the incarnation of Christ but it became true as soon as God's son had taken on flesh. Similarly, that Christ is not risen from the grave was a true *enuntiabile* before the resurrection but it ceased to be true and began to be false at the moment of the resurrection (*In I Sent.*, Dist.39, q.1, art.2).

14.2. Other adherents of the theory of the *complexe significabile*

14.2.1. Elie (1937: 37–40) has expressed the opinion that Nicolas of Autrecourt was a pupil of Gregory of Rimini and that the condemnation of Nicolas' views which took place in 1346 was partly aimed at his master's theory. The evidence for this opinion is drawn from some of the statements that Nicolas was forced to recant, in particular that such contradictories as 'God exists' and 'God does not exist' signify exactly the same, though in a different way, and that what is signifiable in a complex way by the *complexum* 'God is distinct from what is created' (*deus et creatura distinguuntur*) is nothing[2]. To me it seems rather improbable that the first statement could have been regarded as typical of Gregory's position. Although he might not have denied it if taken in a certain sense, it is not at all the kind of statement one would expect him to have used to express the real import of his doctrine (Cf. 15.1.2). The second statement could be representative of Gregory's view if 'nothing' is taken to mean the same as 'not a thing in the sense of an existing substance or accident'. As we saw in 14.1.4, he is prepared to concede that the significate that man is an animal is nothing provided that 'nothing' is understood in the right way. But it is also quite conceivable that exactly the same sentence would be used to score a point against Gregory. As long as we do not know in what kind of context Nicolas of Autrecourt made his state-

[2] Cf. H. Denifle & E. Chatelain, *Chartularium universitatis Parisiensis*, II, Parisiis, 1891, p. 578, p. 580, p. 583.

ments, the question whether he was an adherent of the *complexe significabile* theory or not cannot be satisfactorily answered.

14.2.2. On the other hand, there can be no doubt that Gregory's theory was supported — with certain reservations — by some of his fellow Augustinians, notably by Ugolino of Orvieto and Bonsembiante Beduarius (or Badoer) of Padua. Ugolino, who lectured on the *Sentences* in Paris in 1348—1349, discusses some questions concerning the *complexe significabile* in the *Prologus*, q.1, art.2[3]. He distinguishes between an *incomplexum* and a *complexum*. For him an *incomplexum* is that which is signifiable by a simple concept, by means of a noun, and a *complexum* is that which is signifiable by a concept which is a *propositio*, by means of a noun and a verb (p. 270, 18). Ockham's theory that the object of knowledge and belief is the *propositio formata* is extensively refuted. Ugolino shows that what is primarily true or necessary, known in some way or believed is not the *propositio* but the significate of the *propositio* (p. 290, 15 — p. 296, 3). He then asks what such a *complexe significabile* is and particularly in what sense the words *ens, essentia, aliquid*, and *res* are applicable to it. According to him these words can be understood in four different ways (p. 296, 23 — p. 301, 5). In the first place, there is a very general sense in which every imaginable state of affairs may be called something. Secondly, in a less general sense every true *complexe significabile* is something that is the case. For example, that the Antichrist is capable of sinning (*Antichristum posse peccare*) is something that is the case, although neither the Antichrist nor sinning are actual things. So far Ugolino is in complete agreement with Gregory of Rimini (Cf. 14.1.4). But in elaborating the third and the fourth sense in which the words *ens, essentia, aliquid*, and *res* are applicable to a *complexe significabile* he goes his own way. The above-mentioned words may be applied to a *complexe significabile* in a strict and proper sense if a main part of it is really something or if the significate is many things (*multa aliqua*) instead of one thing. As an example of the first case Ugolino gives the *complexe significabile* that God is capable of creating the Antichrist (*deum posse creare Antichristum*); since the part *deus ens potens* is a real thing, it may be said that the whole significate is an entity in a stricter sense than, for instance, that the Antichrist is capable of sinning, although neither significate is one thing (*unum aliquid*). An example of the

---

[3]The *Prologus* has been edited by A. Zumkeller, in *Hugolin von Orvieto und seine theologische Erkenntnislehre* (*Cassiciacum. Eine Sammlung wissenschaftlicher Forschungen über den hl. Augustinus und den Augustinerorden,* Band IX, 2. Reihe, 3. Band), Würzburg, 1941, pp. 267—391. References are to this edition.

second case is the *complexe significabile* that every man is capable of laughing (*omnem hominem esse risibilem*) or that man is white (*hominem esse album*). In the strictest sense, finally, the words *ens, essentia, aliquid,* and *res* may be applied to a *complexe significabile* in the same way as they are applied to *incomplexa,* if the *complexe significabile* is the content of a *propositio* that asserts the existence of one actual thing, such as *deum esse.* The significate *deum esse* is nothing but God in so far as he actually exists (*deus ens*; p. 300, 20—21). In general, the only difference between such significates and incomplex things is that they are signified and understood in different ways: in a verbal way and in a nominal way. If one asks what *hominem esse* is, the correct answer is that it is a man in so far as he is or exists, signified in a verbal way (*homo ens seu existens verbaliter significatus*). There are, therefore, some cases in which a *complexe significabile* may be said to be something in the sense of one actual entity. Ugolino remarks that others deny this, holding that if we take *aliquid* in the strictest acceptation, *deum esse* is nothing, in the sense of no thing (*nulla essentia*; p. 301, 25). One of the others was no doubt Gregory of Rimini. Ugolino's conception of the ontological status of the *complexe significabile* is an interesting intermediate position between Gregory's view and most of the theories that will be considered in the next chapter.

From Bonsembiante's *Quattuor principia,* which he delivered in Paris in 1363, some fragments concerned with the *complexe significabile* were made accessible in French translation by Elie (1937: 140—145)[4]. Bonsembiante tries to refute several arguments against Gregory's view by pointing out that such a *complexe significabile* as *deum esse,* if it has a purely verbal force, is not an entity in the sense of a thing that can be signified by a single word. It is neither a substance nor an accident, neither a genus nor a species; and consequently all kinds of characterizations that apply to things that can be signified in an incomplex way — for instance, the properties of being perfect or imperfect, finite or infinite, good or bad — simply do not fit a *complexe significabile.* In one important respect Bonsembiante's view appears to be at variance with Gregory's doctrine. He is of the opinion that the identity of a *complexe significabile* is not affected by differences in the tenses of the verb. As we saw in 11.1.3, the *nominales* held that three inflexions of an *enuntiabile* such as *Socratem cucurrisse, Socratem currere,* and *Socratem fore cursurum,* pronounced at different times, form one and the same *enuntiabile* because they signify the same event taking place at a certain moment. Whereas for the *nominales* the *enuntiabile* is a signifying expression, Bonsembiante

---

[4] From the *Codex Latinus Monacensis 26711* and the *Codex Vaticanus Latinus 981.*

applies this doctrine of unity in diversity to the significate. What is signified or signifiable by the *complexa* 'Adam will exist', 'Adam exists', and 'Adam has existed', namely that Adam will exist, that Adam exists, and that Adam has existed, is one and the same state of affairs in spite of the different tenses of the verb by which it is expressed. There is one feature of the world by which these significates and the *complexa* that signify them at different times are rendered true. We are here confronted with the same terminological difficulty as in the case of the identical *enuntiabile* and its different inflexions. On the one hand, the term *complexe significabile* stands for the significates as they are determined by the tenses of the verbs in the signifying *propositiones,* for instance that Christ will suffer, that Christ is suffering, and that Christ has suffered. On the other hand, the same term is used for the identical state of affairs, namely Christ's suffering (*passio Christi*), which is the common content of the different acts of believing and asserting. If we use the word 'meaning' for the tensed significates and reserve the word 'significate' for that which is believed or asserted, we might say that Bonsembiante is trying to state that in spite of the fact that the meanings of the utterances 'Christ will suffer', 'Christ is suffering', and 'Christ has suffered' are different, what is believed or asserted is the same. Bonsembiante mentions some objections which were made against his view. Some argued that there can be no identity between that *a* exists and that *a* has existed, since then it would have to be conceded that there is an identity between that *a* is here and that *a* is there as well. Or it was pointed out that there is a difference between that the Antichrist exists and that the Antichrist does not exist, that further that the Antichrist will exist implies that he does not exist, and that consequently there can be no identity between that the Antichrist will exist and that the Antichrist exists. And it was also objected that such contraries as that *a* exists and that *a* will exist can never form one and the same *complexe significabile.* In all these cases it can be answered, of course, that there is indeed a difference of meaning but that nevertheless what is believed or asserted is the same. This insight was, however, blocked by a too undifferentiated use of the verb *significare.*

14.2.3. Another adherent of the *complexe significabile* theory seems to have been Albert of Saxony, who had been a pupil of Jean Buridan in Paris. In his *Quaestiones super Analytica posteriora* there are a few passages[5] from which it may be gathered that he considered the significate of the conclusion as that which is true and known.

[5] I, q.2; I, q.7; I, q.33 (Venetiis, 1497, f.3 r. B, f.7 r. A, f.23 r. B). Cf. Prantl (1855–1870: IV, 78, n.301).

Further, there is a very interesting passage in his commentary on Ockham's *Expositio aurea*[6]. In connection with *De int.* 16 b 1 Albert states there the following conclusion. Syncategorematic terms do not signify a thing that is a substance or an accident but they signify rather a state of a thing (*modus rei*) which by others is called a *complexe significabile*. That, for instance, a predicate belongs to everything that falls under the subject or does not belong to anything that falls under the subject is not a thing that is a substance or an accident but rather a state or a condition (*dispositio*) of a thing, namely of the subject or the predicate. One can therefore say that a syncategorematic term signifies something (*aliquid*) in so far as the word 'something' designates not only the existence of a thing but also the state or the mode of existence of a thing. The doctrine that syncategorematic terms indicate a characteristic or state (*proprietas, determinatio, modus, dispositio*) of the thing or things to which the accompanying categorematic terms refer is rather well known. It is already found in Abelard (Cf. 9.1.2), and De Rijk (1967: I, 467 and 481) quotes some passages from the *Summae Metenses* in which a distinction is drawn between words that signify things, namely substances or accidents, and words that signify states of things (*modos rerum*); those states may pertain to the subject, or to the predicate, or to the way in which the subject and the predicate are combined (*compositio*). A similar conception is found in Walter Burleigh[7].

What is most interesting is Albert's remark that the *modus rei* was also called a *complexe significabile*. This usage is probably to be explained in the following way. Syncategorematic terms signify only in combination (*complexio*) with categorematic terms; what they signify is therefore something that can be signified only in a complex way, by adjoining the syncategorematic term to a categorematic term. Albert draws a distinction between a *complexio indistans*, a combination of words in which no copula occurs (*homo albus*), and a *complexio distans*, a combination of words by means of the copula (*homo est albus*). Now a syncategorematic term can occur both in a *complexio indistans*, for instance *omnis homo* or *aliquis homo*, and in a *complexio distans*, for instance *Socrates est albus*. In both cases, therefore, the significate is a *complexe significabile*, something that can be signified only by a *complexio*, either with a copula or without a copula. The phrase *com-*

---

[6]William of Ockham, *Expositio aurea et admodum utilis super artem veterem cum quaestionibus Alberti Parvi de Saxonia*, Bononiae, 1496, reprinted Farnborough Hants, 1964.
[7]*De puritate artis logicae tractatus brevior*, ed. Ph. Boehner, St. Bonaventure, N.Y., 1955, p. 220.

plexe significabile can have a wider meaning and a narrower meaning, in the same way as the term *complexum*. Gregory of Rimini concentrates upon the narrower meaning and understands by a *complexe significabile* something that can be signified only by the combination of a subject with a predicate that is brought about by the copula, in a *complexum* that is a *propositio*. But it is clear that this is just a special case of a *complexe significabile* in the wider sense, namely something that is signifiable only by a combination of any syncategorematic term with one or more categorematic terms, either in a *complexio indistans* or in a *complexio distans*. This connection between the significate of a *propositio* and the significate of syncategorematic terms in general is already indicated by Abelard when he says that neither syncategorematic terms nor *propositiones* denote a thing (*Dialectica* 119, 3). And it cannot be a coincidence that both Abelard (*Dialectica* 160, 35) and Bonaventure (*In I Sent.*, Dist.41, art.2, q.2) use practically the same words as Albert of Saxony when they declare that a *propositio* or *enuntiatio* signifies not a thing but a *rerum modus habendi se*.

It may be concluded that there is a close resemblance between the problems that are connected with the signification of syncategorematic terms in general and the problems that beset the significate of a *propositio*. As the syncategorematic copula is an essential ingredient of every *propositio*, it was felt by many that the significate of the whole *propositio* can never be a thing but must be a state of things, a certain way of being (*ita, sic, taliter esse*). The question whether such a state of things is something is, as becomes evident from Albert's conclusion, only a special case of the more comprehensive question whether that which is signifiable only by a combination of any syncategorematic term with a categorematic term can be called something.

15. THE OPPOSITION AGAINST THE THEORY OF THE *COMPLEXE SIGNIFICABILE*

Gregory of Rimini's theory of the *complexe significabile* attracted more adversaries than followers. The five thinkers whose views will be discussed in this chapter — Jean Buridan, Marsilius of Inghen, André de Neufchâteau, Pierre d'Ailly, and Paul of Venice — are alike in their thorough criticism and rejection of the most characteristic part of Gregory's doctrine. Apart from this negative similarity, their positive outlooks too are sufficiently akin to justify our grouping them under one head, in spite of the differences that this juxtaposition will bring to light.

15.1. Jean Buridan

15.1.1. Reina (1959–1960) has given a rather detailed survey of Buridan's conceptions of language and meaning, mainly based upon his *Summulae de dialectica*. I shall therefore confine myself to selecting and emphasizing a few points that are of special importance to get a clear idea of Buridan's attitude towards the *complexe significabile* and the problems connected with it.

Buridan follows Ockham in distinguishing written, vocal, and mental terms, but he restricts the word *significare* to the written and vocal terms. Written terms are conventional signs of vocal terms and vocal terms are conventional signs of mental terms. The mental terms, however, do not signify, not even in a natural way, but they are concepts in the mind by means of which we conceive of things or conceive of things in a certain way. Vocal terms are either categorematic or syncategorematic. Categorematic vocal terms signify both with regard to the mind (*ad mentem*) and with regard to the outside world (*ad extra*); they directly signify concepts and indirectly, *via* the concepts, the things thought of. Syncategorematic vocal terms, such as the copula, negation, and the signs of quantity, signify only certain ways of conceiving; they do not signify any things in the outside world.

Concepts may be simple or complex, and complex concepts are formed either by a *complexio indistans* or by a *complexio distans*. In a *complexio indistans* two simple concepts are combined in such a way that the one determines the other (*per modum determinationis et determinabilis*), yielding, for instance, the complex concept signified by such phrases as *homo albus* or *asinus risibilis* ('an ass that is capable of laughing'). As a rule a complex concept will be signified by a combination of words, but there are also complex concepts that are signified by a single word — for example, by *chimaera, vacuum,* or even *Ilias.* Now a complex concept that is formed in a *complexio indistans* may either have an object corresponding to it in reality or be empty. The complex concept signified by the phrase *homo albus,* for instance, may be related to a really existing thing, a white man, whereas the complex concept signified by the phrase *asinus risibilis* or by the word *chimaera* has no object corresponding to it in the world of real things. In the latter case there are two acts of thinking of existing objects — for example, asses and beings that are capable of laughing — but the composite act of thinking that results from the typical combination of those acts has no application at all. Although the terminology is different, there is a striking resemblance between Buridan's view and what Abelard says about the *intellectus compositus* (Cf. 9.1.3). Such expressions as *asinus risibilis* and *chimaera* have a significate in the mind, namely the complex concept, but they have no significate in the outside world, since the concept is not a thought of a real thing; one might say that they have a connotation but no denotation.

A mental *propositio* is a complex concept formed by a *complexio distans.* The matter of the mental *propositio* consists of the concepts that are the subject and the predicate; the form is the mental copula, a *conceptus complexivus* that is an act of compounding or separating. The mental copula does not signify that the subject-thought and the predicate-thought are related to the same thing or are not related to the same thing. It is, rather, the activity of compounding or separating itself, being a mode of conceiving of a thing in a complex way, either affirmatively or negatively. The mental *propositio* is the significate of the vocal *propositio,* the concepts of things being signified by the categorematic vocal terms and the way of conceiving, the mental copula, being signified by the syncategorematic words *est* and *non est.* If we wish to speak of the significate of a *propositio* as such, we can mean only that the mental *propositio* is the significate of the vocal *propositio* or, in a less important way, that the vocal *propositio* is the significate of the written *propositio.* That there cannot be a specific significate of a *propositio* as such in any other sense is clear from the following considerations. Apart from the signification with regard to the mind, there is only the signification with regard to the outside world, which is restricted to categorematic expressions. Now if we look at the things signified by the categorematic terms in isolation, it is evident that the word *deus* and the expressions *deus est deus, deus non est deus, omnis deus est deus,* and *nullus deus est deus* signify exactly the same thing, namely God, since all the acts of thinking signified by the categorematic words have only that thing for their object. The different ways of conceiving the thing, either in a non-complex manner or in a complex manner, either affirmatively or negatively, do not alter the fact that in each case the same thing is thought of. If, on the other hand, we take into account the way in which the several categorematic words are combined into one complex of words, the signification *ad extra* of a *complexio indistans* and of a *complexio distans* will be the same, since the integrated and composite acts of thinking that correspond to the complexes of words will in both cases be related to the same thing. What is signified in the outside world by the phrase *homo albus* and by the statement-making utterance *homo est albus,* through the corresponding composite acts of thinking, is one and the same thing — namely, a man who is white. And in a similar way the phrase *asinus risibilis* and the statement-making utterance *asinus est risibilis* equally lack a significate in the outside world, since the corresponding composite acts of thinking have no application. Although there is a difference between the *complexio indistans* and the *complexio distans* in that the latter contains an element of assenting or asserting that is lacking in the former, this difference does not affect the signification *ad extra* of the vocal expressions or the reference of the composite thoughts to the outside world.

Buridan tries to minimize the difference between the *complexio indistans* and the *complexio distans.* Although he recognizes that a mental *propositio* has an ingredient that a mere composite act of thinking of something does not have — namely, a mental copula with assenting or dissenting force — he nevertheless tends to treat the mental *propositio* as a complicated act of thinking of a thing and the corresponding vocal *propositio* as a referring expression. This assimilation is reflected in the fact that the terminology which he uses for the *complexio indistans* is closely akin to the terminology that is typical of the *complexio distans.* A *complexio indistans* in which a determining adjective is combined with a determinable noun is either a *compositio,* if it is done in an affirmative manner (*homo albus*), or a *divisio,* if it is done in a negative manner (*homo non albus*). In both cases what is thought of or signified in the outside world is men and white things, but there is a difference in the way these things are conceived of, namely the difference between a *modus intellegendi compositivus* and a *modus intellegendi divisivus*. Now if, in the affirmative case, the acts of thinking terminate in one and the same object, there is a *conveniens* or *debita correspondentia* and the composite act of thinking is true. If, on the other hand, the complex thought is of a golden mountain or of a neighing man (*homo hinnibilis*), there is no due correspondence in reality and the act of thinking is therefore false or empty. One succeeds in thinking of men and beings that are capable of neighing but the resulting combination stands for nothing (*In Met. quaest.* IV, q. 14; VI, q. 6)[1].

15.1.2. According to Buridan the primary bearers of truth and falsity are the mental *propositiones*. Written and spoken *propositiones* are true or false only in a derivative sense. The Boethian definition of a *propositio* as a combination of words that signifies something true or false applies to the spoken *propositio*. The mental *propositio* does not signify something true or false but is true or false. The truth of a mental *propositio* is nothing but the true mental *propositio* itself. Further, the mental *propositio* is that which is primarily and immediately known. Buridan admits that we can also say that the things referred to by the terms of an *enuntiatio* are known, but only in a remote way (*Soph.* VIII, 13)[2].

Buridan rejects the view that a *propositio* is true if its significate exists. If we mean by the significate the mental *propositio,* it would follow that every spoken *propositio* is true, since every spoken *propositio* signifies a mental *propositio*. If, on the other hand, we mean by the significate a thing in the outside world, it would follow that many true statements, for instance about the past and the future, are not true, since the objects referred to do not actually exist (*Soph.* II, Conclusions 1–2). In general, Buridan has serious misgivings about the formula that a *propositio* is true if it is so as the *propositio* signifies that it is (*qualitercumque significat esse, ita est*). In the first place, this formula suggests that there is a specific significate of the *propositio* as a whole, an *ita esse* as conceived of by Gregory of Rimini. Moreover, the formula, being in the present tense, does not cover the truth of, for instance, *propositiones* about the past and the future. In the light of such objections Buridan thinks it better to replace this misleading formula by an elaborate set

---

[1] These references are to *In Metaphysicen Aristotelis quaestiones argutissimae Magistri Ioannis Buridani,* Parisiis, 1518, reprinted Frankfurt, 1964.

[2] These references are to *Sophismata,* Parisiis, 1489. For an English translation, with a good introduction, cf. Scott (1966).

of conditions of truth and falsity by means of which it can in each case be decided whether a certain *propositio* is true or false (*Soph.* II, Conclusions 10–14; *In Met. quaest.* VI, q. 7, q. 8, q. 10). He starts from singular affirmative categorical *propositiones* about the present and without modal qualifications. These are true if the subject-term and the predicate-term stand for the same existing thing – for instance, for this man who is white; they are false if the subject-term and the predicate-term do not stand for the same thing. From this central case he then goes on to the same sort of *propositiones* about the past, about the future, and about the possible; these are true if the subject-term and the predicate-term stand for the same thing which has existed, will exist, or can exist, and false if it is otherwise. In the same way Buridan indicates the conditions of truth and falsity for other kinds of statements, negative, particular, universal, modal, and compounded.

For us the main point is that a *propositio* can be true or false even if no thing signified by the *propositio* exists, has existed, will exist, or can exist. For the falsity of a singular affirmative statement, for example, it is sufficient that the thing that would render the statement true does not exist, has not existed, will not exist, or cannot exist. And for the truth of a negative statement it is sufficient that the thing which would make the corresponding affirmative statement true does not exist, has not existed, will not exist, or cannot exist. In neither case is it necessary to assume a special cause of the falsity and the truth or to posit any other significate, in the case of a spoken utterance, than the corresponding mental *propositio*. Because an affirmative mental *propositio* is fundamentally an act of thinking directed towards the outside world and a spoken *propositio* an intended act of referring to something in the outside world, there are only two possibilities: the thing conceived of or referred to exists, has existed, will exist, or can exist, or it does not exist, has not existed, will not exist, or cannot exist. In the first case the thing renders the act true, in the second case there is no object in the outside world corresponding to the intended act of referring and consequently the act is empty or false and its negation true.

Let us finally, by way of illustration, look at the way in which Buridan treats the contradictories *deus est* and *deus non est*. This may also help to clarify what Nicolas of Autrecourt meant when he said that these contradictories signify exactly the same but in a different way (Cf. 14.2.1). In a passage that is very instructive for the assimilation of the *complexio distans* to the *complexio indistans* (*In Met. quaest.* IV, q. 14) Buridan states that the spoken utterances *deus est ens* and *deus non est ens* have opposite significations in that they signify different and opposite mental *propositiones* of which one is true and the other false. But what is thought of in the outside world by means of the two mental *propositiones* is exactly the same, namely God and being. The difference between the two comes from the way in which these things in the outside world are conceived of. In the affirmative *propositio* God and being are thought of in a *complexio compositiva*; because it has the required correspondent in reality, an existing God, the *propositio* is true. In the negative *propositio* God and being are thought of in a *complexio divisiva*; because God and being are not separated in fact, however, the composite thought of a non-existing God or of God as not existing is empty or false.

15.1.3. In his questions on the *Prior Analytics* [3] Buridan raises the problem of what kind of thing *hominem bibere vinum* (that a man drinks wine) is and mentions four answers. Some say that it is only a *propositio,* the accusative and infinitive phrase standing for *homo bibit vinum.* Others are of the opinion that it is some signifiable *complexum (quoddam significabile complexum)* that in reality (*ex parte rei*) corresponds to the transitory *propositio.* Others again say that it is nothing but a man who is in such a state with regard to wine (*homo taliter se habens ad vinum*). And finally there are some who hold that it is a certain accident inhering in a man, namely that he is in such a state with regard to wine (*quoddam accidens inhaerens homini, ut taliter se habeat ad vinum*). The third opinion is defended by Buridan himself. The second opinion may be Walter Burleigh's view, according to which the ultimate significate of a mental *propositio* is a *complexum* or *propositio in re* (Cf. 13.3). To the first and the fourth opinion I shall return in the next chapter.

Buridan (*In Met. quaest.* V, q. 7) holds that such accusative and infinitive phrases as *Socratem currere* can sometimes be interpreted according to material supposition, in such a way that they stand for a *propositio,* in this case for *Socrates currit.* For example, *Socratem currere est falsum* means that the *propositio* for which *Socratem currere* stands, namely *Socrates currit,* is false. Similarly, 'It is possible (necessary) that Socrates runs' means that the *propositio* 'Socrates runs' is possible or necessary (*In Met. quaest.* VI, q. 10). It may be assumed that Buridan would also interpret such expressions as *scio (credo) Socratem currere* ('I know (believe) that Socrates runs') as meaning that the *propositio* 'Socrates runs' is known or believed.

There are, however, cases in which the interpretation according to material supposition leads to unacceptable results. If we take, for instance, the truth

---

[3] *Quaestiones in libros Priorum* I, q. 5, quoted from a manuscript by Reina (1959–1960: II, 160, n. 181).

hominem esse album est hominem esse coloratum, the material interpretation would yield the falsehood that *homo est albus* is *homo est coloratus* (Cf. *Soph.* II, Conclusion 3). And such an interpretation would be equally unsatisfactory for *'homo est animal' significat hominem esse animal* (Cf. *In Met. quaest.* VI, q. 11). In such cases, therefore, the accusative and infinitive phrase has to be taken in a signifying function (*significative* or *personaliter*) and the question arises what it then signifies. According to Buridan — and now we come to the third opinion mentioned at the beginning of this paragraph — the accusative and infinitive phrase, taken in a signifying function, refers to exactly the same thing in the outside world as does a *propositio* or a *complexio indistans,* namely something in a certain state. What the true *propositio* 'Socrates runs' (*Socrates currit*) signifies *ad extra,* namely that Socrates runs (*Socratem currere*), is nothing but Socrates in so far as he runs (*Socrates currens*). And the same applies to *Socratem cucurrisse, Socratem cursurum fore,* and *Socratem posse currere.* These so-called *complexe significabilia* are nothing but Socrates in so far as he has run, or Socrates in so far as he will run, or Socrates in so far as he is capable of running. If the outside world contains, has contained, or will contain an object in a certain state as determined by the combination of categorematic and syncategorematic terms, then the significate, for instance that Socrates loves God, is precisely that object; if there is no such thing in the outside world, then the significate that Socrates loves God is nothing (Cf. *Soph.* I, 5). Buridan points out that not every *complexe significabile* is simply nothing. If *deum esse causam Socratis* were nothing, it would follow that *deum esse causam Socratis est deum esse causam Socratis* is false, since the subject would not denote anything. In fact, of course, the significate that God is the cause of Socrates is God himself. From this it is also evident that even an object that is absolutely simple can always be signified in a complex way. According to Buridan everything in the world can be signified in a complex way. On the other hand, all such *complexe significabilia* as that God does not exist, that man is not an animal, that a stone is an ass, that the chimaera does not exist, or that the Antichrist does not exist are just nothing (*In Met. quaest.* IV, q. 10).

Our assumption that Buridan interpreted such expressions as *scio Socratem currere* as meaning that I know the *propositio* 'Socrates runs' is confirmed by an interesting remark about the utterance *ego scio chimaeram non esse* (*In Met. quaest.* IV, q. 14). Since he adheres to the rule that an affirmative *propositio* is false if one of the terms stands for nothing, he considers the statements *chimaeram non esse est scibile* and *ego scio chimaeram non esse* as false if the accusative and infinitive phrase is taken in a signifying function. If these statements are to be true, the phrase *chimaeram non esse* has therefore to be taken as standing for the *propositio,* namely *chimaera non est.*

Finally, I want to call attention to a passage (*In Met. quaest.* VI, q. 11; cf. *Soph.* II, Conclusion 3) in which Buridan discusses the *propositio* 'A horse is an ass' (*equus est asinus*). If one asks what this *propositio* signifies, there are two correct answers. The spoken *propositio* signifies the corresponding mental *propositio,* and in the world outside the mind it signifies horses and asses. If someone would answer that it signifies that an horse is an ass (*equum esse asinum*), then it can be asked what this phrase stands for. It cannot be taken according to material supposition, for in that case it would stand for the *propositio* itself and according to Buridan the utterance 'The (spoken) *propositio* "A horse is an ass" signifies the (spoken) *propositio* "A horse is an ass" ' is not a proper locution. On the other hand, if the phrase *equum esse asinum* is taken in a signifying function, it follows that the statement *equum esse asinum significatur per istam propositionem 'equus est asinus'* ('That a horse is an ass is signified by the *propositio* "A horse is an ass"') is false, since the subject stands for nothing, and that consequently the *propositio* 'A horse is an ass' does not signify that a horse is an ass.

What Buridan intends to convey in this passage may be put as follows. If someone utters the words 'A horse is an ass', this utterance is meaningful in so far as it is a conventional sign of the thought 'A horse is an ass'; the significate *ad mentem* is the corresponding mental *propositio.* Further, the categorematic words 'horse' and 'ass' denote, *via* the simple acts of thinking which they signify *ad mentem,* things in the outside world, namely the horses and asses which are the significates *ad extra.* But since there happens to be nothing in the outside world that is both a horse and an ass and since Buridan regards the phrase *equum esse asinum* ('that a horse is an ass'), taken in its signifying function, as equivalent to the phrase *equus ens asinus* ('a horse being an ass'), it must be concluded that the spoken *propositio* 'A horse is an ass' in so far as it corresponds to a composite act of thinking has no significate *ad extra* and that the statement 'The *propositio* "A horse is an ass" signifies that a horse is an ass' is false. The statement 'The *propositio* "A horse is an ass" signifies that a horse is an ass' may be taken to be ambiguous between the following senses. It may mean that the spoken *propositio* 'A horse is an ass' is a conventional sign of the corresponding mental *propositio*; in this sense, with regard to the signification *ad mentem,* it is true. It may also mean — and it is on this meaning that Buridan concentrates — that the spoken *propositio* has, *via* the corresponding composite act of thinking, a significate *ad extra* consisting in something that is both a horse and an ass; in this sense, with regard to the complex signification *ad extra,* it is false.

15.2. Marsilius of Inghen

15.2.1. Buridan's rejection of *complexe significabilia* as interpreted by Gregory of Rimini is based mainly on his conviction that they are superfluous. One of his conclusions (*In Met. quaest.* V, q. 7) is that everything can easily be explained without positing any *complexe significabilia* that are not substances or accidents; and what can be done with fewer assumptions is done in vain with more. He is more concerned to develop his own doctrine which does not require anything but *propositiones* and things in the sense of substances and accidents than to engage in lengthy discussions about something that is not needed to do justice to the object of inquiry. His pupil Marsilius of Inghen, on the other hand, attacks Gregory in a more direct way. In the prooemium to the first book of his commentary on the *Sentences*[4] (q. 2, art. 3) he mentions a widely held opinion which was also shared by Ockham, namely that the immediate object of assent is the *propositio,* that the remote object of assent is the terms in so far as they are signs of things, and that the most remote and ultimate object of assent is the incomplex thing signified by the terms. This thesis – which applies only to *propositiones* that are affirmative, about the present, and without modal qualifications – is elsewhere[5] repeated for that which is knowable. The *scibile propinquum* is the demonstrated conclusion, the *scibile remotum* is its terms, and the *scibile remotissimum* is the thing signified by the terms of the conclusion. In the case of the statement *deus est,* for example, the immediate object of the act of knowing is the *propositio* itself; the remote object is the term *deus* in so far as it is a sign of the first being; and the most remote object is God. Marsilius adds that the most remote object is at the same time the most intended and desired object. Knowledge of *propositiones* and terms is sought only in order to gain thereby knowledge of the incomplex things that are signified by the terms.

In this context Marsilius quotes at length the arguments which Gregory of Rimini had adduced against the *complexum* theory and the *res* theory and also some of the considerations that had led Gregory to regard the *complexe significabile* as the object of assent and knowledge. In the face of Gregory's arguments against the *complexum* theory (Cf. 14.1.2) Marsilius maintains that in proving a conclusion we are aware of that conclusion and that it is the

---

[4] *Quaestiones Marsilii super quattuor libros Sententiarum,* Strassburg, 1501, reprinted Frankfurt, 1966.

[5] *Quaestiones super libros Priorum analyticorum,* Venetiis, 1516, reprinted Frankfurt, 1968, I, q. 1.

apprehended conclusion that we assent to and know. This awareness of the conclusion is not a reflection upon it in the form of the statement that the conclusion is true, since the conclusion and the statement that it is true are clearly different; although one who assents to the conclusion will generally also assent to the statement that the conclusion is true. It is a reflection rather in this sense that the reasoner fixes his attention directly on the conclusion and only *via* the conclusion on that which it signifies. Therefore the conclusion is the first object of assent and the thing signified the ultimate object.

Gregory's objections against the *res* theory are aimed at a doctrine according to which the object of knowledge acquired by scientific proof is primarily or even exclusively a thing in the outside world. It is obvious that Marsilius does not want to defend that kind of doctrine but is only committed to the view that the thing in the outside world is the ultimate object of assent and knowledge, the primary object being the *propositio*. Thus he can admit that the sciences are about contingent things while maintaining that their actual objects, the *propositiones,* are necessary. In the same way he can counter Gregory's argument that from the *res* theory it follows that the same thing is the object of knowledge, belief, opinion, and error by pointing out that this may be true for the thing signified as the most remote object, but that the *propositiones* which are the immediate object of such knowledge, belief, opinion, or error are of course different. The same applies to the case in which someone assents to the *propositio* 'God is eternal' and dissents from the *propositio* 'God is not eternal'. The ultimate object of the act of assenting and the act of dissenting may be the same, but the *propositiones* are different.

15.2.2. As for Gregory's own theory that *complexe significabilia* which are neither substances nor accidents are the objects of assent and knowledge, Marsilius suggests that it may have been prompted by an ignorance of logic. He suspects that the assumption of a *complexe significabile* was resorted to by respondents who were unable to find a cause for the falsity of false *propositiones.* According to Buridan there is no separate cause of the falsity of an affirmative statement (or of the truth of the corresponding negative statement); what makes an affirmative statement false is simply the absence of the cause that would render it true (*In Met. quaest.* VI, q. 8). Only a true affirmative statement has a proper significate in the outside world. A false affirmative statement is false because it has no proper significate in the outside world. Marsilius presumably means that this correct insight was missed by those who introduced a *complexe significabile* for both false and true *propositiones* and then explained the falsity of a statement by saying, according to the Aristotelian formula, that in such a case the thing does not exist or that the *complexe significabile* is not the case in reality. Accordingly, he rejects Gregory's appeal to the authority of Aristotle. The *res* (*pragma*) of which Aristotle speaks in *Cat.* 14 b 19–21 is not a *complexe significabile* but an incomplex thing whose existence (in a certain state) makes an affirmative statement true and whose non-existence (in a certain state) makes it false.

Marsilius attacks Gregory's thesis that the significate that God exists (*deum esse*), being no entity at all, cannot be God. He attempts to refute it by adducing seven arguments which are supposed to establish that *deum esse* is God. In the first place, he invokes the authority of Aristotle (*Metaphysics* 1029 b 13), who states that in essential characterizations (*in dictis secundum se*) the thing itself and that the thing is are the same (*est idem ipsum et esse ipsum*). The same passage had been discussed also by Buridan (*In Met. quaest.* VII, q. 3, for accidental characterizations, and q. 4, for essential characterizations). Secondly, if the word *esse* is joined to a term that stands for an existing thing, it does not add anything from outside (*extrinsecum*); therefore, if *deus est deus* is true, *deum esse est deus* is true as well. Thirdly, cutting (*secare*), being an activity, belongs to one of the categories and is thus an *incomplexum*. Now, according to Aristotle (*Metaphysics* 1017 a 28), 'He cuts' has the same meaning as 'He is cutting'; consequently, if *secare* is an *incomplexum, esse secans* is an *incomplexum* too. But what applies to an accident holds *a fortiori* of a substance; *deum esse* is therefore also an *incomplexum,* namely God. Fourthly, every thing that is not God – for example, an ox – is not that God exists (*non est deum esse*); consequently, it is that no God exists (*est nullum deum esse,* from *est non deum esse*). That no God exists is therefore an *incomplexum* and, since what applies to a negative expression certainly holds of an affirmative expression, that some God exists (*aliquem deum esse*) must be an *incomplexum* as well. Next, if the act of believing by which one assents to the *propositio* 'God exists' would terminate in a *complexe significabile* which is neither God nor any other thing, it is hard to see what would be the use of believing, since its object is apparently nothing at all. Similarly, if the object of the science of medicine consisted of *complexe significabilia,* physicians would have nothing to operate upon. Marsilius adds that the ultimate object of desire, of love, and of knowledge is the same. Since God is the object of desire and love, he must equally be the object of knowledge. In the sixth place, that God exists is either something or nothing. If it is nothing, then the objects of the sciences, being *complexe significabilia,* will be nonentities. If it is something but not God and neither another substance nor a quality, then we shall have to conclude that there are two prime causes (Cf. Buridan, *In Met. quaest.* V, q. 7). For, since there is a hierarchical order of cause and effect among *complexe significabilia,* we must suppose that *deum esse* is the first cause of all *complexe significabilia.* Now this first cause which is not God cannot be dependent upon God either, for then it can be shown to be superfluous, as we shall see in a moment. Consequently, there will be two independent prime causes, a result which, according to Marsilius, cannot be very attractive to a philosopher or a Catholic. He then goes on to consider the question whether *deum esse,* if it is not God, is dependent upon God or not. The supposition that it is not leads to the unacceptable consequence that there is a necessary truth that does not depend upon the first truth. If, on the other hand, *deum esse* is dependent upon God, we must assume that God is free to do with it as he likes. He can therefore destroy it and at the same time keep in existence the *propositio* 'God exists' and a mind that understands it. In that case the mind would assent to the *propositio* without assenting to the *complexe significabile.* This proves that in normal circumstances the *complexe significabile* is not the object of assent either. Lastly, Marsilius calls attention to yet another absurd consequence of the *complexe significabile* theory. If *deum non esse* and *deum esse* are both *complexe significabilia* and if 'God exists' is true because of the *complexe significabile* that God exists, then 'God does not exist' will equally be true because of the *complexe significabile* that God does not exist.

This outline of the way in which Marsilius tries to establish the thesis that *deum esse* is God is sufficient to give an impression of the kind of reasoning that became rather characteristic of the debates concerning the topic of *complexe significabilia.* An excess of ingenuity often leads to arguments of very dubious quality; and, even if the reasoning is correct, the importance of the results as regards the general issue is not seldom severely restricted by the special nature of the example *deum esse est deus.*

15.3. André de Neufchâteau

15.3.1. In André de Neufchâteau's commentary on the first book of the *Sentences* (written around 1360) there are three long passages dealing with questions that are relevant to our subject: *Prologus,* q. 1–3; Dist. 2, q. 1–2; and Dist. 33–34 [6].

[6] *In primum librum Sententiarum,* J. Granjon, Paris, 1514 (I have consulted this extremely rare book in the library of the British Museum in London). Most of the relevant passages were made available in French translation by Elie (1937), who also gives some biographical information about the author.

In the second question of the second distinction the problem is raised whether in the case of the statement 'God is three and one' assent is given to the *propositio* or to the thing signified by the *propositio,* namely God being three and one. André rejects the *complexum* theory and defends a position that is strongly reminiscent of Chatton's view as I have interpreted it in 13.1 and 13.2.3. That the object of the act of assenting or judging cannot be the *propositio* is argued for in the following way. If I judge that God is three and one, the object of assent is necessary and eternal; but no *propositio* is necessary and eternal. Moreover, the object of assent is outside the mind and has existed before my judgment and will exist after it. Further, if I judge that something has been in a certain state or that something will be in a certain state, it is evident that the object of assent is not the *propositio*; this is confirmed by the fact that in claiming that I remember something it is not the *propositio* to which I assent but something in the past. It is also obvious that the object of a negative judgment is not the negative *propositio*; analogously, the object of an affirmative judgment is not the affirmative *propositio.* The same consequence follows from the consideration that in the case of judgments that are based on sense-perception the object of assent is that which is actually observed. Furthermore, André points to cases in which the object of assent remains the same although the *propositiones* involved are clearly different. If I judge and believe today that God is three and one, I judge and believe the same as I judged and believed yesterday; but the *propositio* which I form today is different from the *propositio* that I formed yesterday. Similarly, two persons can have the same belief or give the same evidence although the *propositio* formed by the one is different from the *propositio* formed by the other. It also happens that I am now sure of something which I formerly doubted; then the object of my doubt and of my certitude is the same in spite of the difference between the *propositio* which I previously formed and the *propositio* that I form now. Finally, if I give my assent to something from which Plato withholds his assent, it cannot be said that Plato dissents from the particular *propositio* formed by me. These last four arguments are like those used in the debate concerning the identity of the article of faith.

According to André it is not the *propositio* that is the object of assent but rather the *significate* that God is three and one. Before we judge that the *propositio* is true, we must give our assent to *deum esse trinum et unum* or, in other words, that it is so in reality (*sic esse a parte rei*). But *deum esse trinum et unum* is nothing but *deus ens trinus et unus,* God in so far as he is three and one. On the one hand, André differs from Buridan and Marsilius of Inghen by his rejection of their view that the primary object of assent and knowledge is the *propositio* while the thing signified by the *propositio* is only the most remote object. On the other hand, he sides with them in maintaining against Gregory of Rimini that the *complexe significabile* is not something distinct from all entities in the sense of substances or accidents but rather the thing in some state which renders certain affirmative statements true.

André uses the word *dictum* for such accusative and infinitive phrases as *Socratem currere*. Taken according to material supposition, the *dictum* stands either for the *oratio infinitiva* itself or for the corresponding *propositio*, for example *Socrates currit*. Taken in its signifying function (*significative* or *personaliter*), the *dictum* stands for the total or adequate significate of the corresponding *propositio*. André distinguishes five possible senses of the phrase *totale seu adaequatum significatum* (*Prologus*, q. 3, f. X r.). For him the complete or adequate significate of a *propositio* such as *Socrates currit* is an intelligible thing in a certain state (*intelligibile sic se habens*) as determined by the categorematic and syncategorematic parts of the *propositio*. Since the categorematic and syncategorematic elements of the phrases *Socratem currere* and *Socrates currens* are exactly the same as those of *Socrates currit* as regards the significate in the outside world, both the *dictum* and the phrase *Socrates currens* may be used to indicate the complete or adequate significate of the *propositio*, which is nothing but the thing in a certain state whose existence in the outside world makes the *propositio* true. In the same way the complete significate of *Adam fuit* is *Adam fuisse* (that Adam has existed) and that is nothing but *Adam praeteritus*, Adam in so far as he existed in the past; and the complete significate of *Antichristus erit* is *Antichristum fore* (that the Antichrist will exist) and that is simply *Antichristus futurus*. André says (*Prologus*, q. 3, f. XII r.) that if *a fore, a esse, a fuisse* were not the same as *a* itself in so far as it is first future, then present, and finally past, it would follow that they are distinct objects; and that consequence is incompatible with some passages in Peter Lombard's *Sentences*, namely I, Dist. 41 and Dist. 44, which we already discussed in connection with the problem of the immutability of God's knowledge (Cf. 11.2.1) and from which André extensively quotes. Lastly, the complete significate of *angelus potest esse* ('An angel can exist') is *angelum posse esse,* which is an angel capable of existing (*angelus possibilis esse*). Such things in a certain state are the positive causes of the truth of the corresponding *propositiones*; the conditions of truth and falsity of other kinds of *propositiones* can be stated without resorting to any other things than those which actually exist, have existed, will exist, or can exist.

One of the many objections which André puts forward against Gregory of Rimini's interpretation of the *complexe significabile* is connected with the three senses of the words *ens* and *aliquid* which Gregory had distinguished

(Cf. 14.1.4). André expounds this distinction (*Prologus,* q. 2, f. III v.) and then points out that among the theses because of which Nicolas of Autrecourt was condemned in 1346 was one according to which that which is signifiable in a complex way by the *complexum* 'God is distinct from what is created' is nothing (Cf. 14.2.1). André argues that 'nothing' must here be opposed to 'something' as denoting a substance or an accident, since nobody had denied that the *complexum* is true, so that 'nothing' cannot mean the same as 'not something that is signifiable in a complex way by a true statement'. Because of the condemnation of the contradictory, it must be concluded that the *complexe significabile* that God is distinct from what is created is an entity or a thing in a certain state, namely God himself in so far as he is distinct from what is created. Moreover, if the loose senses of *aliquid* are admitted, one might just as well posit somethings that are signifiable only by a verb, or only by a participle, or only by an adjective, and somethings that are signifiable only in a syncategorematic way. This last remark may be aimed at such a doctrine as was held by Albert of Saxony (Cf. 14.2.3).

15.3.2. In the Distinctions 33 and 34 André deals at length with the objection that there is a fundamental difference between that which is signifiable by a true or false *complexum* and that which is signifiable by such referring expressions as a noun or a nominal phrase. He explicitly maintains that no true or false *complexum,* either vocal or mental, signifies an object that is only intelligible in a complex way and is distinct from all objects that are intelligible in an incomplex way and can be signified by a noun or a combination of nouns. This is already evident from the fact that *complexe significabilia* can be characterized by such incomplex expressions as 'possible', 'impossible', 'intelligible', and 'signifiable'. But the decisive factor is that a true *complexum* and a referring expression that is not a true *complexum* may have exactly the same significate in the outside world. If it is said that such signs signify the same thing in different ways, namely one by a combination of a noun with a verb and the other by a noun or a combination of nouns, André answers that it can easily be shown that such differences are irrelevant as far as the adequate significate in the outside world is concerned. The difference between a mental *propositio* and a spoken or written *propositio* is greater than the difference between a complex and an incomplex concept in the mind or between a complex and an incomplex sound. But such a difference in the signs does not alter the fact that if the one is true the other is also true, because of the identity of the significate. Similarly, the difference between the uncreated sign and a created sign is far greater than the difference between two created signs of the same species or genus; nevertheless, if the one is true

the other is true too. That a sign may be true or false without its being compounded of a noun and a verb is further clear from the gesture-languages that
are used by some monastic orders. Moreover, if a difference in the form of
two signs that signify exactly the same thing in the outside world were a
reason to call one true and the other not, one might just as well say that of
the two *propositiones* 'Socrates runs' and 'Socrates is running' one is true and
the other is not.

In general, André follows Buridan in trying to minimize the difference
between the *complexio distans* and the *complexio indistans.* The distinction
between the *legein*-level and the *onomazein*-level, between *dicere* and *nominare,* or between an *oratio perfecta* containing a copula with assertive force
and an *oratio imperfecta* lacking such a copula, a distinction that was so
much emphasized by previous thinkers, is practically abandoned by André.
For him *Socrates currit, Socratem currere,* and *Socrates currens* are combinations of words that in spite of minor formal dissimilarities have the same
significate. What they have in common is that they all three refer to a thing in
a certain state. If that thing exists, they are true; if it does not exist in the
required state, they are false or empty.

In Distinction 2, q. 2 (f. XXXV v.) André discusses the objection that such
phrases as *iudico lapidem* or *assentio lapidi* are not proper answers to the
question what one believes or assents to. According to him the question of
what one judges (*quid iudicas*) is not only about the objective matter of the
judgment but also about its form and quality. Strictly speaking, what I judge
or believe is not an object but rather that some object is or is not in a certain
state. One proper question is therefore 'What is the object about which I
judge that it is or is not in a certain state?'. And this question can be answered by saying that it is Peter or a stone. If, on the other hand, it is asked
what is the complete and adequate object judged or believed in the judgment
that Peter is white (*Petrum esse album*), then the answer is already contained
in the question, namely 'that Peter is white' (*Petrum esse album*). And if it is
further asked what this complete and adequate object that Peter is white is,
the answer must be that it is Peter in so far as he is white.

The distinction between the thing as such and the thing as being in a
certain state enables André to counter such familiar arguments against the *res*
theory as that someone who believes that God is three and one and someone
who believes that God is not three and one would believe the same thing. The
thing about which it is judged that it is in a certain state and that it is not in a
certain state is admittedly the same; but the things that are determined by each
judgment as a whole, being things in such a state as is required for the truth
of the judgment (*obiectum tale ens et taliter se habens quale requiritur ad*

veritatem illius iudicii; f. XXXVI r.) are of course not the same. In a similar way, it can be said that the person who believes that God exists and disbelieves that God does not exist forms judgments about the same thing, namely God. But what he assents to in the first case is God as existing and what he dissents from in the second case is God as not existing and these qualified objects, being things in a certain state, are different.

15.4. Pierre d'Ailly

The writings of Pierre d'Ailly that are important for our subject are the commentary on the *Sentences* [7], the *Conceptus et insolubilia* [8], and the *Destructiones modorum significandi* [9]. These texts date from the period between 1372 and 1389. Paul of Venice expounds and criticizes Pierre d'Ailly's views in the fourth opinion concerning the significate of the *propositio* [10].

15.4.1. Pierre d' Ailly distinguishes four kinds of terms. Mental terms in the strict sense are natural signs or acts of understanding. Some of these natural signs signify in a nominal way and are therefore by nature nouns, others signify in a verbal way and are therefore by nature verbs; the same applies to other parts of speech. The mental nouns also have natural cases, and agreement in case belongs primarily and naturally to mental speech. Written and vocal terms are synonymous conventional signs signifying immediately the mental terms to which they are subordinated and mediately a thing in the outside world. Pierre rejects the view that the written term is subordinate to the vocal term; it is subordinate only to the mental term which it directly signifies. Further, there are mental terms in a secondary sense, namely likenesses of written or spoken terms; they are conventional signs of a mental term in the strict sense and are subordinate to it in the same way as the written or spoken terms of which they are the mental images.

Similar relations hold between the *propositiones* that are formed by means of these four kinds of terms. Of the *propositiones* that are conventional signs it can be said, according to the Boethian definition, that they signify something true or false. The mental *propositio* in the strict sense, however, does

---

[7] *Quaestiones super libros Sententiarum*, Strassburg, 1490, reprinted Frankfurt, 1968.

[8] For editions cf. Elie (1937: 64–65), who also gives a French translation of relevant passages (66–82). Pertinent quotations are found in Prantl (1855–1870: IV, 108 ff.).

[9] Cf. Pinborg (1967: 202–207).

[10] *Logica magna*, Venetiis, 1499, Second part, *De significato propositionis*, f. 163 r. – f. 164 r.

not signify a truth or a falsity but is that which is primarily true or false. Concerning the question whether the mental *propositio* in the strict sense is made up of partial acts of knowing of which one is the subject and one the predicate or is rather one undivided act Pierre cites the view propounded by Gregory of Rimini (Cf. 14.1.1), which according to him contains only part of the truth. In fact, compound mental *propositiones* such as conditional or copulative thoughts or syllogisms are essentially made up of more than one act of knowing. But no categorical mental *propositio* is essentially made up of partial acts of knowing. Such a mental *propositio* is called complex not on the grounds offered by Gregory, but rather on account of the fact that it is equivalent in signifying to several acts of knowing, which therefore may be called its parts in a figurative sense. What Pierre presumably means is that the mental *propositio* 'Man is an animal' may be regarded as equivalent in signifying to the act of thinking of men or to the act of thinking of animals, and that therefore these acts of thinking are in a way its parts. As we shall see in the next paragraph, Pierre held that the things in the outside world signified by a *propositio* are exclusively those things which are signified by each of its parts. But even if this interpretation is correct, it is far from clear how this doctrine of the essential incompositeness of the categorical mental *propositio* is to be harmonized with the view that it contains nouns, verbs, and other parts of speech, and even cases and agreement in case.

The fundamental bearers of truth and falsity and also of the modalities are the mental *propositiones* in the proper sense. Written or spoken *propositiones* and their mental images are called true or false, possible or necessary, in a derivative way, namely in so far as the corresponding mental *propositio* in the proper sense is true or false, possible or necessary. That Pierre at least sometimes understood *propositio* in the sense of an utterance-type may be gathered from his detailed discussion, perhaps partly inspired by Cicero's *De fato*, of *propositiones* with changing truth-values (*In I Sent.*, q. 11, art. 1, C–D). Such an affirmative *propositio* as 'The Antichrist will exist at the future moment *c*' is said to be true before *c* if the Antichrist exists at *c*, but false (rather than inapplicable) after *c*. It may cease to be true and is therefore mutably true (*mutabiliter vera*), but once it has become false it remains immutably false (*immutabiliter falsa*). In the same circumstances the corresponding negative *propositio* will cease to be false and is therefore mutably false before *c*, but once it has become true it remains immutably true. In this connection Pierre also discusses the rule that every true *propositio* about the past is necessary and that every false *propositio* about the past is impossible (Cf. 5.2.1). He denies that this rule holds universally, citing as counterexamples 'Adam was every man' (*Adam fuit omnis homo*) and 'Something that was every man was an animal' (*aliquid quod fuit omnis homo fuit animal*). These *propositiones* were true before Eve came into existence but they were not necessary, since now they are false. Similarly, 'Every animal that existed after the Flood was in Noah's ark' was true before any other animals were born, but it was not necessary, since now it is false.

In defending the thesis that every truth can be taken to be a true *propositio* (*In I Sent.*, q. 1, art. 1, C–D) Pierre d'Ailly considers the following three objections. In the first place, it might be adduced that God or the divine knowledge is a truth, but that God is not a true *propositio*. Pierre, however, sees no reason why it should not be held that God or the divine knowledge is a true *propositio* for the divine intellect. The only argument for denying this would be that a *propositio* is something complex essentially made up of several parts of which one is the subject, one the copula, and one the predicate, and that such a complexity is incompatible with God's absolute simplicity. But for Pierre, as for Gregory of Rimini, a categorical mental *propositio* is not composite but rather an undivided whole. In the second place, one might object that before there existed anything but God it was true that the world would exist (*mundum fore*). This truth, being contingent, was not God and it was not a *propositio* either, since there were no *propositiones*; therefore this truth was some *complexe significabile*. Pierre's answer to this objection is that the phrase *mundum fore* can be interpreted, according to material supposition, as standing for the corresponding *propositio*, namely *mundus erit*, and that this true *propositio* was God. In that case two difficulties remain. The first is that *mundus erit* seems to be a contingent truth, whereas God is a necessary being. Pierre tries to solve this difficulty by maintaining that this truth was just as necessary as God but that it was a truth in a contingent way (*erat contingenter veritas*). The second difficulty is that the contradictory of *mundus erit*, being from eternity false, could hardly be identified with God. Pierre concludes that this shows only that there has been a truth from eternity to which no contradictory falsehood corresponded. The third objection against the thesis that every truth is a true *propositio* is that even if no *propositio* existed it would still be true that there is no *propositio*. According to Pierre the antecedent must mean that there is no created *propositio*, since it is impossible that God is not a true *propositio*. But then we can say that the truth that there is no created *propositio* is the true uncreated *propositio* which is God.

According to Pierre d'Ailly the object of knowledge is the mental *propositio* in the proper sense (*In I Sent.*, q. 1, art. 3, HH). He establishes the plausibility of the *complexum* theory by rejecting the two alternatives, the *res* theory and the *complexe significabile* theory. Against the *res* theory he advances the well known arguments that then many sciences would be about contingent objects and that knowledge, belief, opinion, and error would have the same object. The other theory is dismissed on the ground that Gregory of Rimini himself admits that the *complexe significabile* is nothing. In the same passage Pierre attempts to refute Gregory's thesis that the conclusion of a scientific proof is identical with an act of assenting and an act of knowing, mainly on grounds that had been discussed and rejected by Gregory himself (Cf. 14.1.1).

15.4.2. Another occasion on which Pierre deals with Gregory's *complexe significabile* theory is a passage in the *Insolubilia* where he treats the question why a *propositio* is true or false. He there proposes a formula according to which a mental *propositio* in the proper sense that is singular, categorical, affirmative, and without modal qualifications is true if in reality it is, has been, or will be so (*taliter*) as (*qualitercumque*) the *propositio* according to its complete signification (*secundum significationem totalem*) signifies that it is, has been, or will be. Now the phrase *secundum significationem totalem* easily leads one to assume that a *propositio* has some significate of its own in the form of something that can be signified only in a complex way. If it is true that 'Every man is an animal' signifies that every man is an animal, it looks as if this truth could also be expressed by 'That every man is an animal (*omnem hominem esse animal*) is signified by "Every man is an animal" '. The second statement is supposed to be true, so the subject-term must stand for something. Since it does not seem to stand for any incomplex thing, it is concluded that it stands for a *complexe significabile*.

At this point Pierre gives a summary of Gregory's doctrine and urges the following objections against it. It is hard to see how a *complexe significabile* can be something if it is neither a substance nor an accident, neither God nor a creature. Further, it would have to be assumed that some of these dubious entities – for instance, that the world would exist or that God exists – have been true from eternity; but only God has existed from eternity. Next, Pierre propounds a question which had already been propounded by Buridan in connection with such particular cases as that the Antichrist will exist or that a horse is not an ass (*In Met. quaest.* VI, q. 8) – the question of the location of the *complexe significabilia*. One cannot say that they are at this place rather than at that; nor can one say that they are everywhere, since only God is everywhere. It must therefore be concluded that they are nowhere, which means that they do not exist. Moreover, if the true *propositio* 'Man is an animal' signifies a true *complexe significabile* existing outside the mind, then it must also be conceded that the impossible *propositio* 'Man is an ass' signifies an impossible *complexe significabile* existing outside the mind, which is absurd. Finally, Pierre points out that everything that exists or can exist is signifiable in a complex way and also that there is no need to posit *complexe significabilia,* since according to Gregory they are not the fundamental bearers of truth and falsity (Cf. 14.1.5).

In this connection it should also be noted that Pierre, in discussing the familiar problems about God's knowledge *(In I Sent.,* q. 11, art. 2, P), explicitly states that he does not recognize any *enuntiabile* in the sense of an object of knowledge that is not a *propositio.* For him an *enuntiabile* is always a *propositio,* an expression that signifies in a complex way. Elsewhere *(In I Sent.,* q. 12, art. 3, FF) he quotes Gregory's reflections on the words *dicere* and *dictum* (Cf. 14.1.3). In practice, he uses the word *dictum* as a synonym of the phrase *oratio infinitiva.*

Although Pierre rejected Gregory's *complexe significabile* theory, he did not follow those who maintained that such a complete significate as *deum esse* is God. He adheres instead to a view which has some resemblance to a theory that is briefly mentioned by André de Neufchâteau, at the very beginning of the first question of the *Prologus.* According to Pierre, as far as things in the outside world are concerned, there is not any one thing that is the adequate or complete significate of the *propositio* as a whole. A mental *propositio* in the proper sense signifies those things in the outside world which are signified by each of its categorematic parts to which it is equivalent in signification. These significates are as a rule several distinct things *(plura ad invicem distincta)* and every thing that is signified by the *propositio* according to its complete signification is also signified by one of its categorematic parts. The *propositio* 'Man is an animal', for instance, signifies the men and the animals in the outside world that are signified by the separate acts of thinking of men and of animals to which the *propositio* is equivalent in signification.

What is specifically signified by the *propositio* according to its complete signification is not one thing in the outside world but a certain mode of being, an *aliqualiter* – for example, that man is an animal – of such a kind as is not signified by any of its parts *(quia haec propositio 'homo est animal' aliqualiter, scilicet hominem esse animal, significat, qualiter non significatur per aliquam eius partem).* Pierre openly agrees with Nicolas of Autrecourt that two contradictory mental *propositiones* signify exactly the same things but in different ways; what makes them different is the *modus* or the *aliqualiter.* Such an *aliqualiter* as that man is an animal is not a something in the sense of an entity. It is true that the *dictum* or accusative and infinitive phrase that corresponds to the *propositio* 'Man is an animal' may be taken according to material supposition; then it stands either for itself or for the *propositio* (for example, in *hominem esse animal est verum*). But if it is taken in a signifying function, it stands for nothing. This is proved in the following way. Since the *dictum* taken in a signifying function signifies all those things in the outside world that are signified by the *propositio,* there is no reason why it should stand for one of those significates rather than for another. Consequently, it stands for anything whatever or for nothing; but not for anything whatever; therefore for nothing. This is confirmed by the consideration that if it is admitted that *deum esse* is God or that *hominem esse animal* is man, it equally has to be allowed that *omnem hominem esse animal* (that every man is an animal) is man, which is false, since of no man it can be said truly that he is that every man is an animal. Similarly, it would be false to say that *hominem esse asinum* is man, because there is no reason why it should be a man rather than an ass.

In order to curb the tendency to regard the *aliqualiter* as a something or an entity Pierre declares that such questions as *quid est omnem hominem esse animal* or *quid est hominem esse animal* are just as ungrammatical and ridiculous as the question *quid est omnem hominem* ('What is every man?', with *omnem hominem* in the accusative instead of in the nominative case). And he denies the validity of the transition from *'omnis homo est animal' significat omnem hominem esse animal* to *omnem hominem esse animal significatur per eam* (*propositionem*), since the second expression is as ungrammatical as *omnem hominem* (in the accusative case) *significatur per 'omnis homo'* would be if it were inferred from the correct expression *'omnis homo' significat omnem hominem.*

Pierre explains this condemnation of certain expressions containing a *dictum* by drawing two distinctions between ways in which infinitives and accusative and infinitive phrases can be understood. The first distinction is that between interpreting them according to material supposition and taking them in a signifying function (*significative* or *personaliter*). In the latter case he again distinguishes between an interpretation in a verbal sense (*verbaliter*) and an interpretation in a nominal sense (*nominaliter*). In the expressions *bonum est legere* and *malum est occidere*, for instance, the infinitive *legere* ('to read') and the infinitive *occidere* ('to kill') may be taken either in their full verbal force or as synonyms of the verbal nouns *lectio* and *occisio.* If they are taken in the second way, *bonum est legere* may be replaced by *bona est lectio* and *malum est occidere* by *mala est occisio.* Now, according to Pierre, every expression in which an infinitive or an accusative and infinitive phrase taken in a signifying function and in a verbal sense is used as the subject-term is ungrammatical. *Sedere est,* for example, where *sedere* is so understood, is ungrammatical in the same way as *sedeo est* ('I sit is') would be. This rule also disposes of the expression *omnem hominem esse animal significatur per propositionem 'omnis homo est animal'*. Furthermore, every expression in which an infinitive or an accusative and infinitive phrase taken in a signifying function and in a verbal sense is used before or after the verb *est* is ungrammatical. Strictly speaking, therefore, the example given by Gregory of Rimini (Cf. 14.1.4), namely *hominem esse animal est hominem esse substantiam animatam sensibilem rationalem* ('That man is an animal is (the same as) that man is a living substance possessed of senses and reason'), is not a properly formed expression. Finally, Pierre offers some examples of constructions in which an accusative and infinitive phrase taken in a signifying function and in a purely verbal sense may be used in a correct manner. They are *volo Socratem currere* ('I want Socrates to run'), *scio hominem esse animal* ('I know that man is an animal'), and *haec oratio significat deum esse* ('This combination of words signifies that God exists').

These attempts to show that accusative and infinitive phrases need not be naming or referring expressions and that the mode of being which they indicate is therefore not a peculiar kind of entity are strongly reminiscent of Abelard's endeavours to convince his readers that what is asserted is not a thing (Cf. 9.3.3 and 9.3.4). On the other hand, Pierre's view differs from Abelard's theory – and from Gregory of Rimini's theory – in that he does not regard the mode of being that is signified by a *propositio* according to its complete signification as a bearer of truth or falsity or as the primary object of knowledge. He categorically refuses to hypostasize the *aliqualiter* in any way at all; it is nothing but a manner in which a *propositio* signifies certain things in the outside world. If the things exist in the manner in which they are signified, the *propositio* is true; if not, the *propositio* is false. Pierre firmly sides with Buridan and other adherents of the *complexum* theory in recognizing only the *propositio* as the bearer of truth and falsity and as the primary object of knowledge. But he rejects the doctrine that the basic affirmative *propositiones,* if true, name one entity in a certain state as determined by the categorematic and syncategorematic parts of the *propositio*; according to him they refer to all the entities referred to by the categorematic parts but they do so in a certain way. This may even be the most literal interpretation of the view mentioned by Abelard (*Glosses,* ed. Geyer p. 365) according to which a *propositio* signifies the things themselves signified by its parts, not however one by one, but all at once in a certain state (Cf. 9.3.1).

15.5. Paul of Venice

The last opponent of the *complexe significabile* theory to whom I want to call attention is Paul of Venice. An Augustinian himself, he is not lacking in sympathy with certain aspects of Gregory's doctrine, but he nevertheless disagrees with him on an essential point. The principal source of information about Paul's views is the voluminous and learned *Logica magna* [11]. Most of what is said there concerning the significate of the *propositio* is strongly dependent upon such predecessors as William Heytesbury [12], Richard Ferry-bridge [13], and Johannes Venator Anglicus [14].

15.5.1. Paul begins the second part of *Logica magna* (f. 101) with a defini-tion of the *propositio* as an *enuntiatio congrua et perfecta veri aut falsi significativa.* He deliberately uses the word *significativa* ('capable of signify-ing') instead of *significans* because he is of the opinion that a well-formed and complete utterance deserves the name *propositio* even if it does not actually signify a truth or a falsehood. There are many utterances in the Bible or in some other closed book which are *propositiones* in spite of the fact that they are not read at a given moment. According to him it would be strange if someone had the power of causing such utterances to exist or to cease to exist by simply opening or closing the book. A *propositio* is not only an utterance-token but also an utterance-type in that it may be used again and again to make one definite statement.

Another remarkable feature of the definition is that it does not contain the element *oratio indicativa.* Paul uses the word *enuntiatio* in a rather wide sense, practically as a synonym of *oratio,* and defends the view that not only the indicative *enuntiatio* but also imperative, deprecative, optative, and sub-junctive *enuntiationes* are rightly called *propositiones.* His first argument is that in all these cases the mind can be said to assent to such *enuntiationes* or to dissent from them. Now only what is true or false can be assented to or

---

[11] Venetiis, 1499. I shall refer to this work by means of the letters *LM,* followed by folio.

[12] Especially *De veritate et falsitate propositionis,* Venetiis, 1494. For a survey of relevant passages cf. Maierù (1966).

[13] *Logica sive de veritate.* I know this work through transcriptions from the manu-script *Padova B.U. 1123* which were kindly put at my disposal by Mr. Francesco del Punta.

[14] *Logica,* especially the chapter *De significato propositionis.* In this case too I am very grateful to Mr. Francesco del Punta for providing me with transcriptions from the manuscript *Codex Vaticanus Latinus 2130.*

dissented from; therefore, all those *enuntiationes* are true or false and thus *propositiones*. That we assent to a subjunctive utterance, for instance, is shown by means of the true conditional *si Antichristus esset albus, Antichristus esset coloratus* ('If the Antichrist were white, he would be coloured'). The antecedent and the consequent are subjunctive *enuntiationes*; since, according to Paul, we assent to them, they are supposed to be true and therefore to be *propositiones*. Paul is aware of the fact that his view is at variance with what Aristotle (*De int.* 17 a 5) says, namely that prayer is an *oratio* (*logos*) but not a true or a false one. He replies, however, that there are more cases in which Aristotle takes a term in a narrower sense than is desirable. For example, he also defines a noun as a spoken sound significant by convention, whereas it is obvious that there are many nouns, namely mental nouns, which are neither spoken sounds nor significant by convention. Further, Paul attempts to show the correctness of his conception by maintaining that imperative, deprecative, optative, and subjunctive *enuntiationes* can be said to have a subject and a predicate and also a certain quantity and quality. The imperative utterance *Petre, lege* ('Peter, read') is singular and affirmative; the implicit subject is *tu* ('you') and the implicit predicate is *legens* ('reading'), while the element *Petre* is a part of the whole *propositio*. As for optative utterances, some are singular affirmative, like *utinam ego essem homo* ('O, that I might be a man'), in which *ego* is the subject and *homo* the predicate, while *utinam* is the mark of a wish (*nota optandi*) and belongs to the *propositio* as a whole. On the other hand, *utinam homo disputaret* ('O, that man might dispute') is indefinite, *utinam aliquis asinus curreret* ('O, that some ass might run') is particular, *utinam omnis homo diligeret deum* ('O, that every man might love God') is universal affirmative, and *utinam nullus homo peccaret* ('O, that no man might sin') is universal negative.

In a second argument for his main thesis Paul goes a step further and contends that all the above-mentioned *enuntiationes* can plausibly be regarded as indicatives, not explicitly, but implicitly, in that they are subordinated to mental *enuntiationes* in the indicative mood. *Lege, Petre* is subordinated to the mental correlate *volo* or *impero quod legas, Petre* ('I want you to read, Peter'); *miserere mei, deus* is subordinated to *deprecor, deus, quod miserearis mei* ('I pray you, God, to have mercy upon me'); *utinam legerem* is subordinated to *ego sum cupiens quod legerem* ('I wish that I might read'). In each case the mental correlate is an indicative *enuntiatio,* a thought which is composed of a subject, a copula, and a predicate, and which indicates that one has an attitude of commanding, praying, or wishing something. Whereas Abelard (Cf. 9.2.2), though reducing the mental counterparts of non-declarative utterances to the mental counterparts of the corresponding statement-making utterances, maintained a difference between declarative vocal utterances and several kinds of non-declarative vocal utterances, Paul of Venice appears to recognize only one kind of complete utterance even on the level of spoken and written speech. For him the formal dissimilarities between indicative, imperative, deprecative, optative, and subjunctive utterances are altogether superficial and secondary. The uniform character of the mental counterparts to which they are subordinated and which determine their implicit or underlying nature is made a decisive criterion to classify them as actually being *propositiones*, statements that are either true or false.

It should be noted that Paul realizes that his two ways of elucidating non-declarative utterances do not necessarily yield the same result. *Utinam non legerem*, for instance, is to be regarded as being of negative quality if taken according to the first way, whereas according to the second way it is identified with *opto quod non legerem*, which is an affirmative statement. If it is objected that the second interpretation is inconsistent with the rules of the grammarians, Paul's answer is that the logician has a mode of discourse different from the grammarian's.

15.5.2. There is some reason to believe that Paul's conception of the adequate significate of a *propositio* underwent a certain development. In commenting upon *Cat.* 14 b 21 in his *Expositio in Praedicamenta*[15] he says that Aristotle in the formula *dum res est vel non est* means by *res* not the significate of the subject or the predicate but rather the adequate significate of the *propositio* as a whole. The statement *homo est,* for example, is true if *hominem esse* is the case and false if *hominem esse* is not the case. This view is in complete accordance with Gregory of Rimini's position. But in discussing Gregory's theory in the third opinion concerning the significate of the *propositio* (*LM* f. 162 v. – f. 163 r.) Paul concludes his criticism of Gregory's use of the terms *aliquid, res,* and *ens* by rejecting the appeal to *Cat.* 14 b 21 (Cf. 14.1.4). Paul now holds that Aristotle calls only such individuals as Socrates and Plato things and not just any significate. What he intends[16] to convey by his formula is that a *propositio* which says that a certain individual thing exists is true if that individual thing exists and false if it does not exist. In general Paul's criticism of Gregory's view is entirely aimed at the thesis that a *complexe significabile* is something but not an entity in the sense of a substance or an accident; it is precisely against this point that he advances no less than a dozen arguments. While he completely agrees with Gregory in regard-

---

[15] The relevant passage is quoted by Pagallo (1960: 185).
[16] I read *voluit* instead of *noluit*.

ing the *complexe significabile* as a bearer of truth-values and modalities and also as that which is known, he seems to have come to disagree with him on the question whether every *complexe significabile* is a something. Concerning this central issue the *Logica magna* puts forward a view which is sharply opposed to Gregory's doctrine and is somewhat like the positions defended by Buridan and André de Neufchâteau and also by Richard Ferrybridge (Cf. *Logica sive de veritate,* especially f. 82 v.). This view is laid down in four conclusions (*LM* f. 164 r. – f. 167 r.).

In the first conclusion Paul states that the adequate significate of a negative *propositio* is never a thing (*aliquid*), more than one thing (*aliqua*), or a mode of being (*aliqualiter*). He extensively defends this thesis against the eighth conclusion of Johannes Venator Anglicus (*Logica,* f. 74 v.), according to which *deum non esse solem* (that God is not the sun) is God.

In the second conclusion Paul maintains that the adequate significate of a categorical affirmative *propositio* to whose implicit or explicit subject or predicate nothing but the sign corresponds in reality is neither a thing nor a mode of being, neither a quality nor a quantity, neither the creator nor a creature. The adequate significates of *Antichristus erit, Adam fuit,* and *hoc potest esse,* namely that the Antichrist will exist, that Adam has existed, and that this can exist, are not actual parts of reality, since the Antichrist does not exist, Adam does not exist, and this does not exist. All one can say is that *Adam fuisse* has been, that *Antichristum fore* will be, and that *hoc posse* can be. Paul agrees with Ferrybridge in rejecting the view – held, for instance, by Johannes Venator Anglicus (*Logica,* f. 74 v.) – that *Adam fuisse* is Adam in the past (*Adam praeteritus*) or that *Antichristum fore* is the future Antichrist (*Antichristus futurus*) on the ground that then it would follow that both significates have some kind of being. He is, however, prepared to admit the statements *Antichristum fore est Antichristus futurus* and *Adam fuisse est praeteritus Adam* if *futurus* and *praeteritus* are taken as participles so that *est futurus* is synonymous with *erit* and *est praeteritus* with *fuit;* for *Antichristum fore erit Antichristus* and *Adam fuisse fuit Adam* are acceptable.

The fourth conclusion states that the adequate significate of a true affirmative *propositio* about the present[17] is in fact (*realiter*) identical with the significate of the subject or the predicate. This means that the adequate significate of *deus est,* namely *deum esse,* is in fact identical with God. Already in discussing Pierre d'Ailly's theory, in the fourth opinion concerning

---

[17] An exception is made for such special cases as *homo est mortuus* ('The man is dead') and *chimaera est opinata* ('A chimaera is thought of') which contain a *terminus distrahens* and a *terminus ampliativus.*

the significate of the *propositio,* Paul had attacked the thesis that what the *propositio* as a whole signifies in the outside world are several distinct things. According to him the significate with which the adequate significate of the *propositio* can be in fact identified is the one thing that, by being in a certain state, renders the *propositio* true.

Paul mentions twelve objections against the fourth conclusion[18]. In order to refute these objections he had introduced the third conclusion which states that, although such adequate significates as *deum esse* may be in fact identical with God, there is nevertheless a formal distinction between that God exists and God. According to him the copula *est* may have the meaning 'is in fact or really identical with' or the meaning 'is formally identical with' (Cf. *LM* f. 167 r.). Only formal identity gives us the right always to substitute one expression for another. Now all the objections he mentions are arguments in which the minor is an identity-statement with a copula that means 'is in fact or really identical with' and in which nevertheless on the ground of this minor one expression is substituted for another. For example, from the premiss 'I can bring it about that I run' (*ego possum facere me currere*) and 'I am that I run' (*ego sum me currere*) the conclusion 'I can bring about myself' (*ego possum facere me*) is drawn. This argument is invalid, since *me currere* is only in fact identical with me and that kind of identity does not justify the replacement of *me currere* by *me.* According to Paul the only conclusion that can be validly drawn from the premisses is *ego possum facere aliqualiter esse qualiter esse sum ego* in which the copula *sum* has the meaning 'am in fact identical with'. This existential generalization may perhaps be paraphrased by 'I can bring about some state of affairs with which I am in fact identical or which is in fact identical with me'. Other arguments are of a slightly different form, for instance this one: 'That God exists is necessary (*deum esse est necessarium*); that God exists is (in fact identical with) that God creates Socrates (*deum esse est deum creare Socratem*); therefore, that God creates Socrates is necessary (*deum creare Socratem est necessarium*)'. The minor does not state a formal identity and the replacement of *deum esse* by *deum creare Socratem* is therefore unwarranted. A correct conclusion from the premisses would be *aliqualiter esse qualiter esse est deum creare Socratem est necessarium* ('Some state of affairs which is in fact identical with that God creates Socrates is necessary').

Paul's third conclusion also enables him to deal effectively with the well

---

[18] For similar lists of objections cf. William Heytesbury, *De veritate et falsitate propositionis,* f. 183 v. − f. 184 r.; Richard Ferrybridge, *Logica sive de veritate,* f. 83; Johannes Venator Anglicus, *Logica,* f. 75.

known arguments that if the adequate significate of a *propositio* is a thing, many sciences will be about contingent objects, that knowledge, belief, opinion, and error will have the same object, and that one and the same person will assent to something and at the same time dissent from it. The adequate object of knowledge and assent is a *complexe significabile* or a *taliter esse,* a state of affairs expressed by an accusative and infinitive phrase. Though an actual state of affairs is in fact identical with a thing, this does not mean that the thing is the proper and adequate object of knowledge and assent. Since there is a formal distinction between the state of affairs and the thing, there are also differences in the roles they can play. Similarly, two states of affairs may be *realiter* identical, by being *realiter* identical with the same thing, but this does not alter the fact that they are formally distinct, and it is this latter feature that matters when we are considering acts of knowing, assenting, or opining. By maintaining a formal distinction between the *complexe significabile* and the thing with which it may be *realiter* identical Paul succeeded in retaining a good deal of Gregory of Rimini's doctrine, while at the same time replacing its most controversial part by insights that were borrowed from some of his opponents.

16. THE SIGNIFICATE OF A TRUE *PROPOSITIO*

From such a statement as *haec propositio 'deus est' significat deum esse* ('The *propositio* "God exists" signifies that God exists') there is an easy transition to the statement that *deum esse* is the significate of *deus est* and from there to the question of what precisely this significate is. In the final phase of medieval thought about the problems concerning the bearers of truth and falsity the discussions became centred almost exclusively around this question. Some, like Pierre d'Ailly, denied that it is a proper question at all and tried to block the road that leads to it (Cf. 15.4.2). But most thinkers considered it a genuine problem of decisive importance and offered various solutions to it. As we saw in 15.1.3, Buridan mentioned four answers to the question of what kind of thing *hominem bibere vinum* is. His own view distinguishes between an interpretation of the accusative and infinitive phrase according to material supposition, in which case it stands either for itself or for the corresponding *propositio,* and an interpretation of the phrase according to its signifying function. In the latter interpretation the phrase was held to stand either for nothing, notably when the corresponding *propositio* is false but also in the case of certain true *propositiones,* or for a thing in the outside world, in the case of a privileged class of true *propositiones.*

As far as we can judge from the available sources, this doctrine that the significate of a true *propositio* is sometimes a thing in the outside world had secured wide acceptance at the end of the medieval period. In one form or another it was also held by Marsilius of Inghen, André de Neufchâteau, Richard Ferrybridge, Johannes Venator Anglicus, and Paul of Venice. It may therefore be called the dominant doctrine. Although dominant, it was not, however, wholly unchallenged. The chief rival theories seem to have been the view that every true *propositio* has a significate and that this significate is never a thing but only a mode in which a thing is (*modus rei*) and the view

273

that there is no significate in the outside world at all. Unfortunately, no writings are known in which these competitors directly present themselves; we have to rely upon what others, mainly adversaries, tell us about them.

16.1.   The significate as the mode of being of a thing

The doctrine that every true *propositio* has a significate which is never a thing but a way in which a thing is, the *modus rei* theory, is discussed by William Heytesbury[1], by Richard Ferrybridge[2], by Johannes Venator Anglicus[3], and by Paul of Venice[4] who, in the first opinion concerning the significate of a *propositio*, copies Ferrybridge almost verbatim. If *quoddam accidens inhaerens homini* is taken as a paraphrase of *modus rei*, it may be assumed that the fourth opinion which Buridan mentions concerning the question of what *hominem bibere vinum* is also represents a *modus rei* theory, the mode consisting in the circumstance that the man is in such a state with regard to wine (*ut taliter se habeat ad vinum*).

The proponents of the *modus rei* theory appear to have supported their view by the following two arguments. In the first place, they started from the premiss that the significate of such a true affirmative *propositio* about the present as 'You exist' (*tu es*) is everywhere, since that you exist may be known at every place in the world and is therefore everywhere true. But nothing except an immaterial substance can be everywhere; thus it follows that the significate of *tu es*, namely that you exist, is not a thing (since you are not an immaterial substance) but rather a mode of a thing. In the second place, it was argued that if the *propositio* 'No chimaera exists' is true, its significate, namely that no chimaera exists, is true and consequently is. But that no chimaera exists cannot be a thing; therefore, it is a mode of a thing. These arguments are clearly aimed at the main tenets of the dominant theory, which denied that there is always a correlate to a true *propositio* in the outside world and maintained that in those cases in which a true *propositio* does have a significate in the outside world this significate is a thing.

The standard objections against this *modus rei* theory were of the following kind. Wherever the significate of a *propositio* is, there the significate of each of its categorematic parts must be. Consequently, if the significate of

[1] *De veritate et falsitate propositionis,* f. 184.
[2] *Logica sive de veritate,* f. 82 v. – f. 83 v.
[3] *Logica,* f. 73 r., f. 74 v., f. 75 v.
[4] *Logica magna,* f. 162 r.

'Socrates exists' is everywhere, the significate of the subject-term, namely Socrates, is everywhere, which is false. Further, if 'Socrates runs' is true, then, according to the *modus rei* theorists, that Socrates runs is a mode of being that is everywhere. Thus Socrates, by beginning to run, would bring it about that it is everywhere the case that he runs. And this would mean that a change can take place nowhere unless it occurs everywhere. Moreover, the theory leads to the consequence that all knowledge has modes of things for its object; this consequence is false, since there is also knowledge of quiddities, which is prior to the knowledge of modes. Next, if the significate of a true *propositio* is a mode, this mode is either simple or complex. If it is simple, then it can be designated by a non-composite expression; but in that case non-composite expressions would not only signify things in the sense of substances or qualities but also modes of things, which is contrary to Aristotle (*Cat.* 1 b 25). If, on the other hand, the mode is complex, it should be possible that something simple exists without its mode existing, since what is simple precedes composition. But this consequence is false; for if God exists, it is the case that God exists, and consequently it is not possible that God (who is absolutely simple) exists unless that God exists (which is the mode signified by a true *propositio*) exists or is the case. Furthermore, if that you exist is a mode, this mode is either in you or outside you. It cannot be outside you, since then it would not cease to exist if you were destroyed. Nor can it be in you, since you are naturally prior to everything that exists in you and it is always possible that what is by nature prior exists without that which is by nature later; so it would follow that you can exist although that you exist is not (the case). Finally, if that you exist is a mode, it is something that is (*ens*); but then it is either a substance or an accident and therefore a thing (*res*).

The first argument which the *modus rei* theorists advanced in support of their view was countered by pointing out, for instance, that from 'At this place it is true that you exist' it no more follows that it is at this place that you exist (*hic est quod tu es*) than it follows from 'At this place I see you' or 'At this place I think of you' that you are at this place. Against the second argument it could be maintained that the adequate significate of a negative *propositio* is neither one thing, nor more than one thing, nor a mode of being (*aliqualiter*); although the significate of *nulla chimaera est* is true, this does not mean that *nullam chimaeram esse* is.

As we saw in 14.2.3, the phrase *modus rei* was typically applied to significates that can be expressed only by combinations of words in which syncategorematic ingredients play a decisive part. Such a *modus rei* was also called a *complexe significabile*. A *complexe significabile* as it was interpreted by Gregory of Rimini may probably be regarded as a special case of a *modus rei* in the wider sense; it is a state of a thing that can be signified only by the combination of a subject with a predicate that is brought about by the copula, in a *complexum* that is a *propositio*. It is therefore plausible to assume that the later *modus rei* theory has to be seen against the background of all those theories, from Abelard onwards, which stressed the point that the significate of a *propositio* as a whole, because of the essential contributions made to it by the syncategorematic elements, cannot possibly be a thing in the sense of a substance or a quality that can be expressed by a categorematic *incomplexum*. This would also account for the thesis that every true *propositio* has a significate in the outside world. If the Aristotelian formula *eo quod res est vel non est* is related to the mode of being that is expressed by the *propositio,* it is precisely the circumstance that this mode of being is realized in the world that renders the *propositio* true. The only thing that remains rather puzzling is that in the above-mentioned sources the *modus rei* theory is treated in such complete separation from those theories that seem to be its proper background.

16.2.   The significate as the mental composition

The theory that the significate of a true *propositio* is a mental composition rather than a thing is mentioned by Richard Ferrybridge[5], Johannes Venator Anglicus[6], and Paul of Venice[7], who discusses it as the second opinion on the significate of the *propositio,* again closely following Ferry-bridge.

In support of this theory it was pointed out that the significate of such a true *propositio* as *Socrates est homo* cannot be a thing outside the mind, since according to Aristotle (*De int.* 16 b 25) the verb *est* signifies a certain composition which cannot be thought without the components and is not itself a thing in the world. What a true *propositio* signifies is therefore a mental composition. Further, the authority of Aristotle (*De int.* 22 a 22) was also invoked to establish the equivalence of *necesse est nullam chimaeram esse* ('It is necessary that no chimaera exists') and *impossibile est chimaeram esse* ('It is impossible that a chimaera exists'). Now it is clear that *nullam chimaeram esse* is neither a thing nor a mode of being (*aliqualiter*) outside the

[5] *Logica sive de veritate,* f. 83.
[6] *Logica,* f. 74 v. – f. 75 r.
[7] *Logica magna,* f. 162.

mind. But as there has to be something that is necessary, we must conclude that it is the mental composition[8]. Thirdly, it was argued that unless the significate of a true *propositio* is a mental composition no true negative *propositio* and no true affirmative *propositio* about the past or the future (whose subject-term does not signify an existing thing) would have a true significate. Apparently, the adherents of this theory shared with the *modus rei* theorists the conviction that, contrary to what the dominant theory held, every true *propositio* must have a significate that has some kind of being. Since they thought that the only thing which all true *propositiones* have in common is the mental composition, they concluded that the significate of a true *propositio* is the mental composition. It is obvious that this view is most plausible (or least implausible) when by the true *propositio* is meant the spoken *propositio,* which can be said to signify the mental *propositio.*

Among the objections put forward against this theory of the significate as a mental composition are the following. If the theory were correct, the argument 'God exists; therefore that God exists is true' would be invalid. For the antecedent is necessary but the consequent would be contingent, since it is possible that there is no act of mental composition and in that case it cannot be true that God exists. Similarly, it would follow that at a time when there are no acts of composition it is impossible that God exists; or that it ceases to be the case that God exists when everybody refrains from performing the required mental act of composition. Further, it was pointed out that a true mental *propositio* signifies something that is not a mental composition but rather something that is the case in the outside world, for instance that God exists. But since the corresponding vocal *propositio* signifies the same as the mental *propositio,* the vocal *propositio* too must signify something in the outside world and not just a mental composition. Moreover, it would follow that you can bring it about that God exists, for that God exists is nothing but a mental composition and you are the efficient cause of that mental composition.

As in the case of the *modus rei* theory, it is evident that the doctrine that the significate of a true *propositio* is a mental composition had many roots in the past. We have only to think of the theory according to which a *propositio* signifies nothing but a composite thought[9], mentioned by Abelard (Cf.

---

[8] Paul of Venice has a somewhat different version of this obscure argument according to which 'It is necessary that no chimaera exists' was held to be equivalent to 'It is not impossible that no chimaera exists' (*impossibile non est nullam chimaeram esse*).

[9] It is remarkable that in Ferrybridge's discussion of the doctrine the phrase *intellectus compositus* occurs once instead of *compositio intellectus* or *mentis.*

9.3.1); of the theory that held that *enuntiabilia* are acts of conceiving produced by the words of a *propositio,* mentioned by the author of the *Ars
Meliduna* (Cf. 10.2.2); and of the view that the articles of faith are identical
with the acts of believing (Cf. 11.1.3). Nothing, however, indicates that there
was any clear awareness of these connections with the past.

Paul of Venice says that from the conception of the significate of a true
propositio as a mental composition two other false opinions had sprouted of
which the first was the view that the significate of a *propositio* is an *oratio
infinitiva,* such as *deum esse* or *hominem esse.* This theory had also been
mentioned by William Heytesbury[10]. It was supported by the simple reasoning '*deum esse* is the adequate significate of *deus est*; but *deum esse* is an
accusative and infinitive phrase; therefore, the adequate significate of the
propositio is an accusative and infinitive phrase'. Besides remarking that the
phrase *deum esse* is taken in different ways in the major and in the minor,
Paul raises four objections against this view. In the first place, since no accusative and infinitive phrase is true or false, there will be no true or false significate of *deus est* and consequently this *propositio* will not be true or false.
Secondly, that I know that God exists or that I exist does not mean that I
know an accusative and infinitive phrase. Thirdly, before the creation of the
world it was the case that God existed (*fuit deum esse*); but at that time there
was no accusative and infinitive phrase. Fourthly, it would follow that I can
bring it about that God does not exist and that you are an ass and even that
two contradictories are simultaneously true; for I can easily produce the
required accusative and infinitive phrases.

According to the second opinion the significate of a *propositio* is the
propositio itself, so that the sign and the significate are the same. In all
probability this opinion is identical with the first opinion mentioned by
Buridan, namely that *hominem bibere vinum* is nothing but a *propositio* (Cf.
15.1.3). This opinion was proved by the reasoning 'Everything that is true is a
propositio; but *deum esse* is true; therefore, *deum esse* is a *propositio*' and
also by the consideration that knowing or believing that God exists is nothing
but knowing or believing the *propositio* 'God exists'. The latter is denied by
Paul of Venice who holds that what is known or believed is something that is
distinct from the *propositio* itself. Furthermore, he objects that it would
follow that it is not the case that God exists or that anything exists if there is
no *propositio* asserting it. Moreover, it is conceivable that everybody sleeps or
keeps silent and that all writings are burnt; in that case there are no created
mental, spoken, or written *propositiones* (the only *propositiones* which ad-

---

[10] *De veritate et falsitate propositionis,* f. 183 v., f. 184 v.

herents of this theory admit) and thus even God would not know any such *propositio* as 'Something exists', which means that he does not know that something exists.

The arguments which are offered for the view that the significate of the *propositio* is the *propositio* itself are strongly reminiscent of arguments that were adduced in support of the *complexum* theory of Ockham and Holkot. And the statement that the sign and the significate are the same (*idem est signum et significatum*) looks like a variant of Holkot's statement that the act of knowing and that which is known are the same (*idem est scientia et scitum*; cf. 12.2.1). It is indeed not difficult to see that there is a certain resemblance between the theory of the significate as a mental composition as it appears in the context we are now discussing and the *complexum* theory of Ockham and Holkot. In the same way as the latter view made that which is true and known (the *verum* and *scitum* which finds its natural expression in an accusative and infinitive phrase) coincide with the mental *propositio,* the mental composition theory took an accusative and infinitive phrase exclusively according to material supposition, as standing for the true mental *propositio*. Such a statement as *'deus est' significat deum esse* was interpreted as meaning either that the spoken sounds *deus est,* if true, have as their only significate the true thought *deus est* or, more paradoxically, that the true thought *deus est* is its own significate. In contrast with the dominant doctrine, the adherents of the mental composition theory did not allow any interpretation of accusative and infinitive phrases according to a signifying function, thereby restricting the significate of a true *propositio* to the mental side and simply ignoring any significate in the outside world.

16.3. Conclusion

We have reached a point where the survey of medieval conceptions of the bearers of truth and falsity may reasonably be regarded as completed in a chronological sense. After the beginning of the fifteenth century no really new or interesting views concerning our topic were put forward; the creative period of medieval thinking had come to an end. I would not claim, however, that the general picture which I have tried to draw is complete in any other sense. In the first place, I am aware that further scrutiny of the sources which are at present available may very well yield results that will show the need of corrections or even drastic changes both in details and in the outlines. But what is more, the sources on which this study has been based are no doubt only a fragment of what may be brought to light and made accessible in the future. While for the ancient period it is unfortunately almost certain that what has disappeared is irrevocably lost, prospects for the Middle Ages seem to be more hopeful. New discoveries and publications may be expected which will throw fresh light on many points that have been left obscure or unsatisfactory in this essay.

SELECTIVE BIBLIOGRAPHY

Editions

Alexander Neckam, *De naturis rerum*, ed. Th. Wright, *Rerum Britannicarum medii aevi scriptores* 34, London, 1863, pp. 1–354.

Anecdota Graeca, ed. Immanuel Bekker, Berlin, 1814–1821.

Apuleius Platonicus Madaurensis, *Liber Peri hermeneias*, in: *Opera quae supersunt* III, ed. P. Thomas, Leipzig, 1908, pp. 176–194.

Caecilius Calactinus, *Fragmenta*, ed. E. Ofenloch, Leipzig, 1907.

F.S. Charisius, *Artis grammaticae libri V*, ed. C. Barwick, Leipzig, 1925.

Commentaria in Aristotelem Graeca, Berlin, 1891–1909 (For Alexander of Aphrodisias, Ammonius, John Philoponus, Porphyry, Simplicius, Themistius).

Corpus glossariorum Latinorum, ed. G. Loewe & G. Goetz, Leipzig, 1888–1923.

Dionysius Halicarnaseus, *De compositione verborum*, in: *Opuscula critica et rhetorica* II, ed. H. Usener & L. Radermacher, Leipzig, 1904.

A. Donatus, *Commentum Terenti*, ed. P. Wessner, Leipzig, 1902–1908.

Grammatici Graeci, Leipzig, 1878–1910 (For Apollonius Dyscolus, Choeroboscus, Dionysius Thrax, *Scholia* on Dionysius Thrax, Sophronius).

Grammatici Latini, ed. H. Keil, Leipzig, 1855–1880 (For Diomedes, Macrobius, Marius Victorinus, Priscian).

Notker Labeo, *Die Schriften Notkers und seiner Schule*, ed. P. Piper, Freiburg-Tübingen, 1882–1883.

Patrologiae cursus completus, Series Graeca, ed. J.P. Migne, Paris, 1857–1866; *Series Latina*, ed. J.P. Migne, Paris, 1844–1855.

Rhetores Graeci XIV, *Prolegomenon sylloge*, ed. H. Rabe, Leipzig, 1931.

Rhetores Latini minores, ed. C. Halm, Leipzig, 1863.

Scholia in Aristotelem, ed. C.A. Brandis, in: *Aristotelis opera*, Prussian Academy edition, IV, Berlin, 1836.

Stoicorum veterum fragmenta, ed. Ioannes ab Arnim, Leipzig, 1903–1924.

William of Sherwood, *Introductiones in logicam,* ed. M. Grabmann, *Sitzungsberichte der Bayerischen Akademie der Wissenschaften, philosophisch-historische Abteilung* 1937, 10, München, 1937.

Other works

Ackrill, J.L.
 1963 *Aristotle's* Categories *and* De interpretatione. *Translated with notes and glossary*, Oxford.
Adams, Marilyn McCord & Kretzmann, Norman
 1969 *William Ockham,* Predestination, God's foreknowledge, and future contingents. *Translated with an introduction, notes, and appendices*, New York.
de Andrés, Teodoro
 1969 *El nominalismo de Guillermo de Ockham como filosofía del lenguaje*, Madrid.

Barwick, K.
 1957 'Probleme der stoischen Sprachlehre und Rhetorik', *Abhandlungen der Sächsischen Akademie der Wissenschaften zu Leipzig, philosophisch-historische Klasse* 49, 3, Berlin.
Beonio-Brocchieri Fumagalli, M.T.
 1964 *La logica di Abelardo*, Firenze.
Bocheński, J.M.
 1962[2] *Formale Logik*, Freiburg-München. First published 1956.
Boehner, Ph.
 1952 *Medieval logic. An outline of its development from 1250 – c. 1400*, Manchester.
 1958 *Collected articles on Ockham*, ed. E.M. Buytaert, St. Bonaventure, N.Y.
Brandt, Reinhard
 1965 *Die Aristotelische Urteilslehre. Untersuchungen zur "Hermeneutik"*, Marburg.
Bréhier, Émile
 1962[3] *La théorie des incorporels dans l'ancien stoïcisme*, Paris. First published 1908.

Cartwright, R.
 1962 'Propositions', in: *Analytical philosophy*, ed. R.J. Butler, Oxford, pp. 81–103.
 1968 'Propositions again', *Nous* 2, 229–246.
Chenu, M.-D.
 1934[2] 'Contribution à l'histoire du traité de la foi', in: *Mélanges Thomistes*, Paris, pp. 123–140. First published 1923.
 1936 'Grammaire et théologie aux XIIe et XIIIe siècles', *Archives d'histoire doctrinale et littéraire du moyen âge* 10, 5–28.
Cornford, F.M.
 1935 *Plato's theory of knowledge. The* Theaetetus *and the* Sophist *of Plato translated with a running commentary*, London.
Courtenay, William J.
 1971 'A revised text of Robert Holcot's quodlibetal dispute on whether God is able to know more than he knows', *Archiv für Geschichte der Philosophie*, 53, 1–21.

Crombie, I.M.
    1963   *An examination of Plato's doctrines* II (*Plato on knowledge and reali-
            ty*), London.

Dal Pra, Mario
    1956a   'Linguaggio e conoscenza assertiva nel pensiero di Roberto Holkot',
            Rivista critica di storia della filosofia 11, 15–40.
    1956b   'La teoria del "significato totale" della proposizione nel pensiero di
            Gregorio da Rimini', *Rivista critica di storia della filosofia* 11, 287–
            311.

Elie, Hubert
    1937   *Le complexe significabile*, Paris.

Frede, Michael
    1967   *Prädikation und Existenzaussage. Platons Gebrauch von "ist" und "ist
            nicht" im Sophistes*, Göttingen.

Gale, Richard M.
    1967   'Propositions, judgments, sentences, and statements', in: *The encyclo-
            pedia of philosophy*, ed. P. Edwards, New York–London, 6, pp. 494–
            505.
Garceau, Benoit
    1968   Judicium. *Vocabulaire, sources, doctrine de Saint Thomas d'Aquin*,
            Montréal–Paris.
Geach, Peter
    1957   *Mental acts. Their content and their objects*, London.
Gochet, Paul
    1972   *Esquisse d'une théorie nominaliste de la proposition. Essai sur la phi-
            losophie de la logique*, Paris.
Goldschmidt, Victor
    1969[2]   *Le système stoïcien et l'idée de temps*, Paris. First published 1953.
Gould, J.B.
    1970   *The philosophy of Chrysippus*, Leiden.
Guthrie, W.K.C.
    1962–   *A history of Greek philosophy*, 3 vols., Cambridge.
    1969

Hadot, Pierre
    1966   'La notion de "cas" dans la logique stoïcienne', in: *Actes du XIIIe
            congrès des sociétés de philosophie de langue française*, Neuchatel,
            pp. 109–112.
    1968   *Porphyre et Victorinus* I, Paris.
    1969   'Zur Vorgeschichte des Begriffs "Existenz". HYPARCHEIN bei den
            Stoikern', *Archiv für Begriffsgeschichte* 13, 115–127.

Haller, Rudolf
    1962   'Untersuchungen zum Bedeutungsproblem in der antiken und mittel-
            alterlichen Philosophie', *Archiv für Begriffsgeschichte* 7, 57–119.

Hay, William H.
    1969   'Stoic use of logic', *Archiv für Geschichte der Philosophie* 51, 145–
            157.
Hossenfelder, Malte
    1967   'Zur stoischen Definition von Axioma', *Archiv für Begriffsgeschichte*
            11, 238–241.

Isaac, J.
    1953   *Le* Peri hermeneias *en occident de Boèce à Saint Thomas. Histoire lit-
            téraire d'un traité d'Aristote*, Paris.

Jackson, B. Darrell
    1969   'The theory of signs in St. Augustine's *De doctrina Christiana*', *Revue
            des études augustiniennes* 15, 9–49.
Jolivet, Jean
    1969   *Arts du langage et théologie chez Abélard*, Paris.

Kahn, Charles H.
    1966   'The Greek verb "to be" and the concept of being', *Foundations of
            language* 2, 245–265.
    1969   'Stoic logic and Stoic *LOGOS*', *Archiv für Geschichte der Philosophie*
            51, 158–172.
Kieffer, John S.
    1964   *Galen's* Institutio logica. *English translation, introduction, and com-
            mentary*, Baltimore.
Kneale, William & Kneale, Martha
    1962   *The development of logic*, Oxford.
    1970   'Propositions and time', in: *G.E. Moore. Essays in retrospect*, ed. A.
            Ambrose & M. Lazerowitz, London, pp. 228–241.
Kretzmann, Norman
    1966   *William of Sherwood's* Introduction to logic. *Translated with an intro-
            duction and notes*, Minneapolis.
    1967   'Semantics, history of', in: *The encyclopedia of philosophy*, ed. P.
            Edwards, New York–London, 7, pp. 358–406.
    1970   'Medieval logicians on the meaning of the *propositio*', *The journal of
            philosophy* 67, 767–787.
Kuypers, K.
    1934   *Der Zeichen- und Wortbegriff im Denken Augustins*, Amsterdam.

Long, A.A. ed.
    1971   *Problems in Stoicism*, London.
Lorenz, K. & Mittelstrass, J.
    1966   'Theaitetos fliegt. Zur Theorie wahrer und falscher Sätze bei Platon
            (*Soph.* 251 d – 263 d)', *Archiv für Geschichte der Philosophie* 48,
            113–152.

Maierù, Alfonso
    1966   'Il problema della verità nelle opere di Guglielmo Heytesbury', *Studi
            medievali* 7, 40–74.

Manthey, F.
    1937   *Die Sprachphilosophie des hl. Thomas von Aquin und ihre Anwendung auf Probleme der Theologie*, Paderborn.
Mates, Benson
    1961 [2]   *Stoic logic*, Berkeley–Los Angeles. First published 1953.
Mau, Jürgen
    1960   *Galen, Einführung in die Logik. Kritisch-exegetischer Kommentar mit deutscher Uebersetzung*, Berlin.
Mignucci, M.
    1965   *Il significato della logica stoica*, Bologna.
Moody, Ernest A.
    1935   *The logic of William of Ockham*, New York–London.
    1953   *Truth and consequence in medieval logic*, Amsterdam.
    1964   'A quodlibetal question of Robert Holkot, O.P. on the problem of the objects of knowledge and of belief', *Speculum. A journal of mediaeval studies* 39, 53–74.
Mühl, Max
    1962   'Der *logos endiathetos* und *prophorikos* von der älteren Stoa zur Synode von Sirmium 351', *Archiv für Begriffsgeschichte* 7, 7–56.
Müller, Ian
    1969   'Stoic and Peripatetic logic', *Archiv für Geschichte der Philosophie* 51, 173–187.

Norden, E.
    1915 [3]   *Die antike Kunstprosa vom 6. Jahrhundert v. Chr. bis in die Zeit der Renaissance* I, Leipzig. First published 1898.

Obertello, Luca
    1969   *A.M. Severino Boezio, De hypotheticis syllogismis. Testo, traduzione, introduzione e commento*, Brescia.

Pagallo, Giulio F.
    1960   'Nota sulla *Logica* di Paolo Veneto: la critica alla dottrina del "complexe significabile" di Gregorio da Rimini', in: *Atti del XII congresso internazionale di filosofia*, Firenze, pp. 183–191.
Pfligersdorffer, Georg
    1953   'Zu Boethius, De Interpr. Ed. sec. I, p. 4, 4 sqq. Meiser, nebst Beobachtungen zur Geschichte der Dialektik bei den Römern', *Wiener Studien* 66, 131–154.
Pinborg, Jan
    1962   'Das Sprachdenken der Stoa und Augustins Dialektik', *Classica et mediaevalia* 23, 148–177.
    1967   *Die Entwicklung der Sprachtheorie im Mittelalter*, Münster–Kopenhagen.
    1969   'Walter Burleigh on the meaning of propositions', *Classica et mediaevalia* 28, 394–404.
Pohlenz, Max
    1964 [3]   *Die Stoa. Geschichte einer geistigen Bewegung*, Göttingen. First published 1948.

Popper, Karl
  1968   'On the theory of the objective mind', in: *Akten des XIV. internationalen Kongresses für Philosophie* I, Wien, pp. 25–53.
Prantl, C.
  1855–   *Geschichte der Logik im Abendlande*, 4 vols., Leipzig.
  1870
Prauss, Gerold
  1966   *Platon und der logische Eleatismus*, Berlin.
Prior, A.N.
  1966   'Some problems of self-reference in John Buridan', in: *Studies in philosophy. British Academy lectures*, ed. J.N. Findlay, London, pp. 241–259. First published 1962.
  1971   *Objects of thought*, ed. P.T. Geach & A.J.P. Kenny, Oxford.

Reina, Maria Elena
  1959–   'Il problema del linguaggio in Buridano', *Rivista critica di storia della filosofia* 14, 367–417; 15, 141–165.
  1960
Ries, John
  1931   *Was ist ein Satz?*, Prag.
De Rijk, L.M.
  1966a   'Some new evidence on twelfth century logic. Alberic and the School of Mont Ste Geneviève (Montani)', *Vivarium* 4, 1–57.
  1966b   'Some notes on the mediaeval tract *De insolubilibus*, with the edition of a tract dating from the end of the twelfth century', *Vivarium* 4, 83–115.
  1967   *Logica modernorum. A contribution to the history of early terminist logic* II, 1–2, Assen.
Riondato, Ezio
  1957   *La teoria Aristotelica della enunciazione*, Padova.
Rist, J.M.
  1969   *Stoic philosophy*, Cambridge.
Robins, R.H.
  1951   *Ancient and mediaeval grammatical theory in Europe*, London.
  1967   *A short history of linguistics*, London.
Rotta, P.
  1909   *La filosofia del linguaggio nella Patristica e nella Scolastica*, Torino.

Sainati, Vittorio
  1968   *Storia dell' Organon Aristotelico* I: *Dai Topici al De interpretatione*, Firenze.
Saw, Ruth L.
  1941–   'William of Ockham on terms, propositions, meaning', *Proceedings of the Aristotelian Society* 42, 45–64.
  1942
Scaglione, Aldo D.
  1970   *Ars grammatica. A bibliographical survey, two essays on the grammar of the Latin and Italian subjunctive, and a note on the ablative absolute*, The Hague–Paris.

Schepers, Heinrich
    1970   'Holkot contra dicta Crathorn I: Quellenkritik und biographische Aus-
               wertung der Bakkalareatsschriften zweier Oxforder Dominikaner des
               XIV. Jahrhunderts', *Philosophisches Jahrbuch der Görres-Gesellschaft*
               77, 320–354.
    1972   'Holkot contra dicta Crathorn II: Das "significatum per propositio-
               nem". Aufbau und Kritik einer nominalistischen Theorie über den
               Gegenstand des Wissens', *Philosophisches Jahrbuch der Görres-Gesell-
               schaft* 79, 106–136.
Schmidt, R.
    1839   *Stoicorum grammatica*, Halis.
Schuhl, Pierre-Maxime
    1960   *Le dominateur et les possibles*, Paris.
Scott, T.K.
    1965   'John Buridan on the objects of demonstrative science', *Speculum. A
               journal of mediaeval studies* 40, 654–673.
    1966   *John Buridan, Sophisms on meaning and truth. Translated and with an
               introduction*, New York.
Searle, John R.
    1969   *Speech acts. An essay in the philosophy of language*, Cambridge.
Seidel, Eugen
    1935   *Geschichte und Kritik der wichtigsten Satzdefinitionen (Jenaer Ger-
               manistische Forschungen* 27), Jena.
Sprague, Rosamond Kent
    1968   'Dissoi logoi or Dialexeis', *Mind* 77, 155–167.
Steinthal, H.
    1890–   *Geschichte der Sprachwissenschaft bei den Griechen und Römern mit
    1891[2] besonderer Rücksicht auf die Logik*, 2 vols., Berlin. First published
               1863.
Sullivan, Mark W.
    1967   *Apuleian logic. The nature, sources, and influence of Apuleius's* Peri
               hermeneias, Amsterdam.
    1970   'What was true or false in the *Old Logic*?', *The journal of philosophy*
               67, 788–800.

Trentman, John
    1970   'Ockham on Mental', *Mind* 79, 586–590.
Tweedale, Martin M.
    1967   'Abailard and non-things', *Journal of the history of philosophy* 5,
               329–342.

Warnach, Viktor
    1937–   'Erkennen und Sprechen bei Thomas von Aquin. Ein Deutungsversuch
    1938   seiner Lehre auf ihrem geistesgeschichtlichen Hintergrund', *Divus
               Thomas* 15, 189–218, 263–290; 16, 161–196.
Watson, G.
    1966   *The Stoic theory of knowledge*, Belfast.

White, Alan R.
    1970   *Truth*, London.
Würsdörfer, Joseph
    1917   *Erkennen und Wissen nach Gregor von Rimini. Ein Beitrag zur Geschichte der Erkenntnistheorie des Nominalismus*, Münster.

INDEX OF PROPER NAMES

INDEX OF GREEK TERMS

premiss: 32, 61, 90, 118
See further: 62, 120, 131
proteinein, propound a question: 32
prothesis, preliminary statement of the case: 118
protropē, exhortation: 101
psektikon (lekton, pragma), censure: 63
pseudesthai, say something that is untrue, be false: 133
pseudorkein, swear falsely: 100
ptōsis, case, noun, name, thought signified by a noun in a certain case: 46, 72–74, 89
pysma, specific question: 63, 98
pysmatikē (erōtēsis), specific (question): 98

rhēma, combination of *onomata*: 13
verb: 14, 15, 16, 17, 18, 20, 24, 27, 28, 29, 37, 38, 47, 51, 69, 72, 73, 74, 89, 93, 94, 95

schēma, figure: 30, 100, 119
form (simple or compound): 200
schēmatizein, give a certain form to something: 100
sēmainein, signify: 14, 29, 31, 38, 55, 68, 70, 91, 133, 134, 151, 152
sēmainomenon, that which is signified: 55, 62, 65, 66, 67, 68, 70, 71, 73, 76, 84, 116, 117, 134, 135
sēmainon, that which signifies: 55, 68, 71
sēmeion, sign: 38, 126
sōma, body, agent or patient: 45, 46, 50, 51, 52, 54, 55, 61, 62, 66, 68, 69, 70, 71, 73, 76, 85, 95, 97
that which is accessible to the senses: 65, 66

sterētikon (axiōma), privative: 59
stigmē, mark of punctuation: 92
syllogismos, argument: 55, 77, 191
symbama, consequence, predicate: 58, 72
symbebēkos, consequence, predicate: 45, 49, 58
symbolon, sign, symbol: 38
symperaioun, make complete: 92
symperasma, conclusion: 57, 80
symplokē, combination: 14, 24, 26, 27, 37, 94
syndesmos, conjunction: 74
synēmmenon (axiōma), conditional: 60
synkatathesis, assent, act of assenting: 19, 78, 79, 190
synkatēgorein, consignify: 124
synkatēgorēma, that which consignifies: 124
synkleiein, conclude, make complete: 93
syntelein, bring to fulfilment, make complete: 92
synthesis, composition, combination: 25, 26, 28, 37, 38
syssēmainein, consignify: 97, 124

telein, bring to fulfilment, make complete: 92
teleios, complete, perfect: 57, 91, 92, 93, 111
teleioun, make complete: 16, 92
thaumastikon (lekton, pragma), expressed admiration or astonishment: 63
ti, something: 12, 52, 68
tynchanon, that which gets a name, denoted object: 68, 69, 70, 71, 73

zōtikē (dynamis), appetitive: 98

INDEX OF LATIN TERMS

mens, mind: 128, 193, 194, 225, 228, 277
    thought: 126
mentalis, mental: 19, 128, 145, 149, 168, 194, 197, 199, 203, 212
moderni, those who live after the coming of Christ: 178, 180, 186, 210
    the moderns: 220, 222, 223, 224
modus, mood of the verb: 129, 130
    way, mode, state: 142, 147, 149, 183, 188, 219, 241, 242, 246, 263, 273–276, 277
monstrare, make known, indicate: 134
multiplex (oratio), ambiguous: 167
mutabiliter (vera, falsa), mutably: 260

negare deny: 145, 151
negatio, denial: 141, 145, 152
negativus, negative: 145
nihil, nothing: 153, 154, 233
nomen, name, noun: 116, 155, 156, 174, 175, 180, 181, 183, 188, 192, 193
nominales, 'nominalists': 180–188, 239
nominaliter, in a nominal sense: 264
nominare, name: 140, 153, 258
non-existentia, not being the case: 158
    non-existence: 218
notio, thought: 116, 192
notitia, act of knowing: 228
nugatorium (dictum, enuntiabile), nugatory, neither true nor false: 174
nuncupativus (sensus), naming: 156

obiective (esse), be in the mind as an object of the understanding: 225
obiectum (scientiae), a conclusion as the object of knowledge: 202, 229
operatio, operation: 190
opinatum, that which is believed: 157, 160
opinio, thought, belief: 145, 157
optativus, expressing a wish: 128, 129, 166
oratio, speech, group of words: 19, 93, 105, 107, 114, 117, 119, 120, 121, 124–129, 132–137, 142–145, 149, 153, 155, 165–170,

175, 187, 188, 192, 195, 197, 202, 256, 258, 263, 266, 267, 278
    prayer: 194

pars (orationis), part of speech: 124
participialis (modus), participial: 130
partitio, division: 189
passio (animae), affection of the soul, idea: 203
pendere, be pendent: 125
percunctativus (modus), interrogative: 130
perfectio, perfection, completeness: 16, 125
perfectus, perfect, complete: 105, 108, 112, 121, 125, 132, 145, 147, 165, 258, 266
perficere, express something that is complete: 110
peri(h)ermenia, categorematic expression: 114, 136
perpetuus (modus), infinitive: 129
personaliter, in a signifying function: 234, 249, 256, 264
plenus, complete: 105, 107, 108, 112, 114, 124, 125
praedicabile, that which is signified by a word: 117
    that which can be predicated: 117, 170
praeteritio, pastness: 215, 218
pro alio positio, assumption made in order to get something else: 166
proculpositio, that which is placed outside the actual syllogism: 137
prodere (sententiam), make known: 125
profari, make known, assert: 107
profatum, that which is asserted: 105, 106, 107, 115
proferre (sententiam), make known: 125
    (dictum), utter: 232
prolatus (terminus), uttered, spoken: 196
prolocutio, = *proloquium*: 113, 114
proloqui, make known, assert: 107, 109, 110
proloquium, that which is expressed in a

speech act of asserting, statement-making utterance: 105–115, 120, 131, 168
pronuntiabilis (oratio), statement-making: 107, 120, 131
pronuntiare, make known, state: 107, 145, 149
pronuntiatio, = pronuntiatum: 107
= enuntiatio: 114
pronuntiativus, statement-making, indicative: 128, 129, 131
pronuntiatum, that which is made known, stated: 107, 115
proponere, make known, assert: 134, 145, 147, 151, 152, 167
propositio, propounded question: 120, 131, 136, 137
premiss: 118, 120, 132
major premiss: 114, 118, 132
statement-making utterance, statement: 32, 81, 107, 114, 115, 119, 120, 121, 131–134, 136, 137, 141, 143, 145–163, 166–168, 172, 173, 188, 197, and *passim; propositio in re:* 221–224, 248
preliminary statement of the case: 118
propositum, propounded question: 131
proprietas, characteristic, state: 141, 171, 241
protensio, propounded question, proposal: 120

quaestio, question: 126, 132, 137
qualitas, mood: 129

ratio, reasoning: 125, 126, 170
realiter, really, in fact: 269, 271
receptio, reception: 191
res, action or passion: 48, 105
that which can only be thought: 55, 66, 125, 126, 127, 170
thing: 116, 140, 141, 149, 153, 158, 159, 173, 174, 178–189, 192, 195, 198, 204, 209–224, 230, 233, 238, 239, 253, 268, 273–276, 277

alleged state of affairs: 156, 158, 159, 233, 238, 268
rogamentum, problem: 120, 121

sanus (intellectus), sound: 144
scibilis, knowable: 249, 251
scientia, act of knowing, scientific knowledge: 202, 204, 228, 229, 279
scire, know: 176, 184, 198, 205, 215, 230, 248, 249, 265
scitum, that which is known: 176, 204, 279
scriptus (terminus), written: 196
semiplenus, half-complete: 128
sensum, that which is thought: 125
sensus, thought, sense: 16, 106, 110, 125, 135, 145, 148, 156, 159, 160, 186
sententia, thought expressed, meaningful expression, sentence: 105–115, 119, 121, 125, 126, 130, 135, 145, 170, 193
sermo, speech, utterance: 118, 128, 131, 232
sic (esse), in a certain way: 201, 202, 218, 230, 246, 255
significabilis, having meaning, significant: 231
signifiable, signified: 194, 227, 231, 232, 241, 242, 248, and *passim*
significans, that which signifies: 117, 169
significare, signify, make known: 48, 105, 114, 123, 132, 133, 134, 136, 140, 145, 151, 152, 156, 166, 167, 182, 187, 188, 189, 209, 217, 218, 219, 232, 240, 243, 263, 264, 265
significatio, signification: 55, 124, 133, 153, 186, 200, 262
significative, in a signifying function: 196, 234, 249, 256, 264
significativus, signifying: 123, 136
capable of signifying: 266
significatum, that which is signified, made known: 117, 135, 152, 153,

INDEX OF TOPICS